BUSINESS AND POLITICS IN INDIA

This volume is sponsored by the
CENTER FOR SOUTH AND SOUTHEAST ASIA STUDIES,
University of California, Berkeley

THE CENTER FOR SOUTH AND SOUTHEAST ASIA STUDIES of the University of California is the coordinating center for research, teaching programs, and special projects relating to the South and Southeast Asia areas on the nine campuses of the University. The Center is the largest such research and teaching organization in the United States, with more than 150 related faculty representing all disciplines within the social sciences, languages, and humanities.

The Center publishes a Monograph Series, an Occasional Papers Series, and sponsors a series published by the University of California Press. Manuscripts for these publications have been selected with the highest standards of academic excellence, with emphasis on those studies and literary works that are pioneers in their fields, and that provide fresh insight into the life and culture of the great civilizations of South and Southeast Asia.

RECENT PUBLICATIONS

OF THE CENTER FOR SOUTH AND SOUTHEST ASIA STUDIES

Edward Conze
The Large Sutra on Perfect Wisdom

William G. Davis
Social Relations in a Philippine Market

Daniel S. Lev
Islamic Courts in Indonesia

Sylvia Vatuk
Kinship and Urbanization: White-Collar Migrants in North India

BUSINESS AND POLITICS IN INDIA

Stanley A. Kochanek

UNIVERSITY OF CALIFORNIA PRESS
BERKELEY, LOS ANGELES, LONDON

University of California Press
Berkeley and Los Angeles, California
University of California Press, Ltd.
London, England

ISBN: 0-520-02377-3
Library of Congress Catalog Card Number: 72-93521

To Pat, Christopher, and Kevin

CONTENTS

TABLES

PREFACE

Groups, like all structures in society, are multifunctional. Patterns of group identity, mobilization, and politicization have a significant impact on the patterning of cleavages within the society, but they may also serve as critical agents of social integration and as channels of communication between the individual and the state.[1] Perhaps the primary function of groups, however, is to serve as mechanisms for the articulation of demands and the pressing of group claims on the political system.[2]

Until recently, most of the interest group literature has focused on developed western nations. It was generally assumed that any extension of such studies, to supposedly less differentiated societies whose pre-

[1] See Sidney Verba, "Organizational Membership and Democratic Consensus," *Journal of Politics* 27 (1965): 467–497; and William Kornhauser, *The Politics of Mass Society* (New York: Free Press, 1959), pp. 13–115.

[2] On the various difficulties associated with the interest group approach to the political process, see Joseph La Palombara, "The Utility and Limitations of Interest Group Theory in Non-American Field Situations," *Journal of Politics* 22 (1960): 29–49; Stanley Rothman, "Systematic Political Theory: Observations on the Group Approach," *American Political Science Review* 54 (1960): 15–33; Roy E. Macridis, "Interest Groups in Comparative Analysis," *Journal of Politics* 23 (1961): 24–45; W. J. M. MacKenzie, "Pressure Groups: The Conceptual Framework," *Political Studies* 3 (1955): 247–55; Mancur Olson, Jr., *The Logic of Collective Action* (Cambridge: Harvard University Press, 1965), pp. 111–131; David G. Smith, "Pragmatism and the Group Theory of Politics," *American Political Science Review* 58 (1964): 600–610; and Harry Eckstein, "Group Theory and the Comparative Study of Pressure Groups," in *Comparative Politics: A Reader*, ed. Harry Eckstein and David Apter (New York: Free Press, 1963), pp. 389–397; Robert H. Salisbury, "An Exchange Theory of Interest Groups," *Midwest Journal of Political Science* 13 (1969): 1–32; Gabriel A. Almond, "A Comparative Study of Interest groups in the Political Process," *American Political Science Review* 52 (1958): 270–282; Gabriel A. Almond and G. Bingham Powell, Jr., *Comparative Politics: A Developmental Approach* (Boston: Little, Brown, 1966), pp. 73–97; Harry Eckstein, *Pressure Group Politics: The Case of the British Medical Association* (Palo Alto: Stanford University Press, 1960), see especially chaps. I and VII; Raymond A. Bauer, Ithiel de Sola Pool, and Lewis Anthony Dexter, *American Business and Public Policy* (New York: Atherton, 1967), pp. 465–490; Lester Milbrath, "Lobbying as a Communicative Process," *Public Opinion Quarterly* 24 (1960): 33–53; Heinz Eulau, "Lobbyists: The Wasted Profession," *Public Opinion Quarterly* 28 (1964): 27–38; Samuel J. Eldersveld, "American Interest Groups: A Survey of Research and Some Implications for Theory and Method," in *Interest Groups on Four Continents*, ed. H. W. Ehrmann (Pittsburgh: University of Pittsburgh Press, 1960), pp. 173–196.

dominant economic activity was agriculture, would require a search for functional equivalents.[3] The politics of influence in such countries would thus be expected to originate in pressures from family or cliques, rather than from pressures generated by the types of complex, bureaucratized associations that operate as interest groups in modern societies in the west. As a result, even where such organizations existed in some of the developing countries, they were actually overlooked. The role of business in India, however, demonstrates that many of these assumptions are in need of some modification.

The study of business and business associations has been almost entirely confined to an examination of western examples because most traditional societies were thought to lack an indigenous business elite.[4] Yet in India, national associations representing both foreign and indigenous business interests have existed since the early part of the twentieth century. Moreover, from an organizational point of view, the associations representing indigenous capital are as well developed as those representing foreign capital, and both are nearly as well developed as their counterparts in the west. Business associations are far in advance of other sections of Indian society. It is also true that business, unlike other major functional groups in India such as the trade unions, student organizations, and peasant groups, has developed associations which are autonomous from India's political parties.

Once this superficial similarity of interest groups in India to their counterparts in the west is probed, a unique and complex pattern of internal relationships is revealed. Behind the facade of the bureaucratized, modern voluntary associations representing business in India, there exists an intricate interplay between these familiar modern forms of organization and primordial loyalties to family and caste. The basic units in Indian business are business houses, most of which are controlled by families who belong to a small group of castes whose traditional occupation is trade. These primordial identities played a critical role as building blocks in the founding and early development of organs of collective action to represent business in the realm of bureauc-

[3] Almond and Powell, *Comparative Politics*, pp. 73–97.

[4] Except for Chitoshi Yanaga, *Big Business in Japanese Politics* (New Haven: Yale University Press, 1968), all other studies of business groups have focused on the west. See Gerhard Braunthal, *The Federation of German Industry in Politics* (Ithaca: Cornell University Press, 1965); Henry W. Ehrmann, *Organized Business in France* (Princeton: Princeton University Press, 1957); Joseph La Palombara, *Interest Groups in Italian Politics* (Princeton: Princeton University Press, 1964); Raymond A. Bauer, Ithiel de Sola Pool, and Lewis Anthony Dexter, *American Business and Public Policy: The Politcs of Foreign Trade* (New York: Atherton, 1967); S. E. Finer, "The Federation of British Industries," *Political Studies* 4 (1956): 61–82; Harmon Zeigler, *Interest Groups in American Society* (Englewood Cliffs, N. J.: Prentice-Hall, 1964).

ratized government. Although these identities are now in the process of losing their old influence, they have inhibited the development of business organizations according to the modern functional pattern more fully achieved by the associations representing foreign capital in India.[5] Thus, the pattern of internal politics within the Indian business community is symptomatic of the evolution and social differentiation within the extremely heterogeneous and yet highly traditional business community, as it transforms itself from congeries of rival castes and families into a well-defined business class with a consistent set of interests and values pursued through cooperative organizational forms. At the present stage, therefore, the business community in India, like other groups in the society, encounters considerable difficulty in mobilizing its resources for collective action, maximizing its capabilities, and developing representative structures which can successfully press its demands on government decision-makers.

The difficulties resulting from the internal characteristics of the business community in India are exacerbated by the environment within which business must function. Interest group activity, in India as elsewhere, is systems dominated. In India, group activity takes place in an environment which not only determines the patterns of access and influence available to groups but sets severe limits on group effectiveness. Four factors in particular help shape the character of interest group activity in India: the political culture, the level of modernization of the society, the structure of decision-making, and the exigencies of public policy.

The level of modernization in India is reflected in the partial pattern of social differentiation which has affected the character and variety of groups in the society as well as the internal dynamics of the groups. The most potent interest articulators in India are not the economic and social formations in the modern sector but rather their caste, community, language, and regional antecedents. With some exceptions, therefore, modern interest groups in India have been slow to develop. They are still characterized by low levels of group mobilization. They are organizationally weak or poorly institutionalized, and they tend to lack functional autonomy.

Interest group activity in India is also influenced by the fact that all interest groups, but especially business, must contend with a political culture which questions the legitimacy of interest group activity and

[5] A similar pattern of development has occurred in Japan. See Takeshi Ishida, "The Development of Interest Groups and the Pattern of Political Modernization in Japan," in *Political Development in Modern Japan*, ed. Robert Ward, (Princeton: Princeton University Press, 1968), pp. 293–336.

treats it with distrust if not outright hostility. Business in particular is highly suspect, because the low status traditionally assigned to business activity in the society has been reinforced by socialist, Marxist, and Gandhian thought, all of which characterize businessmen as exploiters and profit as booty. In contrast, there is strong support for the active intervention of government in the social and economic sphere.

The biases of the Indian political culture are reinforced by the government's highly centralized structure of decision-making. That structure is dominated by an unspoken but widely accepted set of criteria emphasizing an elite-defined national interest, rational calculation, paternalism, and institutional mission. These considerations take precedence over what are conceived to be partial and potentially dangerous pressures from organized vested interests. Policy initiatives usually come from government and not from the larger society, and so most groups are forced to take a negative or defensive rather than a positive stance.

Finally, groups in general (and business in particular) are held in check by the pattern of public policy which has emerged since independence. The commitment to planned economic development leading to a socialist pattern of society has concentrated vast powers in the hands of government officials. This power enables them to control and regulate both the internal affairs and external conduct of business, trade unions, and other organizations. Groups are naturally hesitant to alienate those who wield such vast powers. So, far from being merely an outcome of interest group activity, as group theory would have it, public policy in India exerts a significant impact on group mobilization and on behavior.

Thus the interrelationship between interest groups and the political process in India is much more complex than that implied by early elaborations of group theory, which conceptualized society as nothing more than a mosaic of interacting groups which, individually understood, would elucidate the whole.[6] As the Indian case reveals, the political system itself sets the parameters for group activity, and groups can be understood only as part of a larger and more complex set of relationships which compose the larger political system.

It is the pattern of interaction, between the systemic factors which

[6] See David Truman, *The Governmental Process* (New York: Alfred A. Knopf, 1968); Earl Latham, "The Group Basis of Politics: Notes for a Theory," *The American Political Science Review* 46 (1952): 376–397; Robert T. Golembiewski, "The Group Basis of Politics: Notes on Analysis and Development," *American Political Science Review* 54 (1960): 38–61; Charles B. Hagen, "The Group in a Political Science," in *Approaches to the Study of Politics*, ed. Roland Young, (Evanston, Ill.: Northwestern University Press, 1958), pp. 38–51.

compose the larger environment and the particular attributes and capabilities of the groups, which determines the patterns of access. In the Indian political system, there are several points in the political process at which a group can bring influence to bear: public opinion, political parties and election campaigns, the legislative process, the cabinet and bureaucracy, and the judiciary.[7] Interest groups may also resort to direct action and violence. Business in India was indeed quick to adjust to the post-independence political environment. Dealing with the executive and bureaucracy, which had emerged as the effective centers of power, placed a premium on organization, bureaucratization, and nonagitational methods which suited both the business style and the business budget. Business influence in Parliament and on the political parties, by contrast, was constrained by systemic factors which restricted intervention to a sporadic level and produced limited results.

Although business in India has been rent by the diversity and social fragmentation that characterize other sectors of Indian society, business has been one of the few interests in the modern sector that has been able to develop autonomous structures of interest articulation capable of reasonably sustained collective action. If business can so organize in India, it is surely not inconceivable that other interests will also in time be able to do so. Moreover, to the extent that interest group formation and functioning is shaped by larger systemic factors, the business case, although unique in detail, may in its larger aspects be instructive about future patterns of interest group formation and behavior in India.

The purpose of this book, then, is to help elucidate the complex dynamic relationships which determine the nature and behavior of a single interest group in its political setting and to determine whether the intervention of that group is functional or dysfunctional to the political system as a whole. Part I of the book deals with the systemic factors which set the parameters of interest group activities in India. Part II focuses on the problems encountered by Indian businessmen in organizing themselves for collective action, and it treats in particular the interaction between family business houses and modern associations. Part III deals with the channels of access and influence employed by business, both individually and collectively, in pressing its demands on government decision-makers, and it also assesses the overall impact of business on public policy in India and on the Indian political system.

[7] Due to limitations of space, the relationship between business and the judiciary will not be treated in this volume.

ACKNOWLEDGMENTS

It is possible that some Indian readers, judging this material as political partisans, may feel that I have minimized the influence of business on government in India. Others, particularly some members of the Indian business community, may feel I have occasionally been too severe in my conclusions. To the extent that both cries are heard I shall feel gratified that I have succeeded in striking a proper balance, for I have tried neither to placate nor to vilify in the course of this study.

A third group, composed of economists in my own country, may feel that I have been grudging in my allocation of space to the analysis of the big business role in the Indian economy. To such readers I can only say that the job of economic analysis belongs to others. As a political scientist, I am concerned here with the basic problem of how business organizes itself for collective action, how it attempts to influence government policy, and how effective it is in this endeavor. I might add that the need to assess the role of big business in the Indian polity has been given new urgency by the Pakistan debacle. The contributions of the twenty-two families to Pakistan economic development as such were extolled, but the political and social impact of the resulting distribution of wealth and power were ignored. Industrial development there was, but it led to a political upheaval, which in turn led to severe economic reversals.

The most important data in this book derives from conversations with some one hundred and fifty businessmen, central cabinet ministers and secretaries, Members of Parliament, and business association staff executives,[1] many of whom not only gave their time but extended the

[1] A total of 151 interviews were conducted with two groups of subjects. The first group was composed of 80 knowledgeable persons who were in a position to comment on various facets of business–government interaction. They included 31 staff members of major trade and industry associations, 18 Members of Parliament associated with business and labor, 14 secretaries and upper echelon civil servants drawn from the major economic ministries of the government of India, 10 past and present Congress ministers in charge of major economic portfolios, and 7 economic journalists, academics, and certified public accountants.

The second group of interviews was conducted with a carefully selected sample of 71 members of the business elite in India. Three major criteria were used in

hospitality of their homes to a total stranger. Because I must keep faith with them, I cannot acknowledge their contributions individually, but I must confess that the study could never have been accomplished without their candor and goodwill.

---

defining the elite sample: leadership position in one of the major business associations; executive head of one of the top 75 business houses or 16 independent companies listed in the Monopolies Commission Report of 1965; and regional representation of the major business centers in India. The precise breakdown of these categories exceeds seventy-one because of the overlapping of the criteria selected. The breakdown included the following:

(1) 36 out of 51 members of the committee of the FICCI in 1967–1968.
(2) 14 of the 24 former presidents of the FICCI still living, most of whom are still members of the committee.
(3) 14 members of the executive committees of the Bengal, Bombay, and Madras chambers of commerce who have served as delegates to the annual session of Assocham and who constitute the equivalent of an informal executive committee for Assocham.
(4) The president and four members of the executive committee of the All-India Manufacturers Organization.
(5) The president of the major regional chambers of commerce in India: Indian Merchants Chamber, Bombay; Indian Chamber of Commerce, Calcutta; Southern India Chamber of Commerce, Madras; the Bombay Chamber of Commerce; the Bengal Chamber of Commerce; and the Madras Chamber of Commerce.
(6) 11 executive leaders of the top 75 business houses not represented on the committee of the FICCI or Assocham.

The breakdown of the elite sample by business house included leaders of 39 of the top 75 business houses; of these, 20 were drawn from the top 25 houses. Directors of 5 of the top 16 independent companies listed in the Monopolies Commission Report were included in the group. Each of the major industrial regions of India was represented in relative proportion to its industrial importance.

I conducted all of the interviews. Each interview lasted for one hour. My previous experience in India had led me to be very wary of the problems of interviewing Indian elites. Moreover, because my study concerned a very sensitive area of Indian politics and because many businessmen in India are extremely secretive and suspicious, the only way to get any information was to use a set of open-ended general questions whose results could then be content analyzed. I was primarily concerned about getting accurate information and data on a variety of controversial issues, including the internal politics of business, the relationship between business and government, and individual attitudes toward government and politics. Except for the attitude questions—which took up only a small part of the total interview time—the information collected did not lend itself to aggregation into percentages. A great deal of the information obtained, however, is simply not available anywhere in published form, even in the financial press. The only way I could get straightforward responses was to assure the individual being interviewed that he would enjoy complete anonymity. Thus, throughout the book, I have quoted key figures without attribution. Had I broken faith, I would have created a political storm and damaged the position of the persons who had granted interviews.

In short, the interviews were not designed primarily as a survey of business opinion but to gather basic information about business and its role in the Indian political system. Although some attitude data is presented in Chapter II, it is primarily exploratory and lays the foundation for a future survey of business opinion in India.

Happily there are other contributions that I may acknowledge publicly. I am deeply grateful to Mr. G. L. Bansal, secretary-general of the Federation of Indian Chambers of Commerce and Industry, and to the members of the committee for permitting me to use their facilities in Delhi. Mr. P. Chentsal Rao, secretary of the FICCI, was particularly helpful to me in securing past FICCI reports and in responding to what must have seemed, for a while, an unending stream of questions. Mr. Rao has read the completed manuscript, and so I must acknowledge a special debt of gratitude for his extremely helpful suggestions. The staff of the FICCI, especially the library staff under Mr. V. K. Majmudar and the records staff under Mr. R. S. Sharma, were both helpful and patient in assisting me in the use of their public records, books, and newspaper files.

I wish also to thank Mr. C. A. Pitts, former president of Assocham, for the special interest he took in my project. My appreciation extends to the Assocham staff in Delhi and Calcutta, and to the staffs of the All-India Manufacturers Organization, Indian Cotton Mills Federations, Organization of Pharmaceutical Producers of India, and a variety of other industrial associations and regional chambers of commerce in India, which unfortunately are far too numerous to mention individually.

I am especially appreciative of the enthusiasm and vast knowledge of Rishi Jaimini Kaushik, who acted as a research guide through the history and development of the Marwari community of Calcutta and to the Indian National Archives for permitting me to use their facilities.

I recall with pleasure the long informal conversations with knowledgeable friends in Bombay and Madras. Their knowledge about the role of business in India was as fulsome as their hospitality. Unfortunately they too must remain anonymous.

I had hoped to complete the final version of this manuscript in India during my sabbatical. Like several other American scholars, however, I had to wait outside the gates pending a thaw in Indo-American relations. I therefore owe a special debt of gratitude to Anthony and Hilde Kochanek, who graciously provided work space, living accommodations, and their hospitality, without which the task of revision would not have been completed so expeditiously or in such pleasant surroundings.

For the elimination of those small errors that creep into all manuscripts and for some thought provoking comments, I am indebted to Mr. P. L. Tandon, former managing director of Hindustan Lever, who struggled through the entire manuscript. Needless to say, the responsibility for all interpretations and conclusions and for any errors that may remain is mine.

The transcriptions of my interviews and the typing of the early drafts of the manuscript involved long hours of work by Vandila Blatchford and Darlene Kalada, whose contributions were supported by The Pennsylvania State University work-study funds. The final typing of the manuscript would have taken twice as long had it not been for the demoniac efforts of Susan Sorrell, Lucia Swanson, and Virginia Dansey. The editorial burden fell on the shoulders of my wife Pat, who took time out from her own writing to put the red pencil to mine.

None of these acknowledgments would ever have been necessary or possible, however, without the financial support provided by the American Institutes of Indian Studies, which provided me with a senior research fellowship to carry out my research in India from 1967 to 1968. Financial support for subsequent phases of the work was provided by the Central Fund for Research of The Pennsylvania State University.

A word in connection with spelling is necessary. In cases where alternate spellings are possible, the version accepted was that which seemed to represent the broadest consensus. No doubt, however, there will be those who feel that the choice in some cases was unfortunate. To them I can only respond that, so long as the transliteration problem in regard to Indian names remains in flux, there is bound to be disagreement.

S.K.

Geneva
December 1972

PART ONE

Systems Determinants of Interest Group Behavior

I

PATTERNS AND LEVELS OF MODERNIZATION

An important by-product of the modernizing process for the development of a political system is the stimulus it provides for the emergence of associations representing new sets of values and interests. The modernizing process contributes in several ways to the emergence of new forms of association based on new patterns of interaction. First, it increases the extent of social differentiation within a society by supplanting but more often by supplementing preindustrial patterns of group identity, stratification, and primordial values. Second, it increases organizational capability by developing better communications and more modern bureaucratic forms. Finally, it calls into question the legitimacy of previous forms of authority patterns by making those traditional forms of authority seem less awesome.[1]

In any society, the propensity to form new groups depends on the nature of the society's primordial groups and on its differential rates of group mobilization, which in turn are based on levels of education, socioeconomic status, and attachment of various sectors of society to traditional values. Thus, modernization has a differential impact on heterogeneous traditional societies. As a result, there is enhanced competition for new rewards and there are also widening disparities in the capacities of groups to secure those rewards.

The development of modern voluntary associations began in India during the nineteenth century, as a response to the acceleration of social change under colonial rule and British colonial policy. The extent, duration, and intensity of British rule upset the traditional social order. Groups which had long existed amicably were provoked into novel competition with one another. And new groups came into existence, necessitated by the erosion of traditional patterns of stratification in the urban sector of India's preindustrial society. The process of social differentiation according to nontraditional principles in the urban sector superimposed a new, urban, middle class on a still largely tradi-

[1] Harry Eckstein, "Group Theory and the Comparative Study of Pressure Groups," in *Comparative Politics: A Reader*, ed. Harry Eckstein and David Apter (New York: Free Press, 1963), p. 395.

tional, segmented, rural agricultural society, for the countryside had remained isolated from many of the major forces of change that swept through the cities during the nineteenth century. The resulting duality in Indian society led to an exacerbation of the usual estrangement between the urban elites and the masses of the society residing in the countryside. A tentative rapprochement began in the twentieth century, under the impact of nationalism, and was accelerated with the end of colonial rule and the introduction of the politics of mass franchise.

Indian society in the middle of the eighteenth century was characterized by a strong tradition of localism based on geographic isolation and exclusivity and by a social heterogeneity that seldom transgressed regional boundaries, although it fragmented the society along community, caste, and language lines. Indian localism derived its power from strong loyalties to family, kin, caste, and village and from a nearly complete economic self-sufficiency resulting from and perpetuating a relative lack of commercialization. More specifically, the rural economy was characterized by the outflow of surplus agricultural products from villages to towns or cities, by a limited inflow of specialized products like indigo and cotton, and by a comparative divorce of urban finance and trade from the rural exchange mechanisms.[2]

The level of urbanization in India in particular areas was comparable to that in many other countries at the time of British penetration. But traditionally important urban centers, such as Murshidabad, Dacca, Surat, and Ahmedabad,[3] were to give way to the British-created port cities of Calcutta, Bombay, and Madras. The port cities became the centers of commercial activity and of political and cultural affairs as well. Of the old cities, only Ahmedabad was able to regenerate itself into a modern industrial center and thus ensure its survival as a commercial metropolis. The sustained concentration of development in the coastal cities resulted in patterns of uneven growth and development that called forth new classes of workers to perform new functions in new localities. Thus, development aggravated the tensions and conflicts that the years of East India Company rule had already inspired among and within different sectors of Indian society.

During the long period of Hindu hegemony in India, the tradition of localism was reinforced by the strong attachments to community, caste, region, and language and was left nearly untouched by the ebb and flow of foreign intercultural contact, which over the years left sig-

[2] D. R. Gadgil, *Origins of the Modern Indian Business Class: An Interim Report* (New York: Institute of Pacific Relations, 1959), pp. 1–16.

[3] Kenneth Gillion, *Ahmedabad: A Study in Indian Urban History* (Berkeley and Los Angeles: University of California Press, 1968), pp. 37–40.

nificant deposits of religious minorities like the Parsis, Sikhs, Christians, and tribals. Many of these groups—especially the Parsis, Sikhs, and tribals—were concentrated in geographic areas where relative numbers gave them strength and protection. But one of the most sensitive legacies of the Muslim period of Indian history was the creation of a vast, unassimilated Muslim community scattered across north India. Indian Muslims were never completely integrated in the society. The period of Muslim rule did not encourage Hindu aspirations and was in fact so constituted that it forced Hinduism into a protective shell which was not broken until the Hindu renaissance that followed the introduction of British education. And so Hindus could hardly be expected to embrace the deposed ruling class. Muslim particularism eventually led to the partition of the subcontinent, but migration was not complete enough to eliminate the Hindu–Muslim communal problem in India.

Hinduism had produced a remarkably stable social order which even Muslim rule was unable to destroy. This strong cultural tradition transcended the weakness of its central political authority,[4] perhaps surviving just because it was rooted in the observances of family and caste which external ruling bureaucracies could not replace or penetrate as they could ordinary political institutions. One of the unique features of the traditional Hindu social order called for the division of society into four varnas: Brahmin, Kshatriya, Vaisya, and Sudra. The Brahmins, whose function, strictly speaking, was to provide authoritative interpretations of Hinduism, served as a priestly and learned elite; the Kshatriya were the princes and warriors who were responsible for political functions; Vaisya conducted trade and commerce; and the Sudras provided the work force. These four varnas were supplemented by an additional group known variably today as untouchables, Harijans, or scheduled castes. This group functioned as an essential part of the Hindu social order but was segregated from the other groups because of the low status of its members and their performance of ritually polluting tasks, such as those performed by barbers, laundrymen, and shoemakers. In actuality, however, caste in India comprehends a much more complex phenomenon than the Vedic four varna scheme suggested. Caste, as a working social institution in India, was based on endogamous kinship groups called *jatis.* Defined by marriage and lineage, each Jati was identifiable only on a local basis. Thus, caste consisted not of four great natural groups but of thousands of local jatis which could only roughly, and only at top and bottom levels with any clarity, be

[4] Rajni Kothari, *Politics in India* (Boston: Little, Brown, 1970), pp. 21–41.

assigned to one of the varnas. However, once tradition felt the forces of modernization and change, the difficulty and ambiguity of ranking jatis vis-à-vis varna provided opportunities for groups of related jati to unite in an attempt to raise their status by identifying themselves with a higher varna. For example, a group of related Sudra jati might, as a result of changes in education, wealth, land ownership, or occupation leading to a higher self-image, band together into a caste association to prepare and press their claim to higher status. In time, these caste associations and caste federations expanded their activities to include politics. Thus, an outgrowth of traditional group allegiances transformed itself into an agency of modern social change by urging on society as a whole the demands of segments of the Indian peasantry.[5]

British colonialism had a profound impact on India's strong tradition of localism and created new tensions among India's primordial social groups. British crown rule, following East India Company rule, strengthened a central political authority whose cultural territory, although never congruent with a single political entity, dated back to pre-Muslim days. With almost all of India finally unified under one power, peace and stability were restored to a divided subcontinent. A uniform legal order, although not totally inclusive of all subjects, was extended to all sectors of the diverse Indian society. To administer it, a modern bureaucracy was recruited on the basis of merit through open competition.[6] Thus, an arena for national activity was created.

Of all the changes arising from British colonial policy, the most profound was the change in the pattern of education. The introduction of Western education in 1835 influenced the pattern of Indian modernization more than any other change, for it brought into being a new Indian elite which was to play a dominant role in the development of the country. Yet even here the new was not inconsistent with the traditional pattern of social organization. The introduction of Western education drew its most enthusiastic response from the old literati, consisting in large part of the Brahmanic and other highly placed castes.[7] The men so trained were the first Indians to enter the modern professions of law, medicine, and journalism. Their common experience with the new education led them to conceive of mutually compatible new sets of values which required, for actualization, new pat-

[5] See Lloyd I. Rudolph and Susanne Hoeber Rudolph, *The Modernity of Tradition: Political Development in India* (Chicago: University of Chicago Press, 1967); and Robert L. Hardgrave, Jr., *The Nadars of Tamilnad* (Berkeley and Los Angeles: University of California Press, 1969).

[6] Sir Percival Griffiths, *Modern India* (New York: Praeger, 1962), pp. 51–79.

[7] B. B. Misra, *The Indian Middle Classes: Their Growth in Modern Times* (London: Oxford University Press, 1961), pp. 343–389; Kothari, *Politics in India*, p. 98.

terns of interaction. These professional men therefore led the way in establishing modern voluntary associations designed to bring about the social, religious, educational, and political revitalization of the society.[8] They were also the first to found provincial political associations, and later they were to transcend the localistic tendencies of the traditional Indian social order by banding together at the all-Indian level to create the Indian National Congress in 1885. The Indian National Congress, of course, became the primary instrument for pressing Indian demands on the colonial regime.

The British-trained elite then came to enjoy a primacy in Indian society which they never relinquished. Their dominance was facilitated by the fact that intellectual pursuits had traditionally commanded high status in Indian society. But it was also based on their relative homogeneity and high caste origins, their increasing numbers, their political influence, and their association with modern learned professions. Ironically, although the personal life styles of the educated elite were relatively uninhibited by caste residues, they were able to legitimize their position by drawing on Hindu tradition. For them, the traditional hostility and suspicion of the business function survived, so that the emergent political culture was to be as hostile to business as the old had been.

British educational policy led to the emergence of a new, urban, middle-class, professional and political elite. Similarly, the impact of British trade and commerce and the beginnings of industrialization in the middle of the nineteenth century led to the development of both a foreign and an indigenous entrepreneurial elite. Therefore in India, although not in many other former colonial areas, indigenous capital emerged as force in its own right. Considerable sectors of India's traditional trading communities—especially the Parsis, Gujaratis, Marwaris, and Chettiars—moved as the occasion arose from trade into industry. Most members of the Indian business community felt that British economic and trade policies discriminated in favor of foreign capital, placing the products of Indian industry in an unfavorable trading position compared to those of the British home islands. And so the Indian entrepreneurial elite came into sharp conflict with British colonial rule. Competition between foreign and indigenous capital led to increasing resentment toward British economic policy, and as a result the Indian entrepreneurial elite became strongly committed to the cause of political and economic nationalism. Eventually they sup-

[8] Jyotirindra das Gupta, *Language Conflict and National Development* (Berkeley and Los Angeles: University of California Press, 1970), pp. 69–97; Misra, *Indian Middle Classes*, pp. 367–377.

ported the educated middle class in the founding of the Indian National Congress, which was formed as a pressure group demanding greater Indian participation in the colonial government. Although some businessmen dissociated themselves as the Congress became more radical, Indian business became the chief source of funds for the nationalist movement.[9]

Throughout the period of nationalist agitation, however, the Indian entrepreneurial elite maintained a distinct sense of its own interests and did not neglect to establish its own voluntary associations. These were formed, first at the provincial level and later at the national level, to press their demands and especially to try to counter the influence of foreign capital on British economic policy. Indian businessmen were determined to demonstrate to the British raj that the interests of foreign and indigenous capital were not the same and that the voice of British business in India could not be considered the voice of the entire business community of the country. And so Indian businessmen united to demand that the British colonial government make changes in their discriminatory policies in the fields of trade, tariffs, taxation, currency, and purchasing. Finally, the British were forced to recognize indigenous business associations as the true spokesmen for the Indian business community, and Indian businessmen succeeded in gaining seats in the legislative councils at both the state and national levels. Indian business was, thereafter, also represented on numerous advisory bodies.

Although they came by different paths to share the same commitment to political and economic nationalism, the entrepreneurial elite of India and the urban educated middle class remained distinct groups. It was not yet time for the new Brahmins to become one with the latter day Vaisyas, who had in fact originated among the traditional trading communities of India. With the exception of the Parsis, the business elite remained much more traditional in social customs and personal habits than the professional elite. Up to a point, in fact, their development as a potent national force was aided by these still intact, traditionally strong, family and caste ties. In the long run, however, these bonds tended to inhibit the process of social differentiation and interest group consolidation among them. The strong loyalties guaranteed by localized clannishness intensified the divisions, within the heterogeneous business elite, based on caste, regional origin, and the timing and nature of its response to colonial rule. Thus, unlike the urban middle class, the entrepreneurial elite was never able to develop a strong sense of soli-

[9] Misra, *Indian Middle Classes*, pp. 343–389.

darity. Moreover, unlike the literati, the business elite enjoyed, from the very beginning, a much lower social status because of the opprobrium traditionally attached to business and trade. Nevertheless, business was the only major economic interest in the modern sector which organized itself for collective action and was capable of articulating and pressing its own demands on government independently of the nationalist movement.

The beginnings of industrialization in the middle of the nineteenth century, under the auspices of foreign and indigenous capital, also led to the development of a small but important working class. Even today the working class in the modern sector of India does not exceed ten million out of a population of over five hundred million.[10] Although small in relation to the total working population, the working class became important because of the strategic position it held in the economy and especially in the export trade. The workers were illiterate, desperately poor, and therefore pliant before the omnipresent threat of unemployment due to the vast army of potential workers. And so the working class was not mobilized by its own leaders for class economic gains but by the professional urban middle class as part of the nationalist movement's effort to weaken the British hold in India. As a result, the working class did not develop autonomous structures. It remained dependent on the parent political organization, the Indian National Congress. The tradition of political unionism has continued into the post-independence period. Workers are now mobilized by outsiders, not to gain national independence but to provide electoral support for political parties. The urban proletariat in India still lacks a mechanism for the articulation of specialized demands.[11]

The massive Indian peasantry, which makes up about 70 percent of the entire Indian population, felt the impact of British rule in the form of changes in land tenure, the introduction of an increasingly monetary economy, and expanded commercialization. But the peasantry continued to be dominated by a tradition of localism and functioned as a segmented, caste-dominated social system under the Indian National Congress no less than under colonial rule. Economic and political power in the villages and small towns was exercised by the petty land-

[10] See Harold Crouch, *Trade Unions and Politics in India* (Bombay: Manaktalas, 1966); N. Pattabhi Raman, *Political Involvement of India's Trade Unions* (Bombay: Asia Publishing House, 1967); V. B. Karnik, *Indian Trade Unions: A Survey* (Bombay: Manaktalas, 1966); C. K. Johri, *Unionism in a Developing Economy* (Bombay: Asia Publishing House, 1967); S. D. Punekar and S. Madhuri, *Trade Union Leadership in India: A Survey* (Bombay: Lalvani Publishing House, 1967).

[11] Myron Weiner, *The Politics of Scarcity: Public Pressure and Political Response in India* (Chicago: University of Chicago Press, 1962), pp. 73–96.

lords, the small traders, and the minor officials. Because the routes of access—so far as such routes existed (and for the unorganized majority of the peasantry they simply did not exist)—to these sources of power were personal and local, there was yet little felt need for organization beyond local caste and kinship groupings. Those without personal contact were and always had been unable to articulate their demands or influence local power.[12]

During the nationalist movement, the Congress leadership attempted to mobilize the peasantry from time to time but with mixed success. The left wing of the Congress brought together a series of local peasant organizations to form an all-Indian Kisan Sabha, as a way of pressing the Congress to commit itself to a strong program of land reforms. But the Kisan Sabhas, like the trade unions, eventually became instruments of political mobilization used by political parties for electoral support.[13]

Despite the emergence of a number of functionally differentiated groups in the urban sector, the greatest impact of the social change accompanying British rule and its modernization process was on the political self-consciousness and identity of what Rajni Kothari calls India's "participant communities." [14] Except in the case of Muslim separatism, these stirrings within primordial groups were held in check until after independence. After independence, however, the politics of mass franchise strengthened rather than diminished the role of community interests. Community associations and ethnic interests so proliferated that the most potent interest articulators have been the particularisms of the still pervasive community, caste, language, and regional antecedents, rather than the social and economic interests in the modern sector.

Despite its advantages of early mobilization, autonomy, and clearly articulated organizational structure, business in India was never capable of establishing a "bourgeois dictatorship." [15] The pressures which came from business were important, but they were not the only ones nor invariably the most effective. Business was held in check by the basic attitudes of the political culture which were strongly antibusiness, by the demands of caste, community, language, and regional groups which tended to drown out the concern of the business community, and, as we shall see, by the fact that the predominantly upper-caste, middle-class, intellectual, political leadership eventually became committed to

[12] *Ibid.*, pp. 12–17.
[13] *Ibid.*, pp. 22–23.
[14] Kothari, *Politics in India*, pp. 224–249.
[15] A. H. Hanson, *The Process of Planning: A Study of India's Five Year Plans 1950–1964* (London: Oxford University Press, 1966), p. 241.

socialist and Gandhian ideology which shared with traditional Indian attitudes a hostility to business. Moreover, the business community, itself divided by many of these same forces, was so incapable of acting as a united business class that the very history and development of modern trade and industry is a story of the institutionalization of cleavages within the business community—cleavages wrought by the divisive politics of caste, region, and language.

Because it is such a complex story, anyone who would understand the problems encountered by the business community in articulating their demands and organizing for the purpose of collective action must first examine the origins of modern business in India and the development of the modern entrepreneurial elite. Only then will an analysis of the origins, internal dynamics, and behavior of modern business associations in India become comprehensible.

The Development of British Capital

Beginning in the middle of the nineteenth century, India developed two separate and distinct entrepreneurial elites: one British and one Indian. The British had arrived in India in 1600. Their arrival was part of the great surge of commercial activity which followed in the wake of the age of exploration and predated the industrial revolution. The spearhead of this commercial penetration in South Asia was the East India Company, which was chartered by the British crown and given exclusive trading rights in the East. In order to carry out its trading activity, the company established small trading settlements at Madras in 1639, Bombay in 1662, and Calcutta in 1690. Because of the growing internal political instability in India and the commercial rivalry among the European powers, the company proceeded to fortify these trading settlements. Within these settlements the merchants, therefore, became administrators as well.[16]

Prior to 1750, the company's administrative functions were minimal.[17] When the Mogul Empire began to crumble and political authority passed into the hands of a variety of successor states, the company began moving inland. The earliest major penetration came in Bengal, which eventually became the center of the company's political and economic activity. By the time the industrial revolution was under way in England, the company had already begun to perform several govern-

[16] Bernard S. Cohn, "Recruitment and Training of British Civil Servants in India," in *Asian Bureaucratic Systems Emergent from the British Imperial Tradition*, ed. Ralph Braibanti (Durham, N. C.: Duke University Press, 1966), pp. 87–140.

[17] Gadgil, *Origins*, p. 38.

mental functions. These functions continued to expand as the company increased its territory.

As its political power in India expanded, the company came under increasing attack at home. Successive changes in its charter curtailed its trading activities. In 1813, trade was thrown open to other British merchants and the company lost its trading monopoly; in 1833, the company ceased trading altogether. For the next twenty-five years, the East India Company served not as a body of merchants but as an instrument of the British government. Only after the mutiny of 1857 was political power in India placed directly in the hands of the crown.[18]

At the very time when company rule was coming to an end, India was about to embark on the beginning of industrialization. "(R)ailways reached out from Calcutta, Bombay, and Madras; coal mines began to be seriously worked in Bengal; and the first cotton mills in Bombay Presidency and first jute mill in Bengal were started." [19] It is important to note, however, that in each of these three major centers of economic activity, the pattern, timing, and sources of capital and entrepreneurship varied considerably. Calcutta and Bombay in particular followed such distinctive patterns of development that the result was a longstanding conflict and rivalry within the entrepreneurial elite. In eastern India, development was carried out by the investment of European capital in trade, export, and extractive industries that were concentrated in jute textiles, tea, and coal. In western India, development was financed largely by indigenous capital and was built around the traditional cotton textile industry of the area. Industrialization in Madras drew on both indigenous and British sources, but it was developed at a later time and at a slower pace.

Because Calcutta developed the largest and most exclusive European community in Asia, British interests naturally came to dominate the external trade, banking, insurance, and industry of the city. At first Calcutta was the center of the British export industry based on plantation crops such as indigo, jute, and tea. Later it became the hub of a factory-industry organized around jute textiles. From Calcutta, British capital also controlled the coal fields of Bengal, Bihar, and Orissa. The importance of those coal fields resulted from development of the steamship and the spread of railroads throughout the subcontinent. Because of this overwhelming European presence, Indian businessmen in Calcutta operated more as brokers and junior partners than as independent

[18] Edward Thompson and G. T. Garratt, *Rise and Fulfillment of British Rule in India* (Allahabad: Central Book Depot, 1966), pp. 461–472.

[19] Daniel Houston Buchanan, *The Development of Capitalistic Enterprise in India* (New York: Macmillan, 1934), p. 129.

entrepreneurs until World War I. Although Bengali entrepreneurs had moved into industry as early as the second quarter of the nineteenth century, they tended to be overshadowed by the British presence.

The British business community of Calcutta originated in the small but active group of free merchants and European servants of the East India Company. In the early days of company rule, they were permitted to engage in private trade, even before the company's monopoly of trade was officially ended. Free merchants were British merchants who were permitted to trade in a presidency of India under license from the company. Servants of the company considered the opportunity to participate in private trade as one of the major incentives for going to India. Thus, when the company eventually forbade its employees to engage in private trade, many of them—finding their talents much more suited to trade than administration—resigned from the company.

One of the earliest devices employed by free merchants and company servants to carry out trade and banking was the European agency house, which flourished in Calcutta from 1790 to the mid-1830s. The agency house was the primary means of pooling the rupee savings of company, civil, and military servants for the purpose of developing internal trade in the procurement of commodities for the East India Company's export trade and the provision of supplies for its needs as government.[20] Rungta declares that "between 1790 and 1830 these houses were the center of large capital resources, enterprise, and administration and organizational skills, and wielded great economic and political powers." [21] But the European agency houses collapsed in the mid-1830s, as a result of a commercial crisis in England at the very moment when the East India Company's trading functions were terminated. On the ruins of these old agency houses, however, were built the great managing agency houses which came to play such an important role in the development of industry and the shaping of Indian economic development.

Whereas the old agency houses had been built on the rupee savings of the company servants and free merchants, the managing agency system was the primary vehicle for bringing British sterling capital to India. But the managing agency system, a form of industrial organization "where the promotion, finance, and administration of a vast agglomeration of miscellaneous and unrelated enterprises . . . are controlled by a single firm," [22] was also a method for British investors

[20] *Ibid.*, p. 142.

[21] Radhe Shyam Rungta, *The Rise of Business Corporations in India: 1851–1900* (Cambridge, Cambridge University Press, 1970), p. 21.

[22] S. K. Basu, *The Managing Agency System: In Prospect and Retrospect* (Calcutta: World Press Private Ltd., 1958), pp. 4–5.

to invest in India without having to go to India to supervise their investments.

Supposedly designed merely to maximize entrepreneurial talent, capital, and managerial skills, each company under the managing agency system was in theory functionally and legally independent, with its own board of directors. In practice, however, it was the managing firm and not the individual company's board of directors which exercised the real control. The managing agency contracts were signed for long periods of twenty to thirty years, and many managing agents insured themselves against the loss of a contract by utilizing financial, stock, and voting arrangements to insure perpetual control. From its inception among the insurance companies established in the later years of East India Company rule, the system spread to shipping, coal mining, and sugar under the European agency houses, then to the new factory-industries of cotton and jute textiles which began in the 1850s and to the new tea companies. From the 1870s onward it became the most "generally accepted way of running business corporations in the country,"[23] among both foreign and indigenous entrepreneurs.

The early British managing agents had been free merchants and European company servants. Later they were joined by engineers and technicians, who had been brought to India to install machinery and to teach Indians to operate it. Others who became managing agents came to India in connection with the purchase of raw materials, the sale of finished products, and shipping.[24] For example, one of the most powerful of the managing agency houses, and one which illustrates the scope and complexity of the managing agency system in its British heyday, was Mackinnon Mackenzie, a shipping firm which was part of the British India Company. Mackinnon Mackenzie enjoyed governmental patronage in the form of mail contracts, shipment of government stores, and passage for civilian and military officers. In addition, it was granted a monopoly of the coastal trade. The company was founded in 1856 and

> by the early 70s of the nineteenth century the BIC, still just in its teens, was straddling a large part of the globe. Its operations ranged from London to China, and Australia was coming up over the horizon. It was in virtual command of the India coast trade from Chittagong right around to Bombay and Karachi. The scorched ports of the Persian Gulf were practically its monopoly.

[23] Rungta, *Rise of Business Corporations*, p. 220.
[24] Buchanan, *Development of Capitalistic Enterprise*, pp. 142–143.

> It was the main artery of the vital trade in rice between Rangoon and Calcutta. It carried the enormous surplus of Indian labor from Madras and ports adjacent to Burma, the Straits, and East Africa. Then China, Japan, the Islands of the Bay of Bengal and the Indian Ocean . . . were oysters waiting to be opened in that fabulous period of the sort of expansion that only a maritime race could exploit.[25]

The managing agency firms, unlike the joint stock companies they controlled, could take the form of a partnership, a private or limited company, or an individual,[26] but most British managing agency firms were partnerships. When a partner died or retired, he was succeeded by his son or replaced by a senior official of the firm. Many of England's most prominent business figures made their fortunes in India. Many became influential figures in British politics and acted as advisors on Indian colonial policy. One such figure was James Mackay, later Lord Inchcape, who directed the British India Company. Another was Sir Edward Benthall, a major figure in Bird and Company. After independence, most managing agency partnerships adopted corporate forms of management as a result of changes in tax policy, the need for larger resources, and increasing governmental control and surveillance designed to eliminate abuses which had begun to develop.[27] Despite its long history of adaptability, the popularity of the system declined rapidly after independence. New foreign investment adopted more modern forms of organization, and the government of India, which had continued to place restrictions on its operations, finally decided to abolish the system altogether in 1970.[28]

By the time of its abolition, the managing agency system was notorious for its concentration of power in the hands of a very small number of firms. Just as, in 1911, a group of fifteen foreign owned and operated managing agents controlled 189 industrial units,[29] on the eve of World War II, sixty-one foreign managing agency houses were managing more than 600 companies. Among the top managing agency houses were Andrew Yule which managed 59 units, Bird-Heilgers with 37, Martin Burn with 34, Begg Sutherland with 27, Duncan and Octavius Steel

[25] George Blake, *B. I. Centenary, 1856–1956* (London: Collins Press, 1956), p. 82.

[26] Basu, *Managing Agency System*, pp. 4–5.

[27] *Ibid.*, p. 13.

[28] Matthew J. Kust, *Supplement to Foreign Enterprise in India: Laws and Policies* (Chapel Hill, N. C.: University of North Carolina Press, 1966), pp. 61–66.

[29] M. M. Mehta, *Structure of Indian Industries* (Bombay: Popular Book Depot, 1961), pp. 316–317.

with 25 each, McLeod, Gillanders Arbuthnot and Shaw Wallace with 22 each, and Jardine Henderson with 20. The variety and scope of control can be seen in the case of Andrew Yule, which managed 18 tea companies, 15 coal mining companies, 11 jute mills, 2 jute presses, 3 shipping companies, and one company each in electricity, flour milling, and a number of other spheres.[30] In general, however, the British managing agency houses concentrated largely on banking, insurance, tea, jute, and coal. Based in Calcutta, they towered over their Indian counterparts, which developed around the cotton textile industries of Bombay. When, after independence, the gradual transfer of ownership to the Indian entrepreneurial elite did not appreciably dilute the concentration of economic and productive power, the situation which had been tolerable to a colonial government became politically and ideologically untenable.

The Development of Indian Capital

By contrast with Calcutta or Madras, the development of Bombay as a commercial and industrial center was essentially the handiwork of Indian communities including Hindus, Muslims, Parsis, and Jews.[31] The reasons for this are various and interrelated. In the first place, the west coast—unlike Calcutta, which was no more than a cluster of nondescript villages—was already a center of trade when the British arrived. Explaining why it had been Indian capital which came to play a dominant role in the development of modern industry in Bombay, the Report of the Indian Industrial Commission of 1916–1918 declared:

> If the cause be sought, some indication may be found in the fact that Indians have held a large and important share in the trade of Bombay since the city first came into English hands. The Mahomedans of the west coast, especially, traded by sea with the Persian Gulf, Arabia, and East Africa from much earlier times. The Parsees and Hindus from the northern Bombay coast districts are recorded at the beginning of the British occupation, as taking, with the Mahomedan sects of Khojas, Memons, and Bohras, a most important share in the trade of the port as contractors, merchants, financiers, and shipbuilders, and have throughout shown

[30] Michael Kidron, *Foreign Investments in India* (London: Oxford University Press, 1965), p. 6.

[31] F. R. Harris, *Jamsetji Nusserwanji Tata: A Chronicle of His Life* (Bombay: Blackie and Son (India) Ltd., 1958), pp. 65–66.

> themselves little, if at all, inferior to the English in enterprise, and usually in command of more capital.[32]

British expansion in western India had also been delayed considerably by the existence of strong regional opposition. And, although Bombay did finally become a fortified, commercial outpost of the East India Company,[33] the English settlement there was smaller than its counterpart in Calcutta. As a result of the succeeding long period of relatively light rule, "the competition of races, European and Indian, although as keen as in any other provinces, is tempered by common interests, mutual forbearance, and a certain reciprocal respect, which impart a moderation to Bombay public opinion."[34]

Among the non-Europeans in India, the small Parsi community of one hundred thousand was the first to develop modern industry and banking. Zoroastrian by religion, the Parsis came in the early eighteenth century from Gujarat to Bombay, where they acted as commission merchants and brokers for the East India Company. They became wealthy through foreign trade with Africa, the Near East, and especially China, where they made fortunes in opium and yarn. They were also involved in shipbuilding and real estate and owned some of the most valuable real estate in Bombay. Responding quickly to Western education, the Parsis became one of the most highly anglicized communities in India.[35]

The first successful cotton mill in Bombay was built in 1854 by Cowasjee Davar, a Parsi banker. His success encouraged others to follow his example. These Parsi pioneers succeeded in floating their companies, mainly with the help of members of their own community who formed the directorates.[36] Following the boom in the Bombay cotton market during the American Civil War, the cotton textile industry in western India expanded very rapidly. With Parsis like Sir Dinshaw Petit and Nowrosjee Wadia still in the forefront, leading Muslim, Jewish, and Gujarati trading families began building cotton mills until

[32] Quoted in Misra, *Indian Middle Classes*, p. 248.

[33] Helen B. Lamb, "The Development of Modern Business Communities in India" in *Labor Management and Economic Growth: Proceedings of a Conference on Human Resources and Labor Relations in Underdeveloped Countries*, ed. R. L. Aronson and J. P. Windmiller (Ithaca: Cornell University Press, Institute of International Industrial and Labor Relations, 1954), p. 108.

[34] Quoted in V. I. Pavlov, *The Indian Capitalist Class: A Historical Study* (Bombay: People's Publishing House Private, Ltd., 1964), p. 289.

[35] Lamb, "Development of Modern Business Communities," pp. 109–113.

[36] Rungta, *Rise of Business Corporations*, p. 245.

> from numbers small enough to be counted on the tips of one's fingers, the entrepreneurial ranks expanded substantially in consonance with the growing character of the industry. General traders, shroffs (indigenous bankers), mill managers and technicians, cloth and cotton merchants, machinery agents, other varieties of financiers and speculators serve to fill in the ranks of the expanding group. . . . The growth of the trade in textile machinery, and the creation of a specialized class of persons, who agreed to put up a mill for a financial consideration—both these factors enabled the mere financier or the ignorant cloth trader to start cotton mills.[37]

In the 1870s, the Parsi family of Tata became active in the textile industry. The Tata family were hereditary priests of the Parsis, but Nusserwanji Tata had given up the priesthood in the 1840s to become a Bombay banker and China merchant. As the founder of the managing agency still known as the House of Tata, his son Jamsetji N. Tata became the industrial pioneer par excellence. In addition to building three cotton mills, including the first to spin fine-count yarn, Jamsetji planned the development of the first Indian iron and steel mill and hydroelectric system. Both projects were eventually carried out by his sons. The House of Tata shortly grew into the biggest non-European managing agency house in India, and it simultaneously achieved a reputation throughout India for its honesty and commitment to development, education, science and technology, and social reform.[38]

The second of the traditional trading communities to make the important transition from commerce to industry were the Gujaratis of Bombay and Ahmedabad. *Gujarati* is a term applied to various trading groups originating in the cities of Gujarat and Kutch. These cities are located in western India, north of Bombay in what is now the state of Gujarat. The Gujaratis include a number of caste groups with different customs and traditions, the most important of which are the Shravak Jain Banias of Ahmedabad and the Bhatias and Lohanas of Kutch. Like the Parsis, most of the Gujarati traders enjoyed a reputation for commercial honesty.[39] Among the earliest Gujarati industrialists of Bombay were the Bhatias. The four most prominent Bhatia families

[37] Phiroze B. Medhora, "Entrepreneurship in India," *Political Science Quarterly* 80 (1965): 570.

[38] See Harris on the life of Tata.

[39] Thomas A. Timberg, *Industrial Entrepreneurship Among the Trading Communities of India: How the Pattern Differs* (Cambridge: Harvard University, 1969), p. 64.

were those of Morarjee Gokuldas, Damodar Thackersey, Mulraj Khatau, and Vissanji. Thackersey and Khatau were associated with the Tatas, but they also worked closely with British capital in Bombay. It was Morarjee, Khatau, Sir Lallubhai Samaldas, and Walchand Hirachand, another giant among Gujarati industrialists in Bombay, who in 1919 established the Scindia Steam Navigation Company, the first to successfully challenge the British monopoly in shipping.[40]

Ahmedabad was the second center of Gujarati activity. The first cotton mill there was started in 1861 by Ranchhodlal Chhotalal. Chhotalal himself was a Nagar Brahmin, and the traditional occupation of the Nagar Brahmins was government service. But his financial support came from leading Ahmedabad bankers among whom was Maganbhai Karamchand (Sarabhai), a Jain banker whose family became major industrial innovators. By 1910, forty-eight mills had been built in Ahmedabad by local entrepreneurs. As had the Parsis, the Gujarati managing agents of Ahmedabad depended on community and family to supply joint partners, shareholders, officers, and employees for their companies. "But for the corporate spirit and confidence provided by these ties," wrote Gillion, "it is doubtful if Ahmedabad could have industrialized to the extent that she did."[41]

By World War I, the first phase of Indian industrial development had come to a close. India had developed a factory-industry based on cotton and jute textiles in addition to coal and tea. The preeminent position was enjoyed by the big British managing agency houses of Calcutta. Those houses controlled large numbers of companies.

> With the exception of Tatas, there was no Indian managing house which controlled or managed more than 5 industrial units. In the eastern sector, the only Indian firm which deserves mention was that of Messrs. N.C. Sirkar and Company which managed five big collieries and which had on its board of directors a large number of foreign directors. In the western sector, however, a large number of Indian managing agents, mostly belonging to the Jewish, Parsee, and Gujarati community, were just budding in. Prominent among these enterprising industrialists were Sassons, Khataus, Cowasjiis, Thackerseys, Jeejeebhoys, and Wadias.[42]

But following World War I, the balance of economic power in India began to change. The war had stimulated greater indigenous produc-

[40] Lamb, "Development of Modern Business Communities," pp. 113–115.
[41] Gillion, *Ahmedabad*, pp. 91–94.
[42] Mehta, *Structure of Indian Industries*, pp. 316–317.

tion, economic and political nationalism were beginning to have their impact, and British capital was beginning to hesitate in the face of the changing political and economic climate in India. It was during and after World War I that the Marwaris, the third and most aggressive traditional Indian trading community, began to move from commerce to industry.

Like the term *Gujarati,* the term *Marwari* is applied to a group of endogamous castes with elements of a common culture despite differences in ritual practices, regional origin, and economic activity.[43] Unlike the Parsis and Gujaratis, who tend to remain in their native area, the Marwaris have spread throughout the country so much that they have become the only really national business community. Nevertheless, their most important center of activity has been Calcutta. From there, by the late nineteenth century, they controlled the retail trade of the city and the internal trade of West Bengal.

In the early days of British rule, it had been Bengalis of Calcutta who, like the Parsis of Bombay and the Brahmins of Madras, were the first to take to English education and thus obtain the skills that permitted them to serve as brokers, middlemen, or interpreters and to staff and service British enterprise throughout north India. Rich Bengalis like Dwarkanath Tagore moved into industry as early as the second quarter of the nineteenth century, but the industrial enterprises belonging exclusively to Bengalis were short-lived.[44] By the latter part of the century, the Bengalis withdrew from trade and commerce, leaving a place to be filled by the Marwaris. The Marwaris, because of their business skill and commitment, also replaced Bengalis in the offices of British firms.

The Marwaris were ultraorthodox Hindus with a strong sense of community solidarity and a tight knit family system. As traders who ventured far afield, the Marwaris had to develop special institutions to assist them in their activity and to preserve their distinct identity. They established strong extended families to take care of the women and children left at home; they developed a keen sense of community feeling which enabled the itinerant Marwaris trader to get shelter from his caste fellows while traveling; they developed a unique credit network called the sarafi system, which enabled a Marwari to obtain credit based on his personal reputation instead of on collateral; they established an apprenticeship system within the family to train the young to enter

[43] Timberg, *Industrial Entrepreneurship,* p. 23.
[44] Pavlov, *Indian Capitalist Class,* p. 123.

the business; and they established community panchayats to enforce social mores and mediate business disputes.[45]

The Marwaris migrated to Calcutta in three waves. The first wave arrived about 1564, prior to the British penetration into India. This early group consisted of Oswals and Aggarwals. The Oswals were a very small group who enjoyed a special position as bankers. The famous Jagat Seths, who were said to have provided loans even to the East India Company, were members of this community. The Aggarwals were ultimately to be more important, however, because they emerged as the largest single group in the Calcutta Marwari community.[46] The second migration, which took place in the early nineteenth century, and especially after the end of the East India Company's monopoly of trade in 1813, brought Marwaris from different regions of Rajasthan and from different subcastes. The most prominent of the new groups were the Maheshwaris, who were primarily engaged in the business of sarafi or indigenous banking. The third and largest wave came in the 1890s, with the extension of the railroads and the establishment of Calcutta as the commercial hub of India.[47] As one commentator of the time observed, "The immigration from Rajputana has shown a phenomenal increase in recent years. This increase marks the invasion of the Marwari community into business circles in Calcutta. There are now some four times as many who were born in Rajputana . . . as there were thirty years ago." [48] Even so, the 1921 census shows the size of the Marwari community in Calcutta as only fifteen thousand.

At the turn of the century, Marwari prosperity was closely tied to British capital. Many of the most prosperous Marwaris served as Banyans, or brokers, for major British managing agency houses. A banyanship was a kind of credit and insurance system. British firms wanted to dispose of imported goods as soon as possible after arrival in the port of Calcutta so as to recover their investment without requiring credit or facing the possibility of losses in dealing with retailers or distributors. The banyan solved this problem. He deposited security money with the British importer and took immediate delivery of all goods for distribution. He was paid a commission of 1 percent, but he, in turn, was responsible for any losses which might result in the transaction. Because Marwaris had access to capital and credit, they were

[45] Timberg, *Industrial Entrepreneurship*, p. 7.

[46] Balchand Modi, *Desh-kee Itihas-mee Marwari Jatii-kaa Sthaan* (Calcutta: Ragunath Prasad Singhania, 1940), pp. 591–600 (Published in Hindi).

[47] Timberg, *Industrial Entrepreneurship*, pp. 25–28.

[48] *Ibid.*, pp. 28–29.

ideally suited for this type of function. Thus, for example, when Bird and Co. opened its piece goods department to act as an agency for a large Manchester mill, it enlisted a strong Marwari group as banyans.[49]

With its vast import trade, Calcutta became one of the biggest cloth trade centers in India. As late as 1900, and despite the number of textile mills that had been built in Bombay and Ahmedabad, Indian industry produced only 15 percent of Indian textile needs. The center of the import retail piece goods trade of Calcutta was concentrated in Bara Bazar, which handled 80 percent of the cloth trade of Calcutta and was mostly controlled by Marwaris. The Marwaris completely dissociated themselves from the Swadeshi agitation of 1905, when Indians were admonished to wear only Indian-made cloth. At this point, they opposed the nationalist movement, which seemed to threaten their livelihood.[50]

Marwaris began moving from trade to industry during World War I. From control of the raw jute market, they went into jute baling and finally into jute manufacturing, which up to that time had been dominated by the Scots. The Birla family built the first Indian jute mill in 1919 and was followed by Sir Sarupchand Hukumchand and Soorajmull Jalan. Moving next into cotton textiles, the Birlas built mills in Delhi and Gwalior. Again the Birla example was followed by other Marwaris who established industries in various parts of India. In addition, Marwaris began entering industries in new fields, especially sugar and cement. One of the most active in the cement business was the family of Dalmia. Thus the Marwari entrepreneurs who had migrated to Calcutta maintained their pattern of adaptability. They did not stay in one place or one industry but built various industries in various regions as opportunities presented themselves. Although Birla House remained based in Calcutta, Dalmia-Jain headquarters were located in Bihar, Singhania in Kanpur, Ruia and others in Bombay.[51] The creation of these new Marwari industrial interests led to a division of the Marwari community into two groups, one Nationalist, reformist, and industrialist, and the other orthodox, conservative, and dependent on British trade. The leader of the Nationalists was G. D. Birla, and the leader of the orthodox pro-British groups was Sir Badridas Goenka. Both these men played a major role in the early development of the voluntary associations in Calcutta.[52]

[49] Godfrey Harrison, *Bird and Company of Calcutta* (Calcutta: Anna Art Press Private Ltd., 1964), p. 123.

[50] J. H. Broomfield, *Elite Conflict in a Plural Society: Twentieth-Century Bengal* (Berkeley and Los Angeles: University of California Press, 1968), pp. 33 and 220.

[51] Lamb, "Development of Modern Business Communities," pp. 115–119.

[52] See Chapter VII.

The fourth major community to enter industry were the Chettiars of the south. Although Madras was the third largest center of British commercial activity, it was in many ways a poor trading center. It had no harbor, not even a pier, and losses between ship and shore represented 90 percent of the losses for the entire voyage to India and at least 20 percent of the profit.[53] Yet Madras persisted as a trade center, partly because it was already in existence and partly because there was no better location for several hundred miles on either side. Madras produced very little for export in the early years but instead became an "emporium, supplying foreign markets with foreign goods."[54] It provided banking and insurance services, naval supplies, and freight and passenger agents.[55]

The Chettiars, one of the most important indigenous banking communities in the south, had invested large amounts of capital in Burma in the form of agricultural loans. As a result of the depression of the 1930s, their debtors were in default, and they became large absentee landlords. By 1937, they owned one-fourth of the total cultivated land in lower Burma.[56] The bankruptcy of their traditional economic activities in Burma forced them to look toward their own country. "If we examine the modern incorporated enterprises in which they have some interest at present," reports Ito, "we find that the majority were founded in the 1930s and 1940s."[57] Transforming themselves from big time money lenders into modern entrepreneurs, the Chettiar community became closely associated with the cotton textile industry. Since World War II they have "supplied some of the most energetic and imaginative industrial leadership in south India."[58]

Several distinguishing features of the business community in India emerge from this brief survey of the origins and development of modern industry and entrepreneurship. These characteristics were to have a profound effect on the later mobilization, organization, and cohesion of an emergent business class. First, industrial development was highly uneven and concentrated in a few major port cities, especially in Calcutta and Bombay. Second, the level of industrialization was relatively modest and highly concentrated. Industry was primarily confined to ex-

[53] Hilton Brown, *Parry's of Madras: A Story of British Enterprise in India* (Madras: Parry and Company, Ltd., 1954), p. 5.

[54] *Ibid.*, p. 7.

[55] *Ibid.*, p. 60.

[56] Shoji Ito, "A Note on the 'Business Combine' in India," *Developing Economies* 4 (1966): 360–370.

[57] *Ibid.*, p. 372.

[58] George B. Baldwin, *Industrial Growth in South India: Case Studies in Economic Development* (New York: Free Press, 1959), p. 256.

port, extractive, plantation, and consumer goods, rather than in the field of modern heavy industry. This left a major gap in the Indian economy. Moreover, industry was highly concentrated in the hands of large industrial houses or conglomerates, which represented the major and most successful form of business organization. Third, modern industry was divided between foreign and indigenous capital which, as time passed, developed increasingly divergent and antagonistic interests. As seen in Table I-1, British capital took the lead, and Indian capital did not begin to surge ahead until after World War II. By that time it had succeeded in reversing many of the discriminatory policies of the colonial regime. Fourth, Indian capital was drawn primarily from a small handful of traditional trading communities. Among indigenous entrepreneurs, family and community played a major role because of their ability to mobilize capital. They were also dominant in determining the composition of the management. Moreover, in the relations among Indian entrepreneurs, family and community rivalry came to play a prominent role. This was particularly true of the relationship between the Parsi and Gujarati textile magnates of western India and the more traditional and socially conservative Marwari entrepreneurs of Calcutta. Although the Parsis and Gujaratis were among the first to enter modern industry, their preeminent position was challenged by the rapid rise of the Marwaris. As seen in Table I-1, by World War II, the Marwaris had become the most important single indigenous industrial community in India.

Table I-1

Industrial Control by Community (1911–1951)

	Number of companies			*Number of directors*		
	1911	*1931*	*1951*	*1911*	*1931*	*1951*
British	282	416	382	652	1,335	865
Parsis	15	25	19	96	261	149
Gujaratis	3	11	17	71	166	232
Jews	5	9	3	17	13	0
Muslims	0	10	3	24	70	66
Bengalis	8	5	20	48	170	320
Marwaris	0	6	96	6	146	618
Mixed Control	28	28	79	102	121	372
Total	341	510	619	1,016	2,282	2,622

Source: B. B. Misra, *The Indian Middle Classes* (London: Oxford University Press, 1961), p. 250.

In the attempt to create larger collectivities and to structure a more distinctive business class, the characteristics of the new entrepreneurial elite were extremely important. It was the new business elite, organized into business houses, that provided the leadership, resources, and encouragement for the founding of modern trade and industry associations in India in the nineteenth century. These associations were founded in an attempt to persuade the business community at large of the need to organize to protect its interests. However, in the major business centers of India, strong traditional loyalties based on family, caste, community, language, and region led to the creation of a multiplicity of associations, especially among Indian entrepreneurs. Where organizations made an effort to represent a diversity of interests, differences became reflected in their internal politics. Thus, although the new industrial elite established modern associations to represent their interests, they found that their activities in these strictly functional institutions were muddled by allegiances to family, caste, community, language, and region. Those allegiances became superimposed on interest conflicts between trade and industry and among various types of industry. The tenuity of cohesion and the difficulty of articulating meaningful and specific demands from an exceedingly diverse membership therefore hampered the operations of these business groups from the very beginning and impeded their organizational development.

At the same time, colonial rule and British colonial policy also set in motion a process of change which led to a partial social differentiation of the Indian society. Social differentiation was most extensive within the small but important urban sector consisting of a growing, vigorous, but divided middle class and a small but active urban proletariat. The 70 percent of the population which is still rural and constitutes the mass of Indian peasantry remained socially fragmented and segmented along caste and linguistic lines. Only slowly are class differences beginning to emerge among them.[59] And yet the strongest interests in India tend to remain those that reflect primordial loyalties, not those that represent the demands of the smaller, more class-oriented groups in the modern social and economic sectors, among which the modern business associations are included.

The hostilities and conflicts generated by both traditional and modern interests in the society create serious problems of cohesion and national integration for the political system. The management of conflict is critical to the very survival of the political system, and it is

[59] George Rosen, *Democracy and Economic Change in India* (Berkeley and Los Angeles: University of California Press, 1966), pp. 296–299.

precisely here that the political culture becomes important. The values and attitudes of the society reflected in its political culture affect group activity, decision-making, and the very mechanisms of conflict management. It is to this subject that we now turn.

II

POLITICAL CULTURE

Political culture comprehends the configuration of individual attitudes toward politics as well as the organization of society which underlies the functioning of a political system. These attitudes and social patterns play an important role in setting aspirations and expectations, influencing patterns of decision-making, and otherwise shaping acceptable political behavior. Ultimately this congruence gives legitimacy to the political system whose continuity, in the absence of such endorsement, is likely to be in jeopardy. Although the political system of modern India is modeled after the British example, it must function in a nation whose political experience, individual expectations, social structure, and societal values differ dramatically from those which produced the Parliament of Westminster.

One of the results of British educational policy was to create in urban India what was, for a developing nation, a disproportionally large attentive public. The members of this segment of the population evince a keen interest in politics. They participate in a variety of political activities and hold clearly structured opinions about government policies, programs, and leadership.[1] Although urban opinion is sharply divided on a large number of issues, the intelligentsia as a whole has, in the past, tended to reflect a higher level of frustration and alienation than the rest of the society. In recent years this sense of alienation has also begun to develop within the Indian business community.

Until recently, a more passive view of political life was exhibited by the numerous subsectors of the Indian society that include the illiterates, lower income groups, and rural population. These segments of the population have demonstrated little overt interest in politics and political activity. This relative passivity can hardly have been unrelated to the low level of political knowledge found in these subsectors of the population and their inability to structure opinion on major issues.[2]

[1] Samuel J. Eldersveld, "The Political Behavior of the Indian Public," *Indian Institute of Public Opinion, Monthly Public Opinion Surveys* 9 (1964): 4–9. Although one may question whether the institute's studies are based on perfect samples of all Indian adults, the studies do provide a definite basis for developmental analysis.

[2] *Ibid.*

Under the impact of mass franchise, mass education, and the gradual dispersion and devolution of power that has taken place since independence, there is increasing evidence to show that the political perceptions of these groups are growing more sophisticated, so that the gap between the urban elite and the masses is gradually beginning to close. Thus Indian political behavior is beginning to reflect a keener awareness.

The development, as a result of colonial rule and British educational policy, of a strong central political authority and the superimposing of a new national political elite upon the traditionally segmented masses of Indian society resulted, as we have seen, in the emergence of a dual political culture in India.[3] The split roughly corresponds to the urban-rural distribution of the Indian population. A new elite political culture emerged among the English-educated middle class of intellectuals, senior bureaucrats, the military, the national political leadership, trade union leaders, and sectors of the business elite. But the traditional political culture continued to exist, relatively unchanged, among the massive peasantry which was localized, illiterate, and segmented into a variety of endogamous social units. The wide gap separating these two elements of the Indian political culture began to close slowly under the impact of nationalism, the end of colonial rule, the introduction of politics of mass franchise, and the increasing availability of mass communication and mass transportation.

The existence of a dual political culture obviously presents substantial obstacles to any group desiring to marshall popular support by direct appeals. In India, therefore, according to the Indian Institute of Public Opinion data of the late 1950s and early 1960s,

> only a small minority, the educated and well-to-do, are aware and informed of India's political issues and problems and are able to think intelligently about them. While the lower classes may be interested, so far the politics of their developing society has not penetrated to their political consciousness, nor enabled them to respond meaningfully to political controversies—whether these are controversies over what system shall prevail, or the solution of contemporary problems, or what leadership shall be entrusted with the country's future.[4]

[3] Myron Weiner, "India's Two Political Cultures," in *Political Change in South Asia*, edited by Myron Weiner (Calcutta: Firma K. L. Mukhopadhyay, 1963), pp. 115–152.

[4] Eldersveld, "Political Behavior," p. 9.

During this period of Indian post-independence political experience, one of the most salient issues, a subject of both ideological and symbolic import, was the issue of socialism and a corresponding prejudice against private sector business.[5] Prime Minister Nehru, noted one observer,

> constructed out of the hopes for planning and the public sector the equivalent of a charismatic ideology pointing toward a modern and socialist future. The symbolic function of that ideology, quite apart from its pragmatic implications, were immense. It focused national attention on public, collective, and national goods, and consequently played a considerable role in "nation-building." It made it possible to sustain political hope in a difficult era.[6]

The most deeply committed to a socialist ideology were the urban intellectuals who believed that the socialist pattern implied a vast area of government ownership and that control went beyond mere advocacy of nationalization of large-scale industry and banks to include small-scale and cottage industries, schools, colleges, and hospitals.[7] But most sectors of Indian society had no clear image of precisely what a socialist pattern of society meant. Thus, when surveyed by the Indian Institute of Public Opinion,[8] 95 percent of the urban and rural illiterate and 84 percent of the lower income groups were incapable of responding to queries about expanding the public sector or curtailing the private sector. However, although socialism was most salient to the elite political culture, its symbolic effect was much more widespread despite its vagueness.

The predominant method of reaching the masses in India, and especially the rural peasantry during this period, was to mobilize by using the persuasive powers of local notables and caste elders. What mattered most in rural India at election time was not a candidate's political beliefs or experience but the strength of his rent rolls, his local prestige, his religion, his caste and family, his connections, his wealth, and his benefactors. Traditional loyalties and dependencies thus became and remain an important part of modern politics. Under this system, leaders of the Congress party and of other major political parties were

[5] Indian Institute of Public Opinion, "A Decade of Public Opinion Research: The Sociological Field," *Monthly Public Opinion Surveys* 4 (1964): 26–27.

[6] Susanne Hoeber Rudolph, "The Writ from Delhi," *Asian Survey* 11 (1971): 967.

[7] Indian Institute of Public Opinion, "A Decade of Public Opinion Research," pp. 26–27.

[8] Eldersveld, "Political Behavior," p. 7.

relatively free to formulate and initiate social and economic policies because of the absence of pressures from below. At most, caste leaders within the major parties acted as brokers, who integrated their groups into the larger governing coalition in exchange for relatively modest pork barrel benefits such as schools, roads, and medical facilities. Increasingly, however, these old methods for communicating with the rural masses have been breaking down.[9]

By the late 1960s, there appeared to be an acceleration in the shift away from mobilization on the basis of old loyalties. The political elites which had emerged since independence began making a sustained effort to influence the masses by means of leadership, ideas, and programs designed to appeal directly to the interests of the voters.[10] They were, in short, approaching the illiterate and unsophisticated voter as a unit of opinion rather than as a traditional social unit to be delivered through respected intermediaries based on traditional loyalties and dependencies. A variety of sample surveys of Indian opinion, conducted in the late 1960s, revealed that there was, in fact, an important change taking place in the structuring of opinion in India, and that the strategy of the "new politics" had shrewdly taken into account these changes in voter perceptions and concern with concrete policy issues.[11]

The rhetoric of socialism and development which was used to mobilize support for the government during the past twenty years has resulted in a strong tendency of the Indian electorate to look to government for solutions to their problems. A recent cross-national survey, for example, revealed that Indians, to a greater extent than was the case of citizens of countries like Japan or Nigeria, have high expectations of their government and look to government to solve their problems. A cross-section sample of Indians were asked where they would be most likely to go for help in the event they could not earn enough to support themselves. The respondents were offered two alternatives: relatives not living in the household or the government. Only 31.8 percent of the Indian respondents expected help from relatives, despite the strong traditions of a joint family system. On the other hand, 50.5 percent of the respondents expected aid from government or a government agency. Moreover, when asked whether they *preferred* such help from relatives or from government, only 24.2 percent would look for it from relatives while 69.0 percent considered government aid preferable.

[9] Myron Weiner, "The 1971 Election and the Indian Party System," *Asian Survey* 11 (1971): 1155.

[10] *Ibid.*, p. 1156.

[11] Rajni Kothari, "Continuity and Change in India's Party System," *Asian Survey* 10 (1970): 937–948.

Thus, popular attitudes no less than ideological commitments to socialism seem to support a high level of governmental intervention in the society to solve major social and economic problems.[12]

The existence of high expectations, however, has been accompanied by an increasing feeling that the governmental performance has failed to match these expectations. Surveys taken as early as the 1967 general elections indicated a measurable increase in dissatisfaction with government's inability to control inflation, its failure to ensure the proper distribution of food during periods of scarcity, and its failure to provide strong leadership without which the economy could not function.[13] In particular, the electorate expressed strong disappointment with the effects which poor government performance had had on their livelihood. When asked to evaluate the progress of their personal financial condition during the decade of the 1960s, not only were all respondents capable of expressing an opinion on the subject, but 53.4 percent felt their economic condition had deteriorated, 28.1 percent said it was unchanged and only 16.6 percent felt it had improved. Over half of the respondents felt that their personal financial condition had grown worse, and there was also strong evidence to indicate that discontented respondents were prepared to translate their sense of dissatisfaction into political reprisal. A disproportionate share of those who felt their personal condition had deteriorated supported opposition political parties at the polls.[14] Thus, the strong anti-Congress attitudes reflected in the 1967 elections were at least partly due to a sense of disillusionment with the performance of the Congress party as government.

Popular dissatisfaction with the Congress party resulted in a major reversal of the fortunes of the Indian National Congress in the 1967 election.[15] The popular vote for the Congress party declined from 44.73 percent in 1962 to 40.73 percent in 1967, its strength in the national Parliament dropped from 361 seats to 283, and the party lost control over half of the Indian state governments. The results of the election, however, created a crisis in the Congress party and brought the Indian political system itself under severe strains. The opposition parties, as heirs of popular discontent, had demonstrated they could—when united—bring an end to Congress party dominance, but they also proved incapable of sustaining cooperation long enough to provide stable and

[12] Kothari, *Politics in India* (Boston: Little, Brown, 1970), pp. 285–287.

[13] Kothari, "Continuity and Change," p. 946.

[14] *Ibid.*, pp. 945–946; and Samuel J. Eldersveld, "Elections and the Party System: Patterns of Party Regularity and Defection in 1967," *Asian Survey* 10 (1970): 1021.

[15] See Weiner, "The 1971 Election"; and Lloyd I. Rudolph, "Continuities and Change in Electoral Behavior: The 1971 Parliamentary Election in India," *Asian Survey* 11 (1971): 1119–1132.

effective government in the states they controlled. Far from solving the problems that monolithic Congress party rule had been unable to solve, coalition politics turned out to be a disaster in all but a few states. There was, in most states subject to coalition rule, an endemic defection of legislators from one party to another, a trend toward overstuffed cabinets designed purely to accommodate as many ambitious legislators as possible, a politicization and demoralization of the state bureaucracies, a paralysis of decision-making, and an increase in corruption and with it a growing popular cynicism toward politics, political parties, and the political system itself. Whereas previously the central government might have intervened decisively to counteract such an unwholesome political situation at the state level, there could be no effective corrective action to the politics of defection and instability. Factionalism and later a split in the ruling Congress party had left Prime Minister Indira Gandhi in power, although in charge of a virtually immobilized national government.[16]

Nowhere was the sense of frustration and alienation as strong as among major sectors of the Indian business elite. By early 1968, the steady erosion of political stability was leading sectors of the business community to question openly the viability of the existing political system in India. In a speech before the Indian Merchants Chamber on February 20, 1968, J. R. D. Tata, one of the most respected figures in Indian business, told the assembled businessmen of Bombay that the Indian political system was failing. Moreover, he continued, "the British parliamentary system of government . . . is unsuited to conditions in our country, to the temperament of our people, and to our historical background." [17] He suggested scrapping it in favor of a federal, presidential system. Under such a system, he argued, a chief executive elected for a fixed term would be "irremovable and free to govern through cabinets of experts . . . who may, but need not, include professional politicians." [18] Under a presidential system, then, India would gain both stability and expertise in the management of public affairs.[19]

The Tata critique was endorsed by a majority of the members of the Indian business elite who participated in a series of interviews con-

[16] S. H. Rudolph, "Writ from Delhi," pp. 958–969.

[17] J. R. D. Tata, Speech Delivered at the Sixtieth Annual General Meeting of the Indian Merchants Chamber, Bombay, February 20, 1968. (Bombay: Tata Press, 1968), pp. 21–22.

[18] *Ibid.*, p. 26.

[19] Tata's proposal was not new; it had been raised as early as 1965 by R. Venkataraman, a leading Congress party politician who, as industries minister in the state of Madras had submitted a similar proposal to the Congress AICC at Jubalpore. See *The Statesman* (Calcutta), May 29, 1965.

ducted in 1967.[20] Most of these business leaders agreed with J. R. D. Tata that India needed a more stable and effective government than they believed the existing system could provide. As one Bombay industrialist put it, "We want a stable and able government. With the present system you get a crowd who are ignorant of government and administrative procedures and although government may have a large number of ministers, no real work is done. Moreover, government becomes unstable and when government becomes unstable, business suffers." A young Calcutta industrialist concurred. "There are a lot of people in India who can do the job and deliver the goods," he asserted. "The problem with the parliamentary system is that it doesn't push up the right people. There is a great deal of ability and talent in India which is simply not used and the great tragedy is that a great deal of India's brain power goes unused and the brains simply do not want to work under the present system which is so stifling." The solution, according to this respondent, was to adopt the presidential system, which "gives liberty without destroying the effectiveness of government."

Although most business critics of the existing system were disenchanted with the present system only to the point of having come to advocate its replacement by a presidential system, a substantial number valued efficiency so highly that they rejected all forms of democratic government in favor of some form of dictatorship, military rule, or any system which "would mean more power to individuals to be able to get things done."

Among the business leaders surveyed, the supporters of the present system were clearly in a minority, and they tended to be concentrated in sections of the traditionally pro-Congress party Marwari industrial elite. These businessmen preferred to view the manifold difficulties of the system as temporary and worth countenancing, because they believed that only the existing parliamentary system of government could keep the country united and the government responsive. The present system, they argued, provides a platform for everyone while ensuring that the power of the prime minister is held in check by five hundred Members of Parliament and by party opinion. A presidential system, on the other hand, would lead to a dictatorship which, in turn, would result either in the disintegration of the country or in a Communist

[20] This section is based on interviews with seventy-one industrialists drawn from the active leadership of the major business associations in India and the top seventy-five business houses. Similar attitudes can be found among a smaller group of Baroda industrialists interviewed by Howard Erdman. See *Political Attitudes of Indian Industry: A Case Study of the Baroda Business Elite* (New York: Oxford University Press, 1971). For details of the data gathering process, see Acknowledgments, n. 1.

take-over. As one prosystem businessman put it, "So long as you have democracy, somehow you can pull down the kind of United Front Government that existed in West Bengal after the 1967 general elections. To install a government for five years without being able to get at it would be a mistake and would be a dangerous situation. The center must be strong and must oust such ministries if they come to power."

At best then, the present system in India is viewed by businessmen as manifesting the fewest of the evils to which all political systems are susceptible. Like most sections of the educated middle class, businessmen have become frustrated with and alienated from the present pattern of party politics and parliamentary democracy in India. These feelings of alienation are tempered, among sections of the industrial elite, by their strong loyalties to the Congress party. Thus it would appear that Weiner was excessively optimistic in arguing that business would not react against the system.[21] Not only would business not defend the system if it were to collapse, many members of the business community were ready to see it replaced immediately, whether by a presidential system or by military rule. Above all, however, what each section of the business elite longs for is a strong central government. And they would like the leadership to be recruited on the basis of merit for the purpose of getting a job done, rather than on the basis of criteria intended to satisfy the conflicting forces of caste, language, community, and regional pressures. In view of the characteristic orientations of Indian political culture, however, it would seem that such expectations are exceedingly unrealistic. The role of the strong leader is not to ignore or obliterate all the divisions in society but, like the arbitrator, to reconcile them, to harmonize them.

While growing increasingly alienated from the present political system and envisioning ideal alternatives, the business elite was highly uncertain about India's prospects for the immediate future. When asked, "What do you see as the most likely development in Indian politics in the next ten years," slightly more than half of those interviewed were unable to express much more than vague feelings of optimism or pessimism. Those who were able to project tended to see the future as a continuation of the existing pattern of party politics, with exact developments hinging on questions relating to the future of the Congress party, the possibility of a polarization of political forces, or

[21] See Weiner, *Politics of Scarcity*, p. 129; Erdman found similar expressions of systemic hostility among Indian businessmen. See Erdman "Political Attitudes." See also M. L. Goel, "The Relevance of Education for Political Participation in a Developing Society" in *Comparative Political Studies* 3 (1970): 341–345.

of a shift to the right. Interestingly enough, although many businessmen had expressed a personal preference for some form of dictatorship or military rule, few of them saw much change of such an eventuality occurring.

The pessimists exuded despair. As one Marwari industrialist put it, "I don't know where we are going." Optimistic responses varied from the inarticulate confidence of those who felt that everything would turn out well to the more analytical expectations of those who based their optimism on the spread of education, the growing awareness of the population, and a sense of trust in the Indian masses. As one highly articulate manager put it,

> The problem in India today is a gigantic struggle between the instincts of the people and the products of the electoral system. The democratic instincts of the people are good and strong as witnessed by the fact that when they thought it necessary, they threw out the Congress, and when they found that that didn't work, they brought it back again. When important political leaders did not please them, they threw them out. The problem, however, arises out of the fact that low literacy rates and economic conditions mean that only the lowest multiplier [sic] can get elected. When this kind of person gets elected to Parliament, he simply does not know what to do. He simply loathes the inequalities that exist but cannot think of really building a new society. What is needed more than anything else is a professional politician who knows what his job is. He needs experience. The problem today is that a man gets elected to Parliament and suddenly wakes up to find he is a minister. Moreover, the approach of this kind of politician is an agitational approach and not an administrative approach.

This view reflects a general concern within the business elite about the quality of political leadership in India. They feel that it reflects the lowest common denominator, is unskilled and uneducated, and so must be incapable of dealing with the complex problems faced by the country.

Slightly less than half of the industrial elite were capable of projecting into the future. Some of those who could believed that development is dependent on the future of the Congress party, some envisioned a process of political polarization, and some foresaw a sharp swing to the right. Because these interviews took place before the Congress party split in the summer of 1969, most of those who viewed the future of

Indian politics as based upon the future of the Congress party expected that party to remain intact and to experience a resurgence at the polls as a result of a general improvement in the Indian economy. If the Congress party were really able to cash in on an economic recovery, they argued, then one could expect a return to stability with a continuation of Congress party rule for another five or ten years. A second major segment of business elite opinion was more prescient. The majority of this group expected a breakup of the Congress party, which would result in polarization of the party system followed by regrouping of existing parties around each Congress pole. Another polarization theory was built on the belief that a strong, new, right wing force would emerge from the resurgence of regional and communal parties like the Dravida Munnetra Kazhagam (DMK), Shiv Sena, and Jana Sangh. Although it was not always explicitly stated, those who expected some form of polarization seemed to assume that the right would survive as the dominant force. A small segment of the Indian business elite expected a clear swing to the right during the next ten years. The support for such a movement would come from the newly prospering rural society, and the chief beneficiary would be the Jana Sangh because of its ability to organize and appeal to mass opinion. Those businessmen who looked forward hopefully to a resurgence of the Jana Sangh were not necessarily committed to that particular party's approach, but they were willing to strengthen any right wing party with any chance of success.

Although prophecy is difficult, the business leadership of India seems to have made a very realistic assessment of the relative strengths and weaknesses of India's major parties. Thus, although a vast majority of them would like to see the Swatantra party succeed, they concede that it has little real chance for success. As a result, the actual politics of businessmen tend to reflect three distinct political orientations. One group is pragmatically pro-Congress, a second is ideologically pro-Swatantra, and a third is cynically apolitical.

The pro-Congress group feels that the Congress party, despite its shortcomings, represents the only real alternative for business, because Swatantra is ineffective as a politcal force. The pro-Congress position has been publicly advocated and most forcefully stated by G. D. Birla. In a speech prior to the 1967 general elections, he warned the business community against trying to break or weaken the Congress party:

> I can tell you from my political experience there is not the slightest chance [for] any Swatantra party or any Jana Sangh or any other party to come into power to replace the Congress. You can break the Congress. You can weaken it, but it is not going to

> help. You will be replacing this government by Communist [sic] government and they will be the first to cut your throat. Do not make that mistake. Therefore, I tell you that there is no party in this country except the Congress party [which] I do not fully like. But there is no other party in this country except the Congress which can give stability. It is a question of self-interest. . . . Therefore, I say that with all its faults I support the Congress. Because there is no other alternative. . . . Therefore, for God's sake, forget about breaking the Congress. Because there is no other party which can help you.[22]

Thoroughly disagreeing with G. D. Birla's assessment of the importance of the Congress party prior to the 1967 elections, many business leaders (including B. M. Birla, a younger brother of G. D. Birla) actively supported candidates from major opposition parties, independents, and Congress party dissidents. They hoped to reduce the massive majorities which the Congress party commanded, especially in the Lok Sabha. They succeeded, of course. But many businessmen, and especially those in the Marwari houses, were distressed with the results of even a temporary loss of Congress party hegemony. The weakening of the Congress party, they felt, had hurt business, creating a political vacuum instead of a stable government, strengthening the left and especially the Communists, and increasing labor unrest. Reluctantly conceding that G. D. Birla's assessment had been correct, many businessmen shifted their support back to the Congress party.

Others, however, felt that the weakening of the Congress party had produced mixed, and not purely disadvantageous, results for business. In some states, the political instability that had followed in the wake of the 1967 elections had indeed hurt business, they conceded, but only in states where the left had been strengthened by the election. In states where the right had been strengthened, business had in fact been helped. Moreover, they argued, the weakening of the Congress party had made it less dogmatic and easier to deal with. Finally, the demonstration that the Congress party was not invincible was an important turning point, because it forced business to think of new possibilities. As one industrialist put it,

> The party in power always has an effect on business and thus Indian business must learn to take care of itself whichever party is

[22] *Government and Business* (Text of speeches delivered at the Indian Chamber of Commerce, Calcutta, April 10, 1965) by G. L. Nanda Satyanarain Sinha and G. D. Birla, pp. 8–9.

> in power. In the Congress party most of the leaders were so well known to business because of their associations over five or six decades that when Congress suddenly weakened business contacts with other political parties had not been well developed.

Although the supporters of the Congress party and its critics tend to have the same objective view of the Congress party, they differ on how their assessment should affect business strategy and tactics toward the government party. Most industrialists viewed the united Congress party as a microcosm of the total party system. The Congress party, they argued, consisted of right, left, and centrist tendencies which produced a series of cross-pressures within the party. Dismissing leftism in the Congress party as a product of societal pressures, party supporters believed that their best hope was their ability to influence the right wing or the "more sober sections of the Congress." The critics, on the other hand, declared that the Congress party, as then constituted, ought to be disbanded because it lacked unity, discipline, and a coherent program. Its objectives were too vague and diffuse, proving that the party had no real philosophy. The result was a paralysis at the decision-making level. That paralysis led Congress party leaders to say one thing in private to businessmen and another in public. The most severe critics of the Congress party argued that support of that party would lead to communism. This position has been taken in public by none other than J. R. D. Tata. In his 1970–1971 annual statement as chairman of Tata Iron and Steel Company, he said:

> During the past twenty years, the freedom of action and the scope of operation of the private sector have been subjected to a gradual but continuous process of erosion in the course of which government has achieved a measure of control and ownership of the means of production and distribution, which would have been inconceivable to any of us if introduced all at once at the start and which is unprecedented in any country other than those under totalitarian rule. . . .
>
> I for one believe that our government means well. . . . But I find it difficult to reconcile the public statements on economic policy, made by the prime minister herself or by responsible ministers and officials of government, with the lengths to which, and the speed at which, our country is now being driven on the road to economic totalitarianism.[23]

[23] J. R. D. Tata, "The Future of the Private Sector," *Journal of the Indian Merchants' Chamber* 65 (1971): 43.

Although the vast majority of the industrialists shared pro-Swatantra sentiments, they divided sharply over the advisability of supporting it. Those most strongly committed to the Swatantra party argued that it is the only party which openly fights "for our interests" by supporting the free enterprise system. These advocates view the party leadership as "intelligent," "forward looking," "progressive," and "sensible."

On the other hand, most Swatantra critics and even some of its supporters argue that the party is both too young and too weak to be of much help to business. Furthermore, they point out that it has been unable to establish deep roots anywhere in the country and is especially lacking in appeal in the rural areas. Such a party, with no real programs for the common man, cannot hope to succeed in India. In short, the lack of enthusiasm for the Swatantra party is based on the conviction that, attractive though its program may be to business, it has little hope of becoming a major political force in India.

Although the apolitical business leaders showed almost universal empathy with the Swatantra party as a party of talented and sensible people, they were convinced that no existing party in India really represents business interests. Furthermore, they tended to view politics with disdain and to consider politicians a wholly selfish and power-hungry breed. More pragmatically, the apolitical businessmen usually declared that business should support all rightest parties as the only possible hope.

Even though most business leaders continue to focus their attention on the Congress and Swatantra parties, there was a growing interest in the Jana Sangh. Marwari industrialists, in particular, had formed a very positive image of the effectiveness and potential of the Jana Sangh because of its discipline and its ability to attract and hold mass support. Thus, one industrialist argued, "Their approach appeals to the common man. They have strengthened their roots in the society, and they have also strengthened their base. They preach down-to-earth facts and not ideology." Another felt that "Jana Sangh is beginning to have an impact. Both individuals within the party and the party itself are beginning to make a name and an image, and though the party is not a big force at present it is beginning to gain in performance and reputation." A third commented, "Jana Sangh is spreading its influence among middle-class businessmen especially in the Hindi-speaking states. Their workers are disciplined, organized, active, and loyal."

Even those inclined to stress the positive image of the Jana Sangh recognize that the party suffers from certain drawbacks. These drawbacks include: the party's religious and communal bias, its limited regional appeal because of its language policy, the lack of clarity of its economic policy, and, as with all political parties, the possibility that it might not after all be able to deliver the goods. Despite these disadvantages, the Jana Sangh has gained considerably in stature among Indian industrialists, indicating that the party will be much more effectively financed in the future.

The parties of the left are generally regarded as a direct threat to business interests, although business, if faced by a real Communist threat, would find even some of the leftist parties acceptable. Most businessmen view the Praja Socialist party (PSP) as an ineffective and spent force in Indian politics. Nor are they very sympathetic toward the Samyukta Socialist party (SSP). But parties like the PSP and SSP might receive support in those areas where the most direct threat comes from the Communists, who are an anathema to business. In areas where the Communists are not a force, business would confine its suport to parties of the right.

Thus, business in India is torn between alignments of ideological purity and alignments of convenience, between holding on to what they have left of influence with the ruling Congress party and switching allegiance to some party whose clearcut sympathy with private sector ambitions would promise easy access and certain influence at some future date. Such decisions are never easy, but in India the pragmatic decision is as difficult to comprehend as it is to make, and thus gratitude for support is not likely to be anything but mixed. In fact, the party in power may be so suspicious of business motives that support may actually *reduce* influence. Furthermore, Congress party support at the present avoids the necessity of being involved in public policy debates outside the party. If an ideological party were given sole responsibility for enunciating business demands, business would be more vulnerable to leftist criticism. Support for the Jana Sangh, of course, would go far in defusing Marxist and socialist criticism, for such support would tend to submerge business interests in a party committed to the masses, however conservative in social and religious matters. Any alignment, then, presents problems. Differences of opinion within the business community make the choice of which party to work through difficult. Businessmen are divided politically and have conflicting views about strategy toward particular parties and also about the potential consequences of the support they give to any of the major parties.

The business dilemma became particularly acute when Prime Minister Indira Gandhi shrewdly perceived the underlying changes taking place in voter perceptions and concerns, changes which were only beginning to show themselves at the time of the 1967 elections. She embarked on a new political strategy designed to refurbish her party's radical image in the eyes of the electorate. The "new politics" was designed to appeal to the electorate through leadership, ideology, and program, rather than through traditional vote banks and dependencies. The new program, summarized in the slogan "Gharibi Hatao" (Eliminate Poverty) included, among other things, the nationalization of major private sector banks, the abolition of privy purses granted to India's princes after independence, and ceilings on urban property holdings. In an attempt to ensure that her new radical program received the undivided attention of the electorate, and to free the parliamentary elections from the more parochial concerns which tended to dominate state assembly elections, Mrs. Gandhi dissolved Parliament one year ahead of schedule.

The success of the strategy was evident in the sweeping victory of the new Congress party at the polls, in both 1971 and 1972. In the 1971 parliamentary elections, the new Congress party won 43.7 percent of the popular vote and 350 out of 518 seats for a two-thirds majority.[24] Her triumph was repeated again in 1972, when the new Congress party won 48.32 percent of the votes and 70.76 percent of the seats in the various state assemblies.[25]

Sample surveys showed that both the new Congress party and Mrs. Gandhi had succeeded in projecting a new image on the Indian electorate. The new Congress party was seen by the electorate as a party representing all classes of society and capable of solving India's major problems of unemployment and poverty.[26] The issues raised by Mrs. Gandhi appeared to be much more salient to the electorate than those raised in the 1950s. Whereas Eldersveld had found the electorate incapable of structuring their opinions on issues,[27] a sample survey taken at the time of the 1971 elections showed a sharp decline in such tendencies.[28] For example, only 14 percent of respondents in 1971 had no opinion about the advisability of imposing ceilings on urban property, but 74 percent supported such a policy and only 18 percent opposed it. The symbolic nature of the issue was to some extent reflected in the fact that, although the policy of ceilings on urban property received strong endorsement, few respondents could explain precisely how such a policy would actually improve the lot of the common man.[29] One

[24] L. Rudolph, "Continuities and Change," pp. 1119–1132.

[25] *The New York Times*, March 13, 1972.

[26] Indian Institute of Public Opinion, "After the Assembly Elections: 1972," *Monthly Public Opinion Survey* 17 (1972): iii–ix.

[27] Eldersveld, "The Political Behavior of the Indian Public," pp. 3–9.

[28] Indian Institute of Public Opinion, "After the Assembly Elections: 1972," pp. viii–ix.

[29] *Ibid.*, p. ix.

thing was clear, however. There was a much clearer perception of issues among all subsectors of the society than there had been a decade earlier.

In addition to program and ideology, leadership also played an important role in the 1971 and 1972 elections. Mrs. Gandhi's image as a leader was so striking that the Indian press referred to the sweeping victories of the new Congress party at the polls as the "Indira wave." Sample surveys tended to confirm the impact which her leadership had had on the public. This was especially true after her intervention in Bangladesh, when her popularity soared. In August 1971, shortly after her sweeping victory at the polls, 65 percent of the respondents thought she was doing a good job as prime minister. And by January 1972, following the Bangladesh intervention, 73 percent of the respondents gave her a high rating. At the same time, the proportion of those who were neutral dropped from 22 percent to 5 percent, and those critical of her leadership dropped from 11 percent to only 1 percent.[30]

Overall, then, it would appear that a less segmented political culture is slowly being wrought from the ebbing loyalties and identities of traditional man as the Indian electorate begins to respond to appeals made on the bases of leadership, ideology, and programs. It is more likely, therefore, that past policy conflicts which centered around competition over the relative status of caste, language, and communal groups will give way to greater concern with class issues involving economic policy, unemployment, and poverty. In the process, pressures from below will begin to emerge to focus even greater attention on these issues and, ironically, will give the political leadership less freedom of action on these issues than they enjoyed in the past. Such a process is already evident in the field of agricultural policy and the forces let loose by the green revolution.

Although the Indian electorate is becoming more politicized and issue-oriented, the population as a whole still has a very low sense of political efficacy. Indians have high expectations of government, but they are still uncertain as to precisely how to press their demands on government. Respondents were asked, for example, "Suppose that some action or policy or law is being considered by the government (local [government] in rural areas) which you disagree with, because it was unjust or harmful, or something like that . . . what are the possible things you think you could do about it?" Seventeen percent did not know what they could do, and another 26 percent said they could do nothing. In short, almost half the respondents felt helpless. Of those

[30] *Ibid.*, p. ii.

who felt they could do something, only a small fraction felt they could act through voluntary associations or interest groups. Most felt they could act primarily through friends and neighbors. Among subsectors of the population, the level of efficacy tended to increase with education. However, among illiterates, 27 percent did not know what to do and 34 percent felt they could do nothing.[81] Similar results were obtained when respondents were asked whether they had ever tried to influence a local government decision. Sixty-eight percent of the respondents said they had never tried to influence local decisions, and another 15 percent could not even understand or answer the question.[82]

Government in India is still remote from the population. Citizens are either not sure how they will be treated, or they resort to traditional ways of dealing with the *Sarkar*. When asked, for example, "If you had some problem that you had to talk about with a government official, how do you think that you would be treated?", half the respondents either did not know or felt they would be treated rudely or indifferently. Only 20 percent felt they would be treated politely and with interest shown in their problem, and another 20 percent felt they would be treated fairly only if they gave bribes. Among subsectors of the population, the lower the level of education the higher the nonresponse rate and the greater the expectation that a bribe was necessary. Belief in the effectiveness of a bribe, however, appeared to be directly related to income. The greatest faith in the utility of bribery was found among those whose incomes were over one thousand rupees per month.[83]

Thus, despite increased political awareness, Indians are still primarily accustomed to getting things done through traditional methods such as personal contacts, bribery, and kinship, caste, and community ties, rather than through organized voluntary associations or formalized mechanisms and impersonal procedures. Much of the corruption and talk of corruption which one finds in India is partly due to the existence of a dual system of values that operates in dealings with government. Individuals are afraid to give up traditional modes of action because of fear that the new modes will not work fairly or the way they are supposed to work. Thus the political system often has to cope with the worst features of both value systems. The dilemma is described by one introspective intellectual as follows:

[81] Indian Institute of Public Opinion, "The Fifth Lok Sabha Elections," *Monthly Public Opinion Surveys* 16 (1970–1971): 82. See also M. L. Goel, "Distribution of Civic Competence Feelings in India," *Social Science Quarterly* 51 (1970): 755–768.

[82] *Ibid.*, p. 86.

[83] *Ibid.*, p. 90.

> Those of us who live in large cities have to depend upon a variety of public utilities. These are so organized as to serve citizens uniformly, irrespective of personal considerations. There are rules of procedure according to which every citizen is entitled to make claims on certain services. In practice, however, when someone wants to get something done, he rarely depends on the rules alone. He tries in addition to approach someone in the right quarters through a relative or a friend, or a friend of a relative, just in case the rules do not work or do not work quickly enough for his needs. Those who have no relatives or friends (or "connections," as they are called) find themselves left out in the cold. But it is really amazing how almost everyone in India is able to activate some personal links with at least some persons of consequence.[34]

Thus, beneath the kaleidoscope of changing political attitudes, there persists a set of basic values whose influence continues to play a role in shaping political behavior, patterns of decision-making, and group activity. Although all the ramifications of these themes have not been systematically studied, they are pervasive enough to have been singled out by both foreign and Indian commentators. A number of orientations have been stressed as particularly fundamental: a tolerance of ambiguity, a low level of trust in interpersonal relations, a strong desire to maintain harmony because of a belief in the undesirability of conflict and competition, a hyperrationality in the approach to problem-solving, a belief in the efficacy of norms and law, a tendency to judge by motive rather than action, and a concern with the distribution rather than the creation of wealth. To the extent that each of these orientations contributes to the external and internal conduct of interest groups, these traditional values affect the behavior and impact of interest groups even in the modern sector of Indian society.

Numerous commentators have observed that Indians have a high tolerance of ambiguity. This tolerance is often defined as a facility for the absorption and synthesis of diverse and even contradictory ideas or interests. Historically and culturally, India's response to successive inundations by various groups and ideas has been to graft them onto a system which enabled each to exist, encapsulated, but really secure. Traditional India thus became the quintessence of a stable "plural society." As Hutton has observed, "the caste system has afforded a place in society into which any community, be it racial, social, occupational,

[34] *The Times of India* (New Delhi), November 4, 1968.

or religious, can be fitted as a cooperating part of the social whole, while retaining its own distinctive character and its separate individual life." [35]

If one considers the matter from the point of view of the Muslims or the untouchables, one might say that the integrative stress here is a bit naive. The intersection of these myriad components of Indian society was determined by functional necessity rigidly enforced by tradition, habit, ritual, and law, which may have kept society running but not without deep seated resentments and an inclination to litigiousness whenever expressions of latent conflict were legitimized in village society. Those who attempted to cross caste lines and defy community boundaries were punished by both superiors and peers, as case studies of those who allowed their affections to settle on exogamous objects have abundantly shown.

Still, groups survived in India that could not have survived without such strict enforcement of conformity and orthodoxy. The pragmatic elasticity of the social fabric encouraged culturally diverse groups to preserve their distinctive features and was enhanced by a philosophic system which places major emphasis on self-identity or salvation through self-realization. It is characteristic of Indian philosophy to contend that there are many paths to truth, no one of them worthy to claim unquestioned supremacy. If each social group has its own internally consistent mores, and each path to truth its own rationale, then "both group values and individual morality" must be seen as "transient and situation-specific." Hence, Indian society is known for its legitimizing "of ethical relativism and tolerance of dissent." [36] In the political sphere, this lack of a sense of a singular objective reality enables the "leadership to accept and live with contradictions in policies without submitting them to an analysis and tests of workability." [37] While such an intellectual predisposition may inhibit the ability to establish and implement priorities, it does permit the articulation of policies which create the widest possible following. In ambiguity lies consensus—the notion is not unheard of elsewhere, but in India perhaps the motives for an ambiguous statement may be given a more charitable, and not wholly opportunistic, interpretation.

A second peculiarly Indian orientation stressed by commentators is the strong sense of mutual distrust which appears to underlie interper-

[35] J. H. Hutton, *Caste in India: Its Nature, Function and Origins* (London: Oxford University Press, 1963), p. 115.

[36] Kothari, *Politics in India*, p. 258.

[37] Van Dusen Kennedy, *Unions, Employers, and Government: Essays on Indian Labor Questions* (Bombay: Manaktalas, 1966), p. 20.

sonal relationships in India.[38] Carstairs attributes this sense of distrust to patterns of socialization and child-rearing,[39] which he finds to be characterized by a constant suspicion of favoritism, partiality in the distribution of rewards and punishments, and unfairness or lack of candor in interpersonal relationships. It is as if each member of the family was treated like a separate caste, governed by different rules and yet possessed of the feeling that family membership should imply a uniformity of status and responsibility, in the absence of which jealousy, suspicion, and latent hostility arise. A similar sense of mistrust seems to influence the government's attitude toward groups and also to affect the internal relations of the groups themselves. Thus, bureaucrats feel that business cannot be trusted. "Our businessmen have no self-restraint," they explain. Government must therefore impose restraints.[40] Within groups, as one observer put it, "it is not that Indian businessmen do not want to cooperate, but they feel that they cannot trust the other guy." When businessmen get together, they may agree on a particular course of action as long as they are in the same room. For example, they may agree to refrain from purchasing an agricultural raw material like jute or cotton so as not to touch off a rapid price increase of a commodity in short supply. But as soon as the meeting is over, it is quite likely that the participants will hurry to buy all they can through intermediaries. When such apparent inconsistencies or treacherous actions are questioned, each of the accused disavows personal responsibility. It had to be done, the rationale goes, because the others could be counted on to violate the agreement. In a fragmented and compartmentalized society, it is perhaps not surprising that members of different groups should regard one another with hostility or suspicion, but it is startling that such attitudes should also dominate the way in which members of the same group regard each other.

Where there is such a climate of apprehension at every point of human contact, the third orientation, the Indian passion for harmony and consensus, stands out almost as a wish-fulfillment mechanism. Distaste for conflict and commitment to harmony are fundamental to the epic literature from which the masses draw inspiration every day. And they are basic to the philosophical, intellectual, cultural, and (to a lesser extent) historical norms of the Indian experience, norms that all Indians seek to embody in development of character and the organization

[38] G. Morris Carstairs, *The Twice-Born* (Bloomington, Ind.: Indiana University Press, 1961), pp. 40, 45, 47, and 158.

[39] *Ibid.*, p. 58.

[40] Richard P. Taub, *Bureaucrats Under Stress: Administrators and Administration in an Indian State* (Berkeley and Los Angeles: University of California Press, 1969), p. 169.

of life, whether in village decision-making or in the management of coalitions in the national movement.[41] Like law and order values in other societies, however, the traditional value of harmony and consensus has often been exploited as a means by which dominant groups might preserve the existing patterns of privilege and subordination.

In recent years, the pressure of modern technology, economic change, and the moral ideas which have accompanied them have made it more difficult to justify the old ways. But the old ways are still reflected in the decision-making styles of some Indian leaders. Lal Bahadur Shastri relied on a consensual decision-making style during his brief tenure as prime minister.[42] In contrast, Mrs. Gandhi's refusal to pay lip service to the ideal of consensus—which even Jawaharlal Nehru, at the height of his power and influence, might manipulate but never impugn—was a major factor in the crisis which led to an open rupture in the Congress party.

Inherent in the concern with harmony is a reluctance to use power openly or for obvious personal gain.[43] This customary tacit agreement to subordinate or at least ignore differences, so as to create a harmonious united front, also results in a tendency to view interest groups which flaunt their differences and pursue particularistic demands as potentially disruptive and thus lacking in legitimacy. The fragmentation of Indian society into suspicious isolates, combined with its high regard for the avoidance of open conflict, explains much of the emphasis Indians place on the role of the arbitrator and the peacemaker. The role of the peacemaker is to intervene in disputes and to urge self-control and compromise. "So constantly is the intervention of a third party associated with quarrels," says Carstairs, "that it occurs also in dreams." [44] One of the factors which played an important role in maintaining Congress party cohesion, despite its incorporation of such diverse interests, was the ability of the party to develop arbitrators who could help control factional quarrels within the party. The death of some of the more highly regarded, most trustworthy, of these arbitrators was a key factor in the Congress party split.[45] Because it is difficult

[41] Susanne Hoeber Rudolph, "Consensus and Conflict in Indian Politics," *World Politics* 13 (1961): 385–399.

[42] Michael Brecher, *Nehru's Mantle: The Politics of Succession in India* (New York: Praeger, 1966), pp. 92–137.

[43] For a discussion of the antipower orientation of Indian politics see Myron Weiner, *Party Politics in India* (Princeton: Princeton University Press, 1957), pp. 254–258; Myron Weiner, "Struggle Against Power," *World Politics* 8 (1956): 392–403; and Kennedy, *Unions, Employers, and Government,* p. 16–18.

[44] Carstairs, *The Twice-Born,* p. 47.

[45] Stanley A. Kochanek, *The Congress Party of India: The Dynamics of One-Party Democracy* (Princeton: Princeton University Press, 1968), pp. 251–259, 275, 286;

to rise above suspicion and gain the esteem of members of opposing groups, these pivotal individuals are difficult to replace. With the increasing tendency to accept a clash of ideas as a legitimate mode of resolving differences, few individuals are likely to aspire to such status.

A fourth orientation underlying characteristic Indian behavior is a hyperrationality which leads to a form of optimism based on logical sequences. Their concepts of rationality and public interest lead decision-makers to turn a deaf ear to groups and to be so unresponsive that groups resort to direct action. This hyperrationality leads to a focus on ideological discourse and to a concern with form rather than substance of the sort that has been noticed in the Indian five year plans. "No one reading the plans can fail to be impressed by the frequent unrealism of these assumptions," observes Hanson. "So much appears to be contingent upon the realization of the unrealizable." Admitting that "the sources of this unrealism are complex," Hanson finds it significant "that many of the plan formulators are ideologues in whose minds a variety of Western-derived theories, all too often divorced from Indian reality, jostle for predominance." [46] Among the ideologies which have made the greatest impact on the modern day descendants of the great Indian system-rulers, or the politicians, are socialism, communism, and Gandhianism. The appeal of socialism is particularly strong among the urban educated elites responsible for drawing up and administering the Indian Five Year Plans. As John Kenneth Galbraith once remarked when discussing the problems of the public sector in India, "Above all it is the socialists who are responsible for the paralyzing belief that success is a matter of faith, not works." [47] There had been a predisposition or drawing up but not bringing to adequate fruition these elaborate schemes for economic salvation. That predisposition, when combined with the pervasive sense of distrust and the emphasis on motives, leads to charges that failures or malfunctions spring from public sellouts by bribed officialdom rather than from deficiencies in the planning process. No group is more frequently charged with such peccancies than are organized business interests.

A fifth value is the strong faith in the efficacy of norms embodied in codes of conduct and law. As one cynical former Indian Civil Service official put it, "In India, if you cannot solve a problem, then you pass a law. There is a belief that legislation can do more than it really

Myron Weiner, *Party Building in a New Nation* (Chicago: University of Chicago Press, 1967), pp. 476–480.

[46] A. H. Hanson, *The Process of Planning: A Study of India's Five Year Plans 1950–1964* (London: Oxford University Press, 1966), p. 258.

[47] Quoted in Kennedy, *Unions, Employers, and Government*, p. 15.

can."[48] The result is that legislators keep adding to the fund of legislation even when the existing legislation has not been implemented. Passing laws, as a substitute for grappling with the problems, has in turn reinforced the feeling that there is a gap between expectation and reality which can only be explained by the unreliability or chicanery of others. This gap, Kothari argues, is "filled by pious declarations, a continuous flow of new ideas which were never implemented, and a snobbish attitude on the part of the planners and the administrators who shifted the blame to low motivation of farmers and the rural people."[49] And yet the faith in law and codification may also be seen as the desire to embody the rational, to eliminate the differential and the arbitrary to which the uncodified is susceptible, and so to achieve a system that operates openly and fairly for all who must live by it, no matter who administers it. The rule of law is the orchestration of social harmony, the contract that cannot be broken.

A sixth tendency among Indians is the disposition to judge men's achievements by their motives rather than by their actions. Similarly, the good society must be built by "a spirit of self-sacrifice" and not as a result of motives like enlightened self-interest. Organizations are judged by the characters and personal motives of the members and leaders more than by their program, which after all may be a masterpiece of deception. Ever since Gandhi, politicians have become a new priesthood. It is expected that the politician must be, above all, a moral man.[50] Together, according to Weiner, "these prejudices strengthen the elite's distaste for the profit motive and the private sector and attract it to Socialist ideals."[51] When political leaders apply for party tickets, they tend to stress the sacrifices they have made, their exemplary character, and their previous service to the nation, rather than the experience, education, and position on current issues that would be factors in other systems.[52]

If the politician, like the arbitrator, is the disinterested, evenhanded father one never had and is always searching for, the socialist idea seems to promise an end to conflict, hierarchical privilege, and a mistrust that socioeconomic systems based on competition and self-interest can only intensify. Thus, there is a tendency in India to be concerned

[48] *Ibid.*, pp. 14–15.
[49] Kothari, *Politics in India*, p. 145.
[50] Joseph R. Gusfield, "Political Community and Group Interests in Modern India," *Pacific Affairs* 38 (1965): 137, 139–141; W. H. Morris-Jones, *The Government and Politics of India* (London: Hutchinson University Library, 1964), pp. 52–61.
[51] Weiner, *Two Cultures*, p. 142.
[52] Kochanek, *Congress Party of India*, pp. 272–273.

with the distribution rather than the creation of wealth. Factional struggles within the Congress party, for instance, have been oriented more toward controlling the administration so as to distribute rewards in a slightly different way than toward disputes over means of providing policy initiatives to step up the pace of growth. "Equality," says Weiner, "has also been a cardinal principle of the national leadership, and where this principle has run into conflict with the goal of maximizing the nation's wealth, the latter has often been submerged." [53] Yet, their predisposition would seem to make sense in a society which is not habituated to an annual increase in the gross national product. At this point the reality principle seems to be operating; although there may be no more to distribute, the proper plan and the proper motives may redistribute what already exists, thus providing the just economic basis of the ideal society.

To the extent that these closely interrelated orientations are shared by the political leadership and the masses of the Indian society, they have an important effect on both the form and content of decisions and decision-making behavior in India.

The attitudes and values reflected in the political culture set major parameters on business activity and influence in the Indian political system. The aspirations generated by the nationalist movement and the rhetoric of development have led Indians to look to government to satisfy their expectations. A variety of surveys reveal strong positive orientations toward an activist role for government in the society and the economy. These positive images of government are reinforced by the pervasive influence and symbolic role of socialist ideology, which is especially strong among the urban intellectuals and the urban middle class. Therefore, government policies which have a strong redistributive or radical orientation tend to gain widespread popular support. This was clearly reflected in the popular response to Nehru's socialist pattern of society and to Mrs. Gandhi's nationalization of major private sector banks and her abolition of privy purses and princely privileges. Popular support for such government initiatives, combined with the generally negative images of businessmen and the private sector, makes it very difficult for business to appeal to public opinion in an effort to halt such government actions.

Popular attitudes support not only redistributive policies but also an active policy of government regulation and control. Because of a deep sense of suspicion and distrust, especially of business, it is generally felt that only pervasive government intervention can ensure

[53] Weiner, *Two Cultures*, pp. 144–145.

equitable distribution, fair prices, and social justice for all. Thus, public policy cannot be something that emerges out of a process of group conflict, because such conflict would automatically be unequal and would endanger the development of harmony and consensus.

Despite the general support for an active role for government in the society and economy, government is still viewed as remote and unapproachable. Access to government decision-makers is still sought through personal contacts based on primordial loyalties or bribery, rather than through organized groups and modern voluntary associations. High level decision-makers in fact continue to be suspicious of pressures generated by organized groups. They view such pressures as reflecting the demands of parochial or vested interests which simply distort the process of rational calculation and the ability of the elite to determine what is best in the national interest.

The attitudes and values of the political culture are reflected in the way decisions are made, and also in the very content of public policy itself. Thus, political culture influences both decision-making and public policy, which combine to set major parameters on group activity and performance.

III

STRUCTURES OF DECISION-MAKING

Interest groups respond and adapt to the structure of power in any given political system. Changes in the structure of government or the distribution of power within that structure influence the patterns of interest articulation within the society and the channels of access available to interest groups.[1] Except for its federal rather than unitary form, the structure of government of independent India was basically modeled after the British parliamentary pattern, and the practice and traditions of the past two decades have confirmed its basic outlines. Under the Indian constitution, the executive authority of the Union was formally vested in a president, although in practice these powers came to be exercised by the council of ministers with the prime minister at its head. The prime minister was appointed by the president, and other ministers were appointed by the president on the advice of the prime minister. The council of ministers was collectively responsible to the Lok Sabha, the lower house of the bicameral Indian legislature which is elected on the basis of mass franchise. As a federal system, the constitution provided for a three-fold distribution of power between the center and the states. The central Parliament was responsible for the Union lists, the state legislatures were responsible for the state lists, and both were responsible for a concurrent list.

The change from colonial rule to the politics of mass franchise has led to significant expansion, dispersion and, democratization of political power in India, both within the central government and in the relationship between the central government and the states. Initially, as a result of the legacy of the viceregal tradition, the centralized character of the nationalist movement, and the traditionally hierarchical patterns of Indian leadership, the emergent structure of decision-making was also highly concentrated. Interest groups wishing to exert maximum influence on it were forced to focus their attention on the

[1] See Samuel H. Beer, *British Politics in the Collectivist Age* (New York: Knopf, 1965), pp. 318–390; Samuel H. Beer, "Group Representation in Britain and the United States," *The Annals of the American Academy of Political and Social Science* 319 (1958): 130–141; Bernard E. Brown, "Pressure Politics in the Fifth Republic," *The Journal of Politics* 25 (1963): 509–525; Charles E. Frye, "Parties and Pressure Groups in Weimar and Bonn," *World Politics* 17 (1965): 635–655.

prime minister, the cabinet, and the higher echelons of the bureaucracy. Toward the end of the Nehru era, however, there was a considerable devolution of power from the center to the state as state chief ministers came to exercise increasing control over policy issues in their domain. The most important of those issues were agriculture, land reform, and taxation of agricultural income. At the national level, the increased role of Parliament and the Congress party as critics of executive policy initiatives added additional arenas for interest group activity.

Although the executive authority of the Union was formally vested in the president, who was given an impressive list of formal powers, in intent as well as in practice the president was expected to serve as a constitutional head of state exercising his powers only with the advice of the council of ministers. "The president," said Dr. B. R. Ambedkar, the chief architect of the Indian constitution, "occupies the same position as the King under the English Constitution." [2] All four Indian presidents since independence—Dr. Rajendra Prasad (1950–62), Dr. Sarvapalli Radhakrishnan (1962–67), Dr. Zakir Hussain (1967–69), and V. V. Giri who was elected in 1969 upon the death of Hussain—have accordingly acted as titular heads of state. Although collectively their actions would seem to have established the precedent that the executive power rests with the prime minister and his cabinet,[3] the president may still come to play a more powerful role if India should develop a series of minority governments, succumb to excessive party fragmentation, or suffer from weak party leadership. So far, however, this has not happened, and interest groups therefore do not exert much effort trying to maintain access to the president.

The real powers have thus been exercised by the council of ministers, with the prime minister at its head. India's three post-independence prime ministers—Jawaharlal Nehru (1947–64), Lal Bahadur Shastri (1964–66), and Indira Gandhi (1966–present)—have all been relatively strong executives who have fairly constantly reinforced the preeminent role of the prime minister and the council of ministers. Although the prime minister is theoretically appointed by the president and the other ministers are appointed by the president on the advice of the prime minister, the selection of the prime minister and council of ministers has actually been dependent upon the forces operating within the dominant Congress party. Because the government

[2] M. V. Pylee, *India's Constitution* (New York: Asia Publishing House, 1962), p. 167.

[3] The Indian constitution also provides for a vice president whose role in government is comparatively insignificant. See Pylee, *India's Constitution*, pp. 182–183.

is collectively responsible to the Lok Sabha and must command a majority to stay in power, the prime minister is *de facto* the leader of the majority party. During Nehru's tenure, he was automatically reelected by the parliamentary party at the beginning of each Parliament, but the selection of his successor was determined by the central and state leaders of the dominant Congress party. Similarly, in 1966, 1967, and 1971, Mrs. Gandhi's selection was determined by the internal distribution of power in and between the party and the Congress parliamentary party. In short, the president of India has so far not been able to employ any discretionary powers in the process of selecting the prime minister and the council of ministers, and interest group influence has been indirect at best.

The precise role of the prime minister depends on the stature, personality, and effective power of the prime minister and on the quality of the cabinet members. During the Nehru era, decision-making was highly centralized. Nehru was in a position to obtain from the cabinet any decision he wanted, because he could usually persuade others of his point of view but also because he was willing to be personally responsible for the results.

Although, toward the end of his life, Nehru tended to precede decisions with less consulting than formerly, his habit, in the early years especially, was to consult with his senior colleagues in the cabinet prior to reaching any decision. The failure to consult did not necessarily indicate an increasing authoritarianism on Nehru's part. Over a period of time any prime minister "acquires a sense of the possible," so that he knows even without consultation how far he can press. Furthermore, although Nehru might not always seek consultation, he could have consultation forced upon him. He could be persuaded by others.[4] Toward the end of his tenure, when his health was failing and confidence in his leadership had been shaken by the Chinese invasion which signaled the failure of his foreign policy, Nehru's decision-making became more fragmented. The cabinet, its members no longer compliant as a whole, came to play a more important role, and other, more broadly based organs such as Parliament, the Congress Party in Parliament, and the decision-making structure of the mass organization came to play more significant roles as critics of policy initiatives taken by the executive.

Shastri and Mrs. Gandhi did not come to power with Nehru's overriding, automatic authority. Starting out among equals, each had to depend at first on consensus rather than charisma. When no agreement

[4] Michael Brecher, *India and World Politics: Krishna Menon's View of the World* (New York: Praeger, 1968), p. 241.

with the cabinet was possible, decision could not be forced by fiat. Issues had to be postponed, and as a result issues piled up and tended to clog the operations of government. Under divided leadership or no leadership at all, the civil service also ground to a halt, refusing to review or take any decisions on controversial issues.[5] Forsaking traditional patterns of consensus decision-making, Mrs. Gandhi tried to consolidate her position by centralizing the decision-making process in her hands. She was immediately challenged by her senior colleagues in the cabinet, and the Congress party split into two new entities. After a brief period of heading the first minority government in post-independence India, Mrs. Gandhi succeeded in guiding her new Congress party to a massive victory at the polls in 1971 and 1972. Since then, decision-making has been highly concentrated in the hands of the prime minister and her secretariat. Power has become so concentrated that even the few independent voices among members of the cabinet that could make themselves heard have been stilled.[6] The result has been a stalemate of a different order. Important decisions must be postponed because of the inability of the prime minister to handle the multitude of problems requiring her individual attention.[7]

Because of the pivotal role played by the prime minister in decision-making in India, access to the prime minister is critical for groups seeking to influence major government policies. Despite the socialist rhetoric of Indian prime ministers, they have proven to be extremely accessible to the top echelons of Indian business. On most important issues affecting business, the business community has been reasonably certain that it could plead its case directly before the prime minister. Access to the prime minister, however, does not guarantee that the business community will be able to persuade the prime minister of its point of view.

The prime minister is assisted by a council of ministers, which consists of cabinet ministers, ministers of state, and deputy ministers who assist the ministers in carrying out their duties, doing as much or as little as the ministers permit. Although decisions are taken in the name of the council of ministers, it is really the prime minister, the cabinet, cabinet subcommittees, and individual ministers who make any given decision. The cabinet is an inner circle of the council of ministers and

[5] See, for example, the car price increase as well as statements by business claiming that the reluctance of the bureaucracy to take any kind of decision represented the greatest tragedy of Indian politics. See *Capital,* September 18, 1969, pp. 503–504.

[6] Romesh Thapar, "No More Excuses," *Economic and Political Weekly* 7 (1972): 608–609.

[7] "Political Underpinning for Economic Policies," *Economic and Political Weekly* 7 (1972): 534–535.

consists of the most prominent leaders of the majority party. The cabinet has four functions: it approves all legislative proposals of the government; it recommends major appointments; it settles interministerial disputes; and it coordinates and supervises the execution and administration of government policies.[8]

The composition of Indian cabinets has varied over the past two decades. In the years preceding the first general election, India had a national government in which prominent non-Congress party leaders and even representatives of various interests were given a place. Since 1951, Indian cabinets have been Congress party cabinets whose membership has been determined by the necessity to represent the individuals of real stature in the party, the diversity of views in the party, and the sectional and ethnic interests basic to party power. Thus, although the cabinet theoretically is collectively responsible, each cabinet minister tends to have a different perspective. Over the years some have been convinced socialists, others Gandhians, and still others have been sympathetic toward private sector views. Yet each has reflected one aspect of opinion within the multi-interest Congress party. For this reason, although the policy of the government has remained constant under Congress party rule, the policies of the individual ministries have tended to change with each minister. Thus, as Minister of Labor, for example, G. L. Nanda originated a labor policy which contained a strong dose of Gandhianism, S. K. Patil usually tried to rely on market forces, and K. D. Malaviya attempted to infuse a strong dose of socialism in the ministries over which he was given charge.

In order to coordinate the functions of the various ministries as a whole, the cabinet has established a series of cabinet subcommittees. These cabinet subcommittees have been chaired by the prime minister or by one or another of a small handful of senior Congress party ministers with the experience and esteem needed to play the peacemaker or arbitrator role and reconcile interministerial conflicts and make final decisions. The number of the cabinet subcommittees has varied recently from seven to ten. At times of crisis, small supercabinets have emerged. In 1962, Nehru created the Emergency Committee of the cabinet. This committee, composed of the prime minister and five senior ministers, was formed to deal with policy-making during the Chinese invasion. In her recent attempt to consolidate her control over the Indian government, Mrs. Gandhi created a third type of subsidiary body, called the Political Affairs Committee. The group was formed to handle the functions of three major cabinet subcommittees

[8] Pylee, *India's Constitution*, p. 377.

—internal affairs, external affairs, and defense.[9] The Political Affairs Committee has become the most important decision-making body in India after the prime minister herself. It is a small group of senior ministers who are consulted on all major policy issues involving domestic affairs, regional international affairs, and security policy. Its success in giving political direction to the government resulted in the creation of an Economic Affairs Committee,[10] which it was hoped would provide the same kind of political direction on economic policy issues. So far the Economic Affairs Committee has had little real impact, and major political–economic issues tend to be decided by the Political Affairs Committee of the cabinet.[11] Because the prime minister is the chairman of most of the important committees of the cabinet, she is in a strong position to handle most of the major policy areas dealt with by the government. Moreover, her position is further reinforced by the strong technocratically staffed secretariat that she has developed to assist her in her job as prime minister.

Although almost all policy initiatives emerge from the higher echelons of the executive, India has developed a fairly regularized policy process which it has used in working out the details of major domestic policies. This process includes provision for consultation with organized groups and individuals in the society. The process begins with the appointment of a commission of inquiry, composed of distinguished citizens, to investigate the problem. The commission takes public testimony from various groups and individuals and produces a report which includes a set of specific policy recommendations. The ministry concerned and the cabinet study the report, consider its recommendations, and note public reactions before drawing up a draft bill, which usually includes most of the recommendations of the commission. The draft bill is next submitted to Parliament, where it is usually sent to a select committee. The bill receives a detailed scrutiny, and testimony from interested groups and individuals is again entertained. The select committee report is then debated in Parliament and the bill is passed, usually in a modified form. This step by step procedure was employed in the making of such major decisions as those involving reorganization of the states, monopoly legislation, and patents, although it was not followed in the making of such major ideological reorientations as the nationalization of banks and general insurance or the declaration

[9] *The Overseas Hindustan Times* (New Delhi), August 15, 1970.

[10] "Political Underpinning for Economic Policies," *Economic and Politcal Weekly* 7 (1972): 534–535.

[11] "Quick End to Great Expectations," *Economic and Political Weekly* 7 (1972): 825–827.

in 1955 of the Socialist Pattern of Society as the objective of Indian planning. On lesser matters, the elaborate consultation process is dispensed with. Decisions are made by the prime minister, cabinet subcommittees, the cabinet, or individual members.

Ministers of the government of India are responsible for formulating policy within their sphere of responsibility and for the execution and review of that policy. They are required to coordinate with other ministers in matters affecting the business allocated to another ministry, and in some cases they must seek the approval of the prime minister and the cabinet. Otherwise each minister expects a minimum of interference from his cabinet colleagues. And they are likely to accept such working rules, for each of them has enough problems without creating additional trouble for himself by interfering in the work of others.[12] Because a minister has a great deal of freedom in shaping the policy of his ministry, policy has often changed when the minister changed. Even under Nehru, individual ministers played important roles. A forceful minister could carry his point and have his way. In addition, the prime minister tended to gravitate toward a man who was on top of the job.[13] Especially toward the end of the Nehru era, each minister was coming more and more completely to govern his own department and, by resorting to private agreements with the prime minister and the finance minister, insuring prior acceptance of his own approach.[14] Thus interest groups, in formulating their strategy, must take into account the personality, power, and possible ideological orientation of each minister. For business this means that special attention must be focused on those ministers who are in charge of the major economic ministries of the government of India. It is the economic ministries which are responsible for the detailed implementation of the government's economic policies and which, at the same time, have been delegated extensive regulatory powers over the private sector.

Among the ministries dealing with economic affairs, the Finance Ministry occupies a special place not only within the government of India but for business as well. The Finance Ministry plays a pivotal role within the government, because it must approve all allocations and expenditures of other ministries and in addition exercises special responsibility over administrative personnel. In addition, because most Members of Parliament have very little understanding of economic affairs, sheer expertise in complex policy matters ensures that the

[12] Brecher, *India and World Politics*, pp. 247, 250.
[13] *Ibid.*, p. 241.
[14] *Ibid.*, p. 235.

finance minister will play a dominant role in a vast range of governmental decisions.[15] Because the finance minister occupies such a central position in the highly controlled Indian economy and is responsible for formulating all monetary and fiscal policies, he is a particular target of business groups. The Finance Ministry is flooded with memoranda, representations and petitions from all sectors of the business community—traders, small-scale industrialists and large-scale industry—requesting special exemptions or other changes in government monetary or fiscal policies.

Because of the special relationship between ministers and the higher echelons of the bureaucracy in India, business also expends a great deal of energy in securing access to the administrative levels of government. In India, the minister in charge of the ministry is assisted by a secretary, who is the administrative head of the ministry and principal advisor to the minister on matters of policy and administration. When the volume of work exceeds the capability of one man, one or more additional wings are created within the ministry, and an additional secretary or a joint secretary is placed in charge of each. Normally, however, ministries are divided into divisions, branches, and sections. A section is headed by a section officer, two sections make a branch which is headed by an under secretary, and two branches are headed by a deputy secretary. The higher echelons of the bureaucracy include the under secretary, deputy secretary, joint secretary, and secretary, all of whom are members of the old Indian Civil Service (ICS) or its successor, the Indian Administrative Service (IAS).

Among the top echelons of the bureaucracy, the most important position is that of the secretary. The power of the secretary varies with the talent, skill, and political standing of the minister. If the minister is competent, if he knows his job and is strong politically, then he runs his department. If not, he is heavily dependent on the secretary for advice. Thus, the approach of an outside group dealing with government varies according to the relative standing of the minister and the secretary.

Secretaries, like ministers, vary in their personal ideological predispositions. Some are pro-private sector and others are antagonistic to the private sector, but the majority maintain a professional neutrality that permits them to concentrate on accomplishing their own institutional mission. Exactly how, or how successfully, this balance is maintained, however, is an individual matter of considerable interest to those who must approach a particular secretary for consideration or

[15] *Ibid.*, p. 240.

concessions. Thus, in dealing with government, business or any other organized interest group must vary its strategy and tactics according to the personality of the minister, the personality of the secretary, the ministry, and the issue involved. In general, however, the massive amount of legislation passed in India in the past two decades has transferred such enormous powers to the bureaucracy that the bureaucracy has grown into an almost independent center of decision-making in India. It is generally agreed among business leaders that, regardless of the issue, it is best to clear it with the secretary. Without him you are lost.

Despite its colonial origins, the bureaucracy in India has become very sensitive to political trends as well as to the personality and style of the ministers. Bureaucrats normally function impartially, accepting and implementing the policies set down by the political leadership. When the political leadership becomes uncertain or divided, the bureaucracy becomes reluctant to take even routine decisions and administration grinds to a halt. Since the last years of the Nehru era, the quality of ministers has declined substantially, resulting in an augmentation of the power of the bureaucracy. Most ministers are almost totally dependent on their secretaries for advice. And so a secretary who violently disagrees with a weak minister can delay action by using his detailed knowledge of substantive details, organization, and procedure. Yet no secretary can stop a minister, especially a strong minister, who is intent on doing something from embarking on that course of action. In fact there is increasing evidence that ministers are again assertive in policy-making. As the Administrative Reforms Commission observed,

> there is a disinclination among quite a number of ministers to welcome frank and impartial advice from the secretary or his aides and an inclination to judge him by his willingness to do what they wish him to do. Instances are not wanting of ministers preferring a convenient subordinate to a strong one and thereby making the latter not only ineffective but a sulky and unwilling worker. This has also bred a tendency on the part of an increasing number of civil servants to attempt to anticipate the ministers' wishes and proffer their advice accordingly. A further development of this unhealthy trend is the emergence of personal affiliations leading to an element of "politicalization" among the civil servants. All these cut at the root of the healthy relationship. . . . The prime minister should take special interest to curb this tendency, with

the assistance of the cabinet secretary and the central personnel agency.[16]

The charisma and personal power of the prime minister are important in determining the locus of decision-making. However, the fact that policy, even during the Nehru period, was made at the highest levels and was rarely deflected by pressure from below or from the pluralistic interaction of groups, cannot be attributed merely to the banyan tree effect of which he was so often accused. Government did enjoy a near monopoly over policy-making, and within government policy was indeed determined by a small leadership group. But the leadership and society shared many basic values of which specific policies were a logical outgrowth. The complexity of prospective legislation in major areas like labor policy and economic policy was so great that the ideas of the minister and the experienced men in the upper echelons of his ministry tended to gain baffled acceptance. Except in dealing with ethnic and linguistic demands, which were pressed by well-organized groups with strong localized backing, government dominated policy-making in many areas because the forces opposing government initiatives were weak. Interest groups like labor and business were so dependent on government benevolence and so vulnerable to government administrative actions that they were hesitant to pressure government too extensively or to question its policies. Under these circumstances, groups in India have come to play at best a circumspect negative role in the decision-making process and have exerted themselves mightily for minor concessions.

Access to the prime minister, to ministers, and to the higher echelons of the bureaucracy takes place not only through informal, self-initiated representations by groups but also through formal channels of access created by government as a means of consulting specific sectors of society. The shift, from a laissez-faire policy to a mixed economy in which the state plays a major role in planning and development within the framework of a democratic political system, necessitated the development of formalized patterns of access for the purpose of consulting key groups and interests in the society. The principle of consultation, especially with business, had been firmly established even before independence, and it received a strong additional impetus during World War II.

[16] S. R. Maheshwari, "The Minister-Secretary Relationship," *Journal of Constitutional and Parliamentary Studies* 4 (1970): 73.

Commerical interests were associated with the administration of public bodies in India as early as 1888, in conjunction with the enactment of the Calcutta Port Trust Act. The act provided for the representation of business associations on the Calcutta Port Trust, which was responsible for the operations of the port of Calcutta.[17] During World War II, problems of wartime scarcity necessitated extremely close government and business consultation. The British had further confirmed the principle of consultation through the procedure regularly followed by the various royal commissions and advisory bodies established by the government. After independence, the commitment to planning and government initiative in development resulted in the enactment of a comprehensive system designed to control and regulate business activity. The very comprehensiveness and complexity of this new legislation, as well as the commitment of a government to democratic principles, meant that the government was willing to accept the principle of establishing institutional forms of consultation. As a result, the government of India created two types of consultative or advisory bodies—expert committees and representative committees.

Expert committees were created to secure specialized knowledge and advice from official and nonofficial groups such as the Planning Commission's panels of economists or scientists. Representative committees were designed to secure representative opinions of groups in the society. Each ministry created its own advisory bodies. Thus the Ministry of Education created a central Advisory Board of Education to advise government on education questions; the Ministry of Labor and Employment established the Indian Labor Conference to advise government on matters of labor–management relations; the Ministry of Works, Housing, and Supply set up a Purchase Advisory Council to advise government on general policy and procedural matters relating to central government purchases; and the Ministry of Commerce and Industry formed a whole series of statutory bodies such as the Central Advisory Council of Industries and the Development Councils and nonstatutory bodies like the Export–Import Advisory Council, the Licensing Committee, and the Small Scale Industries Board. Because the function of advisory bodies was purely consultative in nature, government was free to accept or reject any suggestions emanating from them. Yet, having created these bodies, government found it could not treat their recommendations lightly. Even if government did not accept such advice, it had to justify its position. Thus, directly or indirectly the

[17] Federation of Indian Chambers of Commerce and Industry, *Silver Jubilee Souvenir: 1927–1951* (Bombay: India Printing Works, 1951), p. 24.

views of these bodies were important,[18] and interest groups who participated in them had advantages they otherwise would have missed.

One of the most comprehensive systems of consultation, and the one most critical to business interests, exists as part of the mechanism of coordinating the activities of the private sector under planning. After independence, while the debate over the precise role of the private sector was still raging, the government drew on the British Labor party's precedent of establishing a mechanism for consulting the private sector. The government created twenty-seven nonstatutory development committees, each consisting of both government and industry representatives, to discuss questions of productivity, standardization, cost reduction, and so on. The Industries (Development and Regulation) Act of 1951 formalized the pattern of consultation by creating statutory development councils and the Central Advisory Council of Industries.[19] The creation of a regularized and systematized pattern for channeling demands to government gave business a strong incentive to organize specialized associations as a means of presenting their views and difficulties directly to government. Business, meanwhile, also took the initiative in pursuing a whole range of informal and individual contacts with government.

Government officials still tend to make a clear-cut distinction between advice and opinion. In consulting the private sector, they tend to turn to individuals for advice, but they rely on consultative and advisory bodies to obtain a representative view. Advice is looked on as something which one can receive from experts who know their fields, not from committees of businessmen. The latter are suspected of providing the lowest common denominator of agreement, which would be quickly repudiated by individuals in private. Thus, government consults with business in general only on a noncommittal basis; that is, it listens without comment. In private discussions with respected individual businessmen, however, advice is actually sought and followed. And so business influence in the past has tended to become highly individual rather than collective. But this pattern appears to be fading rapidly as business diversifies, becomes more bureaucratized, and develops new leadership which does not enjoy the close contacts which men like G. D. Birla and J. R. D. Tata enjoyed with the older generation of nationalist leaders.

[18] R. C. Dutt, "Hearing and Consultation Procedure in Public Administration," *Indian Journal of Public Administration* 4 (1958): 289.

[19] S. Subbaramaiah, "The Development Councils for Industries in India," *The Indian Journal of Economics* 43 (1963): 251–266.

Although the executive in India is responsible to Parliament, for a variety of reasons the executive has tended to dominate the formulation of public policy. Throughout the Nehru era, the Congress party controlled over 70 percent of the seats in Parliament, and the opposition was scattered among a whole list of parties. A large proportion of the Congress party members were simply men who had been freedom fighters and had little experience in legislative functioning. Most experienced Congressmen had quickly been coopted into the ministerial ranks. The Congress party rank and file followed their leaders, who commanded great respect in the party.

Government introduced almost all the bills discussed in Parliament, and ministers bore the brunt of explaining and defending these policies. "The experience and equipment of the majority of members does not enable them to contribute a great deal, and one consequence is that ministers often feel somewhat lonely and isolated, dependent for encouragement, stimulus, ideas, and argument not on their back-benchers but on their civil servants." [20] Still Parliament was given great respect and was a means of ventilating grievances, passing legislation, and acting as a public forum.[21]

Attempts to develop greater participation—within Parliament by creating consultative committees and within the Congress parliamentary party by developing functionally specialized committees and state groups—have had very limited success. Even the Congress party executive and the general body played only a minor role, for massive Congress majorities enabled the party to permit open criticism on the floor of the house instead of confining it strictly to party forums. For all the latitude given to the expression of views, party discipline was effectively maintained at the time of voting. Thus, although Congress MPs exercised little real control over leadership, they provided the government with a solid majority to govern.

Until recently, the most potent interests in Parliament were not the social and economic interests in the modern sector but their caste, community, and regional antecedents.[22] Thus, although debates on national language and linguistic states were quite vocal and at times effective, complex economic and social legislation passed with little controversy. A leading industrialist, who was a member of the first Lok Sabha, warned his business colleagues as early as 1951 that the business case in Parliament was going by default because of the lack of effective

[20] W. H. Morris-Jones, *Parliament in India* (Philadelphia: University of Pennsylvania Press, 1957), p. 324.

[21] *Ibid.*, pp. 316–333.

[22] Rajni Kothari, *Politics in India* (Boston: Little, Brown, 1970), pp. 215–219.

spokesmen to present the business point of view. "On so many occasions," he told the Bombay Millowners Association, "even in matters where we had a very strong and genuine case we have not even been able to educate either the MPs or the general public outside, to show how on many occasions we have received unfair treatment from government and how all sorts of charges being levied are mostly based on misunderstanding and prejudice." He further warned that "unless we are able to put forth our considered view in proper time it is quite likely that we may be deprived even of whatever reasonable modification or alteration we may otherwise secure." He therefore urged the formation of a national textile body, with a Delhi office for convenient lobbying and greater concentation of study and research to educate public opinion and Parliament.[23] Similar views were voiced by business MPs in 1968.

Parliament began assuming a more creative role as chief critic of the executive in the late 1950s. At that time, as a result of persistent efforts by Feroze Gandhi, a major scandal was uncovered which forced the resignation of T. T. Krishnamachari, one of Nehru's most trusted economic advisors. The Parliament became more restive and critical of government leadership following the first public disclosure of major Chinese border incursions in Ladakh, and the trend, which accelerated toward the end of the Nehru era, received especial impetus following the 1962 Chinese attack and the turmoil following the Congress party split in 1969.

As Parliament became more vocal, so did the Congress parliamentary party. Energized by the onset of the early rounds in the struggle for succession, the Congress parliamentary party became deeply divided over the selection of a deputy party leader to succeed G. B. Pant when he died in 1961. Eventually Nehru was forced to intervene. He first succeeded in postponing the issue and then in modifying the parliamentary party's constitution to provide for two deputy leaders, one from each house.[24] The parliamentary party executive next played an important role in forcing the resignation of V. K. Krishna Menon from the cabinet, despite Nehru's desire to keep him on. The party held that Menon, as defense minister, was responsible for the military setback suffered by India at the hands of the Chinese and should therefore resign.[25]

[23] G. D. Somani, *Confidential Report on the First Session of Parliament May 13, 1952 to August 12, 1952* (Submitted to the Bombay Millowners Association, August 1952).

[24] *The Statesman* (Calcutta), May 2, 1961.

[25] *The Statesman* (Calcutta), November 7, 1962 and November 8, 1962.

When Nehru died, the Congress parliamentary party was formally responsible for the election of the party leader who, because of the Congress party majority, would become the prime minister. But the Congress parliamentary party accepted the consensus of the party leadership as the basis for the selection of Shastri as Nehru's successor. However, the battleground in the fight between Morarji Desai and Mrs. Gandhi in 1966 and 1967 was the parliamentary party itself. Finally, with the Congress party split in 1969, the parliamentary party became, for a brief period, even more important, because its composition and the vote of each of its members counted as never before. The possibility of defection in the face of a less secure majority made the demands of individual MPs more potent than ever before in the history of the Congress party. Thus, interest groups considered the parliamentary party and even individual members as potentially influential and thus worth educating as never before. The restoration of a massive Congress party majority still required some activity at the Parliament level, if only to counter the highly vocal pressure generated by the parties of the left and the left wing within the Congress party.

Parliament's role in the decision-making process is changing. And its composition and the kind of interests it represents are also undergoing a transformation. The Parliament is becoming more interest-based. Ethnic groups are no longer the only active and vocal groups in the Parliament. A farm lobby is beginning to emerge which, although still formally unorganized, is based on individual representation. As seen in Table III-1, the proportion of agriculturalists in Parliament has risen sharply—from 14.7 percent in 1951 to 33.8 percent in 1971—as the richer farmers have begun to take to politics.[26] Moreover, although the proportion of businessmen in Parliament ranged from 7 to 11 percent, the 1967 elections witnessed the entry into Parliament of individuals representing the modern industrial sector rather than the traditional bazaar merchants and traders. Industrialists and business as a whole, however, fared very poorly in the 1971 parliamentary election. The modern professions—lawyers, doctors, journalists, and so on—have been on the decline. Thus, Parliament is becoming more broadly based, with increasing representation of functionally based interests.

Even though Parliament is becoming somewhat more interest-based, the predominant forces still represent individual, caste, community, and region. Ethnic demands continue to dominate parliamentary debates. The average Indian Member of Parliament knows very little

[26] L. M. Singhvi, "The Legislative Process in India," *Journal of Constitutional and Parliamentary Studies* 4 (1970): 126.

Table III-1

OCCUPATIONS OF THE MEMBERS OF THE LOK SABHA

Occupation	*First Lok Sabha*		*Second Lok Sabha*		*Third Lok Sabha*		*Fourth Lok Sabha*		*Fifth Lok Sabha*	
	No.	*Per-cent*	*No.*	*Per-cent*	*No.*	*Per-cent*	*No.*	*Per-cent*	*No.*	*Per-cent*
Full time Social & Political Workers	121	24.7	109	22.0	106	21.2	112	21.6	92	17.6
Lawyers	107	21.9	112	22.6	109	21.8	86	16.6	93	17.9
Scientists, Engineers, Doctors	21	4.3	15	3.0	20	4.0	23	4.4	16	3.1
Teachers	37	7.6	30	6.1	36	7.2	38	7.3	36	6.9
Business	53	10.8	47	9.5	55	11.0	58	11.2	39	7.5
Journalists	38	7.8	33	6.7	19	3.8	27	5.2	30	5.7
Agriculture	72	14.7	93	18.8	114	22.8	135	26.0	176	33.8
Services	24	4.7	22	4.4	24	4.8	25	4.8	12	2.3
Information not available	16	3.2	34	6.9	17	3.4	15	2.5	27	5.2
Total	489	99.8	495	100.8	500	100.0	519	100.0	521	100.0

SOURCES: S. L. Chopra and O.N.S. Chauhan, "Emerging Pattern of Political Leadership in India, *Journal of Constitutional and Parliamentary Studies* IV:1 (1970), 126. *Journal of Parliamentary Information* XVIII:2 (1972), 372.

about modern business and industry and less about company law or finance. In such matters, therefore, the ministers and the ministries retain the upper hand. A strong ideologically based lobby on the right and its complement on the left are constantly attacking each other, and the average Member of Parliament is in the middle. His ignorance of business affairs, or his indifference, do not add up to hostility. Business has learned that the average Member of Parliament can be won over in cases where business has a just case, and thus Parliament in recent years has become an additional arena for business activity.

The increase in the strength of agrarian interests in Parliament reflects the substantial support which the Congress party has received from the owners of large and medium sized land holdings who have gained substantially, economically and politically, as a result of the green revolution. These Members of Parliament have come to act as a commodity lobby, reinforcing the substantial voice already enjoyed by the chief ministers of the states as spokesmen for agrarian interests. Despite the commanding position Mrs. Gandhi occupies in both party and government, and despite her decisive role in selecting Congress party chief ministers, she has not been able to reverse the pattern of center–state relations which emerged toward the end of the Nehru era. At the same time, however, some of the most important new programs which are part of her promise to abolish poverty require action by the state governments. The lowering of ceilings on land holdings and the introduction of an agricultural income tax both fall under the jurisdiction of the states.

An example of the difficulty faced by the central government in implementing the Congress party program occurred in April 1972, at a meeting of the Conference of Chief Ministers. The conference was convened to consider recommendations on the price policy for the 1972–1973 winter crop. An expert government commission had recommended a sharp cut in government price supports for wheat. Members of Parliament from the wheat producing states of Uttar Pradesh, Harayana, and Punjab vigorously lobbied against the recommendations in Parliament. And the chief ministers of those states, sensitive to the pressures of the agrarian sector, resisted any changes in prices from the previous year. At a special meeting of the Political Affairs Committee of the cabinet to which the chief ministers of the wheat producing states were invited on the eve of the Conference of Chief Ministers, they succeeded in persuading the prime minister and her colleagues that any cut in wheat prices would be politically unwise. The leaders of the wheat producing states dominated the debate at the Conference of Chief Ministers the next day and succeeded in getting the conference to endorse their stand. The resistance to changes in wheat support prices reflected similar resistance of the chief minister to even more fundamental issues, such as reducing ceilings on land holdings and enacting an agricultural income tax. Thus the states continue to act as a major check on the implementation of the more radical proposals emanating from Delhi, despite the restoration of strong central leadership[27] as a result of the pressures which the agrarian sector have succeeded in generating.

Patterns of access in India have changed in response to changes in the political system and the distribution of power within the political system. For the first fifteen years after independence, the major targets of the business community had been the prime minister, the cabinet, and the higher echelons of the bureaucracy.[28] Independence had brought to power a strong, capable, and relatively united leadership backed by massive majorities in Parliament. Decision-making was highly centralized in the hands of the prime minister and a small inner circle of his cabinet, all of whom commanded great respect because of their status as leaders of the nationalist movement. To change or to modify executive policy or legislative action, it was necessary to convince the prime minister or one of his chief cabinet colleagues. The Congress party majority in Parliament provided almost unquestioned support to the Congress party government. Congress party discipline at this stage was strong, and the leadership viewed as illegitimate any attempts by outside interests to approach Members of Parliament of any persuasion. Under such circumstances, trying to influence a handful of votes in Parliament was seen as worse than futile; it was potentially counterproductive.

The new government's policy of planned economic growth in the framework of a mixed economy called for the private sector to play an active role in development under the strict supervision of government.[29] The resulting mechanism of government regulation and control included the creation of a highly structured and regularized pattern of consultation with the interests affected.[30] This pattern of interaction through statutory and nonstatutory bodies, by which a me-

[27] "Quick End to Great Expectations" *Economic and Politcal Weekly* 7 (1972): 825–827.

[28] Michael Brecher, *Nehru's Mantle* (New York: Praeger, 1966), pp. 92–137; Michael Brecher, "Succession in India 1967: The Routinization of Political Change," *Asian Survey* 7 (1967): 423–443.

[29] Matthew J. Kust, *Foreign Enterprise in India: Laws and Policies* (Chapel Hill, N. C.: University of North Carolina Press, 1964); see also *Supplement*, published 1966.

[30] *Ibid.*, pp. 117–118.

dium of governmental control was also a potential medium of business influence, placed a premium on organization. The business associations, therefore, became the predominant instrument for allocating seats on government advisory committees. Participation on these committees gave business a chance to conduct a legitimate, direct dialogue with ministers and secretaries of the government of India. Yet legitimacy and effectiveness are far from synonymous. These consultative bodies were purely advisory, serving primarily as policy-reviewing agencies and certainly not as policy-making bodies. So far as business was concerned, their impact on government was indirect. Outcomes depended heavily on the initiative of government and on the attitudes of the various ministers and ministries involved. Nevertheless, an important precedent was set. Government was thereby accustomed to the principle of seeking the advice of business and providing politically acceptable channels of business access to government decision-makers.

The passing of the old nationalist leadership and the trend toward a more participatory decision-making process enabled business to expand its efforts to intervene at an earlier stage in the policy process. The prime minister, cabinet, and bureaucracy were forced to pay greater attention to pressures generated in Parliament and within the Congress party itself. At the same time, however, there was a decline in the old style of highly personal access to political elites, as more regularized patterns of access became safer and less subject to attack. Business began playing a more active role in elections, leadership selection, and lobbying, and began to speak out more openly in pressing its demands. However, public hostility toward the private sector has acted as a major check on the effectiveness of this more broadly based intervention.

The overwhelming 1971 election victory of Mrs. Indira Gandhi's new Congress party, however, brought a return of Congress party dominance, strong political leadership, and a recentralization of decision-making. At the same time, that election victory also marked the beginning of greater concern, on the part of the Indian electorate, with government policy outputs. Thus, unlike the earlier years after independence, the government of India will be faced with increasing pressure from functional interests and less pressure from the more familiar ethnic demands of the past. Emerging interests will focus greater attention on social and economic issues, and government will be compelled to pay greater attention to these demands and to the difficulties of balancing the demands for social and economic equality with the need for more rapid economic growth, increased employment, and expanding productive facilities. In short, Indian politics will become more interest-based, as pressures generated by emerging functional interests are felt at all levels of decision-making and groups increase their demands on the political system. Business will continue to play an active role but will also face increased competition from other groups.

IV

PATTERNS OF PUBLIC POLICY

Patterns of public policy play a major role in shaping interest group behavior, determining the channels of access, and conditioning the style of interest articulation. Even while interest groups are working to influence public policy which impinges on their sphere of action, they are themselves shaped by the very public policy they seek to influence. To a very large extent, the level of government intervention in the society also determines the number and variety of groups in the system. Groups not only make demands, they respond to government policy initiatives. These policy initiatives, which may originate within government itself or in other parts of the political system, in turn may make it easier for interest group leadership to mobilize support and resources. The perceived threat may be strong enough to permit businessmen, for example, to subordinate their divergent views to a united response to government actions, such as tariffs or labor legislation. Government, however, may find it necessary—in order to accomplish its public objectives—to seek support and cooperation from groups in the society. Thus government may even encourage group formation to provide channels of communication or to accomplish larger public purposes. War, for example, may necessitate the creation of groups to allocate scarce resources. Public policy may also play an active and overt role in determining patterns of access to government. Legislation may contain statutory provisions for consultation with groups affected by its enactment, or government may create voluntary public bodies whose function is to seek advice and counsel. The very response of groups to government may determine the style of interest articulation in the political system.

Interest groups are not concerned with all public policy but only with those policies which have a redistributive, distributive, regulatory, or developmental impact on their activities.[1] Although they may be affected by some aspects of foreign policy, most interest groups do not, under normal circumstances, take stands on foreign policy issues.

[1] This system of classification is a modification of the one suggested by Theodore J. Lowi, "American Business, Public Policy, Case Studies, and Political Theory," *World Politics* 16 (1964): 677–715.

Among domestic policy issues, redistributive policy is that policy which establishes an inverse relationship between subgroups in the system. It seeks to facilitate socioeconomic change by taking something from one group of people in order to supply it more abundantly to another group. Property relations thus are altered by nationalization or by the introduction of a progressive income tax. Distributive policy relates directly to single groups, so that benefits to one group do not necessarily, and by definition, entail sacrifices by another group. Subsidies, tax concessions, and protective tariffs are all distributive measures designed to aid specific categories of industry.

Regulatory policy restricts the alternatives open to individuals and groups by imposing controls over prices, production, and distribution, by supervising business activities through company regulation, by specifying the model for labor–management relations, and so on. Developmental policy includes all steps taken by government to provide business with incentives to accomplish larger public purposes. Such measures may include tax rebates to increase exports or concessions of various kinds to encourage specific types of investment and entry into socially desirable activities. Each type of public policy creates a different arena of political action. Therefore the political process, so far as interest groups are concerned, varies according to the nature of the issue.

Public Policy During the Colonial Era

In India, the pattern of public policy affecting the business community changed radically between the period of colonial rule and the post-independence era, but both before and after independence public policy played a major role in mobilizing business for collective action. British economic policy in India, dominated by the doctrine of laissez-faire and free trade, reflected the predominant economic philosophy of the nineteenth century. But in the "free play of market forces," clearly some were regarded as more equal than others. And so, where government interceded with business activities, it tended to favor the demands of British industrialists and the pressure of British capital in India. Thus, both monetary policy toward rupee exchange rates and the purchases of government stores tended to favor British over Indian interests. British shipping was granted a monopoly of the coastal trade, received lucrative mail contracts, and obtained the right to carry civil and military government cargoes and personnel.[2]

[2] Michael Kidron, *Foreign Investments in India* (London: Oxford University Press, 1965), pp. 11–19.

The associations of British capital in India, therefore, concentrated on maintaining the British beachhead on privileges against the rising tide of Indian political and economic nationalism represented by associations dedicated to the redistribution of benefits in favor of indigenous capital.

Thus, Indian capital mobilized, through their own business associations and through their spokesmen in the Indian National Congress, to protest the preferential policies of the colonial government. Protesting discriminatory tariff, currency, and transportation policies, and the undue influence of foreign capital, demanding that exploitation of Indian resources be curtailed and that the state take a more active role in encouraging national development and indigenous industry, the style of Indian capital at this time was mainly vocal protest—overt condemnation of government actions welling up at last from a long felt antagonism toward foreign capital. Ideologists like Dadabhai Naoroji, Fherozeshah Mehta, and M. G. Ranade provided an intellectual critique of the British economic exploitation of India. The philosophical and financial aspects of economic nationalism were given popular appeal in the call to boycott British goods and purchase only swadeshi or Indian-made goods. Indian traders as well as industrialists organized in an attempt to rectify the discriminatory trade policies of the colonial government.

Above all, during the colonial era Indian business demanded protective tariffs. The free trade philosophy had achieved nearly religious status among British liberals. But "the theoretical free-trader hardly exists in India at present," said the Montagu-Chelmsford Report of 1918:

> Educated Indian opinion ardently desires a tariff. . . . Whatever economic fallacy underlies his reasoning, these are his firm beliefs; and though he may be willing to concede the possibility that he is wrong, he will not readily concede that it is our business to decide the matter for him. He believes that as long as we continue to decide for him we shall decide in the interests of England and not according to his wishes; . . . so long as the people who refuse India protection are interested in manufactures with which India might compete, Indian opinion cannot bring itself to believe that the refusal is disinterested or dictated by care for the best interests of India.[3]

[3] Daniel Houston Buchanan, *The Development of Capitalistic Enterprise in India* (New York: Macmillan, 1934), p. 469.

Free trade had not always been the rule in British India. Under the East India Company and in the early years of crown rule, moderate duties on both imports and exports were levied as a revenue device. Under pressure from British industry, rationalized by the pervasive influence of liberal free trade philosophy, India was ordered to abolish all customs tariffs in the late nineteenth century. Lord Curzon, the governor general of India from 1898 to 1905, admitted that "Lancashire pressure" had been the source of "successive readjustments" in tariff policy.[4] The Indian response to this policy was the formation in Bombay in 1875 of the Bombay Millowners Association.[5]

For fiscal reasons, small duties were again imposed in 1892 and extended in 1894. In 1895, Lancashire textile interests complained that the depressed state of textiles in Britain was entirely caused by the imposition of import and excise duties in India.[6] Therefore in 1896, when a duty of 3.5 percent was levied on cotton textile imports, the government placed an equivalent excise tax on all cotton textiles manufactured in Indian mills. Both remained in force until 1925.[7] What the indigenous cotton millowners could not avert, however, British capital could. Despite pressures from the British mills of Dundee, the Scottish-owned jute mills in Bengal succeeded in blocking similar discriminatory policies.[8] The Bombay cotton mills, however, did not obtain meaningful relief until after World War I, when India gained fiscal autonomy. Protection then became official policy, and a tariff board was set up in 1923 to review applications for tariff protection.[9] Subsequently many indigenous industries were granted protection, but only in return for establishing preferential tariffs for British goods.[10] The most controversial of the concessions granted during this period stemmed from the Lees-Mody Pact, which was worked out in October 1933 between the Bombay Millowners Association and the Lancashire mills. Under the agreement, Indian mills were granted limited protection against British goods but strong protection against textiles from other countries, especially Japan. The pact was condemned as a sellout by the nationalists and by sections

[4] *Ibid.*, p. 465.
[5] S. D. Saklatvala, *History of the Millowners' Association: Bombay 1875–1930* (Bombay: for private circulation, 1930), p. 5.
[6] *Ibid.*, p. 42.
[7] Buchanan, *Development of Capitalistic Enterprise*, pp. 163–164.
[8] *Ibid.*, p. 467.
[9] Kidron, *Foreign Investments*, p. 13.
[10] Buchanan, *Development of Capitalistic Enterprise*, p. 467.

of Indian business.[11] From 1923 to 1939, thirteen industries received protection.[12]

After protection, the most important demand of Indian business was for government to play a positive and active role in encouraging development. The most comprehensive expression of this demand was the Bombay Plan, which was drawn up by the business elite of India: Sir Purshotamdas Thakurdas, J. R. D. Tata, G. D. Birla, Sir Ardeshir Dalal, Shri Ram, Kasturbhai Lalbhai, A. D. Shroff, and John Mathai. The Bombay Plan called for the establishment of centralized planning, the imposition of rigorous economic controls, the development of heavy industry, and the introduction of radical agricultural reforms. Planning had also become part of the program of the Indian National Congress. Under the direction of Nehru, the Congress party had prepared a series of development plans for post-independence India.[13]

The British response to Indian demands for a positive governmental role was sporadic and ambivalent. The government of Madras had established a Provincial Department of Industries. But the venture was abandoned under pressure from British business, which had, according to the Indian Industries Commission, interpreted it "as a serious menace to private enterprise and an unwarrantable intervention on the part of the state in matters beyond the sphere of government." [14] Although an Imperial Department of Industries had been created in 1921, it had never played a very active role in economic planning. Even World Wars I and II did not produce any appreciable government initiative in industrialization.[15] Many of the administrative devices that government used to control a wartime economy, however, were to play an important role in post-independence development. Among Indians, the industrialists and the nationalists were especially hostile toward foreign capital.[16] Foreign and indigenous capital had grown up in competition with each other. British capital organized to protect its privileges, and Indian business organized to demand that British economic policy be restructured to shift distributive benefits from foreign to Indian capital. Indian businessmen joined with the nationalist movement to protest continued British control

[11] D. R. Mankekar, *Homi Mody: A Many Splendored Life* (Bombay: Popular Prakashan, 1968), pp. 67–81; Kidron, *Foreign Investments*, p. 26, n. 1.

[12] Matthew J. Kust, *Foreign Enterprise in India* (Chapel Hill, N. C.: University of North Carolina Press, 1964), pp. 185–187.

[13] Baldev Raj Nayar, "Business Attitudes Toward Economic Planning in India," *Asian Survey* 11 (1971): 850–865.

[14] Kidron, *Foreign Investments*, p. 14.

[15] *Ibid.*, p. 16.

[16] *Ibid.*, pp. 65–74.

over India, insisting that Indian economic policy be made in New Delhi by Indians, not in London by Englishmen.

Public Policy in Post-Independence India

The pattern of public policy in India was radically altered after independence. The doctrine of laissez-faire was replaced by a dedication to rapid economic development through centralized planning to create a socialist pattern of society or a mixed economy within the framework of a secular, democratic political system. These policy objectives enjoyed a very broad base of support within India. The detailed implementation of this goal led to the adoption of a series of policies which have helped determine the targets and channels of access available to business in post-independence India. These policies and their effects fall into the redistributive, distributive, regulatory, or developmental category. The most far reaching redistributive policies were incorporated in the policies which implemented the philosophy and objectives of the newly created system of centralized planning within a democratic framework. The basic framework of development was set out in the industrial policy resolutions of 1948 and 1956. Those resolutions acted as the basic guidelines in formulating the first, second, third, and fourth Five Year Plans.

The basic strategy of development in India was worked out over a period of years and was a synthesis of three basic streams of thought which had developed within the Congress movement. First, there were those who supported the Gandhian philosophy of Sarvodaya, which placed major emphasis on the self-sufficient village economy based on village and cottage industries rather than large-scale industrialization. The Gandhians wanted all basic consumer goods such as cloth, edible oils, and paper to be produced in decentralized village and cottage cooperatives protected from the competition of large-scale industry. They believed that only such a policy could raise the standard of living in the rural areas, reduce unemployment, and preserve a distinctive way of life which would otherwise be threatened by the introduction of large-scale industrialization.

A second important stream of thought existed among the small but highly influential group of Western educated Congressmen who were committed to a variety of socialist doctrines. Nehru was generally identified with this segment of the Congress movement. Socialist-oriented Congressmen wanted new investment in industrial expansion concentrated in heavy industry in the public sector.

The third approach was supported by Congress party leaders like

Vallabhbhai Patel and Rajendra Prasad. They had extremely close ties with the Indian industrial elite and were prepared to press for a major role for private sector investment aided by government.

The Gandhian and socialist view received major emphasis in the Report of the Congress Economic Programme Committee of January 1948. This report recommended a radical revision of government economic policy. It called for a ceiling on incomes, land ceilings, the reservation of food production, cloth production, and consumer goods production for village and cottage industries, the abolition of the managing agency system, a maximum profit of 5 percent on venture capital, and the nationalization of public utilities, defense production, and other key industries.

Despite its endorsement by the Congress party, the government disavowed the Economic Programme Committee report and prepared its own Industrial Policy Resolution of 1948. That resolution went a long way toward alleviating business fear and uncertainty by toning down the more radical proposals advocated by the party. The Industrial Policy Resolution of 1948 was an effort to halt the lag in industrial production, which resulted from the loss of business confidence, and to clarify the economic objectives of the government. The Industrial Policy Resolution of 1948 provided for a mixed economy. Exclusive ownership was confined to three industries: munitions, atomic energy, and railways. In six other fields, government reserved for itself the exclusive right to start new ventures: coal, iron and steel, aircraft manufacture, shipbuilding, telephone and telegraph materials, and minerals. As far as the existing private sector facilities were concerned, the government guaranteed that no redistribution through nationalization would take place for at least ten years.

The advent of planning in March 1950, and the decision halfway through the first Five Year Plan to accelerate the growth of the economy through more rapid industrialization, led to a restatement of the Industrial Policy Resolution of 1948. In late 1954, therefore, the cabinet declared that the Industrial Policy Resolution of 1948 "had to be interpreted in terms of the socialistic objective." By December, Parliament had passed a resolution making the "Socialist Pattern" the official policy of the government and a guide to the Planning Commission in drawing up the second Plan.[17] The nature of the socialist pattern was spelled out more clearly in the Industrial Policy Resolution of 1956.

The new Industrial Policy Resolution expanded the scope of the

[17] Stanley A. Kochanek, *The Congress Party of India* (Princeton: Princeton University Press, 1968), pp. 164–181.

public sector. The number of industries reserved for the public sector rose from six to seventeen. Included in this category were all basic and strategic industries, public utilities, and industries requiring large investments. Specifically, heavy industries such as iron and steel, machine tools, heavy electricals, and mining fell under the jurisdiction of the public sector. A second category consisted of a concurrent list of twelve industries in which private sector investment was expected to supplement the dominant public sector enterprise. The concurrent list included the production of machine tools, essential drugs, aluminum, basic chemicals, and sea and road transport. All other industries were to be left to the private sector. In addition, the Industrial Policy Resolution of 1956 guaranteed existing facilities against nationalization, provided for expansion of existing facilities under specific circumstances, and permitted public–private cooperation in development of some of the reserved sector.[18]

Despite the expanded scope of the public sector provided for in the Industrial Policy Resolution of 1956, that resolution was welcomed by the business community. The new policy clarified precisely which sphere would be open to the private sector, it removed the immediate threat of nationalization, and it convinced business that there would be more than ample scope for the private sector. During the next decade the private sector in fact underwent a very rapid expansion which ensured that it would continue to play an important role in Indian industrial development.

The Industrial Policy Resolutions of 1948 and 1956 did not call for the nationalization of existing private productive facilities. But the resolutions were still redistributive, in the sense that all subsequent planning was guided by the objective of achieving a socialist pattern of society or a special kind of welfare state in which the public sector was given a dominant role. In practice, therefore, the Industrial Policy Resolutions were redistributive in three ways.

First, they defined spheres of activity for the public and private sectors in such a way that the economic future of India was taken from the hands of private capital and placed in the public sector. The Industrial Policy Resolution of 1956, in particular, contained a strong bias in favor of the public sector. Thus, although only about 10 percent of the total industrial output was in the public sector even at the end of the second Plan, the public sector was so favored that it could not help but eventually close the gap between its total share of industrial investment and that of the private sector. Table IV-1 shows

[18] Planning Commission, Government of India, *The New India* (New York: Macmillan, 1958), pp. 387–396.

Table IV-1
PUBLIC AND PRIVATE SECTOR INDUSTRIAL INVESTMENT

	Public sector		*Private sector*		*Total percent of plan*	
	Rupees crores	*Percent*	*Rupees crores*	*Percent*	*Rupees crores*	*Percent*
Second Plan	870	56	675	44	1,545	23
Third Plan	1,520	59	1,050	41	2,570	25
Fourth Plan	3,298	62	2,000	38	5,298	23.4

SOURCES: Second Plan, Hanson, *The Process of Planning*, p. 206. Third Plan, *Ibid.* Fourth Plan, *Fourth Five Year Plan* (Faridabad: G.O.I., Press, 1970), p. 314.

that, under the second Plan, public sector investment in organized industry was 56 percent of the total plan allocation for organized industry. Its share increased to 62 percent by the time of the fourth Plan.[19] These targets, however, have not always been met.

Second, the Industrial Policy Resolutions were redistributive to the extent that the government nationalized most important financial and credit mechanisms in the society. In order to finance development and insure the ability of government to dominate the commanding heights of the economy, the government nationalized the life insurance industry and the Imperial Bank of India, the largest private bank in India.[20] Much later it nationalized the remaining private sector banks along with general insurance. In addition, the government introduced a comprehensive series of new taxes: a graduated surtax on dividends, compulsory deposits, a capital gains tax, wealth and expenditure taxes, and gift taxes.[21] Thus, through nationalization of financial and credit mechanisms and a severely progressive tax system, government policy was designed not only to attempt to produce redistributive justice but also to determine the precise sphere of all future private sector development.

Third, the Industrial Policy Resolutions were redistributive in that they led to a total reconstruction of the legal framework within which the private sector would have to operate. Constitutional sanctions and Supreme Court interpretation have given the government of India wide powers of economic regulation over the private sector. This power was utilized to pass and implement the Industries (Develop-

[19] Planning Commission, Government of India, *Fourth Five Year Plan: 1969–1974* (Faridabad: Government of India Press, 1970), p. 51.

[20] Kust, *Foreign Enterprise*, pp. 99–104.

[21] *Ibid.*, pp. 361–369.

ment and Regulation) Act of 1951.[22] That act provides for the most complex and comprehensive system of control and regulation of private business in the world, in addition to creating the administrative institution for the coordination of public and private sector development. Thus, policies which are redistributive in their broadest social and economic implications give rise to subsidiary policies which are essentially distributive, regulatory, or developmental in nature.

Although the Industries (Development and Regulation) Act of 1951 gives the bureaucracy vast powers to control and regulate private industry, its jurisdiction over the awarding of industrial licenses gives it a predominantly distributive impact. Under the act, all existing scheduled industries were required to register with the government, and a license was required before any new facilities could be built. Once registered, the industries became subject to government regulations which included the powers to: investigate their operations and issue directives for changes; assume management and control of industries where warranted; and control the supply, distribution, and prices of their production. Covered under the act were thirty-eight industrial categories involving over 150 articles of manufacture. Section 30 of the act delegated to the central government the power to develop detailed rules for implementing the provisions of the act but preserved parliamentary control by requiring that rules be subject to parliamentary consent. The machinery subsequently created under the rules involves the activation of a complex system of interministerial and intergovernmental coordination before a license for a new industrial undertaking can be granted. The steps include clearance by the following: the Licensing Committee, the Department of Technical Development, the Foreign Agreements Committee,[23] the Capital Goods Committee, the Chief Controller of Imports and Exports, the Controller of Capital Issue, the Company Law Administration, and the Reserve Bank of India.

An application for an industrial license is submitted to the Ministry of Industries, which then refers it to the Licensing Committee. The Licensing Committee is composed of one or more representatives of a variety of ministries, which most recently included representatives of the Ministries of Industry, Railways, Finance, Steel, Mines and Fuel, and Labor. The Planning Commission was also represented. Other

[22] Government of India, Ministry of Law, *The Industries (Development and Regulation) Act, 1951* (Delhi: Government of India Press, 1967).

[23] The primary concern of the Foreign Agreements Committee is to ensure that foreign collaboration, if undertaken, is necessary and that the terms and conditions are reasonable and acceptable.

ministries may be invited. The Licensing Committee, after reviewing and investigating each license application, must prepare a report with recommendations to the Industry Ministry on the disposition of the application. In studying the application, the Committee must consider

> the approved plans, if any, of the central government for the development of the scheduled industry concerned and, where no such plans exist, to the existing capacity of the scheduled industry, the demand and supply position, availability of raw materials and plant machinery. The report should, among other matters, contain recommendations regarding capital and its structure, suitability of the location proposed from the point of view of the approved plans for the industry, capacity of the plant to be installed, availability of rail-transport capacity, availability of technical and other skilled personnel required, and collaboration, if any, with foreign manufacturers.[24]

The Directorate General of Technical Development is the primary technical unit of the government. It advises the Ministry of Industry in the formulation of industrial plans and in the regulation and development of industry in the private sector. It also advises private sector entrepreneurs on the formulation and execution of their industrial projects.[25] Because most new projects involve imports of capital goods and many also involve foreign collaborations, projects must be cleared by the Capital Goods Committee and the Foreign Agreements Committee, both of which, like the Licensing Committee, are interministerial in composition. After receipt of approval from the Capital Goods Committee, specific application for an import license must be made to the Chief Controller of Imports and Exports, who checks to see that the goods are not indigenously available. Meanwhile the Controller of Capital Issue and the Company Law Administration must both approve of all public issue of shares and debentures. The Controller of Capital Issue must evaluate the proposal to raise capital from the public, and the Company Law Administration evaluates the prospectus which is to be issued to the public. The Reserve Bank is responsible for the control and regula-

[24] Quoted in Kust, *Foreign Enterprise*, p. 122.

[25] For a full list of the functions of the Directorate General of Technical Development, see Ministry of Industry and Supply, Government of India, *Report of the Study Team on Directorate General of Technical Development* (*Part 1*) New Delhi: Government of India Press, 1965), pp. 4–5.

tion of all transactions involving foreign exchange and foreign securities in India. All together, then, administrative complexity makes the licensing procedure extremely time-consuming. The system can involve interminable delays at any level. The majority of applications take five to six months and must be watched over so that they do not take longer.[26] And so it is no wonder that the private sector found it advantageous to create industrial embassies in New Delhi, to keep track of license applications and to move applications through the bureaucracy.

The policy tools designed to manage the economy have made government controls all pervasive. A recent World Bank Report[27] concluded:

> The result is that a large part of a businessman's time and creativeness have to be devoted to manipulating the various control systems. Some enterprises do this very successfully, and in fact all large firms keep representatives in Delhi simply to expedite the issuing of various clearances. The system produces a very heavy dependence on government for initiatives or judgments of all kinds; a glance at the financial press shows that not a day passes without representation from some section of industrialists for a concession from government to meet a particular problem.

In addition to endowing government with vast regulatory powers, this licensing procedure provided an almost unlimited reservoir of benefits which it could distribute to individual businessmen in the private sector. The industrial license was the most important benefit bestowed by government, because it almost automatically provided a near monopoly in the field. Large profits were equally predictable because of the government's protectionist policies. The licensing system, therefore, generated fierce competition among business houses for a share in the available licensed capacity. Such cutthroat competition tended to inhibit the development of collective action to deal with larger policy issues. A recent study by the government of India concluded that the system of licensing worked largely to the advantage of a few big industrial houses.[28]

[26] *Ibid.*, p. 17; See also Jagdish N. Bhagwati and Padma Desai, *India: Planning for Industrialization* (London: Oxford University Press, 1970), pp. 261–262.

[27] International Bank for Reconstruction and Development, *India: A Review of Trends in Manufacturing Industry* 3 vols. (Washington: International Bank for Reconstruction and Development) I, 17 (hereafter referred to as *World Bank Report*).

[28] Government of India, *Report of the Industrial Licensing Policy Inquiry Committee* (New Delhi: Government of India, 1969), p. 184.

> Our study . . . shows that the large industrial sector, as a whole, did not obtain a disproportionate share of the overall licenses in any significant sense of the term. The twenty larger industrial houses obtained a share which was slightly higher in some respects than others in the private corporate sector. But . . . disproportion is observed only in the case of a few, the most prominent among them being Birla. These houses apparently understood the mechanics and the weaknesses of the licensing system as well as the manner in which the maximum benefit could be obtained out of it, organized themselves effectively for that purpose, and were thus able to obtain a significantly large share both aggregatively and in terms of certain important products. Our case studies also show that the system not only made it possible for undue advantage to be secured but that this undue advantage accrued very significantly only to some houses in the large industrial sector.[29]

The licensing system thus worked to the advantage of organized business, but it has not contributed as much as was expected to the attainment of the redistributive social and economic objectives of the Industrial Policy Resolution.

The "discovery" that industrial licensing, by aiding predominantly a few of the larger business houses, had led to increased concentration resulted in government enactment of a new monopoly law to control future growth. Ironically, the device that was to be relied on to inhibit monopoly under the new regulations was the very device which had earlier helped to create it. But under the new licensing system, small and medium industry would not require a license to establish a factory which cost less than ten million rupees. Only the top twenty industrial houses of India would have to apply for a license to set up a new unit or to expand an existing unit involving investment of less than ten million rupees. Big business would then be expected to invest in industries requiring large capital outlays and long gestation periods before a return on investment could be expected. Moreover, under the new law, loans—obtained by big business houses from public credit facilities for realizing this newly licensed capacity—were to be written with an option permitting conversion of loan value into equity. This proposal had been raised before and had been vigorously opposed by business. Thus, these credit institutions would be enabled to play an important role in control or management of

[29] *Ibid.*, p. 74.

the private sector facilities in which they had made a substantial investment.[30]

Despite repeated pressure from the Communist party and the left wing of the Congress party, the government has refused to nationalize India's top business houses.[31] The government has offered several arguments in defense of its position. First, government should be careful not to bite off more than it can chew. Before embarking on a program of massive nationalization, it was important to ensure that existing public sector industries and financial institutions were working effectively. The public sector has been bedeviled by managerial and manpower problems at the decision-making levels and faced a variety of other problems as well. Second, the Monopolies Commission had been created only recently and should be given a chance to prove its effectiveness in curbing monopolies and the concentration of economic power. Third, such drastic action, it was argued, would frighten private foreign investors whose importance had increased as a result of the cutoff of American foreign aid at the time of the Bangladesh war.[32] Finally, the government was deeply concerned about the sharp drop in industrial production which resulted from business uncertainty over the precise dimensions of the Congress party government's new radical programs. The government has tried to temper business fears by promising a clear statement of its objectives in formulating its fifth Five Year Plan and by stressing the development of a joint sector involving undertakings that would be jointly owned and operated by government and the private sector. Government would provide the major source of credit, and the private sector would build and operate the plant under the direction of a board of directors consisting of representatives drawn from government financial institutions and private entrepreneurs. In short, despite much of the radical tone and socialist rhetoric of recent political debates, the concept of a mixed economy, as defined in the Industrial Policy Resolution of 1956, appears to remain the basic guide to government policy and planning.

Although regulation and control are inherent in distributive policy, some public policy may be considered as predominantly regulatory in nature. The Essential Commodities Act controls the price, supply, and distribution of essential commodities like cotton, cement, and steel. Government's power in this sphere is final and cannot be challenged in courts. The elaborate system of control, administered by a vast

[30] *Capital* (Calcutta), February 26, 1970, pp. 329–330.
[31] *The Economic Times* (Bombay), May 17 and May 18, 1972.
[32] *The Economic Times* (Bombay), May 5, 1972.

government apparatus under the Essential Commodities Act, was considered necessary, because the government was convinced that the private sector could not be trusted to avoid the temptation of taking advantage of the conditions of scarity in India. Another instrument of regulatory policy is, of course, the Industries (Development and Regulation) Act of 1951 itself. Controls are also exercised over imports and foreign exchange. Although India established tariff barriers after independence to protect its infant industries and to systematize the arbitrary scheme left over from the British period, tariffs shortly were superceded as regulatory devices when foreign exchange shortages dictated the imposition of direct import controls. Import licenses, which are issued only for goods not produced in India, involve a complex system of administration and an equally complex effort by business to obtain them.

The most comprehensive regulatory device in India is that which created the legal framework for planned, democratic socialism in India. India enacted one of the most comprehensive systems of company law regulation in the world to secure two major objectives. The new policy was, first, to bring company law and business practice into conformity with the new socioeconomic policies of the government. Second, it was to protect shareholder interests against mismanagement and abuse. The need for a comprehensive revision of company law is well summarized in the first annual report of the Working and Administration of the Companies Act of 1956, which declared:

> During the period of forty-three years while the Companies Act of 1913 was in force, a great many changes of far reaching consequence had taken place in the organization and working of joint stock companies and also in the character of company management in this country. These changes required a thorough overhaul of the existing law and of the administrative machinery responsible for its enforcement. *At the same time, the compelling needs of a planned economy and the underlying postulates and motivations of the pattern of society, which the country had accepted as the goal of its economic and social policy, called for a new definition of public interest in relation to the working of joint stock companies, and also for the integration of the activities of the corporate sector with the basic values implicit in this policy in more positive terms than had been hitherto attempted.* This explains the detailed and the relatively novel features of the provisions of several parts of the new Companies Act, particularly of those relating to the man-

agement of companies, the powers and duties of directors, managing agents, managers, and shareholders.[33]

Public policy, in its distributive, redistributive, and regulatory aspects, tends to inhibit, limit, or circumscribe private sector activity. Developmental policy incorporates incentives to elicit the active cooperation of business in achieving economic growth and increasing the volume of exports and foreign exchange earnings. Perhaps the biggest incentive to private investment in India has been the vast sheltered market created by government tariff and import policies, and the quasi-monopolistic system created by selective allocations of capacity under the successive five year plans. Both of these factors enabled business to realize returns on capital of 12 to 14 percent.[34] In addition, for some especially desired types of investment, government has provided a variety of tax concessions, including partial tax holidays, rebates on high priority industries, development rebates, and special depreciation allowances.[35] Needless to say, this type of governmental interference is not discouraged by business.

Whatever the type of public policy, the decision to replace the modified laissez-faire system of the British Raj with a system of centralized planning in a mixed economy resulted in government dictating what the private sector could and could not do and also necessitated a complex system of interaction between public and private sectors to the extent that they were expected to play a role in economic development. The private sector could make, within limits, important contributions to the planning process. Integrating public and private sector investment required a vast amount of consultation and coordination with individual companies, industrial groups, or the business community as a whole, at both planning and implementation stages. On the part of business, too, new organizational structures were required for securing an industrial license and responding to details of government regulation and control. Thus, individual business houses set up Delhi branch offices, known as industrial embassies, to deal with the bureaucracy. The larger problems of planning and development, however, required collective liaison with government. Government itself, in fact, recognized the need to create some formalized, legitimate mechanism for consulting the private sector. Thus, the Industries (Development and Regulation) Act of 1951 also provided for statutory consultation between govern-

[33] Quoted in Kust, *Foreign Enterprise*, pp. 229–230.
[34] Kidron, *Foreign Investments*, p. 246.
[35] Kust, *Foreign Enterprise*, pp. 386–393.

ment and the private sector thereby placed so directly under its control. The development of these statutory bodies and the creation of a large number of nonstatutory consultative committees forced business, in turn, to recognize the need for converting its business associations by expansion, democratization, and professionalization into effective mechanisms for collective dealings with government. Many new industry associations were brought into being during the second Five Year Plan. Consequently, as government control has grown more extensive and detailed, business ironically has grown stronger as a collectivity.

Public policy in India thus plays a major role in shaping interest group behavior, determining the channels of access, and conditioning the style of interest articulation. Government controls are pervasive, and government policy tools for managing the economy are so plentiful that business is totally dependent on government. Government in India has the power to intervene in a variety of major business decisions, including the choice and size of the projects undertaken, the location of the factory, the form and remuneration of top management, the company's capital structure, and even the selling price of the product. These decisions affect individual firms, entire industries, and the business community in general.

Business has developed a series of organizations to handle the variety of problems that arise in its dealings with government. The industrial embassies of the major business houses are concerned primarily with development, expansion, and operations of their own plants. Industry associations are concerned with those policies that affect their sector of production. The apex organizations are concerned with attempting to counter broad redistributive policies, policies that affect the business community as a whole and act as barometers of government–business relations in general. Government–business relations take place within the basic framework of the broad general policies outlined in this chapter. Although the policy content is fixed, its principles are sufficiently general so that the nuances fluctuate with changes in the political climate, as will be seen in Chapter X.

PART TWO

Internal Dynamics

V

BUSINESS IN POST-INDEPENDENCE INDIA

Systemic factors determine the parameters of group behavior and provide the environmental setting within which groups must function. The actual political potential of any specific group in the society is nevertheless determined by the attributes of the group itself and by the political capital it can mobilize to press its demands. Among the most important attributes which determine group effectiveness are the size and resources of the group, the degree to which these resources can be mobilized on a sustained basis to accomplish specific goals, and the patterns of organization and leadership which the group is capable of developing to define and secure its goals. In short, access and influence are not automatic. They must be earned, and the process requires time, money, and effort directed and coordinated by a system of group organization.

Despite the socialist rhetoric of Indian politics and heavy investment in the public sector, the private sector—which includes agriculture, trade, small-scale industry and handicrafts, as well as modern, large-scale industry—still holds a predominant position in the Indian economy. Prior to the first Five Year Plan, the private sector generated 92 percent of India's gross national product. It continued to generate over 90 percent during the 1950s and slightly over 85 percent in the 1960s. By contrast, the private sector in Japan provides less than 80 percent of the gross national product and even in the United States it accounts for under 75 percent.[1]

The public sector in India is concentrated primarily in the capital goods sector of the economy. Public sector units account for one-seventh of the total output of capital goods and have played a significant role in helping to restructure the character of Indian industrial production. In the 1950s, two-thirds of Indian production was confined to consumer goods, and capital goods and intermediate goods accounted for only one-sixth each. By the 1960s, however, the propor-

[1] Wilfred Malenbaum, "Politics and Indian Business: The Economic Setting," *Asian Survey* 11 (1971): 843.

tion of the three sectors was about equal.[2] In some subsectors of the economy, the public sector dominates completely. For example, Hindustan Machine Tools Ltd. accounted for half the output of machine tools in India; Hindustan Steel Ltd. produced 60 percent of all finished steel; and Heavy Engineering Corporation (Ranchi) and Heavy Electricals (India) Ltd. (Bhopal) were the sole producers of some types of heavy machinery. At the same time, however, although the public sector dominates the commanding heights of the economy, the total gross sales of public sector manufacturing, excluding Indian Oil Corporation, amounts to little more than 10 percent of the industrial sector.[3]

Private sector business in India is therefore still quite important. It is not only responsible for the bulk of the total output in the industrial sector but also plays a dominant role in internal trade and commerce. The elements which make up the private sector, however, are extremely heterogenous and consist of traders, small-scale manufacturers, and large-scale indigenous and foreign manufacturers organized into conglomerates called business houses and modern corporate units. It is this very size and diversity of the business community that has made it so difficult to mobilize into organized cohesive groups and which has inhibited the development of a united business class.

In terms of numbers and diversity, the largest sector of the business community consists of 6.7 million persons employed in wholesale and retail trade. Assuming an average family of five, the total strength of the trading community in 1961 would be over 33 million out of a population of 437 million.[4] Moreover, transport, communication, and commerce contributed 14.9 percent to the national product of India in 1967–1968.[5]

The middle-class trader in India feels threatened and insecure. He feels he is being systematically destroyed by the actions of government and big business. Government has been slowly eroding traditional trading functions by channeling more and more trade through the government-owned State Trading Corporation. At the same time, private business has steadily encroached on the traditional livelihood of traders by opening retail outlets and channeling all their products through their own marketing organizations. Feeling insecure and

[2] *World Bank Report*, I, 26.

[3] *Ibid.*, I, 28–29.

[4] National Income Estimates 1960–1961 information supplied by Federation of Indian Chambers of Commerce and Industries.

[5] *World Bank Report*, Annex, Table 2.

threatened, large sectors of the trading community have become closely identified with the revivalist politics of parties like the Jana Sangh.

Despite their numbers, the vast majority of small businessmen and traders in India remain an unorganized reflection of the fragmentation of the larger society, each basing his behavior on family, caste, and community norms rather than on any large appreciation of class identification or interest. Because most small businessmen are still not conscious of the potential benefits of collective action,[6] they have proven difficult to organize; their demands on the political system tend to be sporadic and anomic in origin and uncertain in impact. It has, thus, generally been the representatives of the unorganized or intermittently organized traders and small business sector who have resorted to demonstrations, strikes, and violence. Such groups as have agitated for specific demands from time to time have been bus fleet owners, restaurant owners, cycle shop owners, grain traders, vegetable sellers, and sweets sellers.[7] It is also this vast army of traders, shopkeepers, and middlemen belonging to the noncorporate, largely unorganized sector of Indian business that has generated the greatest amount of public resentment because of highly questionable practices, including food adulteration, creation of artificial shortages, price gouging, black marketeering, and petty bribing. Such offenses, more visible than abstruse white-collar crimes, go far toward creating anti-business sentiments, even among those with no particular commitment to the socialist pattern or to another more radical pattern of society.

Although smaller in size than the group of small businessmen and traders, manufacturing contributed 13 percent to the national product of India in 1967–1968. Within the manufacturing sector, large-scale industry contributed 8 percent to the national product, and the small-scale sector contributed 5 percent.[8] The small-scale sector in India has grown very rapidly in recent years, as a result of strong encouragement from government. As late as 1961, there were only 36,000 small-scale industrial units registered with the various directors of industries in the states, but by March 31, 1971 there were 281,781 units registered. It is estimated that small-scale industrial units covered

[6] Robert W. Hunt, "Some Personal Roots of Modernity Among Small Industrialists in India," *Asian Survey* 11 (1971): 886–899; Richard N. Blue, "Political Participation and Group Behavior of Indian Small Scale Entrepreneurs," *Asian Survey* 11 (1971): 900–915.

[7] M. V. Namjoshi and B. R. Sabade, *Chambers of Commerce in India* (Bombay: Asia Publishing House, 1967), p. 81; *The Statesman* (Calcutta) October 16, 1967.

[8] *World Bank Report*, Annex, Table 2.

under the programs of the Small Industries Development Organization had a fixed investment in 1970 of Rs 475 crores and an output of Rs 4050 crores, and that they employed 3.3 million workers.[9] Half the manufacturing product and 92 percent of all registered factories in India—that is, one-half the value added in the industrial sector—was produced by the small-scale sector.

The small-scale sector is primarily concentrated in the consumer goods sector of the economy and accounts for 77 percent of the value added in that sector. The small-scale sector produces such things as buckets, trunks, nails, hand tools, plastic goods, electric fans, sewing machines, bicycle parts, pharmaceuticals, and a wide variety of other consumer products. The predominant field, however, was textiles, and in 1967 the small-scale sector produced 43.7 percent of all cloth manufactured in India as opposed to only 56.3 percent for the large-scale, organized mill sector.[10] The government of India has specifically reserved 128 items of manufacture for the small-scale sector. At present, 33 items are exclusively produced by the small-scale sector, and the bulk of production of another 54 items is contributed by the small-scale sector.[11]

The small-scale industries sector of the Indian economy faces a host of problems which are quite different from those of the large-scale sector. Although small scale industries have proven difficult to organize and somewhat ambivalent toward joining business associations,[12] they are now represented through their own apex organization: The Federation of Associations of Small Industries of India (FASII). The federation maintains close liaison with a whole host of government bodies especially created to assist in the development and finance of small-scale industry.[13]

The organized large-scale sector of Indian industry has grown proportionately even faster than the small-scale sector, as a result of government planning, tariff protection, national development policies, and its own initiative. Unlike the small-scale sector, which is scattered throughout the country, big business is highly concentrated. It is

[9] *The Economic Times* (Bombay), May 19, 1972.

[10] *World Bank Report*, I, 22–23.

[11] *The Economic Times* (Bombay), May 19, 1972.

[12] See Hunt, "Some Personal Roots," and Blue, "Political Participation."

[13] The government of India provides a variety of special concessions to small-scale industries, which are defined as enterprises with fixed assets of up to 750,000 rupees (one hundred thousand dollars). The rapid growth of small- and medium-sized industry has added a new dimension to business–government relations. However, the role of this sector and the Federation of Associations of Small Industries of India are not dealt with in this book. The primary emphasis is on the role of big business in Indian politics.

centered in the older industrial regions of India, is drawn from a small group of traditional trading castes, and is responsible for a substantial share of the total industrial production. The gross output of organized industry in 1968–1969 was Rs 5,421 crores based on Rs 4,500 crores gross investment.[14]

The private, organized sector of the Indian economy grew very rapidly during the decade from 1955 to 1965. Investment between 1955 and 1957 doubled, from Rs 100 crores to Rs 200 crores, and then jumped to Rs 350 crores at the beginning of the third Five Year Plan. Private sector growth hit its peak in 1965–1966, before falling off sharply in response to a recession in the Indian economy and renewed political uncertainty.[15]

Despite the government's commitment to reduce disparities in levels of development between various regions, the fastest growing areas tended to be the old port cities of Madras, Calcutta, and Bombay. From 1953 to 1961, 40 percent of all industrial licenses were granted for units in these areas. Of the three areas, the Greater Bombay area grew the fastest[16] and was to have a significant impact on the post-independence development of business associations in India.

During the decade of growth, many of the old business houses were able to expand, diversify, and develop into major forces in the Indian economy. Because of its historical development, Indian capital had been highly concentrated, even at the time of independence. In 1951–1952, the total share capital of all nongovernment-owned companies was estimated at Rs 13,960 million. "In that year the four largest business groups—Tatas (a Parsee firm), Birlas and Dalmia-Jain (Marwari groups), and Martin Burn (a Bengali-English group) —had full control by sole ownership or majority stock holding of approximately 15 percent of the total share capital of both nongovernment public and private limited companies." [17] If their minority holdings were added, their proportionate share of the total was 19 percent. The top thirteen business houses had complete or partial control of 28 percent of the total share capital.

The effect of a decade of rapid growth was to increase the absolute number of large business houses and to change their relative ranking. A government study in 1965 revealed that the modern industrial sector of business in India was dominated by seventy-five British and

[14] *World Bank Report*, Annex, Table 2.

[15] *Ibid.*, I, 31–32.

[16] Irvin Roth, "Industrial Location and Indian Government Policy," *Asian Survey* 10 (1970): 390–391.

[17] George Rosen, *Democracy and Economic Change in India* (Berkeley and Los Angeles: University of California Press, 1966), p. 41.

Indian conglomerates or business houses which controlled almost half of the nongovernmental, nonbanking assets of the country.[18] The top thirty-seven business houses were predominantly drawn from the traditional trading communities. Despite their later start, the Marwari houses ranked first, with Rs 7.5 billion in assets, followed by the Parsis with 4.7 billion, and the Gujaratis with 3.8 billion.[19]

Another study revealed that, although the proportion of assets controlled by the top six houses (Birla, Tata, Martin Burn, Mafatlal, Associated Cement, and Bangur group) remained relatively unchanged from 1958 to 1966–1967, increasing from 20 percent to 21 percent, there were dramatic changes in the fortunes of specific houses. The Tatas held over half of the assets of the top six houses in 1958 but only one-third in 1966–1967. The Birlas, on the other hand, doubled their assets during the same period and came to equal the Tatas in relative size. The Mafatlal and Bangur groups grew at a relatively rapid rate. The progress of Associated Cement was slowed by government attempts to break its near monopoly in the cement industry, and the position of Martin-Burn declined.[20]

Foreign controlled assets in India represented a relatively small but important part of the total. In 1961, foreign capital controlled more than two-fifths of the total assets in the organized large-scale private sector. The bulk of this investment was new investment which had flowed in after independence.[21] Foreign investment in 1961 was heavily concentrated in a small number of industries. Some of these had been the long-standing original preserve of foreign capital, and others had grown up since independence. Three areas—tea, petroleum, and manufacturing—together accounted for three-fourths of the total foreign investment in India. Half of the investment in manufacturing was concentrated in a relatively small group of industries—chemicals and drugs, cigarettes and tobacco, jute textiles, and light electrical goods. Generally speaking, older forms of

[18] Government of India, *Report of the Monopolies Inquiry Commission, 1965*, vols. 1 and 2 (Delhi: Government of India Press, 1965), pp. 119–122.

[19] Thomas A. Timberg, *Industrial Entrepreneurship Among the Trading Communities of India: How the Pattern Differs* (Cambridge: Center for International Affairs, Harvard University, 1969), p. 5.

[20] *World Bank Report*, I, 61–62; Annex, Tables 59 and 60.

[21] From mid-1948 to the end of 1961, 438 crores gross of foreign, nonbanking, private investment flowed into India, more than doubling the original total of 256 crores; Michael Kidron, *Foreign Investments in India* (London: Oxford University Press, 1965), pp. 31–32. By March of 1967, the total outstanding foreign private investment in India was 11,376 million rupees, or 1.5 billion dollars. See Rajya Sabha *unstarred* question no. 593, May 12, 1970. Parliamentary Debates, *Rajya Sabha Official Report* 72 No. 12 (May 21, 1970), pp. 54–55, col. 1–2.

investment, like tea and jute manufacturing, grew slowly or declined in relative importance after independence, because most fresh foreign capital was directed into petroleum and into newer, technologically complex and patented manufacturing industries.[22]

Originally foreign capital in India meant British capital. At the time of independence, three-fourths of foreign investment in India was British.[23] Although British capital continues to play an active role in India, its power and influence have been diluted. The substantial influx of foreign capital in the last twenty years has resulted in a greater diversity of the national origins of capital. Indian affiliates have been developed by American, German, French, Swiss, Japanese, and Italian corporations.[24] These affiliates were usually established in collaboration with the larger Indian business firms, thereby augmenting the trend toward closer liaison between foreign and indigenous capital.[25] Thus, despite the original hostility of the government of India and the ambivalence of foreign investors, foreign investment in India has increased in size, diversity, sophistication, and national origins. It has also played an important role in Indian development.

Unlike the activities of the traders and small-scale businessmen, the activities of the organized corporate sector of the business community are neither sporadic nor anomic. Demands are articulated through two types of permanent structures. The first is the business house itself, functioning through its industrial embassy in Delhi. The embassy is capable of continuous and calculated self-representation based on family and kinship structures. It also employs the highly personal system of liaison and lobbying developed after independence as an attempt to influence the political elite largely for individual benefit, although some collective benefits might incidentally accrue. The second type of representational structure includes a series of specialized structures for interest articulation: chambers of commerce, trade and industry associations, employers' associations, and peak associations.[26] Together these associational groups constitute the oldest,

[22] Kidron, *Foreign Investments*, pp. 185–223.

[23] *Ibid.*, p. 3. By March 1967, British investment was down to 57.6 percent of the outstanding foreign private investment in India.

[24] Matthew J. Kust, *Foreign Enterprise in India: Laws and Policies* (Chapel Hill, N.C.: University of North Carolina Press, 1964), pp. 65–74.

[25] Soviet investment, of course, has been channeled toward public sector industries and projects.

[26] Business in India had adopted the British practice of maintaining a functional division between labor policy and economic policy. The Federation of Indian Chambers of Commerce and Inductry (FICCI) and Associated Chambers of Commerce and

most bureaucratized and politically autonomous structures for interest articulation in India. They function through a highly regularized and formalized pattern of access and are designed primarily to achieve collective rather than individual benefit. And—because of their growing organizational capacity—they have become one of the few kinds of groups in the society capable of sustained rather than intermittent action. Because the leadership of the specialized business organizations is provided by the leadership of the top seventy-five houses, the two structures are linked and capable of more or less coordinated action.

The advent of planning and the introduction of a pervasive system of government controls made business heavily dependent on government initiatives. Business houses immediately organized themselves for the purpose of securing maximum benefit from the system of licensing and controls under which they were expected to function. In the early years of planning, individual businessmen had been principally concerned with the expansion and growth of their own business empires and made limited use of associations. Individual growth and protection of individual interests were of such primary importance that each business leader used the influence acquired through individual contributions to Congress party leaders, patronage, and hospitality to obtain benefits for his own house. As one leading industrialist put it,

> Until now everybody had been attempting to build and improve his own units and has concentrated on his own development and expansion. Business houses existed before independence, but they did not really operate on a very big scale. Since independence, however, these houses have increased three to four times in size, and they were all very engrossed in their own problems. In the process they were reluctant to extend aid to others. They concentrated on their own capacity and getting their own licences and other kinds of government assistance.

Another added, "Some are more interested in furthering their own house than in the business community as a whole."

As business grew it became more complex, and with complexity

Industry (Assocham) deal with economic policy. The All-India Organization of Industrial Employers in New Delhi is the sister organization of the FICCI and handles all labor problems. Most Assocham members belong to the Employer's Federation of India, which is closely associated with the Tatas. This book does not deal with employer organizations.

came the need to consider the organizational dimension of business. Indian business had moved relatively quickly from the traditional manufacture of textiles to more complex types of industry requiring greater organizational skills and expertise. In addition, as enterprises began to grow larger and more complex, traditional family patterns of control and organization no longer sufficed. The Sarabhai organization, for example, was made up in its early years of a series of informal personal relationships between the managing agents and other managers within the organization. This series of relationships was complicated by close family ties between the managing agents and other members of the company. Although no organization chart with formal lines of communication existed, there was a recognized and accepted order of seniority among managers and direct contact between managing agents and managers at all levels.[27] "The pattern was not dissimilar to that of the management of family business in other countries than India, but in India, more than in the West, it was supported by the traditional joint family system . . ." The eldest male was the head of the firm. All other members looked to the head of the family for decisions and accepted his authority, whereas "authority and responsibility among the other members of the family are diffused, informal, and personal." In hiring, also, the needs of the family prevailed. The tendency was to find jobs for people, not people for jobs.[28]

As Indian business grew, it became more efficiently organized; it began to emphasize professional and managerial skills in recruitment; and the slow process of dissociation of management and ownership was begun. The older generation of industrial giants began to die out and a new generation of owner-managers began to emerge, not just as sons and heirs of the old boss but as competent managers in their own right. More self-confident, more highly educated, politically and socially more aware than their elders, the members of the younger generation were all also more alert to the importance of organization.

Interest in organization extended beyond concern with the internal organization of the individual business firm to the value of links to others in the same industry and the business community at large. Businessmen were faced by a common set of problems emerging from business interactions with government. And so they become more

[27] A. K. Rice, *Productivity and Social Organization: The Ahmedabad Experiment* (Bombay: Tavistock Publications, Ltd., 1958), p. 26.

[28] *Ibid.*, pp. 182–183.

concerned with the substance of government policy which impinged upon business activity collectively, rather than being preoccupied solely with gaining individual distributive benefits for their firms. In addition, they became concerned with the problem of building a better image for business. Their conviction of the worth of the business contribution for the society left them no longer content with merely affecting the detailed implementation of public policy. Businessmen, they felt, must be concerned with influencing the actual formation of public policy in the open and direct manner employed by any legitimate interest group.

Thus businessmen have become more aware of their common interest, more socially conscious, and more mindful of organization. Although India may not yet have a united business class, the business communities are moving in that direction under the impact of technology, modern organization, and higher levels of education and management training. These changes in business attitudes have not obviated the need for industrial embassies in the highly controlled and regulated Indian economy, but they have resulted in the development of greater concern for building stronger organs of collective action.

Specialized structures for articulating the collective demands of business had emerged in India as early as the nineteenth century. However, the historical development, diversity, and heterogeneity of the business community in India had a major impact on the patterns of group mobilization, on leadership, and on patterns of institutionalization of these modern business associations. The present configuration of these associations and their orientation toward government can only be explained in terms of their historical origins. Business associations in India exhibit a number of distinctive characteristics.

First, two parallel systems of apex business associations have come into existence in India. Modern business associations developed first among the European merchants of the port cities of Calcutta, Bombay, and Madras in the early nineteenth century. By the end of the century, parallel Indian associations had emerged. Both of these loose networks of regional associations federated after World War I. These two groups, the Federation of Indian Chambers of Commerce and Industry (FICCI) and the Associated Chambers of Commerce and Industry (Assocham), traditionally reflected the conflicting interests between indigenous and foreign capital, respectively. But this is no longer true.

Second, although the pattern of organization of both resulting apex structures was federal, each reflects years of uneven economic development in India leading early to the founding of the original regional organizations in Calcutta and Bombay. The representation in Calcutta and Bombay continues almost completely to overshadow in ability, experience, numbers, and financial backing the representation of all other areas. As a result, the larger regional associations in Bombay and Calcutta have come to play a disproportionate role in the control and decision-making of the apex associations.

Third, unlike the business associations in most countries, in India both the major apex organizations combine industrial and trade interests within a single organization. Because business associations in India antedate the introduction of industry, they retain elements of their origins as chambers of commerce. It was the distinctive nature of the managing agency system for the various managing agency houses to provide common service to the firms it controlled. Similarly, the existing chambers tended to provide common services to newly formed industrial associations. As a result, the old chambers of commerce were transformed into chambers of commerce and industry, creating a unified system in dramatic contrast to the separate structures existing in most other countries.[29] The combination of these interests under one roof, although a potential source of great strength, has more often raised serious problems in maintaining cohesion, especially in the larger and more diverse FICCI.[30]

Fourth, even in any one major commercial and industrial center of India, a multiplicity of chambers exist where one would suffice in other countries. This fragmentation reflects the historic split between indigenous and foreign capital, the partial differentiation of the Indian business community, and the survival—among those with common economic interests—of traditional social divisions of caste, community, family, language, and regional loyalties. These loyalties weaken group solidarity and tend to prevent the emergence of a united business class. They also play an important role in the internal politics and organization of Indian chambers, where they are a major cause of factional conflict. As a result, Indian business lacks the degree of unity exhibited by British business associations.

[29] "The Associated Chambers of Commerce and Industry of India" (Speech by H. K. S. Lindsay, president of Assocham 1964–1965, at the Rotary Club of Calcutta, June 8, 1965), reprinted by Assocham, p. 3.

[30] The one exception to this rule among the three apex business associations in India is the All-India Manufacturers Organization (AIMO), which is strictly an organization of manufacturers. It was created in 1941, represents medium sized industry, and draws its membership predominantly from Bombay. Although it had its origins in the associational politics of Bombay, AIMO does have branches throughout India.

Another distinctive aspect of Indian business associations is that the dominant leadership role in both the FICCI and Assocham is performed by the executives, officers, and directors of the older managing agency houses. These houses also provide the bulk of the resources. Those who provide leadership and funds are likely to control the organization.

Finally, compared to those in many other countries, business associations in India developed a more intense political orientation and tended to be less concerned with performing other functions. Indian business associations came to put primary stress on the political element, for several reasons. During the early colonial period they were one of the few nonofficial bodies available, and thus they were uniquely able to express independent views. Later, business organizations were given direct functional representation in the colonial legislatures. The termination after independence of functional representation, the lack of a business party to fill the gap, and the underrepresentation of business and businessmen in Parliament made business associations the only viable means by which business can formulate positions on public policy and articulate its demands. Finally, the difference in origins and in original orientation toward government of the FICCI and Assocham has had a major effect on their style. Although often critical of the British colonial government, the leaders of Assocham preferred to work through a system of quiet diplomacy in close contact with their countrymen. The preference for quiet diplomacy survives. By contrast, the chambers of indigenous businessmen, like the nationalist movement itself, developed a highly vocal and critical style which is employed to this day. Although the importance of caste and community may be declining, their effect on the organizational behavior of the business community still cannot be ignored. Divisions between indigenous and foreign capital persist in post-independence India, and family, caste, region, and language continue to play a role in business politics. In addition, the more managerially oriented British, Parsi, and Gujarati firms disagree fundamentally with the family-dominated Marwari groups over such critical issues as business ethics, strategies of dealing with government, and political philosophy.

In many ways, the character of business associations in India began to change under the impact of changes in the Indian political system after independence. The emergence of Congress party dominance, the centralization of decision-making in the hands of the cabinet and bureaucracy, and the development of a government policy emphasizing planning, rapid industrialization, a mixed economy, protectionism, regulation, and control and restrictions in regional disparities—these factors forced business to develop institutional patterns of access and professional staffs to handle the complexity and all-embracing nature of government action. Big business in India felt compelled to pour large amounts of resources into business associations so that they could work at both the personal and institutional level. Individual problems could be taken up personally with ministers and the higher echelons of the bureaucracy. But business still needed a way to formulate collective views and reactions to government policy as a means of setting limits on Nehru's socialism, of securing greater government protection and support, and of handling more generalized problems of policy or administrative action. At the same time, the government policy of reducing regional disparities, encouraging new entrepreneurship, developing new methods of finance, and increasing emphasis on organized and systematized liaison with the business community were all beginning to transform the character of Indian business. Under the impact of planning, the size of the entrepreneurial elite increased, and caste and community became much less important in determining entry into industry. Thus, in a study of south Indian entrepreneurship, James Berna concluded "that sociological factors such as caste, attachment to traditional activities, and approval or disapproval of the social groups to which a potential entrepreneur belongs are less important than economic factors such as access to capital and possession of business experience and technological knowledge."[31] Presumably this unequal access to capital is one advantage that nationalization of banks was designed to prevent.

Small and medium sized businesses also became more organizationally conscious. Big business had always enjoyed relatively easy access to government on an individual basis, but small and medium business had to approach government through organizational channels or not at all. Government in fact encouraged them in their efforts, for it was becoming clear that unless business approached government jointly through organized channels, the channels of access would become flooded by a multitude of individual petitions. As a result of this complex of recent developments, business associations in India have grown phenomenally in size, variety, resources, organization, and even in unity as business has become more organizationally conscious.

No complete census exists of the exact number of business associations in India. But there are numerous indications that, as a result

[31] James Berna, *Industrial Entrepreneurship in Madras State* (Bombay: Asia Publishing House, 1960), pp. 212–213.

of planning and controls, the number of associations has increased and that they have become more geographically dispersed, functionally differentiated, professionalized, and bureaucratized. In 1951–1952, a study by the Gokhale Institute of the ten largest industrial centers (as measured by labor employed) found a total of 25 chambers of commerce and 408 associations in these areas. An estimate in 1954 listed 123 chambers of commerce and 1,075 associations located in 226 Indian towns. A census in the state of West Bengal listed 7 chambers of commerce and 393 associations in the state.[32] Another indication of the rapid growth of associations can be seen in the trend of FICCI membership alone. The number of associations and chambers of commerce that were members of the FICCI increased from 102 in 1947 to 220 in 1971. The rapid growth of organizations took place among both chambers of commerce and trade and industry associations. The number of chambers of commerce and their membership increased rapidly in the new industrial centers, in mofussil areas (outside the major cities), and in medium sized cities. Major gains were also made in cities like Ahmedabad, Madurai, Bangalore, and Poona.[33] However, membership in the older centers of Bombay, Calcutta, and Madras remained static.

Perhaps even more important than the rapid increase in numbers was the process of consolidation of industry associations in response to government pressure, public policy, and the growing diversity and differentiation of industry. A large number of new associations came into being toward the end of the second Five Year Plan, as new industries encountered difficulties of supply, pricing, and overproduction. New associations were also formed to represent the rapidly developing pharmaceutical and cement industries. Meanwhile, older associations had begun to consolidate, under government pressure, through coordinating committees, merger, and federation. The government had, moreover, called for the creation of central associations "with a view to insuring that all common problems connected with price and quality, standards, market practices, rationalized distribution, negotiations with state and central government, and so forth, are dealt with from a common angle." As a result, the two bicycle manufacturers associations merged in 1958. The two paint associations merged in 1960.[34] Where the regional diversity of the industry made

[32] M. V. Namjoshi and B. R. Sabade, *Chambers of Commerce in India* (Bombay: Asia Publishing House, 1967), p. 25.

[33] *Ibid.*, pp. 24–25.

[34] Michael Kidron, *Foreign Investments in India* (Oxford: Oxford University Press, 1965), pp. 58–60.

merger difficult, as in tea and coal, coordinating bodies were established. Within the widely dispersed textile industry, by contrast, a federation was created. Federations were also formed for glass, plastics, and wool interests. Finally, changes took place within industrial associations, such as the engineering association, which found it necessary to establish regional committees and specialized panels. Although no such consolidation or coordination has transformed the old rivalry between the two major apex associations, there has been a rapid trend toward dual and overlapping membership, a trend which may eventually bring such a unification process about.

The necessity of dealing with detailed administrative decisions and negotiating with experts in the Indian bureaucracy has forced business associations to increase their organizational capacity through professionalization and bureaucratization. To do so, business organizations have had to mobilize to obtain greater resources. The FICCI had a budget in 1947 of Rs 131,423, a large part of which was provided by donations from members of the committee. By 1970, the FICCI had total revenues of Rs 1,981,995. The need for elastic forms of revenue led to the creation of a new type of membership in 1951.[35]

Assocham meanwhile has also substantially increased expenditures. Business associations have deployed the bulk of the increased revenues for hiring professional staffs. Although the British chambers spend more on staff than do the Indian chambers, part of the difference is attributable to the continued existence of the highly paid expatriot staffs in the British chambers. The development of research facilities, libraries, and public relations materials, all made possible by increased funding, have all been designed to support the representational function of business associations. Finally, the FICCI secretariat has grown from a modest support facility for a single secretary to an elaborately specialized bureaucracy, and Assocham is also in the process of creating its own specialized staff.

Even the major regional chambers have increased their activities. In 1961, forty-five chambers filing returns with the Company Law Administration had a total income of 9,111,456 rupees. The thirty-five major chambers accounted for 8,096,001 of the total.[36] These chambers spent 62 percent of their income on staff salaries.[37] The large regional chambers, especially the Bengal Chamber of Commerce and Industry and the Indian Chamber of Commerce of Calcutta, have very large professional staffs, because they provide secretarial

[35] See Chapter VIII.
[36] Namjoshi and Sabade, *Chambers of Commerce in India*, p. 37.
[37] *Ibid.*, p. 41.

services for a whole host of industry and trade associations. The Bengal chamber also serves as the secretariat for Assocham. The Indian Chamber of Commerce of Calcutta has an income almost as large as that of the FICCI. In addition, there are many industry associations which command even greater resources. The total income of 278 trade associations which filed returns with the Company Law Administration in 1961 was 18,412,132 rupees.[38] In addition, several of these specialized associations have been given special functions to perform by government, such as export promotion and the allocation of raw materials.

Thus, although the bulk of the business community remains unorganized, business has made major strides in the last twenty years in mobilizing its potential resources for sustained collective action. Interest articulation is moving from a highly personal system of elite representation to the use of more specialized structures like chambers of commerce, trade and industry associations, and employers associations. The difficulties of mobilization arising from the diversity and heterogeneity of the business community have had a significant impact on the nature of business organizations, on their leadership, and on the pattern of cohesion and conflict within the organized sector. Many of the peculiar features of the pre-independence period —features that were products of the particular condition of India and the origins of business associations—continue to play an important role in the developing and functioning of the major business associations.

The next four chapters will deal in greater detail with the origins, patterns of institutionalization, leadership, and problems of cohesion of India's two most important apex associations—Assocham and the FICCI. A few words of introduction are in order.

The distinctions between Assocham and the FICCI are beginning to blur as a result of Indianization of Assocham membership and the increase in overlapping memberships. And foreign and indigenous capital are drawing closer and closer together in other ways. But the separate organizational structures persist, and the two associations differ from each other in several ways. First, Assocham through its constituent chambers represents 2,500 large public companies staffed by professional managers and employing about two million workers.[39] The FICCI, in contrast, is both larger and more varied in the types of interests it represents. Through its many member bodies, the

[38] *Ibid.*, p. 96.
[39] Lindsay, p. 3.

FICCI represents one hundred thousand business firms employing over five million workers, including both medium and large industry as well as retail trade.[40] The politics of the FICCI, moreover, is dominated by large family firms which, although they may employ professional managers, retain the final decision-making power within the family. Second, the organization of Assocham is much simpler in theory and more federal in character than that of the FICCI. Assocham has only eleven members,[41] and no individual firm can be a member of Assocham except through membership in one of the regional chambers.[42] The FICCI, on the other hand, has as members both constituent bodies, like the trade associations, and individual firms. Even though an individual firm must be a member of one of the member bodies, this membership pattern has had a major impact on patterns of control in the FICCI. Third, Assocham's style is one of "quiet diplomacy" which focuses attention on the higher echelons of the bureaucracy and the ministries. Publicity is shunned, and generally there is no attempt to lobby in Parliament. Unlike Assocham, with its defensive, unobtrusive, and nonagitational approach, the FICCI is quite vocal and at times even publicly critical of government. It functions at all levels of access, including lobbying in Parliament and financing political parties. It also has a vigorous public relations program. Finally, Assocham tends to focus on issues which are of particular interest to foreign business, whereas the FICCI takes a stand on almost all issues. In short, Assocham is smaller and more homogeneous than the FICCI. It represents the larger, managerially controlled units of Indian business, and, at least until very recently, it has employed a much less visible style in penetrating the administrative levels of the Indian government.

[40] Federation of Indian Chambers of Commerce and Industries, "Presidential Address of L. N. Birla" (delivered at the Forty-first Annual Session of the FICCI, New Delhi, March 30, 1968), p. 20.

[41] The eleven constituent members of Assocham are: the Bengal chamber, the Bombay chamber, the Calicut chamber, the Cocanada chamber, the Cochin chamber, the Coimbatore chamber, the Madras chamber, the Punjab and Delhi chamber, the Travancore chamber, the Tuticorin chamber, and the Upper India chamber.

[42] After the manuscript went to press in December 1972, Assocham instituted three major structural changes. Many of these changes were anticipated in the manuscript, First, the secretariat of Assocham has now become completely independent of the Bengal chamber and is located in New Delhi. Second, Assocham has created an executive committee which will play a major role in policy making. Third, Assocham has created the equivalent of an associate membership to insure adequate funding. These changes now make the structure of Assocham and the FICCI quite similar.

VI

THE ORGANIZATION OF FOREIGN CAPITAL IN INDIA: ASSOCHAM

Foreign capital in India articulates its demands and attempts to protect its interests through two distinct and yet interrelated levels of organization. The most important level consists of the wide variety of India-based business associations. These are designed primarily to protect existing foreign investment and enable it to function at a profitable level in a tightly regulated, planned economy. A second level of foreign business activity in India consists of the indirect support received from the business associations abroad who represent potential investors and from the economic missions attached to the embassies of major aid-granting nations of developed Western countries such as the United States and Japan. Foreign embassies also exert pressure on behalf of foreign capital interests emanating from their countries.

Together these organizations seek to stimulate the flow of private, foreign capital by evaluating the climate for foreign investment and facilitating such investment through government-to-govermment agreements on such matters as double taxation, repatriation of profits, and guarantees against expropriation and nationalization. Although these two levels are somewhat separate and independent, they tend to be mutually reinforcing. Aid missions and embassies try to persuade the government of India to adopt policies which will encourage foreign investment, and Indian business associations that represent foreign capital try to protect the investment already in place to ensure that it is profitable and receives equal treatment.

Foreign capital in India enjoys the unique advantage of having a variety of well organized and effective business associations to represent its interests. These associations, which grew up during the colonial era, not only survived the transfer of power to Indian hands, but in the process were able to retain access to the government of India and especially their informal contacts with the Indian Civil Service bureaucracy which had been cultivated over the decades. At the same time, the very changes in the nature of foreign investment have had a profound impact on the traditional pattern of control and the style of these associations.

Origins of Foreign Business Associations

Modern business associations first developed in India in the early nineteenth century. They were organized by the European merchants of the port cities of Calcutta, Bombay, and Madras, in response to the end of the East India Company's monopoly of trade in 1833. The form of organization adopted was the chamber of commerce, a voluntary association organized on territorial rather than functional lines, with origins in eighteenth-century England.[1] Although a few Indian merchants were associated with the chambers of commerce in Calcutta and Madras, and to a larger extent in Bombay, the new associations spoke largely on behalf of European interests. The regional chambers were dominated by the managing agency houses. Thus, when industrialization fostered the development of functionally specialized associations among the concerns controlled by the same managing agency houses developed in the last quarter of the nineteenth century, they were incorporated into the framework of the existing chambers. As a result, the division between trade and industry which is so common in other countries did not take place in India. The conversion of chambers of commerce into chambers of commerce and industry, however, facilitated the retention of control by the managing agency houses over business associations in India.[2]

The chamber of commerce became a powerful organizational instrument in the hands of the British business community in India. It flourished for several reasons. First, because so few outlets existed for the expression of independent opinions in India, the chamber of commerce gave the mercantile community an important voice in British colonial policy.[3] Second, the chamber of commerce was sustained and supported because it performed vital service functions for the trading community. Chambers developed an arbitration function for settling disputes arising from commercial transactions. They performed survey functions, licenced measurers, and later provided advice on labor problems. Finally, the chamber became

[1] Geoffrey Tyson, *The Bengal Chamber of Commerce and Industry 1853–1953 Centenary Survey*, stenciles (Calcutta: The Bengal Chamber of Commerce, 1953), pp. 8–9.

[2] *Ibid.*, pp. 46–51.

[3] Raymond J. Sulivan, *One Hundred Years of Bombay: History of the Bombay Chamber of Commerce 1836–1936* (Bombay: Times of India Press, 1937), p. 256.

the basis for a system of functional representation which gave the British business community a direct voice in the self-governing institution that developed in the late nineteenth and early twentieth centuries. Thus, the chambers of commerce and business, as the best organized interests, came to play an inordinately influential role in India during the colonial period.

The character and development of British chambers varied considerably from region to region. The chambers functioned in different regional environments, varied considerably in size and type of membership, represented slightly different interests, and developed varying levels of organizational capability. Although about a dozen British chambers eventually emerged, the earliest developed in the port cities. One, the Bengal Chamber of Commerce, became so rich and powerful that it towered over the rest—so much so that when a federation was finally formed after World War I, the Bengal chamber easily dominated it.

The first chamber of commerce in India, the forerunner of the powerful Bengal Chamber of Commerce, was established in Calcutta in 1834. The end of the East India Company's monopoly of trade in 1833 created considerable disruption in Calcutta. As a result, in 1834 a circular letter was sent to firms in the city suggesting the utility of preparing a consolidated half-yearly inventory of stocks on hand among the principal importers of Calcutta. Despite some hesitancy, seventy-nine firms, some of them Indian owned, came together to form the Calcutta Chamber of Commerce. Having gathered together for this very limited purpose, the participants discovered that a much broader common interest existed. This common interest was institutionalized in the Calcutta Chamber of Commerce whose functions, according to its constitution, were:

> To watch over and protect the general interests of commerce; to collect information on all matters of interest to the mercantile community; to use every means in its power for the removal of evils, the redress of grievances, and the promotion of the common good; to communicate with authorities and with individual parties thereupon; to form a code of practice whereby the transactions of business may be simplified and facilitated; to receive references and to arbitrate between disputants.[4]

The Calcutta chamber, however, proved to be abortive. When, in 1852, a committee was appointed to study the functioning of the

[4] Tyson, *Bengal Chamber*, p. 14.

chamber, it was found that almost none of these activities were being carried out. The chamber had almost ceased to correspond with government or to collect information; it had never drawn up any code of practice; and disputes were seldom referred to it for arbitration. The formation of the chamber had been a response to a particular crisis. Once the crisis was over, the chamber had become defunct. Even so, the committee that studied the situation was convinced that such a chamber was necessary. Within two years, a new body—the Bengal Chamber of Commerce—was created from the ruins of the Calcutta chamber.

The timing was fortuitous. The Bengal Chamber of Commerce was formed on the eve of major changes in India. The end of company rule was imminent, industrialization was in the wind, and the powerful managing agency houses had begun to emerge. The Bengal chamber was, from the beginning, much more aware of the importance of collective action in relation to government than its predecessor had been. This predisposition was clearly stated in a report of the committee of the chamber on its first year of operations: "Much may not yet have been done, for hitherto government has rarely received—still more rarely adopted—suggestions from commercial men as a body; but in proportion as the chamber hereafter shall represent the collective feeling of the mercantile community; so will the disposition of the authorities to attend to its representations increase."[5] Specifically, the chamber began to demand better services from government—port development, improved mail, and other services to enable trade to function more effectively. With the assumption of direct rule by the crown after the mutiny of 1857, the Bengal chamber began taking a stand on political issues affecting its interests. Thus, the members of the chamber solidified their relationship to the colonial administration in Calcutta, and they also began to exert political pressure directly on Parliament at home.

Now that the British business community was in a strong position to influence the new colonial regime, control of the chamber passed into the hands of the rapidly emerging managing agency houses, which represented such major industries as tea, jute, coal, banking, and insurance. From the records of the chamber, it is clear that the managing agency houses began to play a dominant role in the chamber by the 1850s and 1860s. By 1870 the chamber had become firmly established as the voice of the British managing agency interests in Bengal. The managing agency interests, moreover, were prepared to

[5] *Ibid.*, p. 20.

back their organization with resources in men, management, and finances.[6]

The last quarter of the nineteenth century saw the emergence of the powerful shipping interests represented by Mackinnon Mackenzie, as well as the formation of special associations to represent tea (1881), jute (1884), and coal (1892). All of these were integrated into the rapidly expanding organizational structure of the chamber. Although each association had created its own managing committee, the administrative work was to be handled by the Bengal Chamber of Commerce secretariat, which came to function somewhat like a managing agency for associations. The Bengal chamber provided some common, general, and yet specialized services. Each association was able to handle its own specific and detailed problems. This pattern reinforced the control of the managing agency houses over the Bengal chamber and at the same time strengthened the resources available to the chamber. These three associations, which even today contribute a large portion of the total revenue of the chamber, were to give the Bengal chamber an overpowering role in the future.

The Bengal chamber thus emerged as an influential force in Calcutta, representing the views of the small but wealthy British business community[7] at just the time when the new class of educated Indians were demanding a greater voice in the affairs of the country. Although this new Indian elite was encouraged by a sector of British liberal opinion in government and business, the great bulk of the Indian Civil Service (ICS) and the nonofficial community were disturbed by the motives of the new elite. Thus, while men like Sir William Wedderburn, A. O. Hume, George Yule, and Henry Cotton assisted the new, educated elite in establishing the Indian National Congress and supported the aspirations for wider participation in the offices of the country, the bulk of nonofficial British opinion in Calcutta supported the ICS and its paternalistic approach to governing India.[8] George Yule, director of the managing agency house of Andrew Yule and Company, served as president of the Bengal chamber from 1878–1879. But it was certainly no accident that his firm's role in the chamber declined as, from the 1880s onward, George Yule became identified with the Indian National Congress, even serving as its

[6] *Ibid.*, p. 84.

[7] J. H. Broomfield, *Elite Conflict in a Plural Society: Twentieth-Century Bengal* (Berkeley and Los Angeles: University of California Press, 1968), p. 43. Note that the nonofficial British community in Calcutta at this time numbered about 23,000 persons.

[8] *Ibid.*, pp. 21–25.

president in 1888. Not one member of the firm of Andrew Yule was to hold the post of president of the Bengal chamber again until 1940.

The British community in Calcutta, and especially the business community, having developed a close and intricate relationship with the British administration in India, counted on the ICS to help protect its interests. As the president of the Indian Tea Association said in 1936, "For years past we, in common with very nearly every other industry, have relied upon that splendid body of civil servants to mother and father our political interests." [9] Contacts in Calcutta were reinforced by a powerful lobby in Whitehall and Westminster.[10] Thus, as Indian political and economic nationalism grew, the well entrenched British community could hardly fail to view it with foreboding. "Never before in the history of this chamber," said the president of the Bengal Chamber of Commerce in 1918, "have its members assembled together at a more momentous occasion, seldom perhaps in the history of the world has any community in similar circumstances, small in number yet vast in interests, been asked to face a future which presents to all sane, steady-thinking men of our community such far-reaching possibilities for evil to the country and its people." [11] British business and the Bengal chamber responded to these changes by organizing the previously isolated provincial chambers into an all-India federation, the Associated Chambers of Commerce (Assocham), and by taking a more active role in the politics of the country.

A large but secondary center of British trade and investment in India, Bombay, had developed a totally different character from Calcutta. Because Bombay was more cosmopolitan, British business had to share the center of the stage with members of the Parsi, Gujarati, Jewish, and Muslim business communities. These differences between Calcutta and Bombay were reflected in their business associations. The Bombay chamber, created in 1836, two years after the formation of the Calcutta chamber, was a very different organization. First, the chamber was a joint venture of the British and Parsi trading communities. Parsi firms belonged to the Bombay chamber, and three seats on the ten-member executive committee were held by Indians. Among these was Dadabhoy Pestonjee, a descendant of the famous shipbuilding Wadias of Surat.[12] Second, the Bombay chamber was the creation of the smaller trading firms of Bombay. The big four Bom-

[9] Sir Percival Griffiths, *The History of the Indian Tea Industry* (London: Weidenfeld and Nicholson, 1967), p. 526.

[10] Broomfield, *Elite Conflict*, p. 43.

[11] *Ibid.*, p. 109.

[12] Sulivan, *One Hundred Years*, p. 7.

bay houses of Forbes, Remington, Leckie, and Shotten stayed out until 1867.[13] Although it eventually included importers and exporters, banking, shipping, railroad, and engineering interests, every kind of wholesale business carried on in Bombay, and also professional men such as lawyers and accountants, the Bombay chamber remained dominated by merchants.[14] For the first one hundred years—except for 1922–1923, 1928, and 1932, when the post was held by two exchange brokers and a chartered accountant respectively—the chairman of the chamber was always a merchant. This is in sharp contrast to the dominance of managing agency houses in the Bengal chamber.[15] Third, the Bombay chamber was much more outspoken than the Bengal chamber. Distance had something to do with this stance. The Bengal chamber was located in the capital of the raj, where business could and preferred to discuss its problems informally with a British administration which it expected would protect its interest. The interests of the Bombay chamber, by contrast, were not so closely identified with the interests of Bengal's managing agencies. The Bombay chamber was much less hostile to Indian interests. On several occasions, the chamber tried to identify itself with Indian aspirations. This earned it the contempt of the Calcutta business community.[16] Finally, the Bombay chamber never developed the elaborate secretariat which grew up in Calcutta with the support of the managing agency houses and their associations. The Bombay chamber did supply secretarial services to the Bombay Millowners Association from its creation in 1875 until 1923. In that year the Bombay Millowners Association decided to create its own secretariat to handle the increased work lord of the organization. In addition, while the Bombay chamber included both British and Indian business, the Bombay Millowners Association always tried to represent indigenous textile interests.[17] Thus, although Bombay had a modest secretariat to help in supplying services—such as trade information, measurement of cargo for freight purposes, and arbitration machinery for its members—it lost the financial backing of the millowners asso-

[13] *Ibid.*, p. 11.

[14] *Ibid.*, p. 274.

[15] *Ibid.*, p. 271.

[16] For example, the chamber supported limited protection of the Indian steel industry over the objection of the Bengal chamber in 1923; in 1930 the chamber expressed sympathy with Indian nation aspirations during the civil disobedience movement only to be criticized by the other Europeans for weakness. Sulivan, *One Hundred Years*, pp. 153, 161.

[17] S. M. Rutnagar, ed., *Bombay Industries: The Cotton Mills* (Bombay: The Indian Textile Journal Ltd., 1927), p. 535.

ciation, which would have enabled it to develop a more elaborate secretariat. In short, the Bombay chamber was smaller, less exclusive, more heterogeneous, and failed to develop a secretariat equivalent to that of the Bengal chamber, a fact that was to have important implications at the time of federation.

Although Madras was the third largest city in India in the nineteenth century and was administrative capital of a presidency, its major strength lay more in its educational facilities than in its trade or commerce. Calcutta and Bombay towered above Madras as commercial and industrial centers. Yet on September 29, 1836, one week after the formation of the Bombay chamber, a small group of merchants met at Binny and Company to form the Madras Chamber of Commerce. When the governor of the province was notified of its creation, he expressed regret that no Indians had been enrolled. In response to this objection, the chamber recruited two Indian members. As late as 1936, however, the chamber had not been able to improve on this figure.[18] The Madras chamber was extremely weak financially and organizationally. The duties of the secretary were performed by a member of the staff of the Madras *Mail*. In 1841, when the incumbent secretary left for England, the chamber resolved "that the situation (sic) of the secretary be abolished and that hereafter the chairman be requested to undertake the duties; that the establishment of the chamber be limited for the present to one writer and one peon; and that the newspapers . . . be discontinued." [19] The position of the secretary remained vacant until 1854. The voice of the Madras chamber carried little weight until well into the twentieth century.

Not until 1925 do the chamber records annotate a sense of being consulted and listened to by the government of Madras. Yet, as the originator of a scheme for political representation which would be part of and yet independent of normal chamber functions, the Madras chamber did make a unique contribution to British business in India.

Thus, within a few years of the end of the East India Company's monopoly of trade, chambers of commerce came into existence in Calcutta, Bombay, and Madras. Later chambers were formed in Cochin (1857), Karachi (1860), Cocanada (1868), Upper India (1888), Punjab (1905), Tuticorin (1906), and Chittagong (1906). In 1920, these chambers federated to form the Associated Chambers of Commerce.[20]

[18] *Madras Chamber of Commerce Centenary Handbook 1836–1936* (Madras: The Madras Chamber of Commerce, 1936), p. 10.

[19] *Ibid.*, p. 13.

[20] Other regional chambers were formed after 1920 in smaller trading centers. Be-

The formation of Assocham was largely a response by British business to the growth of Indian political and economic nationalism at a time when the raj had found it politic to try to meet some of the growing aspirations of its subjects. The shift in government policy was first signaled in 1912 when the capital was moved from Calcutta to Delhi, thus ending European dominance in policy-making. It was reinforced by the statement on August 20, 1917, of Edwin Montagu, the secretary of state for India, that the objective of British colonial policy in India was the development of self-government. Although reforms came too late to placate the rising tide of Indian nationalism, the development of political nationalism and the move toward even limited self-government frightened the Europeans into action and drove a deeper wedge between foreign and indigenous capital. British capital joined the European community in fighting the reforms, arguing first that the time was not ripe for constitutional changes of this kind and that changes, if made, must be modest so as to avoid "experiments on a large scale that might mean large disaster." [21] The mere discussion of the political reforms convinced the Europeans, and especially British capital, of the need to pay greater attention to the rapidly emerging structure of self-government. It was also clear that the British would have to organize themselves more effectively to protect their special position. In addition to creating the Associated Chambers of Commerce to represent their interests in Delhi, they joined with the European community in establishing the Central Commercial Representation Fund, a separate political secretariat to assist their elected representatives.

The first steps toward federation of British business associations had taken place in January of 1905, when a conference of British dominated chambers of commerce in India and Ceylon was held in Calcutta. Despite the rapidly growing sense of economic nationalism reflected in the Swadeshi movement of that year, the British chambers were unable to develop any permanent organization. According to Assocham records, "When that conference was held the intention was to make it an annual gathering, but for some reason or other this idea was not carried out; perhaps the reason was that there was no real moving spirit behind the conference." [22] Although informal consultations among the chambers did take place, a second conference was

cause of the membership changes that took place at the time of partition, Assocham was reduced to eleven members. For a list of members see Chapter V, n. 41.

[21] Broomfield, *Elite Conflict*, p. 108.

[22] Assocham, *Proceedings of the Annual General Meeting of the Associated Chambers of Commerce* (Calcutta: Assocham, 1920), p. 15.

not held until 1917. In that year a conference was held in Delhi to consider postwar political and economic developments. By then the growing integration of an all-Indian economic policy, the increasing amount of legislation, the rapid growth of Indian business during the war, and the sharper spirit of trade rivalry all led to increased pressure for federation. The most important impetus for federation was fear of the implications of the 1917 declaration on self-rule and of the growing mobilization of important Indian industrial financial support for political purposes.[23]

Although originally conceived as a federation, the Associated Chambers of Commerce became dominated by its richest and most powerful constituent, the Bengal Chamber of Commerce, which in turn represented the British managing agency interests of Bengal. The Bengal chamber provided the leadership and resources to support the organization and was willing to supply these services to others in return for its position of dominance within the organization.

Concomitant with creation of the Associated Chambers of Commerce, British business in cooperation with the European community in India formed a small political secretariat in Delhi, called the Central Commercial Representation Fund, to assist the European members of the Central Legislative Assembly. The Central Commercial Representation Fund enabled the British business community to separate its chamber functions and its political functions. British chambers had received separate representation as early as 1892, under the Indian Councils Act, when the viceroy nominated representatives of the commercial community to his legislative council. Later, under the Morley-Minto Reforms of 1909, commercial interests were given direct representation in both the state and central legislatures. At first, British business had paid little attention to the legislatures. It was difficult to find people who would devote the time to the job, and turnover was quite high. Instead, the business community "relied upon their personal contacts with senior members of the ICS, with governors and viceroys, and with civil servants and politicians in London to maintain their considerable privileges." [24]

The Montagu-Chelmsford reforms of 1919 forced the British business community to change its attitude toward legislative councils, for the reforms gave the European community in India a large representation at both the state and national levels. Thus, as early as March 1919, the president of the European association warned the Euro-

[23] Tyson, *Bengal Chamber*, p. 101.

[24] Broomfield, *Elite Conflict*, pp. 106–107; Griffiths, *History of Indian Tea*, p. 535.

pean community that it would have to pay more attention to the legislative councils. To do this they needed a fund to pay the salaries of representatives who could devote full time to this work.[25]

The earliest steps to develop a system of paid representation for business were taken in 1928, when United Planters Association of South India (UPASI) decided to hire a full-time representative of the planting community in the Madras legislative council. The representative would also serve as the general European political secretary. In order to secure a strong financial base and to broaden its activities, a group of European trade, commercial, and planting organizations banded together to create the South Indian Planting and Commercial Fund in 1931. The fund was to be controlled by a committee consisting of the chairman of the Madras chamber, the chairman of the Madras Trades Association, the chairman of the Madras branch of the European Association, the chairman of UPASI, and one representative elected by the mofussil chambers. The purpose of the fund was to provide a political secretariat which would be able to undertake political work and coordinate the political activity of the community.[26]

In the early 1930s, when the planter member of the Madras legislature was elected to the Indian legislature in Delhi, the Madras chamber urged Assocham to bear the cost of secretariat services for a European commercial representative in the legislature and to create, for the purpose, a separate political fund and secretariat in Delhi. A central fund was created on October 1, 1934. Once again the bulk of the money was provided by the Bengal chamber. Of the Rs 120,000 which was pledged, the Bengal chamber provided half.[27] Thus, in effect, British business tried to segregate the political and economic function of their association. As the president of the Bengal chamber said, "the chamber committe henceforward will, we hope, then largely be able to have political interests in the hands of the group organizations and will be able to confine itself more rigidly to the vast volume of business problems which are constantly presenting themselves." [28] Considering the rapidly rising feeling of nationalism which had spread across India, the principle was undoubtedly a sound one.

As a consequence of colonial experience, India entered independence with a strong hostility toward foreign capital on the part of both government and indigenous entrepreneurs. But government

[25] Broomfield, *Elite Conflict*, p. 110.
[26] *Madras Chamber Centenary Handbook*, pp. 25–27.
[27] Tyson, *Bengal Chamber*, p. 120.
[28] *Ibid.*

policy and elite attitudes slowly shifted from antagonism to grudging acceptance and then to active encouragement as preoccupation with issues of foreign control and economic power progressively gave way to concern over balance of payments difficulties and a desire for rapid growth.[29] Thus, despite all its foreboding, British business interests and Assocham not only survived the final transfer of power to Indian hands in 1947 but continued to grow and prosper. Its very growth and prosperity, however, had a major impact on the distribution of power in the organization and on its style of interest articulation and influence.

Internal Politics

Traditionally Assocham represented British business, and especially British managing agency interests in Calcutta. But several post-1947 changes have sharply modified this situation and so profoundly affected the internal politics of Assocham. The end of the British raj and the advent of planning altered drastically the nature of foreign investment in India, with repercussions in the ownership, management, and diversity of interests represented in the constituent units of Assocham. First, following independence, many firms that were wholly Indian-owned joined the constituent units of Assocham, especially in Bombay, thus ending the sharp separation between foreign and indigenous capital. Second, many old British-owned firms Indianized both their management and capital. Although this change took place throughout India, the most dramatic changes occurred in Calcutta, the heart of the British business settlement. Third, the process of rapid industrialization—stimulated by the government of India and the advent of planning—involved numerous collaborations between Indian and foreign firms. This has changed the entire complexion of both Indian and foreign business in India.

The impact of these changes in the nature of foreign investment in India was felt in different ways within each of the two largest constituent members of Assocham—the Bengal Chamber of Commerce and the Bombay Chamber of Commerce. The Bengal chamber and its managing agency interests have seen their monopoly of power challenged from both within and without by the growing power of new manufacturing-oriented industrial interests. The membership of the Bengal chamber was substantially modified after independence.

[29] Michael Kidron, *Foreign Investments in India* (London: Oxford University Press, 1965), pp. 97–103.

The changes were brought about by the repatriation of profits and the sale of many old managing agency houses to Calcutta Marwaris, by the growing Indianization of capital and management of both individual firms and managing agency groups, and by the rapid growth of the large multinational corporations like Imperial Chemical, Metal Box, Union Carbide, and Guest, Keen, Williams. As a result, the monopoly of power formerly exercised in the Bengal chamber by the old managing agency houses was successfully challenged in the 1960s, when a *de facto* agreement was reached to rotate the presidency each year between the established managing agency houses and the new industrial interests. In addition, the former monopoly of British nationals on the executive committee of the Bengal chamber has given way to gradual Indianization and the inclusion of American interests.

The changes in the Bengal chamber have been slow and incremental. The rapid growth and development of the Bombay chamber has produced much more dramatic results. The city of Bombay did not experience the disruption of partition which shook Calcutta, nor have its politics been as mercurial. As a result, industrial development in the region has outstripped development in Bengal and substantially reduced the gap in levels of industrialization between the two areas. Bombay became the home of new foreign investment in pharmaceuticals, oil, medium and light engineering, and chemicals. These new industries have been developed by both foreign capital and foreign collaborations between large multinational corporations and indigenous capital. The new firms joined the Bombay chamber, swelling its ranks and its treasury and infusing the organization with a new, more professional, and more dynamic leadership. This leadership has been drawn largely from the new generation of Indian managers recruited by large multinational corporations. Indians play a major role on the executive committees of the chamber, and the first Indian president was elected as early as 1958. According to past president N. M. Wagle, the Bombay chamber has

> changed from a gentlemen's club of distinguished and able merchants to a modern, professional organization as much concerned with industry as with trade. . . . Our committee and officers are no longer the owners of capital but are usually professional managers, with all the differences of outlook which that implies. Similarly, the secretariat has professionalized itself. Secretaries are no longer mainly to turn a good phrase on information provided by committees. The secretariat have them-

> selves to be experts in taxation or company law or labor matters or whatever. And the advice the chamber gives these days is not the pontifical declaration of former years decreeing what will be the practice in the port, but it is a matter of detailed consideration of the individual problems of a large and extraordinarily varied membership.[30]

Wagle's description of the Bombay chamber was also meant as a parody of the Bengal chamber and Assocham, and of the "East India Company atmosphere" which pervades both. The growth in Bombay of managerial, professional, and antitraditional attitudes led to a demand for an end to the Bengal chamber's traditional control of the affairs of Assocham and for a complete reorientation of its leadership, organization, and style of action.

The Bombay chamber did not challenge the formal structure of power in Assocham, but it did question the informal traditions and relationships which had led to the domination of the organization by a small oligarchy of managing agency houses from the Bengal chamber. In fact, the Bombay chamber demanded that the organization return to the practices envisioned by its founders. The constitutional arrangements adopted by Assocham in 1920 took into account the nearly one hundred years of parallel developments on the part of the older constituents in Bengal, Bombay, and Madras. Therefore, Assocham was designed to have almost no separate apex structure. Its sole officers were a president, two deputy presidents, an auditor, and a secretary. With the exception of the auditor and the secretary, all officers served without pay. The constitution called for the eleven member bodies to meet annually to elect officers, receive a report of the proceedings, and consider the yearly accounts, but there was no provision for an executive committee.[31] Traditionally, therefore, the bulk of the work of Assocham was done by correspondence among the constituent members and not by formal meetings. In practice, even the annual meeting took on a highly formalized style in which the most important event was the speech by the chief guest. The chief guest was usually the viceroy of India. His presence gave the delegates of the chamber a chance to confer with him and his aides on the

[30] *Report of the Bombay Chamber of Commerce and Industry 1960* (Bombay: The Bombay Chamber of Commerce and Industry, 1960), p. 23.

[31] Assocham, "Articles of Association of the Associated Chambers of Commerce and Industry of India," *The Associated Chambers of Commerce and Industry of India, Forty-Eighth Annual Report, 1967* (Calcutta: Assocham, 1967), pp. 74–82. See also n. 42, chapter V.

problems facing the business community. The occasion also provided an opportunity for expressing displeasure with government policy by unanimous passage of a series of resolutions agreed on in advance. After independence the pattern continued, except that the chief guest was a high ranking member of the Indian cabinet and at times the prime minister.

The election of officers at the annual meeting of Assocham was a simple, *pro forma* affair, because the election was not direct but indirect. Each year specific chambers were designated to nominate the president, the secretary, and the two deputy presidents. The original assumption was that these four positions would be rotated among the major chambers each year. Although the principal of rotation was followed for a few years, it proved not to be feasible. Henceforth, control passed into the hands of the richest and most powerful constituent, the Bengal chamber. Thus, although the Bombay chamber nominated the president and the secretary in 1923 and 1928 and Upper India did so in 1926, a convention developed from 1929 onward that the responsibility for nominating the president and the secretary belonged to the Bengal chamber. The official justification for this tradition, according to Tyson, arose from the experience, quite early, "that the heavy volume of work, calling for detailed study and documentation, could not be moved from one center to another without loss of efficiency," from which it was concluded "that only a chamber of commerce with a large and experienced staff could provide the requisite secretariat services."[32] The principal of rotation was continued only in the selection of the two deputy presidents, who were selected from the larger chambers in Bombay, Madras, Punjab-Delhi, and Upper India.

Control of the presidency and the secretariat enabled the Bengal chamber, and through it a handful of managing agency houses in Calcutta, to dominate Assocham policy-making. In this way, the voice of the Bengal chamber and its managing agency interests could be legitimized as the voice of British business in India. Because it was control over the nomination of the president and secretary which facilitated the Bengal chamber's domination of Assocham, it is not surprising that when pressure for change came three decades later, it focused precisely on these two areas.

The dominance of the Bengal chamber meant *de facto* dominance by a small group of managing agency houses who controlled the Bengal chamber. These "managing agency interests have always been to the fore in the affairs of the Bengal Chamber of Commerce and

[32] Tyson, *Bengal Chamber*, p. 102.

Table VI-1

SOURCES OF RECRUITMENT OF PRESIDENTS OF THE BENGAL CHAMBER OF COMMERCE AND INDUSTRY (1853–1967) AND ASSOCIATED CHAMBERS OF COMMERCE AND INDUSTRY (1920–1967)

	Bengal chamber	*Assocham*		
		Pre-Independence	*Post-Independence*	*Total*
Firm	*1853–1967*	*1920–1946*	*1947–1967*	*1920–1967*
Mackinnon and Mackenzie	22	9	1	10
Andrew Yule	11	2	7	9
Bird and Company	10	5	3	8
Jardine Henderson	13	1	4	5
Gillanders Arbuthnot	6	2	1	3
Other Firms	64[a]	8	8	16[b]
	128[c]	27	24	51[c]

[a] During this period, only thirty-two firms were able to elect one of their leaders president of the Bengal chamber.

[b] During this period, only seventeen firms elected one of their leaders president of Assocham.

[c] On several occasions during this period, the Bengal chamber had more than one president during a single calendar year due to death, resignation, or departure from India. The same is true of the Assocham.

Industry and, as leaders of business opinion, ready and willing to back their views with their resources in men, management, and finances." [33] The concentration of control of the Bengal chamber and the resulting control of Assocham by a few managing agency houses is vividly portrayed in Table VI-1, which shows the firms that provided presidents to the Bengal chamber and Assocham from 1920 to 1967. The presidency was the preserve of a total of seventeen firms, all of which until recently were managing agency houses. However, it is clear from the table that the circle of control was in fact even smaller that it first appears. The presidency of the Bengal chamber and Assocham was actually the private preserve of five houses: Mackinnon Mackenzie, Andrew Yule, Bird and Company, Jardine Henderson, and Gillanders Arbuthnot.[34]

For the first decade after independence, the presidency of the Asso-

[33] *Ibid.*, p. 84.

[34] Although it was important, the firm of Gillanders had resigned from the chamber in 1863 because of a dispute and remained outside the chamber until 1889.

cham continued in the hands of four large managing agency houses of Calcutta. The importance of some managing agency houses decreased as that of others increased. Andrew Yule and Jardine Henderson moved into greater prominence, although Bird and Company and Gillanders were still quite active and powerful. The power of shipping interests decreased substantially with the Indian government's move to strengthen Indian shipping. Many of the smaller managing agency houses that had played a role in the pre-independence period passed into the hands of the Marwaris.

By structure and tradition, the president and secretariat of Assocham were encouraged to play key roles in decision-making for the organization. Although individual chambers could request action on any issue, it was the president who was in touch with the day-to-day developments and in daily contact with the secretariat. Thus, Assocham initiatives depended on the president aided by the secretariat, which could advise him on major issues and also assist him in drawing up responses to various government policies. This advice, upon which the president became very dependent, tended, however, to draw heavily on traditional Assocham policy. In fact, the conservative bias in the secretariat was so strong that some critics argued that about 75 percent of the policy of Assocham consisted of replays of reactions to the past problems of the jute, tea, and coal industries.

When the president of Assocham needed advice on policy issues, the pattern of consultation depended on the time available. If time was short, the most immediate guidance available to the president came from the committee of the Bengal chamber. Thus, for example, Assocham's reaction to the annual budget speech of the finance minister of the government of India was determined by an informal meeting, held the night of the budget speech, of the president, the secretary, and the committee of the Bengal Chamber of Commerce. However, if long-term policy was involved, issues were first studied by specially constituted, *ad hoc,* all-India subcommittees which prepared an Assocham position for circulation and comment by the constituent chambers. A great deal of the consultation within Assocham, in fact, took the form of circulating memoranda for chamber reaction. Yet it was the secretariat's responsibility to collect these reactions and prepare a consolidated memorandum. The secretariat was thus in a position to insure that the dominant interests of the Bengal chamber were not ignored. At all times, then, the secretariat played a key role in both initiating and finalizing official Assocham policy.

Even during the period of almost absolute Bengal chamber dominance, the president, of course, was not completely isolated from the other constituent members. He undertook frequent visits to member bodies, and he could consult with his deputy vice presidents from other chambers. More recently Assocham has begun to convene periodic meetings of chamber delegates. At these informal meetings, which began to take place about five times a year, two or three delegates from each chamber could hold informal discussions. The effect of these periodic meetings has been the emergence of something like a *de facto* executive committee, which tends to reduce the dominant position of the Bengal chamber. This group might be consulted more frequently in the future by presidents who are not drawn from the Bengal chamber. In the past, however, the Bengal chamber clearly had a disproportionate say in Assocham policy, because it selected the president, provided the secretary, and informally guided the policy through the Bengal chamber committee. By the 1960s this longstanding *de facto* control of Assocham was successfully challenged by the industrial interests which had grown up between 1947 and 1960.

In the early 1960s, a "ginger group" of Indian managers from the Bombay chamber began demanding an end to monopoly control of the presidency of Assocham by the Bengal chamber, a return to the original concept of rotating the presidency and the restoration of a truly associated chamber. In fact, most of these Bombay insurgents demanded the even more radical step of abandoning regional rotation for selection based purely on talent. This demand encountered bitter but subtle resistance from the Bengal chamber. Although the Bengal chamber had actually come to look upon the selection of an Assocham president as its right, whenever the issue was raised by the Bombay chamber, the Bengal chamber's public position asserted that the president must come from where the secretariat was located. Any other arrangement, it was argued, would be impossible to operate. This argument held little sway with the Bombay leadership, which had come to view the Bengal chamber secretariat itself as somewhat anachronistic and unprofessional. After debating the issue for a few years, Bombay finally threatened to secede unless its right to nominate presidents of Assocham was recognized. The Bombay chamber also made it plain that, if necessary, it was prepared to shift the Assocham secretariat to Bombay as an answer to the traditional argument. In addition, the men from Bombay argued, the Indian government itself was unhappy with the existing situation by which Europeans continued to represent Assocham in Delhi.

When, finally, at a general meeting held on February 4, 1965, the

Bengal chamber conceded Bombay's demand for access to the presidency, it was only with the insistence that Bombay would also have to pay a large share of the cost of running Assocham. In 1962, Bombay had contributed only Rs 3,200 toward the Assocham budget of Rs 150,000. The subsequent changes, which equalized the contributions of Bombay and Calcutta, resulted in substantially increasing Bombay's financial responsibility to the organization.[35]

Although the Assocham people had pretended to debate the issues of the location of the secretariat and the sources of financing, the major reason for the Bengal chamber's reluctance to give up its prerogatives was desire to ensure that the interests of the managing agency houses would receive proper attention. Another more subtle problem involved the British character of the chamber. Over the decades, a tradition had developed whereby the president of Assocham, usually a senior British businessman who had spent his entire career in India, was given special recognition and, as reward for his long service, a knighthood. It was well known among British businessmen in India that the presidency of Assocham carried with it a title. The selection process reflected the delicacy of the issue. The consultation format included representatives of the British High Commission in Calcutta, the chairman of the India Burma Pakistan Association, and the top British managers in Calcutta. Because the vice president of the Bengal chamber by tradition became president of the chamber the following year, each president and vice president wanted the system perpetuated for at least one more year. And so, it was traditional prerogatives rather than inertia which had prevented any change until Bombay forced the issue.

Thus, after a long fight and a carefully arranged transition, Bombay had won its point, and the Bombay chamber selected Mr. N. M. Wagle as its first president of Assocham since 1928. Wagle's election in 1968 broke two established traditions. He was the first Indian president of Assocham, and he was the first non-Calcutta president in three decades. In a sense, the decisive change was the shift from Calcutta to Bombay, because that decision made the selection of an Indian inevitable. Wagle deserved the honor, because he was the senior man on the committee of the Bombay chamber and also because he had been one of the Bombay managers who had fought for the change.

Although the transition took place smoothly on the surface, it left behind a considerable amount of grumbling. The rapidly diminishing

[35] *Report of the Bombay Chamber of Commerce and Industry, 1962* (Bombay: The Bombay Chamber of Commerce and Industry, 1962), pp. 24–25.

old guard of the Bengal chamber resented the change. Many of them, after twenty-five years in India, do not have much longer to serve, and they realize that rotation of the presidency is bound to deprive some of them of their title. In addition, they realize that the changing internal politics of the Bengal chamber will also diminish their already jeopardized chances for the big honor, as top executives of the international corporations find their way to the presidency of the Bengal chamber and as Indian executives begin to increase in number and also demand their turn. These dispossessed British members of the Bengal chamber, therefore, tend to argue that the new rotation experiment has not worked and that the deputy president of Assocham resident in Calcutta has had to do most of the work. There are even some who feel that the issue of Bengal supremacy has not really been settled and that the chamber will fight to return the presidency to Bengal permanently. However, it would seem that this approach will simply lead to even further changes and that the next chief target of reform will be the nature and location of the secretariat itself. Moreover, it has now become clear that the issue is settled.

The attack on the tradition of selecting a president from the Bengal chamber was designed as an opening wedge to disentangle and reorient the entire style and functioning of Assocham. One of the major targets in this attack was the secretariat of the Bengal chamber. As a result, along with the decision to change the presidential selection process, modest but significant changes were made in the secretariat arrangements of Assocham. These changes were designed to develop a small but independent secretariat for Assocham in Delhi, by strengthening the Delhi office of the organization. Until then the secretariat function of the Delhi office had been performed largely in Calcutta, by the Bengal chamber secretariat which continued to be run by British expatriots. This was done in two ways. First, although the Assocham had maintained a Delhi office, it was, until recently, staffed by one of the senior secretaries of the Bengal chamber who was given the title of Delhi advisor of Assocham. Second, the Bengal chamber provided all of the back-up support for this Delhi advisor, and for this service it received a fee from Assocham.[36] The occasion for the reorganization of the Delhi office was provided by the retirement of one of the senior secretaries of the Bengal chamber. As a result, the Delhi advisor of Assocham was moved back to Calcutta to become the new head of the

[36] The total financial picture of the Delhi operation was, however, somewhat more complex. The Delhi advisor of Assocham and his small staff were paid, not by Assocham, but rather out of funds collected by a separate organization called the Central Commercial Representation Fund.

secretariat of the Bengal chamber. This gave the reformers a chance to demand personnel changes in the Delhi office. Instead of replacing the Delhi advisor with another senior European secretary of the Bengal chamber, Assocham recruited an Indian who had recently retired from the ICS as a senior officer in the Labor Ministry. In addition, two other new positions were added to the staff of Assocham, an assistant to the Delhi advisor and an economic specialist who was to provide independent economic analysis for the use of Assocham. Thus Assocham, as an apex organization, now has three people on its staff who are relatively independent of the Bengal chamber.

The attack on the Bengal chamber secretariat was an attack on the amateurish tradition of the highly paid British expatriot staff which manned the Bengal chamber. This staff, in Wagle's words, consisted of "journalists well known for their ability to turn a phrase," men whose real concern was limited to the traditional problems of jute, tea, and coal, and the tax implications of home leave. What the reformers wanted instead was a specialized staff of economists, statisticians, and analysts capable of discussing alternative development strategies with their counterparts in the government of India. Assocham, they felt, should cease to be a defensive body which confined itself to responding to external stimuli. It should become an innovative organization capable of initiating creative approaches to policy. For such purposes, the renovation of the secretariat was essential.

Thus, the internal politics of Assocham in the years after independence reflected a restructuring of informal relationships in response to the changing character of foreign capital in India. The members of Assocham today are quite different from those who dominated it in 1920. For that matter, they differ from those who dominated in 1947. Both the new companies and the old are in the middle of a major process of professionalization which they wish extended to their business associations. Moreover, they want business in India to develop in new and different ways. They are not interested in the traditional forms of adjustment associated with mining and plantation or with traditional industries of jute and coal. They are interested in the more modern sectors of industry. As a result, they have been in conflict with those who, as representatives of the more traditional industries, have given to Assocham the defensive style of functioning. That style has been consistent with their preference for the preservation of traditional investment rather than for development and expansion of new investments.

The Indianization of capital and management has made the leadership of foreign investment in India much less insecure than the old holdover British managers. The new Indian management is much more aggressive, and although they may disapprove of some of the things which the FICCI does, they tend nevertheless to sympathize with its approach. As a result, the traditional barriers between British and Indian capital are beginning to break down. There is today even a degree of overlapping membership between the two organizations. It is unlikely that the two organizations will merge for some time to come. But one would certainly expect that, within the next decade, there will be very substantial overlapping membership and that if the business community in India is threatened even further it may, in fact, unite the two in a way which would end the historic split between foreign and Indian capital in India. Moreover, as Indian business begins to gain a greater and greater sense of solidarity so, too, this sense of solidarity will transcend the difference between Indian and foreign capital and the two organizations will be closer together.

Assocham, then, is the primary organized means through which foreign capital in India formulates its demands, develops a response to policy initiatives of the government of India, and raises questions concerning the detailed implementation of government policy. Assocham submits its views to the government of India on a wide variety of issues such as taxation, budget policies, and major legislative proposals; makes recommendations concerning export promotion, import policy and regulation, and industrial licensing policy and procedure; and provides a mechanism for submitting the views of foreign business to government commissions and select committees of Parliament. In general, Assocham handles issues which are of a general concern to the entire foreign business community. In addition, however, Assocham works in close liaison with a variety of specialized industry associations, some of which are closely integrated into the structure of Assocham member bodies. Thus, although organizations like the Indian Jute Mills Association, the Indian Tea Association, the Indian Engineering Association, and the Indian Mining Association elect their own presidents and executive committees, their secretarial function is performed by the Bengal chamber and the same managing agency houses which play a dominant role in their respective industry associations. The industry associations, in turn, also try to coordinate their views with existing nonaffiliated associations which might represent the industry.

The movement in Assocham is toward the development of a stronger, more Indianized apex structure. That structure would be supported by a professional staff, which would maintain day-to-day contact with the operating levels of government and also would be capable of developing alternative policies to those proposed by the government of India. Assocham is also beginning to develop closer contact with the FICCI, and the two organizations may be expected to coordinate their activities more frequently in the future. The historic split between indigenous and foreign capital is rapidly declining, and the time may yet come when the two groups will speak with one voice.

VII

THE ORGANIZATION OF INDIAN CAPITAL: REGIONAL ORIGINS

When Indian businessmen began to sponsor their own business associations, a half century had elapsed since the establishment of the first British chambers. These Indian business groups arose in the 1880s in response to a divergence of interests between Indian and British business. These differences were based specifically on Indian discontent with British economic policy and more generally on the emergence of political and economic nationalism. Like their British counterparts, Indian businessmen in the port cities of Calcutta, Bombay, and Madras were the first to organize. They federated into an all-Indian body in 1927. To chart the genesis of modern Indian business associations and their patterns of institutionalization, one must examine both the regional chambers and the all-India bodies, focusing particular attention on the mobilization and the nature of their membership, their contrasting organizational styles, and their relation to the national movement.

The circumstances surrounding the creation of Indian chambers varied considerably from region to region and case to case, and yet some common characteristics are detectable. First, the organizational pattern of the British chamber of commerce was adopted. Unlike the British, however, the Indians lacked a tradition of organized business life, and so the process of organization proved difficult. Because the average Indian businessman proved to be exceedingly resistant to the idea of mobilizing for collective action, the founders had to expend their personal resources on the organization. Thus, many chambers became identified with particular families.

Second, the Indian pattern of business mobilization reflected the fragmentation of the Indian business community. In all the major centers, a multiplicity of chambers emerged. These were symptomatic of limited social differentiation in the modern sense, and of the survival of strong traditional loyalties of religion, language, and caste which inhibited the formation of large collectivities. Thus, as late as 1945, there were in India chambers which restricted their memberships to certain language groups, chambers which were entirely or predominantly composed of one caste, and even eight chambers composed entirely of Muslim businessmen.

Third, substantial differences, based on the uneven commercial and industrial development of the various regions, tended to overlap between caste and community boundaries and to intensify the divergence of interests between Calcutta and Bombay. Yet, despite these nationwide centrifugal tendencies, the major chambers in Calcutta, Bombay, and Madras sought to establish organizations based on unrestricted membership. These literally cosmopolitan chambers are the ones which came to play the most active role in representing indigenous business interests. Thus, they set an example, and their success has resulted in some erosion of parochial loyalties. Although a large number of chambers based on one extrinsic criterion or another continue to exist, there is an increasing overlapping of membership among the chambers, and they have become less parochial and more responsive to the collective business interest.

The origins of the Indian chambers have had a major impact on their style, functioning, and orientation toward government. They developed as critics of British policy and had to fight hard to achieve recognition as spokesmen of Indian capital. Although they maintained close contact with the nationalist movement and supported it in various ways, they did so from a distance, relying on their own organizations to press for their interests. They remained, moreover, predominantly concerned with economic policy. Their style was based on protest against various unfair practices and on demands for greater government interaction and support. They protested against the exploitation of India's resources by foreigners, including the unregulated incursions of foreign capital; they complained about differential railroad rates; and they denounced excessive military and governmental expenditures. At the same time, the Indian chambers demanded greater and more effective government support for industrial development, fiscal autonomy, protective tariffs, development of a merchant marine, and support for technical and commercial education. Above all, the Indian business groups attempted to impress upon their countrymen "that the country was much more exploited through trade, industries, currency, and exchange policy of the government than through a few jobs given members of a foreign bureaucracy." [1]

[1] L. R. Das Gupta, *Indian Chambers of Commerce and Commercial Associations* (Calcutta: Eastern Chamber of Commerce, 1946), pp. 34–36.

The Rise of Indian Business Associations in Calcutta

The earliest associations of Indian businessmen developed in Calcutta —the capital of British India, the administrative center of Bengal, and a major commercial, cultural, and educational center. Culturally the city was dominated by the Bengali bhadralok composed of three socially dominant castes—Brahmins, Kayasths, and Baidyas. The bhadralok had been drawn to the city by the opportunities for advancement provided by the British settlement. By the nineteenth century they had made Calcutta the center of Bengali culture and were in the forefront of the nationalist movement. Cultural leadership, however, was not power. Because Calcutta was predominantly a commercial city, real dominance was in the hands of the European agency houses and the Marwari traders. The former controlled the foreign trade, shipping, and banking of the city, and the latter virtually monopolized internal trade. In addition, Calcutta, like all of Bengal, had a very large Muslim population. These four groups—the British, Muslims, Bengalis, and Marwaris—were separated into almost watertight compartments. Each of these groups eventually formed an association for the protection and furtherance of its own economic interests. European business was the first to organize, and although some Indians were initially associated with the Calcutta Chamber of Commerce established in 1834, the two communities in time began to drift further and further apart. The Bengal National Chamber, organized in 1887, was the earliest Indian chamber, but because the Bengalis played only a minor role in the trade and commerce of Bengal, the chamber's greatest significance grew out of its political activities and its relationship to the emerging nationalist movement.[2] Somewhat later, when Hindu–Muslim relations became embittered, the Muslims of Calcutta created their own chamber. However, the major associational achievement for indigenous capital and trade in Calcutta centered around the Marwari community, which dominated the internal trade of Calcutta and Bengal.

The development of modern associations among the Marwaris of Calcutta offers an interesting case study of the impact of social differentiation and secularization on one of the most traditional caste communities in India. The Marwari community of Calcutta passed through a three-phase process of change as it moved from traditional

[2] Bengal National Chamber of Commerce and Industry, *Souvenir Volume: 1887–1962* (Calcutta: Bengal National Chamber of Commerce and Industry, 1962), pp. 43–47.

to modern forms of association. The Marwaris first organized a traditional caste panchayat, whose function was to regulate the social and economic behavior of the community and to maintain community norms. Next, a group of the wealthier and more highly educated Marwaris created a caste association for the purpose of uplifting the community. Finally, the community shattered into a whole spectrum of modern associations reflecting the different interests and goals of different groups within the community. In short, as a result of their experience in the commercial city of Calcutta, the Marwaris moved from a pure caste group to a modified, class-oriented group, creating new associations to represent their different interests.

The Marwari community, like all such traditional groups, originally consisted of a group of endogamous castes, with a common culture but separated by differences in ritual, regional, and economic activities.[3] The Marwari community, in particular, was ultraconservative in terms of social and religious orthodoxy, and it had achieved a very high sense of community solidarity. These characteristics were in many ways the product of their extremely successful following of traditional occupational pursuits. After the accelerating migration of Marwaris from Rajasthan to the socially heterogeneous and cosmopolitan city of Calcutta in the early nineteenth century, Marwaris established the Bari panchayat, a caste council to handle common problems of the community and to regulate community norms.[4] The authority of the panchayat was so strong that few were in a position to challenge it. As the size and diversity of the community in Calcutta grew, however, the Bari panchayat shrank into the panchayat of the Aggarwals, and each of the other Marwari subcastes established its own panchayat to regulate its particular norms. The Bari panchayat continued until the late nineteenth century to function as a mechanism for enforcing the norms applicable to the Marwari community as a whole.

By the turn of the century, however, with Marwari caste solidarity and orthodoxy yielding to the forces of differentiation and secularization, new forms of organization replaced the traditional Bari panchayat. Traditional caste unity was undermined by a growing sense of individualism, by conflicting economic interests, by the growth of nationalism, and by the insinuation of processes of social change within the community itself. In comparison with other elite castes of

[3] Thomas A. Timberg, *Industrial Entrepreneurship Among the Trading Communities of India: How the Pattern Differs* (Cambridge: Center for International Affairs, Harvard University, 1969), pp. 23–24.

[4] Balchand Modi, *Desh-kee Itihas-mee Marwari Jatii-kaa Sthaan* (Calcutta: Ragunath Prasad Singhania, 1940), p. 591 (published in Hindi).

Calcutta, the socially conservative Marwari community had lagged in English education. Literacy, for example, was almost nonexistent among Marwari women.[5] In 1898, concerned about such examples of social backwardness, some of the younger, more highly educated members of the Marwari community established a new type of caste association based partly on ascriptive status and partly on voluntary association—the Marwari Association. Unlike the Bari panchayat, the purpose of the Marwari Association was not to enforce social norms but to "promote and advance the moral, intellectual, commercial, economic, political, and social interests of the Marwari community and to protect its rights and status." It was also intended to "found and support establishments for disseminating commercial, technical, and general education in different branches of art and science in the Marwari community." [6] The Marwari Association represented a revolution in organizational development from the traditional caste association, and it signaled the beginning of a process of differentiation within the community. As the association came to focus on gaining political representation for the Marwari community, other newer and more functionally specialized groups came into being to carry out separate economic and social functions.

And so, within two years of the founding of the Marwari Association, a large group of piece goods traders split off to create the Marwari Chamber of Commerce to represent the economic interests of the cloth merchants.[7] At that time two-thirds of India's cotton piece goods, including the material for dhoties and saris, was imported from British mills, while Indian mills and the hand loom section together produced only 15 percent. Within Calcutta, however, members of the Marwari chamber handled about 80 percent of the trade.[8] The priorities of the Marwari chamber included a resolution to change the contract relationship between the traders and the British, and alteration of the system by which the arbitration of disputes arising out of business activities was automatically controlled by the British-dominated Bengal Chamber of Commerce. The fact that the chamber handled 1,198 arbitration cases in its first year of existence[9] demonstrates the importance of this function. The attempt by these retailers to strengthen

[5] Timberg, *Industrial Entrepreneurship*, p. 41.

[6] Quoted in Helen B. Lamb, "The Indian Business Communities and the Evolution of an Industrialist Class," *Pacific Affairs* 28 (1955): 107.

[7] Rishi Jaimini Kaushik, *Anandilal Poddar* (Calcutta: Jaimini Prakashan, 1964), pp. 134–136 (published in Hindi).

[8] Bharat Chamber of Commerce, *Golden Jubilee Souvenir: 1900–1950* (Calcutta: Alliance Press, 1950), pp. 9–11.

[9] *Ibid.*, p. 6.

their position in their trade relationships with the British was challenged, ironically enough, not by the British directly, but rather by a group of Marwari middlemen or banyans. The Marwari middlemen, encouraged by the British, had tried to destroy the new organization which jeopardized their interests in the very process of protecting the interests of their caste fellows. Thus, economic interests came to transcend caste solidarity, even among the unusually cohesive Marwari community.[10] The Marwari Chamber of Commerce nevertheless prospered and remained in the hands of Marwari traders dependent on British imports until 1937, when control of the chamber was captured by a group of young Marwari Swadeshi nationalists led by Anandilal Poddar. This change in control was made possible largely by the rapid decline of textile imports. That decline resulted from the British government's accession to the nationalist demands that the government place protective tariffs on British textiles. The ensuing shift to domestic consumption[11] placed Poddar and his colleagues in a strong position, for they had been specializing in Indian products all along.

The Marwari Association was only four years old when yet another group left to form an organization called the Vaishya Sabha. The organizers believed that the Marwari Association had fallen under the domination of a group of rich and conservative Marwaris who were closely associated in their business affairs with the British and interested solely in personal and political gain. The new organization, in contrast, was going to live up to the old association's stated objectives by focusing on the social reform of the community. They wished to eliminate illiteracy, change undesirable customs, and end extravagance. In their own way, they were also politically motivated, for they began to trade only in Swadeshi goods. In short, they were both nationalists and reformists, but they were perhaps most concerned with problems of education and caste uplift. One of the most prominent figures in the organization was Naurang Rai Khaitan, whose son Devi Prasad Khaitan was to become a highly educated Marwari lawyer and chief lieutenant of the Marwari industrialist G. D. Birla.[12] The creation of the Vaishya Sabha was symptomatic of the widening cleavage based on social, political, and economic differences between the two groups in

[10] Modi, *Desh-kee Itihas-mee Marwari Jatii-kaa Sthaan*, pp. 611–616. The term banyan used in this manuscript refers to native brokers attached to houses of business in Calcutta. *See* William Crooke (ed.). *Hobson Jobson: A Glossary of Colloquial Anglo-Indian Words and Phrases, and of Kindred Terms, Etymological, Historical, Geographical and Discursive*. Delhi: Munshiram Manoharlal, 2nd edition, 1968, p. 63.

[11] Bharat Chamber, *Golden Jubilee*, pp. 9–11. By the late 1930s, imports fell to only 15 percent of total consumption.

[12] Modi, *Desh-kee Itihas-mee Marwari Jatii-kaa Sthaan*, pp. 616–625.

the Marwari community. One group was reformist and nationalist; it was part of the emerging Marwari industrial class. The other was socially conservative, religiously orthodox, and pro-British. Its members tended to serve as banyans to the British managing agency houses.

Although the split between traditionalists and reformists in the Marwari community of Calcutta had originated in the early twentieth century among the Aggarwals in the Bari panchayat, it soon engulfed the entire community of the city. It was reinforced some years later as a result of a similar fight within the Maheshwari community, a smaller but important sector of the larger Marwari community. The Bari panchayat of Calcutta was traditionally controlled by a group of wealthy Sanatanists,[13] as the members of an ultraorthodox sect of Hinduism are called. At the turn of the century, however, Jai Narayan Poddar, a Marwari member of the Arya Samaj,[14] had arrived in Calcutta. Poddar became very successful in a large British firm and a very prominent member of the Marwari community. The Sanatanists, opposed to his reformist ideas, organized a group to counter his growing influence in the community. Their opportunity came in 1906, when the wife of one of Poddar's sons died. The Sanatanists charged that the funeral had not been carried out in keeping with the prescribed tradition. The issue was raised, of course, in the hope of discrediting and outcasting their enemy. Poddar, however, claimed that the charges were false. Both sides sought to mobilize support within the Marwari community, but not within the traditional panchayat structure. Instead, the debate was carried on in public in specially created newspapers.[15] To settle the dispute, a council of famous pundits was convened. After one and a half months of deliberations, they ruled against Poddar. Although Poddar agreed to sign a statement declaring himself to be a Sanatanist, his supporters charged that the verdict of the pundits had been improperly influenced by rich members of the community.[16] Thus, although the incident ended with victory for the conservatives, the Marwari community had become irrevocably divided into two groups, one reformist and one traditionalist.

The schismatic tendencies in the Marwari community were reinforced some years later as a result of a similar contention over community traditions within the Maheshwari community. This dispute involved the Birlas, a rapidly emerging industrial family. In 1922, Rameshwar Das Birla, a widower and one of the four famous Birla

[13] Sanatan Dharam was an ultraorthodox sect of the Hindu community.
[14] Arya Samaj was a reformist sect of Hinduism.
[15] Modi, *Desh-kee Itihas-mee Marwari Jatii-kaa Sthaan*, p. 675.
[16] *Ibid.*, pp. 669–681.

brothers, married a woman from a caste whose inclusion in the Maheshwari community was questioned. Like the Aggarwals, a few decades before, the Maheshwaris emerged from this conflict divided more firmly than ever into traditionalist and reformist factions. G. D. Birla, who had become deeply involved in his brother's cause, emerged as the spokesman for the reformist group in the Marwari community.

The cleavages which developed over social and religious issues coincided with differences in economic interests and political commitment. The Marwari community in Calcutta had become wealthy and prosperous largely because of its symbiotic relationship with British business and especially foreign trade. But it was precisely these interests that were challenged by the development of militant nationalism, especially as manifest in the Swadeshi movement of 1905, and the boycott of foreign goods, including cloth. Because it attacked the very source of their livelihood, the Calcutta Marwari community had bitterly opposed the Swadeshi agitation of 1905, and they were never forgiven by the Bengali nationalists for taking this stand.[17] By the end of World War I, however, some Marwaris had begun to move from trade to industry. Their traditional dependence on the British thus ended, they were brought into direct conflict with the raj and with a sector of their own community as well. The most prominent of these new industrial families was the Birla family, led by G. D. Birla. The new Marwari industrialists of Calcutta simultaneously began to develop interests similar to those of their counterparts in the Bombay industrial community. Like the Bombay industrialists, many of them became attracted to the Congress movement then led by Gandhi.

It might be said, however, that G. D. Birla became a nationalist quite early in life. Although he admired British organizational and business methods, he had come to resent their racial arrogance. He once described the origins of his nationalism as follows:

> When I was sixteen (1908) I started an independent business of my own as a broker, and thus began my contact with Englishmen who were my patrons and clients. During my association with them I began to see their superiority in business methods, their organizing capacity, and their many other virtues. But their racial arrogance could not be concealed. I was not allowed to use the lift to go up to their offices, nor their benches while waiting to see them. I smarted under these insults, and this

[17] J. H. Broomfield, *Elite Conflict in a Plural Society: Twentieth-Century Bengal* (Berkeley and Los Angeles: University of California Press, 1968), p. 31.

created within me a political interest which from 1912 until today I have fully maintained.[18]

G. D. Birla openly identified himself with the Congress and, along with other prominent Marwari industrialists, became one of the major financial backers of the Congress.

The split between the conservative, pro-British group and the reformist, nationalist group in the Marwari community had developed mainly over internal social norms. In 1923 that split took on a more intense political tone as a result of the Montagu-Chelmsford reforms, which granted the Marwari community of Calcutta a seat in the national legislature. A struggle as to who was to become the political spokesman of the community developed in the Marwari Association, which had fought for Marwari representation ever since the principle of representation of special interests and minority communities had been conceded in 1909. The association, however, was controlled by conservatives led by Sir Badridas Goenka, a banyan of the British house of Ralli Brothers, and association secretary Ramdev Chokhany, a banyan for the British house of Hoare Miller. G. D. Birla, leading the reformist challengers, attempted to secure the legislative seat for his group, but his candidate was defeated.[19] As a result, G. D. Birla withdrew from the Marwari Association. In 1925 he established his own organization, the Indian Chamber of Commerce, Calcutta to represent new Marwari capital and industry.

Thus, by the end of the first quarter of the twentieth century, the traditional caste solidarity of the Marwari community, which had been centered in the Bari panchayat of Calcutta, had shattered into a series of organizations representing the conflicting interests within the community. The Marwari Chamber of Commerce represented the cloth merchants, the Marwari Association represented the pro-British Sanatanists, and the Indian Chamber of Commerce, Calcutta, came to represent the new and rapidly expanding Marwari industrial class. Only the latter, however, was to have importance on the national scene. This was the group which joined with its counterparts in Bombay to form the Federation of Indian Chambers of Commerce and Industry.

[18] G. D. Birla, *In the Shadow of the Mahatma* (Bombay: Orient Longman's Ltd., 1955), pp. xiv–xv.

[19] Rishi Jaimini Kaushik, *Shri Ramdev Chokhany* (Calcutta: Jaimini Prakashan, N.D.), pp. 133–135 (published in Hindi).

The Indian Chamber of Commerce, Calcutta had immediately be-become the Indian counterpart to the Bengal chamber for Indian capital in Calcutta. It began with sixty-two members and achieved power as well as responsibility by providing secretarial services for a whole host of industrial associations which it fathered. At the time of the constitutional revision of 1935, the Indian Chamber of Commerce, Calcutta pressed for a separate seat in the legislature, claiming itself as the only true representative of Indian commercial interests in Bengal. Although this attempt failed,[20] the chamber grew in size and power to become one of the strongest in India and the base of Birla operations.

Because the Marwari industrialists now had their own base of power, it was left to other reformist Marwaris to renew the nationalist assault on the citadel of the pro-British Marwari organizations—the Marwari chamber and the Marwari Association. The job was performed by Anandilal Poddar, a young Marwari Congress activist who was associated with the Bengal Congress leader, Subhas Chandra Bose, and who was, appropriately, a distant relative of Jai Narayan Poddar. Poddar began his assault on the Marwari Chamber of Commerce in 1937, by organizing a group of young, educated middle-class Marwari traders to capture control of the chamber.[21] By this time the Marwari chamber was almost defunct, because the rapid expansion of Indian textiles and the Swadeshi movement had caused a rapid decline in the sale of foreign cloth in India. Having accomplished this objective, Anandilal Poddar turned to the Marwari Association and its coveted seat in the state and national legislatures. He succeeded in gaining control of the Marwari Association in the early 1940s, thereby ending forty years of control by the conservatives.[22]

Thus, by 1940 the caste solidarity of the Marwari community in Calcutta had literally disappeared. A process of differentiation and secularization had divided the community into numerous organizations representing interests so diverse that it is almost impossible to organize a new group in the name of community solidarity. The Bari panchayat was dead. The Marwari Association, having lost its special representation after independence, became defunct. And attempts to organize an all-Indian Marwari Federation had failed.[23] Only two major economic organizations survived the internal struggles within the Marwari community. The first, the Indian Chamber

[20] Kaushik, *Anandilal Poddar*, p. 135.
[21] *Ibid.*, pp. 99–100.
[22] *Ibid.*, pp. 136–140.
[23] Modi, *Desh-kee Itihas-mee Marwari Jatii-kaa Sthaan*, pp. 702–704.

of Commerce, Calcutta grew into a very powerful industrial association which came to represent Indian industry in eastern India and was instrumental in the founding of the Federation of Indian Chambers of Commerce and Industry.[24] Meanwhile, the Marwari Chamber of Commerce had come to represent largely the middle-class Marwari traders of Calcutta. It joined the Federation of Indian Chambers of Commerce and Industry only in 1939, after Poddar had gained control. In 1949, the chamber cooperated with the government's attempt to discourage emphasis on caste and community by changing its name to the Bharat Chamber of Commerce.[25] Since then, the Bharat chamber has become a platform for some large Marwari firms in Calcutta. Among them are the Singhanias, who feel that the close identification of Indian Chamber of Commerce, Calcutta with the Birlas cannot give them the greater freedom of action they enjoy within the Bharat chamber. Today there is a considerable overlap in membership among the large Marwari houses between the Indian Chamber of Commerce and the Bharat Chamber of Commerce, but their long history of conflict continues to have an important impact on the internal politics of the FICCI.

The Rise of Indian Business Associations in Bombay

The origins and development of modern business associations in Bombay followed a pattern totally different from the associations that developed in Calcutta. The relations between Indians and the British were not only much less strained, there actually existed a common interest between the two. Furthermore, the multi-ethnic character of the two cities resulted in diametrically opposed methods of articulating business interests, the one fragmented, the other cohesive. Indian capital developed much earlier in Bombay than in Calcutta, and it was more widely spread among the different communities within Bombay. Furthermore, Bombay businessmen as a group were more highly educated and more politically and socially advanced than their counterparts in Calcutta. Finally, with some exceptions, the politics of the associations in Bombay took place between, not within, organizations. They were multi-ethnic and not concentrated in one community.

Both of the first major business associations which came to dom-

[24] The rift between G. D. Birla and Sir Badridas Goenka was healed in 1939, and Goenka was made President of the Indian Chamber of Commerce, Calcutta, in 1941. Goenka was even given the honor of presidency of the FICCI in 1945.

[25] Bharat Chamber, *Golden Jubilee*, pp. 7–8.

inate the Bombay scene were centered around the cotton textile industry. The earliest, the Bombay Millowners Association, was founded in 1875 to protest British tariff policy. It represented the major European, Parsi, Gujarati, and Muslim millowners of the presidency. The second was the Indian Merchants Chamber and Bureau, which was founded in 1907 to represent the trading interests of the large number of Gujarati cotton piece goods traders of Bombay. Its membership was similar in origin to the membership of the Marwari Chamber of Commerce. It differed in that it was more concerned with promoting Indian, rather than foreign, cloth. The Bombay Millowners Association, primarily concerned with the textile industry, followed an extremely independent policy in defending its interests. It was much less politicized than its rival, the Indian Merchants Chamber, which enjoyed both the advantages and disadvantages of its broadly based membership. Although the Indian Merchants Chamber eventually gained the support of prominent millowners, bankers, financiers, and export-import merchants, its various members were divided over political strategy. The leadership of the Indian Merhcants Chamber for its first twenty-five years was dominated by influential industrialists who represented "the largest amount of capital and enterprise in western India." [26] Their control was challenged in the 1930s by a pro-Congress group representing small traders, shroffs, stockbrokers, and insurance interests in the city. The result was the development of a party system within the chamber, the remnants of which survive even today.

Through their own associations,[27] through their encouragement and financial assistance of the creation of the Indian National Congress, and through the creation of an Indian Industrial Conference which met annually at the time of the Congress sessions to discuss economic problems facing the country, Bombay business was the first to speak out for purely Indian economic interests and to attack British economic policy in India. Thus Bombay business at first was very closely allied with the new Congress movement. However, as the Congress moved from its early moderate, constitutional stage, it became more militant and identified with Hindu revival. As it became less of a pressure group making demands on the British government and more of a political force, Bombay business grew hesitant and divided. The division increased to the point of significantly affecting

[26] *The Times of India* (Bombay), November 11, 1932.

[27] In addition to the Indian Merchants Chamber and the Bombay Millowners Association, Bombay also had Muslim, Marwari, and Marathi chambers reflecting religious, caste, and language cleavages in the city.

associational politics after the emergence of Gandhi and the adoption by the Congress of his program of civil disobedience.

Gandhi, the son of a Gujarati Bania family, was venerated by the vast majority of Gujarati traders in Bombay who wished to openly support the Congress. However, the larger industrialists and traders, and especially the Parsis among them, wished to keep both the business community and its business associations aloof from Congress politics. The Congress civil disobedience movements of 1920–1921 and 1930–1933 were, therefore, accompanied by a rift in the chamber which resulted in resignation of many top industrialists and the development of a pattern of party politics within the chamber.

The first Congress civil disobedience campaign took place in the early 1920s. Its profound impact on Bombay business politics was most openly expressed in the Indian Merchants Chamber through rank and file pressure at the annual meetings of the chamber. Following the Nagpur session of the Congress in 1920, a rank and file movement was begun in the Indian Merchants Chamber to commit the chamber to the Congress program of noncooperation. A requisition was submitted which demanded a discussion of the chamber's attitude toward the boycott of councils, one of the items in the Congress program. A resolution was moved from the floor which would have committed the chamber to refusing to send its representatives to the councils as a symbol of the chamber's commitment to the Congress cause. The president ruled the resolution out of order, but this ruling did not end the affair. Shortly thereafter, the pro-Gandhian group in the chamber was presented with an irresistible opportunity when the chamber president, Lalji Naranji, made the tactical blunder of agreeing to associate himself and the chamber with the visit of the Prince of Wales to India in the autumn of 1921.[28] Gandhi and the Congress had not only opposed the visit but used it as the occasion to proclaim a nationwide hartal. Rank and file pressure within the chamber took the form of a requisition which demanded the convening of a general meeting to rescind the apparently pro-British resolution of the committee of the chamber to present an address of welcome to the Prince of Wales on behalf of the chamber. The resolution this time was pushed to a vote, after a bitter and protracted debate. The vote by a show of hands was so close that a petition was filed to conduct a full poll of the members on the issue. The poll produced a tie vote of 111 for and 111 against, with 55 invalid votes. However,

[28] Frank Moraes, *Sir Purshotamdas Thakurdas* (Bombay: Asia Publishing House, 1967), pp. 40–41.

the chairman, casting his vote against the resolution, declared the motion defeated. His decision provoked an open rift in the chamber which threatened to destroy it. The issue was defused when a movement was begun by some of the members to depoliticize the chamber's activities by focusing on economic and not political activity. As part of the compromise, Sir Purshotamdas Thakurdas was elected president.[29]

Sir Purshotamdas Thakurdas emerged from a Gujarati Bania family and had been educated as a lawyer. He became a highly successful cotton trader in his uncle's firm of Narandas Rajaram and Company.[30] At the age of twenty-eight he had been selected by Sir Manmohandas Ramji, the founder of the Indian Merchants Chamber, to become the organization's first vice president, because his firm "rates very high in the trade." [31] Although he was a caste fellow of Gandhi, he "did not generally agree with Gandhiji's politics" [32] and was opposed to his tactics in particular.[33] On the issue of the Prince of Wales visit, however, he had, while in London, advised the British government against it on the grounds that the political temper of the country made the gesture ill conceived.[34] Like many of the big Bombay industrialists, Thakurdas did not believe in mixing politics and business, wishing to keep the Indian Merchants Chamber free from political involvement so that it could concentrate on representing the interests of the business community. "So far as the commercial community was concerned," he once said, "in my youth, I was instructed by elder businessmen in Bombay that it was not for a businessman to bother about politics and we had the example of an eminent man . . . the late Mr. Jamsetjee Tata, who, till the last day of his life, abstained from political activities and gatherings of any kind." [35] Not that Thakurdas was politically inactive. In fact, he was one of the major spokesmen for Indian business in the central assembly. He fought for the rights of the Indian commercial community and was committed to the principle of swaraj, although he thought it best obtained by a process of negotiation between the British and all Indian concerned interests.[36] Thus, while in the assembly, he acted as an independent nationalist spokesman for business and joined no political party.

A large number of big industrialists in Bombay shared these views

[29] Indian Merchants Chamber, *Fifty Years 1907–1957* (Bombay: Indian Merchants Chamber, 1958), p. 16.

[30] Moraes, *Sir Purshotamdas Thakurdas*, pp. 1–24.

[31] *Ibid.*, p. 40.

[32] *Ibid.*, p. 203.

[33] *Ibid.*, p. 202.

[34] *Ibid.*, pp. 40–41.

[35] *Ibid.*, p. 114.

[36] *Ibid.*, p. 115.

which, for the most part, received expression through the Bombay Millowners Association. The chief spokesman for these interests was Sir Homi Mody, a Parsi who was associated with the House of Tata. Mody served as president of the Bombay Millowners Association in 1927 and from 1929 to 1934, and as president of the Indian Merchants Chamber in 1928. He was also a member of the committee of the Indian Merchants Chamber for many years. Perhaps even more strongly than Thakurdas, Mody rejected the Gandhian Congress "whose political philosophy and methods the constitutionalist in him could never stomach." [37] As a representative of the Bombay Millowners Association in the assembly, Mody had to steer a middle course: "he could neither quarrel too much with the government" because of the industry's desire to retain the protection which the government had provided it against British goods, "nor could he completely alienate the nationalists, some of whom do not exactly love Bombay millowners." [38]

Men like Sir Purshotamdas Thakurdas, Sir Homi Mody, Sir Chunilal V. Mehta (a cousin of Thakurdas), Sir Fhiroze Sethna M. A. Master, and Walchand Hirachand dominated Indian Merchants Chamber politics and were typical representatives of the dominant business interest in Bombay. Despite the pressures from the small traders, these men tried to keep the chamber out of politics so that it could concentrate on representing the interests of the business community. However, they succeeded in doing so only during periods of political inactivity. With the second civil disobedience campaign of 1930–1933, their moderation was almost completely overcome by a new group of pro-Congress insurgents.

The first civil disobedience campaign in 1920–1921 had resulted in pressure from the rank and file for an active commitment to noncooperation through the annual meeting of the chamber. This pressure was successfully resisted by the leadership, but tactics invoked by the call for a second civil disobedience movement were more radical. This time the pro-Congress elements decided to capture control of the chamber leadership by organizing themselves to gain control of the executive committee of the Indian Merchants Chamber committee.[39] In the

[37] D. R. Mankekar, *Homi Mody: A Many Splendored Life* (Bombay: Popular Prakashan, 1968), p. 82.

[38] *Ibid.*, p. 83.

[39] The major source of information concerning the 1932 political conflict in the Indian Merchants Chamber has been drawn from a series of newspaper accounts in which the two groups exchanged public criticism of each other. As far as the election is concerned, the old dominant group charged that, in January 1931 at the time of the Indian Merchants Chamber election, a new group was able to come to power by using illegitimate means. "The secret of the group's coming in the open

January 1931 elections of the Indian Merchants Chamber, the insurgents succeeded in winning a block of twenty-five seats in the forty man executive of the chamber, and then they began to function as an organized group within the committee. They would meet in advance of all executive committee meetings to consider the agenda and decide on a position. Then they would attend the regular meeting of the executive and vote as a bloc on critical issues.[40] The key members of this group were J. C. Setalvad, A. D. Shroff, Manu Subedar, Ratilal M. Gandhi, K. S. Ramchandra Iyer, and Gordhandas G. Morarji. At first the group was known by various names, but eventually it became known as the Nationalist group. The group publicly admitted to functioning, from 1931 onward, as a compact party. Its purpose was to chalk out lines of policy which would improve on methods which "appear to have been established by the continual control of the chamber visiting in a small clique." [41]

For almost two years the Nationalist group carried on a running battle with the old leadership, led by Thakurdas, who dubbed themselves the "old Nationalists" before the crisis finally came to a head. The process of compromise through which unity had been preserved proved too difficult to maintain under the extraordinary political conditions of the day. The rift finally broke into the open on October 31, 1932,[42] pushed to the breaking point by the resumption of civil disobedience in India in January of 1932.

On the morning of January 4, 1932, the government of India had attempted to head off a new wave of Congress agitation by arresting and confining without trial Gandhi and Vallabhbhai Patel, president of the Congress. The government simultaneously issued four ordinances giving far-reaching powers to the authorities to suppress all political activity in India. Nevertheless, the arrest of Gandhi led to the resump-

---

election two years ago was the defective system of voting for committee members. Here blank forms are sent to members to be ticked and returned to the chamber through post or otherwise . . . instead of the voting by ballot by personally calling at the chamber's office. . . ." It was charged that the group, taking advantage of the political turmoil of the time, collected large numbers of blank forms from the bazaar merchants and other members of the Indian Merchants Chamber and filled them in at leisure, thus insuring their election (*The Times of India*, Bombay, November 11, 1932). These charges were partially confirmed in a *Times of India* editorial, which charged that the coterie of politically-minded individuals were able to gain control as a result of the way in which the committee was selected. The editorial argued that the provision for committee selection did not adequately represent the large concern and thus control came to rest with the numerically strong (November 8, 1932).

[40] *The Times of India* (Bombay), November 11, 1932.

[41] *The Times of India* (Bombay), November 17, 1932.

[42] *The Times of India* (Bombay), November 11, 1932.

tion of civil disobedience which, although begun in 1930, had been suspended pending a possible negotiated political settlement with the British through a series of round table conferences.

Bombay business reacted in various ways to the events of January 4, 1932. Even before the resumption of civil disobedience, the Bombay Millowners Association met privately with Gandhi and Patel and informed the Congress leaders that depressed economic conditions and problems in the industry would prevent them from supporting a resumption of civil disobedience.[43] Once the movement had begun, British intelligence confirmed that the millowners in general opposed the boycott and refused to support it financially.[44]

Specialized organizations representing Gujarati traders—such as the Indian Piece Goods Merchants Association, Bombay Cotton Brokers Association, the Native Share and Stock Brokers Association, and the Bombay Shroffs Association—were incensed by the arrest of the venerated Mahatma.[45] They passed resolutions advocating the boycott of goods from those countries which were "opposed to India's national aspirations," they advocated boycotting the shipping, banking, and insurance houses of those countries,[46] and they were reported to be providing financial and other aid to the Congress movement.[47] These groups were all members of the Indian Merchants Chamber.

The reaction of the Indian Merchants Chamber was mixed. It reflected the internal struggle that was taking place in the committee between the Nationalist group of small traders and the Thakurdas group of industrialists. For the most part the resolutions passed by the Indian Merchants Chamber were obvious compromises worked out between the two sides. Thus, in responding to the arrest of Gandhi, the chamber president, a member of the Thakurdas group, issued a statement which deplored the viceroy's refusal to meet with Gandhi prior to his arrest, yet expressed their inability to participate in the movement or to pronounce judgment on its advisability. At the same time the statement assured the Congress of the group's support in obtaining full self-government and of the movement's program of excluding foreign cloth and promoting hand spun and hand woven khadi.[48]

[43] Mankekar, *Homi Mody*, p. 101.
[44] Government of India, Home Department, Political, *Fortnightly Report on the Internal Political Situation*, first half, January 1932 (New Delhi: Home Department, Government of India, 1932), hereafter cited as Government of India, *Fortnightly Report*.
[45] Government of India, *Fortnightly Report*, second half, February 1932.
[46] Government of India, *Fortnightly Report*, first half, January 1932.
[47] *Ibid.*
[48] *Ibid.*

When the full committee met in early February, however, a sterner resolution was passed protesting the arrest of Gandhi and the propagation of prohibitive ordinances and proposing the calling of a public meeting of chamber members and other commercial bodies to endorse the protest. Before actually taking this action, the committee decided to submit the resolution to the government to ascertain whether its passage would be unlawful. When the Bombay government refused to preaudit such a resolution,[49] the dissidents in the chamber decided to hold the meeting anyway. The Thakurdas group responded by refusing to attend the meeting, and the president of the chamber refused to preside.[50] The meeting was never held. The Bombay government issued ordinances preventing such a gathering.[51] Again crisis was avoided.

The struggle over political strategy within the chamber continued throughout the year. Finally, on October 31, 1932, a resolution of censure was introduced by Ratilal M. Gandhi, a pro-Congress trader, and supported by J. C. Setalvad, A. D. Shroff, Manu Subedar and several others. The resolution was directed against Sir Purshotamdas Thakurdas for his decision to accept an invitation from the British to attend a small scale round table conference, an action which was interpreted as a violation of the Congress policy of noncooperation. The resolution said: "The committee of the Indian Merchants Chamber have learnt with regret that Sir Purshotamdas Thakurdas has accepted the invitation to attend the Third Round Table Conference, and entirely disapprove of his action." [52] The resolution went on to state that "neither Sir Purshotamdas Thakurdas nor any other person has the right or authority to speak in the name of the commercial community of India." [53] In pushing the resolution of censure, the Nationalist group refused to accept any compromise.[54]

The action of the Nationalist group produced bitter criticism from the Bombay press. An editorial in the *Times of India* said that, instead of accepting a compromise resolution, "some lesser lights in the chamber" were determined to attack Thakurdas "in what can only be described as a spirit of petty vindictiveness." Moreover "they refused to listen to the advice of many of the senior members of the chamber . . . and pushed their vendetta to a successful vote by weight of numbers." [55]

[49] Government of India, *Fortnightly Report*, first half, February, 1932.
[50] *Ibid.*
[51] Government of India, *Fortnightly Report*, second half, February 1932.
[52] Indian Merchants Chamber, *Annual Report for 1932* (Bombay: Indian Merchants Chamber, 1932), p. 61.
[53] *Ibid.*
[54] *The Times of India* (Bombay), November 1, 1932.
[55] Editorial in *The Times of India* (Bombay), November 1, 1932.

The significance of the event, said another editorial,[56] "in which a body of leading businessmen, who represent great indigenous industrial and trading interests and who have really made the Indian Merchants Chamber what it is today, were overthrown by a group of politically-minded lesser lights . . ." cannot be lost on the Bombay business community.

The censure vote led to an open split when thirteen influential senior members of the committee, including the president, resigned from the chamber. They charged that the work of the committee was being conducted on party lines and that decisions were being made by a clique before the committee formally met.[57] This action was followed by threats to establish a new chamber.[58] The Nationalist group called the charges against them "unwarranted allegations," insisting that their action had been in keeping with the policy set down by the Federation of Indian Chambers of Commerce and Industry and that all efforts to seek a compromise had failed. They chided the Thakurdas group for not taking their case to the general body of the chamber, a procedure they were safe enough in recommending, because the Nationalists knew they controlled the majority.[59] When those who had resigned refused to withdraw their resignations, the Nationalist group coopted new members to the committee and elected a new president.

The Thakurdas group now had two alternatives: either establish the threatened new chamber or try to recapture control of the Indian Merchants Chamber. Choosing the latter course of action, they began mobilizing support for the Indian Merchants Chamber elections to be held late in 1932. There ensued a prodigious effort on the part of two competing elites to mobilize rank and file support. The great test of strength, however, never took place. Instead, when both sides indicated a willingness to compromise, Sir Manmohandas Ramji, the founder of the chamber, was persuaded to come out of semiretirement to become president of the chamber. He was charged with the task of drawing up a compromise slate of committee members representing the two groups.[60]

The compromise proved short-lived. Again the Nationalist group

[56] *The Times of India* (Bombay), November 8, 1932.

[57] *Ibid.*

[58] *The Times of India* (Bombay), November 11, 1932.

[59] *The Times of India* (Bombay), November 17, 1932.

[60] Indian Merchants Chamber, *Annual Report for 1932*, pp. 55–56. Ramji, however, resigned shortly after his election as president of the Indian Merchants Chamber as a result of a conflict with the committee over the Lees-Mody Pact. See Indian Merchants Chamber, *Annual Report of 1933*, p. xxxvi; Mankekar, *Homi Mody*, pp. 67–81.

succeeded in gaining control of the chamber, and again some of the older members drifted away from the chamber. Those who remained behind organized a minority group which eventually became known as the Democratic group. The Democratic group had learned its lessons well. They functioned as an organized opposition, with their own constitution and rules. However, the Nationalist group retained control of the Indian Merchants Chamber until independence, when it too broke up. So many of its members thereupon joined the Democratic group that the two-party system in the chamber came to an end. The Democratic group became the only organized group in the chamber.

Membership in the Democratic group is open to any member of the Indian Merchants Chamber with a "democratic and national outlook." The group has its own managing committee, which is elected at the ordinary general meeting. It also publishes its own annual report. And even though it is not recognized by the secretariat of the chamber as having any existence at all, the Democratic group has an independent office in the chamber. Its numerous stated objectives notwithstanding, the chief function of the Democratic group is to control the elections to the Indian Merchants Chamber. This intent is clearly spelled out in the group's constitution, where the managing committee of the group is given "the power to approve or disapprove the nomination of the candidates for election to the committee of the chamber or to any other committee, council, or public body to which the chamber may be entitled to elect its representatives." In addition, the constitution states that "any member desirous of contesting any such election (that is, to the chamber) shall intimate his intentions to the managing committee, who shall have the right either to authorize the member to contest such an election or otherwise," and "any member who acts in contravention of this rule shall be liable to such disciplinary action including expulsion from the group as the members of the group assembled in an extraordinary general meeting may decide." [61]

Within the Democratic group, there are still those with strong Congress party sentiments along with others who have slowly drifted from noncommitment into opposition. The pro-Congress party faction is led by Babubhai Chinai, an old Congress party MP and chief lieutenant of S. K. Patil, the Congress party political boss of Bombay. When the Congress party split in 1969, Babubhai Chinai and S. K. Patil both remained with the Congress party organization faction which opposed

[61] See Constitution of the Democratic Group (Bombay: The Democratic Group, n.d.).

the continued stewardship of Mrs. Indira Gandhi as prime minister. The leader of the Democratic group was the late Murarji Vaidya, who led a pro-Swatantra party group in the chamber. These two groups, or subgroups, draw up a common slate of candidates for all offices in the Indian Merchants Chamber and thus dominate the electoral process. The compromise slate invariably provides a group parity on the executive committee and alternation from year to year in the selection of a president. The Indian Merchants Chamber has thus moved from a two-party system to a one-party system with two factions.

Thus, business politics in Bombay reflected the multi-ethnic character of the region, conflicting interests between trade and industry, and divergent views within the business community toward the Congress party and the nationalist movement. The conflict had caste and community overtones, but it also revealed the divergence between the industrial pioneers of Bombay and the rank and file traders and merchants. The majority of Parsi and Gujarati industrialists sought to exclude politics from the activities of the Indian Merchants Chamber so that it could concentrate on its primary objective of representing business interests. The small traders, shopkeepers, shroffs, and native stockbrokers and insurance brokers sought to commit the chamber to public support of the Gandhian Congress. The ensuing struggle in Bombay, like the conflicts within the Calcutta business community, was to have significant repercussions on the internal politics of the FICCI as well.

The Rise of Indian Business Associations in Madras

Just as the development of business associations in Calcutta centered around the Marwari community and in Bombay around the Parsis and Gujaratis, so the development of business associations in Madras centered around the traditional, indigenous south Indian banking community of Nattukottai Chettiars. The Nattukottai Chettiars, a branch of the Chettiar community deriving from a region of southern Madras known as Chettinad, began as landowners who branched out into banking and later into industry.[62] Among the most prominent Chettiar families of Madras and leader of the Nattukottai Chettiar community in the early twentieth century was the family of Muthiah Chettiar. Muthiah Chettiar had two sons, Rajah Sir Annamalai Chettiar and Dewan Bahadur Ramaswami Chettiar, both of whom became ac-

[62] George B. Baldwin, *Industrial Growth in South India* (New York: Free Press, 1959), pp. 262–264.

tive in business and community affairs. Annamalai Chettiar, in particular, became extremely prominent as a philanthropist and as founder of Annamalai University, which still bears his name. In gratitude for his donation of twenty lakhs to start the university, the British granted him the hereditary title of Rajah.[63]

Annamalai Chettiar and his brother Ramaswami came to play an important role in the finance of Madras when, in 1907, they joined with a group of leading Madras citizens to found the Indian Bank, the first indigenous joint stock bank in Madras. Prior to the founding of the Indian Bank, modern banking in Madras was controlled by British banks and by a few British trading firms with a sideline in banking. Indian banking, meanwhile, rested largely in the hands of Chettiars who functioned as indigenous bankers. In 1906, two leading trading firms of Madras, Arbuthnot's and Binny's, were faced by a crash. On October 26, 1906, Arbuthnot's declared insolvency and suspended payments. Although Binny's very nearly followed suit, it somehow survived the crash. In response to these troubling financial events, the Indian elite of Madras assembled to discuss the need for establishing a "native bank in Madras." The creation of the Indian Bank followed.[64] Later a rival bank, which was called the Indian Oversea Bank, was created by a relative of Muthiah Chettiar.[65]

The formation of the Indian Bank is significant to the study of Indian business associations, because it also heralded the imminent founding of the Southern India Chamber of Commerce (SICC). Eventually the bank and its leadership came to play a prominent role in the chamber.

On May 29, 1909, the rising tide of political and economic nationalism, which had led to the formation of the Indian Bank in Madras and two years earlier to the Indian Merchants Chamber in Bombay, surged again. A notice was sent out in Tamil, Telugu, and English calling for the foundation of an Indian chamber. (A British chamber had existed in Madras since 1836.) Forty-seven people responded and the meeting, held at the Indian Bank, was presided over by the Honorable Shri P. Thyagaraya Chettiar, a leading Chettiar politician who later became one of the co-founders of the Justice party.[66] Dr. Rajah

[63] *Ibid.*, p. 262.

[64] The Indian Bank Limited, *The Indian Bank Limited Golden Jubilee: 1907–1957* (Madras: Associated Printers, 1957), pp. 13–16.

[65] Baldwin, *Industrial Growth*, p. 263.

[66] The Justice party was a non-Brahman party which sought to end Brahman dominance of Madras politics. The party received strong support from south Indian trading communities and for a time was anti-Congress.

Sir Muthiah Chettiar of Chettinad, the son of Annamalai Chettiar, came to play a dominant role in the chamber, representing the Muthiah family.[67] In addition, two members of the Indian Bank were chosen as provisional secretaries of the new chamber. As the official history of the chamber describes it, "From the choice of the first honorable secretaries of the chamber dates a connection between the Southern India Chamber [of Commerce] and the Indian Bank, a connection that is unbroken, cordial, and beneficial." [68]

Because the SICC was the south Indian business community's response to Indian nationalism, it attempted to represent all groups in the province—Muslims, Tamils, Telugus, and non-south Indian business. Special care, in fact, was taken to insure that the Muslim community of the city received due recognition, and a Muslim was elected president periodically. Chamber politics, however, were dominated by the Chettiar community, in particular the Muthiah Chettiar family. This Chettiar dominance, as well as the growing expression of latent linguistic, regional, caste, and community differences, eventually led to the fragmentation of the Madras business community and to the creation of a multiplicity of competing chambers in the city.

The earliest groups to found their own chambers were the Telugus and the Muslims. The Telugus of Madras came together in August of 1928 to form the Andhra Chamber of Commerce. Its membership was confined to speakers of Telugu, and the chamber became a strong champion of the cause of a separate Andhra state.[69] The increasing expansion of subnational loyalties was accompanied by a greater emphasis on communal differences, which led to the creation of a Muslim chamber.[70]

The formation of a separate chamber to represent the non-south Indian business communities grew out of a split within the SICC. Along with the British, Madras had attracted its share of Marwari and Gujarati entrepreneurs. Among the most prominent non-south Indian business houses in Madras was Kothari and Sons, founded in 1918 by C. M. Kothari. He was a Gujarati trader who started the first indigenous share, stock, and exchange brokerage firm in Madras and later

[67] Eugene F. Irschick, *Politics and Social Conflict in South India: The Non-Brahman Movement and Tamil Separatism, 1916–1929* (Berkeley and Los Angeles: University of California Press, 1969), p. 176.

[68] Southern India Chamber of Commerce, *Southern India Chamber of Commerce Jubilee: 1910–1960* (Madras: Commercial Printing and Publishing House, 1960), p. 3.

[69] Andhra Chamber of Commerce, *Andhra Chamber of Commerce Souvenir, 1963* (Madras: Andhra Chamber of Commerce, 1963).

[70] The Muslim Chamber in Madras is now known as the National Chamber.

moved from finance into industry.[71] C. M. Kothari became active in SICC politics and was also a prominent member of the FICCI, where he was given strong backing by Purshotamdas Thakurdas, who was the uncle of Kothari's wife.[72] In 1944, C. M. Kothari had been selected vice president of the SICC, and by tradition he should have succeeded to the presidency. His election to the presidency, however, was blocked by Dr. Alagappa Chettiar. Kothari's failure to be elected president of the SICC resulted in his withdrawal from the chamber and in the founding of his own organization—the Hindustan Chamber of Commerce—in 1945. The Kothari family played the dominant role in the politics of the Hindustan Chamber of Commerce, which came to represent non-south Indian business interests in Madras. Because the Hindustan chamber developed into a large, well-financed, and effective organization, it also served as an effective platform to support Kothari's activities in the FICCI.

Concurrently with Kothari's withdrawal from the SICC, another dispute was being carried on between the Chettiars and another Tamil community, the Mudaliars. These differences led to the establishment of the Tamil Chamber of Commerce. Although it took on a linguistic designation, it was, unlike the Andhra chamber, a product of underlying caste conflict between Chettiars and Mudaliars.

Thus Madras started with a single unified business association dedicated to minimizing caste, community, language, and regional differences, only to end up with a multiplicity of chambers reflecting precisely these differences. Since independence, this multiplicity has been somewhat overcome through a process of overlapping membership. The Muslim chamber and the Tamil chamber are almost defunct, but the Madras chamber, Andhra chamber, and the Hindustan chamber continue to function. Within the SICC, the old dominance of the Muthiah family has been successfully challenged by the highly successful Murugappa House, which has developed into one of the most rapidly expanding industrial families in the south.[73]

Throughout India, in all the major commercial centers, the growth of political and economic nationalism drove a wedge between indigenous and foreign capital. This resulted in efforts by leaders of the emerging Indian industrial elite to organize modern associations to counteract the influence of British business by mobilizing indigenous business and providing it with an effective voice. Major Indian cham-

[71] J. Walter Thompson Company Limited, *Kothari and Sons* (Madras: Associated Printers, n.d.).

[72] Thakurdas made C. M. Kothari president of the FICCI in 1951.

[73] Baldwin, *Industrial Growth*, p. 263.

bers were founded in Calcutta, Bombay, and Madras. In each case, they came to be dominated by those communities which had moved from trade to industry—the Marwaris, Gujaratis, Parsis, and Chettiars. However dedicated they might at times have been to the ideal of representing the entire Indian business community, conflicts developed sooner or later in each center. Thus, the fragmented nature of Indian business received organizational form through the establishment of independent chambers reflecting caste, language, community, and regional differences. When a national federation was eventually created, the persistence of the almost irreconcilable factions tended to inhibit organizational development and the articulation of business demands.

VIII

THE ORGANIZATION OF INDIAN CAPITAL: THE FICCI

Although the creation of an apex structure to articulate Indian business interests of national scope was dependent on the development and solvency of regional chambers, the mechanisms of the nationalist movement facilitated all-India contacts among Indian businessmen before the creation of Assocham or the FICCI. The emergence of the Indian industrial elite was concurrent with the rise of the Westernized, educated middle class, and so there was at first a substantial convergence between their interests. The Indian National Congress was their joint creation, and the early Congress party leaders demanded changes in the economic as well as the political policies of the British raj. As the nationalist movement began to grow in size and appeal, however, it became so concerned with predominantly political issues that the business elite decided to establish an autonomous organization for the purpose of pressing their economic demands on the British government. Thus, unlike other sectors of Indian society like labor and kisans or peasantry who were mobilized by the Congress leadership for political ends, business organized itself, thus becoming one of the few autonomous structures for the articulation of interests in India.

The creation of an all-India organization to represent Indian business interests was not easy because, as we have seen, the emerging business elite was an extremely heterogeneous group. Calcutta Muslims, Bengalis, and Marwaris were divided along religious and linguistic-cultural lines. And within the Marwari community, divergence between those who were closely tied to British business and the nationalistically inclined emerging industrial class continued to widen. In Bombay, a clash of interests existed between the politically neutral, large British, Parsi, Gujarati, or Muslim millowners and the smaller pro-Congress traders, shroffs, native stockbrokers, and insurance groups. In Madras, the rise of business associations involved clashes between northern immigrants and southern natives and among native south Indian castes. Considering the nature of Indian society and the fact that the Indian business elite had not reached the stage of differentiation in which a true national business class could exist, the remarkable development was the ability to create any national organization rather than the conflicts which accompanied its founding process and continue to affect its internal politics. Despite the obstacles and the setbacks, a group of organizational pioneers had fought to establish a national apex structure to promote their common interests and combat British economic interests. This structure, intended for cooperation, has often served as another arena for conflict, but it has also provided the framework for the mobilization of the business community and thus has aided in the development of a truly national business elite.

The Origins of the FICCI

Indian capital prior to World War I was primarily concentrated in Bombay. And so the earliest efforts to form an all-India body originated with leading Bombay industrialists and, as I have remarked, was closely connected with the nationalist movement. In the early days of the Congress, Congress leaders fought for tariffs to protect the infant textile industry of Bombay and advocated that the government of India follow a positive policy of industrial development.[1] The earliest national efforts to call attention to India's nascent industry can be traced to the Congress decision in 1901 to hold an industrial exhibit in conjunction with its annual meeting in Calcutta. Exhibits to focus attention on Indian development were subsequently held at Ahmedabad in 1902, Madras in 1903, and Bombay in 1904. The success of the 1904 industrial exhibit in Bombay gave rise to the idea of holding an industrial conference along with the annual meeting of the Indian National Congress. The first Indian industrial conference met in Benares, in December of 1905, under the presidency of Ramesh Chandra Dutt, a leading political figure in Bengal and former president of the Congress. The conference passed several resolutions urging the government to establish technical schools, encourage industry, and foster the use of Indian over foreign goods. Committees to study and encourage industry were established in Calcutta, Bombay, Madras, Allahabad, Lahore, and Nagpur. They included outstanding businessmen such as Dinshaw Wacha, Sir Vithaldas D. Thackersey, and Sir Lallubhai Samaldas from Bombay, Pandit Madan Mohan Malaviya from Allahabad, Lala Lajpatrai and Lala Harkishen Lal from Lahore, and Rao Bahadur Mudholkar from Nagpur.[2]

[1] P. C. Ghosh, *The Development of the Indian National Congress, 1892–1906* (Calcutta: Firma K. L. Mukhopadhyay, 1960), pp. 28–41.

[2] FICCI, *Silver Jubilee Souvenir: 1927–1951* (Bombay: India Printing Works, 1951), p. 7.

Just as Bombay business had been the earliest to support the young Congress, it was among Bombay businessmen that the need for a separate and more vigorous organization to represent business interests was most keenly apparent. The leadership for the establishment of such a vehicle was provided by the newly formed Indian Merchants Chamber and Bureau, which convened the Indian Commercial Congress in 1915 in Bombay. The Honorable Sir Fazulbhoy Currimbhoy, a leading Bombay millowner presided, and Dinshaw Wacha, a Parsi, acted as chairman of the reception committee. After Currimbhoy had stressed, in his presidential address, the need for an apex body to represent Indian business, the group adopted a resolution approving the motion to establish an Associative Chamber of Commerce and approved a draft outline of its constitution. Although a committee consisting largely of Bombay businessmen was empowered to take all necessary steps to establish the new associative chamber,[3] provincial jealousies and divergent interests prevented the resolution from becoming a reality at that time. The new associative chamber never came into being.[4]

Attempts to establish a permanent all-India business association were not renewed until after World War I. By then the war had stimulated the Indian business community to develop and diversify, national policy had become more important, and British business had joined forces to create its own apex organization—the Associated Chambers of Commerce. These changes gave renewed impetus to those who wished to create a national organization to represent Indian business. The first step came in 1920, when the Indian Industrial Conference and the Indian Commercial Congress merged into the Indian Industrial and Commercial Congress. That development had been prompted by a desire to eliminate duplication of effort, as well as by a feeling that the Indian commercial community was not sufficiently vocal and the realization that the political tempo of Congress sessions had all but eliminated time for discussion of economic problems.[5] In 1926, at its third annual session, the Indian Industrial and Commercial Congress passed a resolution to dissolve itself and create a nationwide associative organization. The name finally chosen for this organization was the Federation of Indian Chambers of Commerce and Industry, which came into being in 1927.

The prime movers behind the creation of an all-India federation of Indian business were G. D. Birla, the leader of the emergent Marwari industrial interests in Calcutta, and Purshotamdas Thakurdas, a cot-

[3] *Ibid.*, p. 19.
[4] *Ibid.*, pp. 231–232.
[5] *Ibid.*, p. 10.

ton trader and leading figure in the Bombay business community. Both Birla and Thakurdas believed that, unless Indian business organized itself effectively, the government of India would be guided solely by the views of the recently created apex body of European business, the Associated Chamber of Commerce. In the words of Purshotamdas Thakurdas, "The original object of starting the federation was to get a proper foothold before the executive at Delhi, so that the claims of Indian commerce and industry would not be at a disadvantage in comparison with those of European interests." [6] It was this same concern which prompted federation leaders to go all out to get the viceroy to inaugurate its annual session, as he had for the Associated Chambers of Commerce. As Purshotamdas Thakurdas said,

> It was suggested by several that unless we got the viceroy to inaugurate our annual meetings, as he used to inaugurate those of the Associated Chambers of Commerce, representations of the federation would not command much respect in the eyes of the central and provincial governments. Sir Geoffrey Corbett, the secretary of the Commerce Department at that time, agreed to recommend to Lord Irwin, who was the viceroy then, to attend the session. The meeting was held accordingly and was a great success. The Clive Street people did not like the idea of the viceroy coming to the federation meeting, but Lord Irwin's attendance at our second meeting had this effect that the federation's views carried considerable weight with India Office.[7]

In order to launch the federation, Thakurdas joined G. D. Birla, Shri Ram of Delhi, and Fakirji Cowasji of Karachi in pledging fifteen thousand rupees each to the new venture. An additional Rs 2,500 was put up by Devi Prasad Khaitan, a highly educated Marwari lawyer and chief lieutenant of G. D. Birla. Khaitan handled the organizational and constitutional problems.[8] His role was best indicated by Shri Ram, who once remarked: "If Sir Purshotamdas Thakurdas and Mr. Birla are the parents of this body, there is no doubt that Mr. Khaitan has been the wet nurse of the federation." [9]

The creation of the FICCI in 1927, as a permanent body to represent

[6] *Ibid.*, p. 184.
[7] *Ibid.*, pp. 183–184.
[8] Frank Moraes, *Sir Purshotamdas Thakurdas* (Bombay: Asia Publishing House, 1967), p. 42; FICCI, *Silver Jubilee Souvenir*, pp. 183–184.
[9] FICCI, *Proceedings of the Tenth Annual Meeting, 1937* (Delhi: FICCI, 1937), p. 136. The federation added the word industry to its official title in 1929.

the interests of Indian capital, was in many ways a remarkable achievement. The federation came into being despite innumerable family, community, and regional rivalries and was able to survive despite the development of strong conflicting interests and differences over political strategy and tactics. Thus, even though the new federation has never really represented *all* of the Indian business communities, it was clear that the new apex chamber, with its twenty-four members drawn from Bombay, Calcutta, Madras, Lahore, Karachi, Delhi, and Ahmedabad, was the most representative Indian business association in the country. Furthermore, it marked the beginning of sustained associational activity at the all-India level. The FICCI became an important forum for the expression of Indian views on all economic policies affecting the subcontinent.

Although the leadership of the FICCI worked hard to give the new organization an all-India character, the federation from the very beginning came to reflect the family, caste, regional, and political differences that divided the Indian business community as a whole. Despite the creation of a tradition of rotating the presidency among the major regional centers of Bombay, Calcutta, Madras, and Delhi, with occasional resort to some of the smaller centers, and despite the attempt to ensure regional representation in the executive committee, it was clear from the very beginning that for all the sprinkling of Parsi, Muslim, Bengali, and Chettiar names, the federation was actually dominated by the Calcutta Marwaris and Bombay Gujaratis.[10]

Thakurdas succeeded in persuading Sir Dinshaw M. Petit, the famous Bombay Parsi millowner, to become the first president of the FICCI. But the Bombay Millowners Association, the premier organization representing the most important Indian-controlled industry in the country, refused to join so broadly based an organization. The millowners were further alienated by the presence, in the FICCI leadership elite, of such men as G. D. Birla, Shri Ram, Padampat Singhania, and Kasturbhai Lalbhai, all of whom were known for their strong nationalist views and pro-Congress sympathies.

Thus, in the early days of the FICCI, the committee roster was conspicuous by the absence from it of such major industrial families as

[10] Although represented in the federation, the south took little interest in its activities. The Calcutta Marwari community was divided, and as a result the anti-Birla Marwaris stayed out of the federation for the first decade. The Marwari Chamber of Commerce did not join until 1939, and the Marwari Association, although it was one of the original twenty-four members, withdrew in 1933 and did not return until 1939. The Bombay business groups were also divided, and although Thakurdas succeeded in persuading Sir Dinshaw M. Petit to become the first president of the FICCI, he never succeeded in getting other prominent millowners to join.

the Tatas, Khatau, Thackersey, and Sarabhai.[11] The Tatas stayed out of the federation, except for a brief period in the late 1930s when, according to Shri Ram, "I went to Sir Saklatwala, who is head of the big Tata business house in this country. I begged him that it was high time that Tatas took some interest in our federation and helped us generously with men and money. He generously agreed that Mr. Dalal could become a member of our committee. He is a very great acquisition to our committee. He is far above average and we will have the biggest business house in the country represented on the committee." [12] The acquisition was short-lived, however. The Tata representative dropped out of the federation on the eve of the 1939 crisis between the Congress and the British government.

The absence of the larger Bombay industrialists meant that the Bombay interests represented in the federation were substantially different from those of Calcutta. Calcutta interests were represented in the FICCI through the Indian Chamber of Commerce, Calcutta, whose orientation was industrial. By contrast, the Indian Merchants Chamber, which was the key member vehicle of Bombay business, represented traders predominantly. Thus, because of the absence of major Bombay millowners, the representation stressed the needs of traders, although the Calcutta contingent had a primary interest in industry. This division continues even today.

The FICCI *and the Congress*

Although the FICCI likes to portray itself as the economic arm of the freedom movement whose leadership and policy were "wholly in conformity with the views of the Indian National Congress," [13] conflicting objectives and political divisions within the business community ensured that the relationship was not always quite so harmonious. The FICCI was primarily concerned with economic issues. It conceived of its role in negative terms as acting as critic of British economic policy and in positive terms as the voice of the views of the Indian business community in its dealings with the British government. Its primary objective was to counter the influence of foreign capital on the government of India and so to win concessions for Indian industry. As a result of this primarily economic focus, the federation appeared at times to take an ambivalent attitude toward both the Congress and the

[11] Ambalal Sarabhai served on the committee in 1931 as a co-opted member.

[12] FICCI, *Proceedings of the Eleventh Annual Meeting, 1938* (New Delhi. FICCI, 1938), p. 86.

[13] FICCI, *Silver Jubilee Souvenir,* p. 13.

British government. The alternating periods of attraction and repulsion conformed, to a very large extent, to the political condition of the nationalist movement and the attitudes and policies of the British government.

The FICCI became embroiled in political issues almost immediately after its creation, when the Congress began its second major civil disobedience campaign in 1930. At first, the Congress received full support from the federation and its leaders. For example, when the viceroy announced, in May of 1930, the establishment of a round table conference of Indian leaders to settle the political question and the Congress refused to attend, the FICCI passed a resolution withholding its cooperation and requested its member bodies to do likewise, unless the conferences were attended by Gandhi or at least had his approval.[14] Later, when Gandhi and the working committee were released from jail, in January 1931, the Congress negotiated the Gandhi-Irwin Pact. An agreement was reached to convene a second round table conference, and the FICCI established a three-man committee to represent the FICCI, with instructions to follow the lead of Gandhi.[15] In April of the same year, Gandhi was even invited to inaugurate the fourth annual session of the FICCI. At this time he was asked for a pledge to consult the FICCI in the formulation of Congress economic policy.

Close cooperation between the Congress and the FICCI, however, was ended by the historic decision of the Congress to resume civil disobedience on January 4, 1932. The resumption of civil disobedience sharply divided the FICCI and the Indian business community as a whole. Not only did the Bombay millowners withhold financial support[16] from the Congress, they went so far as to conclude a separate agreement with British industry. This agreement, the Lees-Mody Pact, was tantamount to treason according to Nehru, who later wrote in his biography,

> the Bombay mill industry in a body, during the continuance of civil disobedience and when we were preaching the boycott of British goods, had the temerity to conclude a pact with Lancashire. From the point of view of the Congress, this was a gross betrayal of the national cause, and it was characterized as such. The representative of the Bombay millowners in the assembly

[14] *Ibid.*, pp. 62–64.

[15] The government at first accepted only Thakurdas but after a fight agreed to accept the three-man delegation.

[16] D. R. Mankekar, *Homi Mody: A Many Splendored Life* (Bombay: Popular Prakashan, 1968), p. 101.

> also consistently ran down the Congress as extremists while most of us were in gaol.[17]

Even the federation condemned the millowners action, calling the agreement a "sectional" act lacking the seal of national approval.[18]

The FICCI became embroiled in the controversy surrounding the national movement's decision to resume civil disobedience. At first the FICCI appeared to support Congress noncooperation, but later it tried to temper its endorsement because of the sharp reaction of the British government to the original federation stand. The attempt to modify the federation's position toward the resumption of civil disobedience led to the emergence, within the organization, of a dissident minority which was determined to challenge the policies and authority of the federation leadership. The emergence of the dissidents was to have a profound, long-term impact on the functioning of the federation.

The controversy began in January 1932, when Sir Purshotamdas Thakurdas was invited by the viceroy to serve on a consultative committee of the round table conference.[19] The committee of the FICCI officially advised Thakurdas not to accept the invitation. The government of India, however, chose to interpret this advice as an act of noncooperation by the federation and therefore refused to permit any government members to attend the annual meeting of the federation.[20] The FICCI leadership was deeply troubled by the government stand and set about to modify the federation's position.

Each of the FICCI founders played a critical role in trying to revise the federation's stand, but each was motivated by different factors. Although G. D. Birla was perhaps the most pro-Congress of the big three, he did not always agree with Gandhi's policy.[21] He, too, had been offered a seat on the consultative committee.[22] Like Thakurdas,

[17] Quoted in Michael Kidron, *Foreign Investments in India* (London: Oxford University Press, 1965), p. 26, n. 1.

[18] FICCI, *Proceedings of the Seventh Annual Meeting, 1934* (New Delhi: FICCI, 1934), p. 9.

[19] Sir Purshotamdas Thakurdas, a member of the committee, was invited by the British prime minister through his deputy, the viceroy, to serve on a consultative committee of the round table conference. The consultative committee was considered a working committee of the round table conference, which was to prepare the groundwork for a third round table conference.

[20] FICCI, *Report of the Proceedings of the Executive Committee, 1932* (New Delhi: FICCI, 1932), pp. 8–9.

[21] Howard L. Erdman, *The Swatantra Party and Indian Conservatism* (Cambridge: Cambridge University Press, 1967), pp. 40–41.

[22] G. D. Birla, *In the Shadow of the Mahatma* (Bombay: Orient Longman's, Ltd., 1955), p. 44.

G. D. Birla rejected the offer, but he committed himself to reversing the FICCI's position of January. "The best service I can render to my own country, as well as to the cause of cooperation, is to persuade the federation to officially offer its cooperation." [23] Birla later explained to the viceroy that he did this because "I had thought that by offering you our cooperation, however qualified, I would convince you that we were true friends who were very eager to see permanent friendly relations restored between the two countries and I had expected that once we could get your trust and confidence it would not be difficult for us later on to convince you of the wisdom of our advice." [24] In short, Birla's motive for reconciliation was increased influence, not capitulation.

Purshotamdas Thakurdas' and Shri Ram's motives for reversing the federation's stand were economic rather than political. Shri Ram took the initiative to change the policy in order to "stop any harm being done" to business interests. Surveying business opinion, Shri Ram found "there was not the same enthusiasm in our members to give cooperation to the Congress as there was in 1930. There were those who would follow the Congress. There were some who were not prepared to go as far; there were still others who were trying to rehabilitate their position with the government. Again there were some who were lukewarm." Concluding that a revision of the January resolution was in order, Shri Ram contacted G. D. Birla and an agreement to reconsider the January resolution was reached.[25]

The leadership confronted major obstacles, however, in its attempt to change the January resolution. The committee had previously consulted the member bodies. It turned out that the overwhelming majority favored nonparticipation and noncooperation. Support for this position was particularly strong in Bombay, where the leadership of Thakurdas was being openly challenged by a group of pro-Congress businessmen who had seized control of the committee of the Indian Merchants Chamber. They threatened a revolt at the annual meeting of the FICCI if the January resolution were changed.

Meeting prior to the annual session, the FICCI committee passed a modified compromise resolution which committed the federation to a policy of cooperation. The resolution had three parts: the first paragraph requested the government to change its policy of repression; the second paragraph repudiated the government's interpretation of the

[23] *Ibid.*, pp. 44–45.
[24] *Ibid.*, p. 59.
[25] Khushwant Singh and Arun Joshi, *Shri Ram: A Biography* (Bombay: Asia Publishing House, 1968), pp. 204–205.

January resolution; and the third paragraph offered limited cooperation by proposing the appointment of a committee to "examine and come to an agreed solution in all financial matters." [26] In effect this resolution would enable the FICCI to participate in the consultative committee. Thus, the committee changed its position and offered conditional cooperation despite the opposition of its members. Recognizing that it faced a possible rank and file revolt, the committee agreed unanimously to resign if their resolution was defeated by the organization.[27]

The group from which the committee faced an open challenge at the annual meeting was led by J. C. Setalvad, A. D. Shroff, and a group of pro-Congress traders, shroffs, and insurance brokers. These men controlled the Indian Merchants Chamber in Bombay, and they demanded an *in camera* meeting to discuss the committee's resolution.[28] The *in camera* session was a "tempest and storm," for the resolution in question was one that has been characterized as "the most controversial resolution that has ever come before the federation." [29] The Bombay group insisted that the committee inform the group of the results of the survey of the member bodies, most of whom they knew had opposed any about-face in policy. The committee agreed only to "read to the house all the letters from eleven member bodies which have expressed that the said resolution should be reconsidered either unconditionally or under certain conditions." [30] The pro-Congress group finally succeeded in forcing the committee to change the action clause of its resolution. The new third paragraph was sterner in tone, and only in a highly qualified way did it accept the principle of cooperation. Thus, as finally passed, the resolution condemned British repression in no uncertain terms but indicated a reluctant willingness to attend a consultative conference so long as specific conditions were met.[31] In writing to Sir Samuel Hoare, G. D. Birla argued that the substance

[26] It is interesting to note that this particular suggestion had been made by G. D. Birla to the viceroy, who turned it down. See Birla, *In the Shadow of the Mahatma*, p. 44.

[27] *Ibid.*, pp. 46–47.

[28] Only three *in camera* meetings have been held in the history of the federation. Despite the fact that these *in camera* sessions were held in the 1930s, the federation still refuses to permit anyone to see the records. However, enough information is contained in the public meetings to construct the events.

[29] FICCI, *Proceedings of the Fifth Annual Meeting, 1932* (New Delhi: FICCI, 1932), p. 68.

[30] *Ibid.*, p. 62.

[31] Paragraph one of the resolution condemned the repression policy of the government, and paragraph two regretted the interpretation given the FICCI resolution of January 22, 1932. For a full text of the changes made, see Birla, *In the Shadow of the Mahatma*, p. 281.

was unaltered and reluctantly conceded that "In some respects this resolution is better than the one passed by the committee because it is not vague and definitely offers cooperation under certain conditions." [32]

Despite disagreements with the Congress over strategy and tactics, most of the top federation leaders prior to independence were closely associated with the national movement and were among its chief financial backers. This close association with the Congress, however, was contrary to the views of a large sector of the old Bombay business aristocracy, who argued that business should remain aloof from political controversy and concentrate its attention on furthering the economic interests of the business community. These political differences kept a large number of Bombay millowners out of the federation and tended to exacerbate previously existing regional, caste, and family differences.

Internal Politics Prior to Independence

What began as a split over political strategy produced a permanent, dissonant minority that continued to challenge the leadership of Birla, Thakurdas, and Shri Ram in the federation for the next decade. The leadership, however, attempted to fight back, by developing procedural rules to curb the potential challenge of an active minority and by restructuring the election constituencies for the selection of the federation executive. The result was to strengthen the oligarchical tendencies within the FICCI, rather than to develop the kind of competitive party politics which for some time characterized the internal politics of the Indian Merchants Chamber.

Among the most important procedural changes made were the restrictions placed on the moving of amendments to resolutions submitted to the annual meeting. These restrictions required the permission of the chair to move amendments and also gave the executive the power to refuse a resolution for submission to the annual meeting unless previous notice had been given. These restrictions made it very difficult to change FICCI policy resolutions once they were approved by the committee, and the dissidents, to no avail, charged that the rules were designed by the leadership to stifle minority rights.[33]

In the long run, the dissidents' charge proved to be correct. Instead of opening up greater possibilities for participation by a relatively

[32] *Ibid.*, p. 49.

[33] FICCI, *Proceedings of the Sixth Annual Meeting, 1933* (Delhi: FICCI, 1933), pp. 139–140, 142.

small membership, the rules centralized decision-making power in the hands of the committee and strengthened the oligarchical tendencies within the organization. Tight control was exercised by the leadership over the annual meeting at a time when the annual meeting was still small enough for meaningful debate. Thus, as the size of the membership and consequently the size of the annual meeting increased and the dissidents ceased their activities, the annual meeting became embarrassing—as G. D. Birla himself finally admitted by 1942:

> We every year just put the report before the house and pass it without any comment. We do not get any opportunity of knowing the views on various important questions which may at the moment be agitating the mind of the country, of our brother delegates. As a matter of fact, all the resolutions which we put forward before the house are more or less revised and redrafted in the final form by the members of the committee and the speakers are fixed in consultation with member bodies, but as we do not allow any amendment on any of the resolutions or any new resolution, it becomes almost impossible for us to know the views of the delegates who come here from such long distances about the various questions which they may have in mind.[34]

An even more significant change took place when the original constitution, designed "more as a skeleton for the purpose of gaining experience," [35] was rewritten in the late 1930s. The showdown over the proposed new constitution was held *in camera* in 1937. The extent of the struggle between the two "warring camps" is evident in the fact that 104 amendments were offered during the proceedings.[36] The reverberations continued for two years, pitting a large section of Bombay business—led by the pro-Congress leadership of the Indian Merchants Chamber joined by Karachi business—against Calcutta, the south, and the smaller disadvantaged chambers. The key to the successful restructuring lay in the change in the composition of the committee and in its method of selection. Instead of a committee selected from among the total membership by the annual meeting, the new constitution called for the representation of specific industries and

[34] FICCI, *Proceedings of the Fifteenth Annual Meeting, 1942* (Delhi: FICCI, 1942), p. 67.

[35] FICCI, *Proceedings of the Tenth Annual Meeting, 1937* (Delhi: FICCI, 1937), pp. 131–132.

[36] *Ibid.*, p. 136.

interests. In effect this created on the committee watertight compartments designed to prevent the capture of the federation by a dissident group.[37] In addition, a new set of rules reduced the power of the larger and richer chambers, by instituting a mailed ballot instead of holding the vote at the annual meeting, and by reducing the voting strength of each chamber at the annual meeting from four to one.

At the time of the adoption of the constitution in 1937, the dissidents were evidently promised that if they would endorse the constitution, the details of the method of voting and the voting strengths of the chambers would be discussed further at a special session of the federation. However, the nature of the compromise itself became a matter of dispute. At a special session called in 1938, the old voting method was restored, thereby rescinding the mailed ballot idea.[38] Whereas the dominant group argued that in return for this change the dissidents had agreed to accept the reduction of chamber voting strength from four to one,[39] the dissidents insisted that the two issues were entirely separate. They sought to change the voting strength at the 1939 annual meeting.[40]

The knockdown, dragout battle between the leadership and the dissidents that was the 1939 annual meeting ended in a complete rout of the dissidents. The dissidents charged that the new constitution unjustifiably reduced the number and strength of the delegates who attended the annual meeting and that they would be unable to exercise the influence they had commanded in the past. If the voting power of each chamber was cut from four to one, they argued, attendance would drop sharply because there would be little point to sending a full complement of nonvoting delegates.[41] Moreover, they charged the leadership with throwing out a red herring in attacking those chambers that could afford to send four delegates as merely buying themselves an unfair edge in decision-making, for there were "at least a dozen 'members' who are really pocket boroughs." Some of the member chambers, they meant, were only paper organizations dominated by

[37] FICCI, *Proceedings of the Eleventh Annual Meeting, 1938* (Delhi: FICCI, 1938), p. 144. After the 1937 reforms, the committee was elected along functional lines as follows: (1) textiles were given two seats; (2) sugar, insurance, banking, plantations, and transport were given one seat each; (3) three seats were allotted to unspecified industries; (4) eight seats were allotted to unspecified trade and commerce; (5) six seats were co-opted. This pattern remained unchanged until 1962, except for the addition of the associate members constituency in 1951.

[38] *Ibid.*, pp. 138–139.

[39] FICCI, *Proceedings of the Twelfth Annual Meeting, 1939* (Delhi: FICCI, 1939), pp. 62–65.

[40] *Ibid.*, pp. 65–67.

[41] *Ibid.*, pp. 55–56.

large institutions and designed by them to gain the votes needed to control committee elections.[42]

The vote on the issue clearly demonstrates the distribution of power in the FICCI and the nature of the division in the Indian business community at that time. In 1939 there were sixty-four member bodies in the FICCI and forty-four attended the session. Each member body could cast one vote. The dissidents were defeated by a vote of thirty-three to eleven. The regional distribution was unmistakable. Bombay and Karachi supported the amendment; Calcutta, the south, and the smaller chambers opposed it.[43] This defeat ended Bombay's dominant role in the FICCI and initiated the ascendency of Calcutta. The dissidents all but ceased to operate as a group. Later, in 1944, their leader, J. C. Setalvad, totally coopted by the leadership, was made president of the FICCI. The defeat of the dissidents ended the united check they were able to exercise over the leadership. The role of the Bombay dissidents was philosophically summarized in 1944 by A. D. Shroff, who said in retrospect,

> It was about thirteen years ago that Mr. Setalvad, myself and company started taking interest in the affairs of the federation as rebels. The big bosses of those days, they still exist, looked upon us as young Chokras and occasionally as interlopers. Under the leadership of Mr. Setalvad we continued to struggle [until] we got the senior men in the federation to allow us to have a look in. With the ingenuity and strategy of Mr. Setalvad, we completely duped the seniors into accepting us as their colleagues, and it is a matter of no small gratification that on the initiative of the senior members Mr. Setalvad was last year brought to the chair of the federation." [44]

[42] *Ibid.*, p. 68.

[43] All the Bombay associations voted for the amendment, except the East India Cotton Association controlled by Purshotamdas Thakurdas, the Indian Steamship Owners Association controlled by Scindia Steamship Company led by Walchand and Master, the Maharashtra Chamber of Commerce controlled by Walchand, and the Marwari Chamber of Commerce, Bombay, which voted with the Calcutta Marwaris. Voting for the amendment were the Indian Merchants Chamber dominated by J. C. Setalvad, the Bombay Shroffs Association led by Chunilal V. Mehta, the Grain Merchants Association, and the Seed Traders Association led by Ratilal Gandhi, and the Indian Insurance Company Association and Indian Life Assurance Officers Association which were connected with Setalvad. For some reason, the Native Share Brokers Association, although controlled by members of the group, was not represented in the 1939 meeting.

[44] FICCI, *Proceedings of the Eighteenth Annual Meeting, 1945* (Delhi: FICCI, 1945), pp. 196–197.

The absence of the major Bombay industrial houses from the federation and the defeat of the Bombay traders resulted in the ascendency of Calcutta in the affairs of the federation. This ascendency was translated into organizational dominance in the 1950s, as a small group of Marwari business houses, led by Birla house, succeeded in translating financial support into organizational control. This pattern of control was not successfully challenged until the 1970s. Thus, the circumstances surrounding the origins of the federation and its early organizational development were to continue to have a profound effect on the organization throughout the decades following independence.

Internal Politics after Independence

In size, resources, and diversity of interests represented, the FICCI grew very rapidly after independence to become the largest and most prestigious apex business organization in India. From its modest beginning in 1927, it had grown by 1971 to include over two hundred trade and industrial associations and over four hundred individual firm members drawn largely from the top seventy-five Indian-controlled business houses.[45] Many of the chambers of commerce and industrial or trade associations which are members of the federation are themselves large organizations, with membership in some cases in the thousands. Through such member bodies and its individual members, it is estimated that the FICCI represents one hundred thousand business firms employing over five million workers.[46] Thus, as B. M. Birla once said, "I think it is the largest party, in a sense, next to the Congress party, which is so well organized." [47]

Table VIII-1 indicates the wide variety of interests comprehended by the FICCI. Of the 170 ordinary members in 1965, for example, 49 were chambers of commerce, 39 were trade associations, and 82 were industrial associations. In addition, the 366 associate members included banking, insurance, and shipping firms, as well as manufacturers. Like Assocham, the FICCI is unusual among world business associations in that it attempts to represent both industry and trade. As India has grown increasingly industrialized, however, the traders have been reduced to the status of a minority within the federation, even though

[45] FICCI, *Report of the Proceedings of the Executive Committee for the Year 1966* (Delhi: FICCI, 1966), pp. 7, 181–191.

[46] FICCI, *Presidential Address of L. N. Birla, Forty-First Annual Session, March 30, 1968* (Delhi: FICCI, 1968), p. 20.

[47] FICCI, *Proceedings of the Twenty-Ninth Annual Meeting, 1956* (Delhi: FICCI, 1956), p. 185.

Table VIII-1

MAJOR FUNCTIONAL INTERESTS OF THE MEMBERS OF THE FICCI

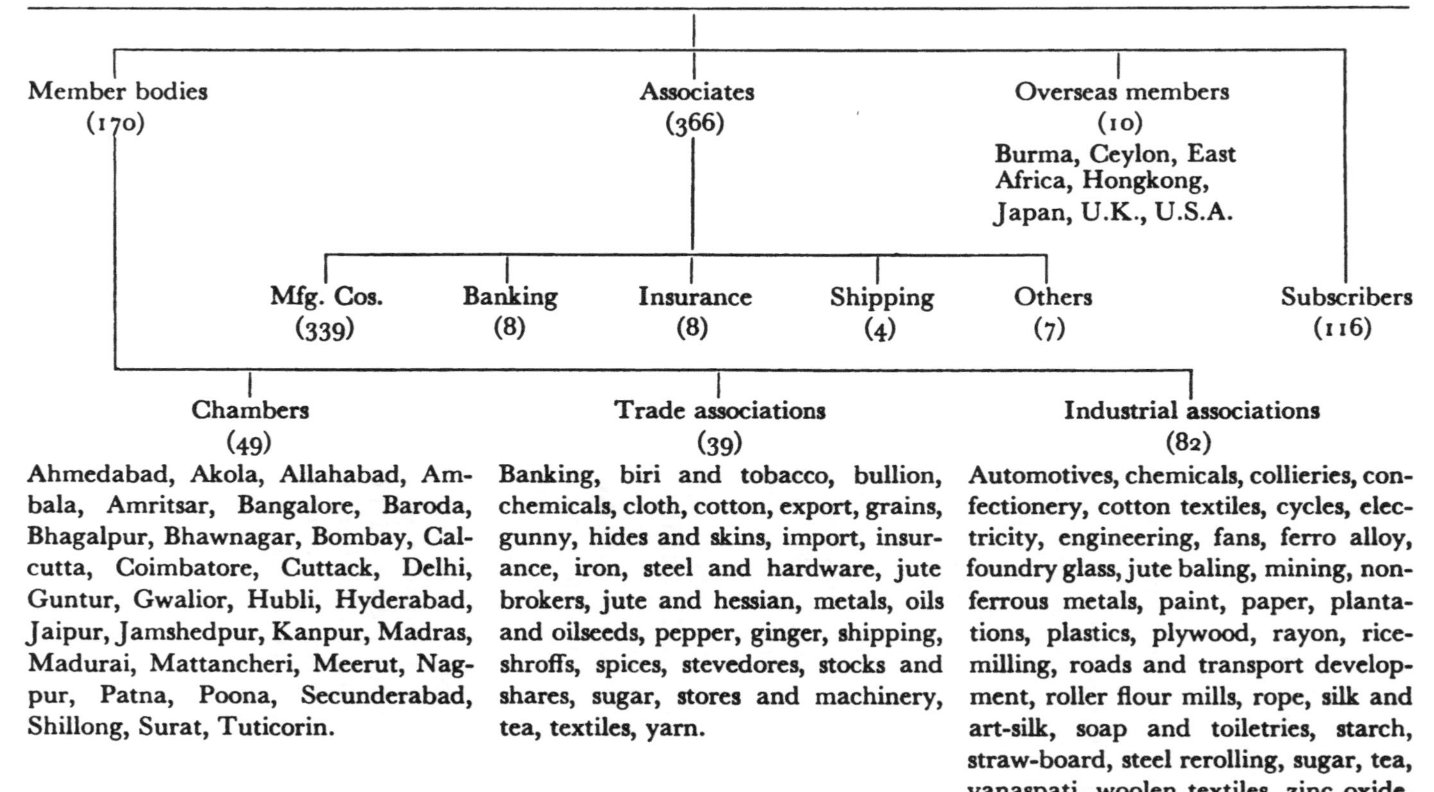

SOURCE: FICCI, *Federation of Indian Chambers of Commerce and Industry: Organization and Functions* (New Delhi: FICCI, 1965), p. 6.

in terms of absolute numbers they far exceed the handful of industrialists in the country. Within the federation, therefore, the 82 industrial associations and the associate memberships held by industrial firms are far more powerful than the 39 trade associations and the handful of small chambers representing trade. The imbalance is even greater than it might seem on the surface. Many of the chambers of commerce are actually industrial associations controlled by large industrialists who use them as a base of power in federation politics. In addition, some of the chambers are closely interlocked with trade and industrial associations. The Indian Chamber of Commerce in Calcutta, for example, provides secretariat services for a host of specialized associations, including such major organizations as the Indian Sugar Mills Association, the Indian Paper Mills Association, the Engineering Association of India, and the Tea Association of India. Finally, although the associate members may not vote on resolutions at the annual meeting, they are represented there. They speak on resolutions and elect almost 30 percent of the members of the executive committee, which is the chief policy-making body of the federation.

The resources of the FICCI as seen in Table VIII-2 have increased dramatically, from Rs 131,423 in 1947 to Rs 1,981,995 in 1970. This income has been devoted primarily to the development of an increasingly specialized secretariat to carry out the expanding activities of the federation. However, the pattern of finance has come to exert a significant influence on the distribution of power and control in the FICCI. The character of the organization was, in fact, substantially altered in 1951 when, in order to ensure a steady source of revenue, the federation created a new category of membership. Prior to that time, only chambers of commerce and industry or trade associations could be direct members of the federation. Yet the federation found that these members were reluctant to pay the costs of the organization.[48] Every attempt to increase subscription fees was resisted, and the leadership had to make up deficits from its own sources. These recurrent financial crises were finally overcome by the creation of an associate membership, which permitted individual firms to join the federation directly instead of depending entirely on representation through the various constituent trade associations.[49] Some 70 percent of the federation's income now comes from associate membership contributions, and, as Table VIII-3 shows, the associate membership in 1966 was drawn pre-

[48] FICCI, *Proceedings of the Twenty-Second Annual Meeting, March 1949* (Delhi: FICCI, 1949), pp. 90–92.

[49] See FICCI, *Silver Jubilee Souvenir*, pp. 227–230.

Table VIII-2

MEMBERSHIP AND SOURCES OF FINANCE OF THE FICCI (1927–1970)

Year	*Ordinary members*	*Associate members*	*Total income in rupees*	*Total paid by associate members*	*Percent paid by associate members*	*Individual contributions made by committee*
1927	24	—	—	—	—	—
1937	57	—	—	—	—	—
1947	102	—	131,423	—	—	42,500
1948	112	—	159,679	—	—	47,500
1949	121	—	163,973	—	—	51,500
1950	117	—	197,104	—	—	40,500
1951[a]	123	79	221,978	78,000	35.1	—
1952	115	115	255,869	89,000	34.8	—
1953	113	143	299,903	104,000	34.7	—
1954	113	177	310,690	160,000	51.5	43,502
1955	113	186	335,099	184,000	54.9	—
1956	117	207	368,825	197,000	53.4	—
1957	116	209	368,825	197,000	53.4	—
1958	116	221	488,473	224,000	45.9	—
1959	126	270	570,068	317,000	55.6	—
1960	137	285	561,228	327,000	58.3	—
1961	144	293	586,317	371,500	63.4	—
1962[b]	170	366	1,001,817	751,086	75.0	—
1963	178	364	1,187,710	912,666	76.8	—
1964	177	369	1,176,036	893,750	76.0	—
1965	170	361	1,272,503	933,000	73.3	—
1966	179	384	1,395,270	1,013,250	72.6	—
1967	193	392	1,508,511	1,086,500	72.0	—
1968	192	378	1,592,838	1,105,250	69.4	—
1969	201	390	1,751,183	1,315,500[c]	75.1	—
1970	220	402	1,981,995	1,324,740[c]	66.8	—

[a] Associate membership created in 1951.

[b] Constitutional revision increased fees in 1962.

[c] Includes special surcharge and only those fees paid as of date of annual audit.

SOURCE: FICCI, *Report of the Proceedings of the Executive Committee, 1927–1970* (New Delhi: FICCI).

Table VIII-3
SOURCES OF ASSOCIATE MEMBERSHIP IN THE FICCI IN 1966 WITH AN ESTIMATE OF VOTING POWER BY SIZE

Source of membership	*Number of firms*	*Per-cent*	*Estimated[a] voting strength*	*Per-cent*
41 of top 75 Houses[b]	196	51	312	58
Individual firms with assets over 1 crore	68	18	88	16
Other	119	31	139	26
	383	100	539	100

[a] The estimates of voting strength in tables VIII-3, VIII-4, and VIII-5 are based on the List of Associate Members of the FICCI with their representatives given in appendix C of *The Proceedings of the Fortieth Annual Session* April 1967. The number of delegates is assumed to represent the voting power of each associate member. Where no name is listed it is assumed that the member is entitled to at least one vote because that is a minimum given to all those who pay a subscription of less than 2,000 rupees.

[b] The remaining 34 houses did not have any member firms as far as can be determined.

SOURCES: Tables VIII-3, VIII-4, and VIII-5 are based on a comparison of the companies listed by business house in the *Monopolies Inquiry Commission Report* of 1965 and the 383 associate members of the FICCI in 1966.

dominantly from 41 of the top 75 business houses. Even more striking, however, is the fact revealed by Table VIII-4, which indicates that a group of six out of the top ten industrial houses in 1966 made up a dramatically disproportionate share of the total. The six were Birla, Thapar, Jalan, Sahu-Jain, Bangur, and Singhania. All, except for Thapar, are Marwari. Together, from their many constituent firms, they provided about 60 percent of the large house membership or about one-third of the total associate membership of the federation in that year. The enrollment of such a large number of firms from these six houses gave this group a block of votes within the federation's general body or annual meeting which was large enough to enable them to control entry into the committee of the federation from the associate member constituency.

Even more striking was the phenomenal associate membership generated by Birla House. As Table VIII-5 shows, with seventy-four individual firms providing approximately Rs 242,500, or 24 percent of the income generated by the associate membership in 1966 (in addition to whatever Birla House firms contribute via subscriptions to the various member bodies of which they are members), Birla easily ranked as the largest contributor to the FICCI and commanded the largest single block

Table VIII-4

DISTRIBUTION OF THE NUMBER OF FIRMS CONTRIBUTED BY THE TOP SIX SUPPORTERS OF THE FICCI AND AN ESTIMATE OF THE VOTING POWER OF EACH

						Estimate of[a] voting strength	
House	*Caste*	*Region*	*Rank by assets*	*Number of companies*	*Percent*	*Number*	*Percent*
Birla	Marwari (Maheshwari)	Calcutta	2	74	64.3	137	25.4
Thapar	Hindu (Khatri)	Calcutta	6	10	8.7	10	1.8
Jalan	Marwari (Aggarwal)	Calcutta	10	9	7.8	9	1.6
Singhania	Marwari (Aggarwal)	Calcutta	9	8	7.0	13	2.4
Sahu-Jain[b]	Jain-Bania	Calcutta	7	8	7.0	15	2.7
Bangur	Marwari (Maheshwari)	Calcutta	4	7	6.1	8	1.4
				116	100.0	192	35.3

[a] All percentages are based on an estimate of 539 possible votes in the associate membership constituency.

[b] The strength of Sahu-Jain would be 21 votes if the entire Dalmia-Jain group was counted as a single unit.

of votes at the annual meeting of the federation. It is estimated that Birla House in 1966 controlled about 25 percent of the total associate membership delegates. The voting blocks of the other houses did not exceed 3 percent each. Thus, with only a few allies, Birla could play a dominant role in the election of the members of the committee chosen from the associate membership constituency. To block the Birlas required a very large coalition of other business houses. Such a coalition did not emerge until 1971 when, despite strong opposition by Birla House, modest steps were taken to dilute the voting power of individual associate members.

The composition of the federation and the nature of its membership have had a significant impact on the informal structure of power in the FICCI. As seen in Table VIII-6, the constitution of the federation provides for a general body or annual meeting, an executive committee, a standing advisory committee, the president, and the secretariat. In

Table VIII-5

ESTIMATE OF THE VOTING STRENGTH AND CONTRIBUTIONS OF BIRLA HOUSE TO THE FICCI

	Estimate of number of votes by size of company			
Vote	*Number of companies*	*Estimate of vote*	*Subscription categories*	*Estimate of total subscription paid*
1 Vote	44	44	1,750	77,000
2 Votes	13	26	3,500	45,500
3 Votes	4	12	5,000	20,000
4 Votes	10	40	7,000	70,000
5 Votes	15	15	10,000	30,000
	74	137		242,500[a]

[a] 242,500 is 23.9 percent of the 1,013,250 rupees paid in 1966 by the associate membership. It would represent 17.3 percent of the total FICCI budget of 1,395,270 rupees for 1966.

SOURCE: This table is based on a combination of the annual subscriptions payable by each company based on its turnover and the number of delegates each associate member is entitled to nominate to attend the annual meeting based on the amount of subscriptions it pays. These categories are contained in *Memorandum and Articles of Association of the FICCI*, pp. 13–16 and 19. Thus, for example, where the annual subscription of a company is up to 2,000 rupees, it is entitled to nominate one delegate. Because the minimum subscription is 1,500 on turnover of up to 1 crore and 2,000 if the turnover is from 1 to 2½ crores, it is assumed that the 44 Birla companies which have 1 delegate must pay an average in subscriptions of 1,750 rupees each.

theory, the general body, which consists of about one thousand delegates nominated by the member bodies and associate members, is supreme.[50] The general body is responsible for reviewing and endorsing the annual report of the work of the committee and the budget. It elects the president, the treasurer, and members of the committee. It passes on resolutions submitted by the committee and on "such other resolutions as may be brought forward in accordance with these rules." [51] However, because they control large blocks of general body votes, either directly through a block of associate members or indirectly through their control over various member bodies, the big houses are able to control entry into the executive committee—the true locus of power within the federation.

This committee consists of sixty-one members including the president —thirty-six representatives of the member bodies, seventeen represen-

[50] FICCI, *Memorandum and Articles of Association* (Delhi: FICCI, 1970), pp. 8–11.

[51] *Ibid.*, pp. 18–19; Appendix A, pp. 28–31.

Table VIII-6

FEDERATION: HOW IT FUNCTIONS

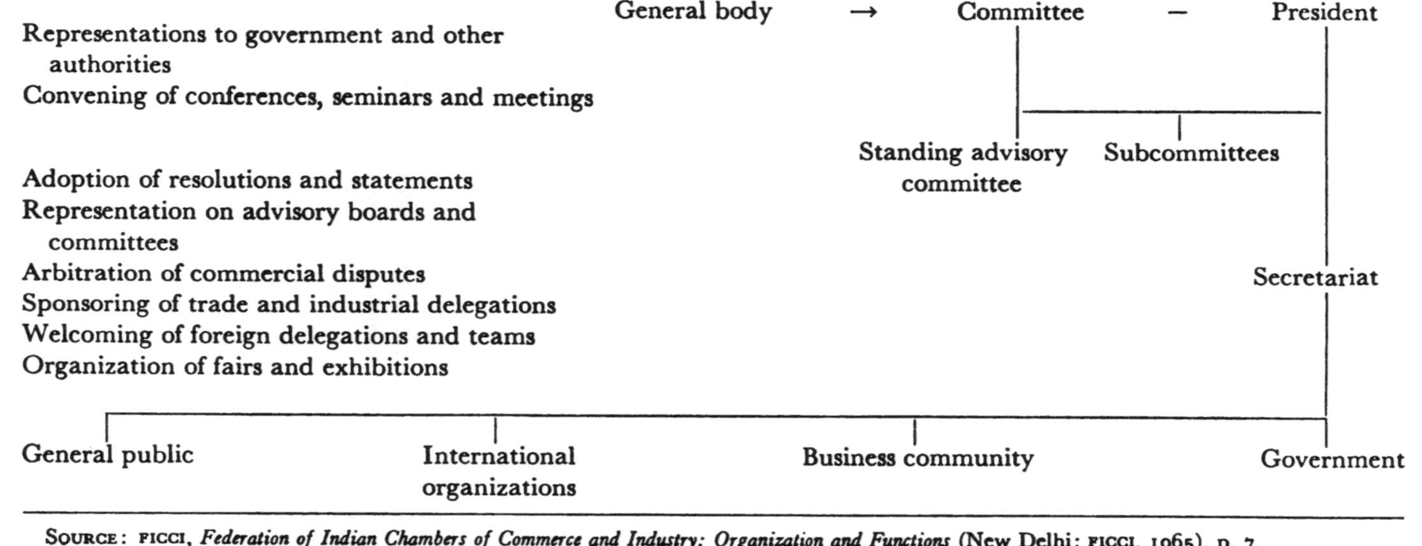

SOURCE: FICCI, *Federation of Indian Chambers of Commerce and Industry: Organization and Functions* (New Delhi: FICCI, 1965), p. 7.

tatives of the associate membership, and seven coopted members. Of the thirty-six committee members representing the ordinary membership, twenty must be drawn from industry and sixteen from trade, banking, insurance, and transport. Formally, then, provision is made for a broadly representative membership. In actuality, however, because managing agency houses are so ubiquitous and various in their operations, they can qualify under almost any category. Thus, a *de facto* concentration of membership and control is easily achieved.

As the real center of decision-making and control in the FICCI, the committee manages the business of the association. It is the chief policy-maker for the federation, it performs all executive duties, and it exercises all powers not exclusively conferred on the general body.[52] In addition, the committee elects the vice president from among its own members. By custom, the vice president is unanimously elected by the general body to succeed to the presidency, and so the actual power of choosing the president lies in the hands of the committee rather than with the general body. Although the president is the executive head of the FICCI and is responsible for directing the work of the secretariat,[53] he is elected for just one year, and by tradition he can serve only that one term. In this way tradition prevents the development of an executive authority independent of the committee whose members, by contrast, enjoy an extremely high level of continuity in power. In consultation with the committee, the president appoints a standing advisory committee to meet once a month and serve in an advisory capacity. Although up to five members of this fifteen member subcommittee can be drawn from outside the federation, in practice the standing advisory committee has always consisted of an inner circle of key committee members. Formally speaking, the executive authority continues to reside in the hands of the full committee, but there is a tendency for most important issues to be delegated to the standing advisory committee for action.

In sum, through control of large voting blocks in the general body, a small group of major business houses, which supply the bulk of the financing of the federation, were able to dominate by controlling entry into the executive committee. Control of entry into the committee in turn meant control over the selection of the president and determination of what shall constitute organization policy.

The pattern of oligarchy in the FICCI is clearly visible in the pattern

[52] *Ibid.*, pp. 22–24; Appendix B, pp. 32–42.
[53] *Ibid.*, p. 21.

Table VIII-7
REGIONAL ORIGINS OF FICCI PRESIDENTS
(1927–1972)

Bombay	15
Calcutta	16
Madras	6
Delhi	3
Ahmedabad	3
Kanpur	1
Karachi	2
	46

of recruitment of federation presidents since 1927.[54] The presidency of the FICCI is rotated on a regional basis, with careful parity for representation from Bombay and Calcutta, frequent representation from Delhi and Madras, and occasional inclusion of one of the smaller business centers. Thus, as Table VIII-7 indicates, of the forty-six presidents from 1927 to 1972, fifteen were from Bombay, sixteen were from Calcutta, and the remaining fifteen were drawn from Delhi, Madras, Ahmedabad, Kanpur, and (before independence) Karachi. The dominance of Bombay and Calcutta is the result of the uneven development of industry during the British period. Despite the growth of other centers since then, Bombay and Calcutta still reflect the loci of business power in India.

The selection of presidential candidates within each region is based mainly on the size of the business houses in the area. Although pre-independence procedures also provided for the selection of leading business personalities as such, FICCI presidents since 1947 have been drawn from the major business family groups which dominate the federation.[55] Table VIII-8 shows that twenty-three houses have provided a total of thirty-four out of forty-six presidents since 1927. The distribution of the twenty-three houses reveals three levels within the oligarchy.

The preeminent position is monopolized by Birla House, which has

[54] For a more detailed treatment see Stanley A. Kochanek, "Interest Groups and Interest Aggregation: Changing Patterns of Oligarchy in the FICCI," *Economic and Political Weekly* 5 (1970): 1291–1308.

[55] Since 1947, only two presidents have not been connected with a major business house: Lalji Mehrotra in 1948 and Sir B. P. Singh Roy in 1958.

Table VIII-8
DISTRIBUTION OF FICCI PRESIDENTS BY BUSINESS HOUSE
(1927–1972)

No. of presidents from each house	*No. of houses*	*Names of houses*
4	1	Birla (1929, 1936, 1954, 1967)
3	1	Scindia (1932, 1942, 1947)
2	6	Thakurdas (1928, 1953); Shri Ram (1930, 1963); Singhania (1935, 1956); Dalmia-Jain (1952, 1962); Goenka (1945, 1964); Kothari-Madras (1951, 1970)
1	15	Lalbhai (1934); Kumararajah Muthiah Chettiar (1943); Jalan (1949); Kilachand (1950); Mangaldas Jaisinghbhai (1955); Chinai (1957); Ruia (1959); Murugappa Chettiar (1960); Thapar (1961); Kirloskar (1965); Amin (1966); Modi (1968); Podar (1969); S. S. Kanoria (1971); Madanmohan Mangaldas (1972)
	23	Total number of FICCI presidents from 1927 to 1972 drawn from the top 75 business houses was 34.

supplied four presidents since 1927. Birla, now equal to Tata in size of assets, was instrumental in founding the federation, remains the largest financial contributor, and traditionally had two seats on the FICCI executive committee.

The second level of the oligarchy is composed of six houses, each of which has elected at least two presidents since 1927. All except Purshotamdas Thakurdas were elected from among the top sixteen houses in India. (The presence of Thakurdas within this group is the result of his role in founding the federation and his leadership of a section of Bombay business. His influence was eclipsed even before his death.) The remaining five houses, along with Birla, represent the inner core of the federation oligarchy. The important thing to note, however, is that there is here no absolutely united or coherent clique. Each constituent has his own set of allies within the executive committee and within the larger business community. Although allied with one another for some purposes, each remains in competition with all the others. Thakurdas was a close ally of Shri Ram, and Kothari was related to Thakurdas by marriage. Shri Ram in turn was a close friend of Padampat Singhania.[56] Goenka presents a separate point of power. The Goenka family has carried on a longstanding feud with Birla in Calcutta Marwari politics.[57] Dalmia-Jain, which also represents an independent point of power, has earned a reputation for being a maverick; yet, despite repeated difficulties, it continues to grow rapidly. Thus, far from constituting a cohesive and unified elite, each member of the oligarchy strives to limit the others by getting as many of its own supporters into the all important executive committee as possible. Until recently, however, the group was not strong enough to overcome the preeminent Birla position in the federation.

The third level of fifteen houses which have provided at least one president each depended for support on the upper two levels. Two of these houses, Thapar and Jalan, were among the top ten business houses in India. They rank among the major financers of the federation and were considered to be allies of Birla. Two others, Kirloskar and Amin, represent the younger generation of Indian businessmen who were elevated to the presidency in an attempt to give the FICCI a more dynamic image.

The pattern of leadership reflected in the selection of presidents is also present in the executive committee and tends to reflect the level of financial support provided by the large houses through their associate membership.[58] Conspicuous by their absence at both membership and leadership levels of the federation are some of India's largest and oldest business houses: Tata, Mafatlal, Associated Cement, and Sarabhai. Their absence is deliberate and reflects continuing differences over political strategies, organizational style, and levels of modernization, as well as caste, regional, and family rivalries. The Tatas and Mafatlal had joined the federation in the 1950s but resigned in protest of the refusal of the federation leadership to take a strong stand on the Dalmia-Jain scandal. The Dalmia-Jain group was accused by a specially appointed government investigating commission of damaging irregularities and stock manipulations. Shriyans Prasad Jain, one of the leading figures in the Dalmia-Jain group, happened to be president of the FICCI in 1962–1963, when the scandal became public. The Tatas and

[56] Moraes, *Sir Purshotamdas Thakurdas*, pp. 38–48; Singh and Joshi, *Shri Ram*, pp. 217–227.

[57] Rishi Jaimini Kaushik, *Shri Ramdev Chokhany* (Calcutta: Jaimini Prakashan, n.d.), p. 135.

[58] Kochanek, "Interest Groups," pp. 1291–1308.

Mafatlal argued that Jain should resign immediately, but the top leadership held that a hasty resignation would damage the prestige of the federation. The Tatas and Mafatlal strongly disagreed with the decision and resigned.[59]

The Tatas' disagreement with the federation leadership, and especially with the Birlas, went beyond the specific issues raised by the Dalmia-Jain case. The Tatas strongly believe that business in India must become more politically active, must openly espouse the virtues of free enterprise, and must ostracize the antisocial elements in the business community. The Tatas have provided strong support to organizations designed to propagate these views, including the Fair Trade Practices Association, the Forum of Free Enterprise, and the Swatantra Party. In a speech in December 1969, J. R. D. Tata even went as far as to call for the formation of a new trade and industry organization confined to businessmen with a proven record of straight dealing. He condemned those guilty of tax evasion, black marketing, illegal foreign exchange transactions, bribery, corruption, and political intrigues for tarnishing the image of the private sector. The reputation of the private sector had been damaged, he said, "through degradation, misdeeds, and conspicuous expenditure of a few individuals heading large enterprises and who in their pursuit of wealth, profit and self-aggrandizement have wantonly disregarded the public interest." [60]

The continued aloofness of the Tatas has weakened the federation in terms of men, money, and resources, and there has been a concentrated effort to get them back into the FICCI. A major step in this direction came in 1970, when the federation undertook its second major reorganization in less than a decade. Pressure for a fundamental restructuring of the FICCI came from Bombay. In April 1969, Babubhai Chinai submitted a proposal for reorganization of the federation. Ramnath Podar, president of the federation and an active Bombay industrialist, convened a special meeting of the committee of the federation to consider the proposals, and he also took the unusual step of inviting all presidents of member bodies to attend. The major theme which emerged from the meeting was that the base of the federation had to be broadened to make the organization more representative. A committee was appointed to draw up specific recommendations.[61]

Three basic reforms emerged which were ultimately approved by the committee and ratified by an extraordinary general meeting of the

[59] *Ibid.*

[60] *The Economic Times* (Bombay), December 16, 1969.

[61] FICCI, *Proceedings of the Executive Committee for the Year 1969* (Delhi: FICCI, 1969), p. 187.

federation on November 20, 1970. First, the size of the executive committee was expanded from fifty-one to its present sixty-one. Second, in an effort to placate the traders, the federation endorsed the principle that only those whose predominant interest was trade could seek election to represent trade on the committee. Finally, and perhaps most significantly, the federation revised the subscriptions payable by the member bodies and the associate members but at the same time did not increase the voting power of associate members.[62]

The adoption of the reforms and the new leadership which emerged at the time of the election of the enlarged committee, in April 1971, indicated that a new coalition had emerged which was intent on reducing the level of Birla influence. Birla House had vigorously opposed any reorganization of the federation and was especially opposed to increasing the subscription level for associate members without at the same time increasing their voting power. When the changes were adopted despite their objections, the largest Birla companies paying the highest subscriptions resigned their associate membership in the federation.[63] In order to offset these financial losses, and to strengthen their position, the new leadership attempted to get the Tatas and Mafatlal to join the federation and promised further changes in the structure of the federation, if necessary, to accomplish this objective.[64]

The new leadership of the federation is composed of a coalition of younger industrialists drawn from the major business centers of Calcutta, Bombay, Madras, and Delhi. It includes, among others, Goenka, Singhania, Sahu-Jain, the Murugappa group, and the Shri Ram group. These larger houses have been joined by a variety of smaller houses in their attempt to offset Birla influence in the federation.

The slow process of restructuring taking place in the FICCI is a reflection of the gradual process of change taking place within the Indian business community. The rapid rise to power of the Marwari houses of Calcutta in the 1950s is now being slowly offset by the development of new groups and the strengthening of some older groups in Madras, Bombay, and New Delhi. These groups have succeeded in gaining support from some of the large Marwari houses in Calcutta that have never had very close relations with Birlas. Undoubtedly Birla dissatisfaction with their decline in influence is real. The Birla family, more than anyone else, has contributed a great deal to the development of the federation and helped nurse it during its early period of growth.

[62] FICCI, *Proceedings of the Executive Committee for the Year 1970* (Delhi: FICCI, 1970), pp. 162–163.
[63] *The Economic Times* (Bombay), April 12, 1971. They rejoined in 1973.
[64] *Ibid.*

Their financial support, however, had become so large that it was unhealthy for the organization itself, especially because the Birlas always took the attitude that those who pay the bills should have a dominant voice in the leadership and decision-making of the organization. Thus, although the loss of Birla revenue will be missed, it was a necessary development if the FICCI was ever to become the representative of the Indian business community as a whole. A sharp drop in Birla financial support could easily be made up by the reentry of the Tatas and Mafatlal into the federation. Undoubtedly the next decade will see additional organizational changes, as the FICCI adjusts its internal structure to conform to the rapidly changing nature and composition of business in India.

In short, if the pattern of oligarchic control over the federation which was achieved by some big business houses has sometimes been a source of strength, it has also and increasingly had some negative implications for the maintenance of organizational cohesion. Once the leadership had passed into the hands of the big industrialists from Calcutta, and especially after the creation of the associate membership in 1951, the federation came to reflect the views of the big industrialists rather than the views of the Indian business community as a whole. When FICCI spoke, it spoke loudly and clearly to the issues which concerned large-scale industry in India. Considerably less attention was paid to the problems of the traders, small and medium business interests, and newly developing regions such as the south and Punjab.

But with the increase in number and size of medium and small industry, with the emergence of new giants, and with the dispersion of new industrial development throughout the country as a result of government encouragement, all gradually reflected in a changing FICCI membership, pressure from these and other long ignored interests within the federation began to build up.[65] The FICCI leadership found itself faced with demands for broader representation on the committee and for a larger voice in federation affairs and policy-making. As these demands became more and more insistent, the leadership was forced to respond or face the threat of succession. The reorganization of the FICCI, in 1962 and again in 1971, was largely a response to these pressures. To have ignored these pressures for change would have resulted in the fragmentation of business into a multiplicity of apex business organizations which would have destroyed completely the credibility

[65] See, for example, FICCI, *Proceedings of the Twenty-Sixth Annual Meeting, 1953* (Delhi: FICCI, 1953), p. 178; *Proceedings of the Twenty-Eighth Annual Meeting, 1955* (Delhi: FICCI, 1955), pp. 130, 134; *Proceedings of the Thirtieth Annual Meeting, 1957* (Delhi: FICCI, 1957), pp. 4, 13.

of the federation's claim to represent the entire Indian business community and thereby would have diminished its influence with government.

Elite Politics

The internal politics of the FICCI are still basically an elite affair. Elite politics centers around the committee, which acts as the chief executive of the federation and is thus the center of decision-making. As chief executive of the FICCI, the committee is responsible for making decisions which affect the structure and finance of the organization. These organizational policy recommendations must be ratified by the annual meeting. Because most organizational changes involving such issues as increases in fees, changes in the constitution, or major changes in the secretariat have tended to generate substantial debate and controversy among the members, the elite has never had a totally free hand, although it has usually had the upper hand.

Policy resolutions, on the other hand, ever since the defeat of the Bombay dissidents in 1938–1939, have become more exclusively an elite affair. Policy-making in the FICCI involves the formulation of FICCI demands on government, the framing of a reaction to government policy initiatives or changes, and the determination of the strategy and tactics to be employed in attempting to influence government decision-makers. One of the primary functions of the FICCI is to provide a mechanism for the formulation of a collective view of the business community toward government and to articulate the demands of the business community. Because committee resolutions on policy are seldom rejected, amended, or modified by the annual meeting, organizational issues involving the size and composition of the committee have been regarded as critical by the FICCI membership and leadership.

Prior to the reorganization of the FICCI in 1962, policy decisions in the committee were made by a group of five or six senior members representing Birla house, the Singhania, Goenka, Dalmia-Jain, Shri Ram, and the Bombay trading interests through either Thakurdas or later Babubhai Chinai. Although they are part of the inner circle, Jalan and Thapar generally followed the Birla lead. At all times Birla influence was pervasive; Tata played a minor and indirect role, through various members of the committee, from 1953–1963. Decisions reached by the inner circle were simply ratified by the committee as a whole, much as committee decisions in turn were ratified by the general body.

The expansion of the size of the committee, in 1962 and again in 1971, has brought into the FICCI leadership a wider diversity of interests, regions, and houses. This change was accompanied by the entry of a younger, more highly educated and managerially oriented generation of businessmen. This new generation holds views which differ considerably from those of the older generation, both in the area of public policy and on the issue of the larger role of the FICCI in India.

Voting blocks and levels of financial support play a dominant role in leadership selection. But once selected, the leadership operate on the basis of consensus and not by majority vote. Moreover, the views of the senior people in the committee no longer automatically prevail. Although the large Marwari houses have a great deal of influence in the committee as a result of their ability to elect their friends and allies, they are no longer in a position to impose their views on the committee. Committee members insist that decisions in the FICCI are no longer based on seniority or size of holdings but on persuasion, negotiations, and the merits of the case. The old guard is also increasingly aware of the desire for change among the younger generation and has sought to accommodate their views.

Thus, for example, in the late 1960s a major controversy developed within the committee over the legitimacy and status of the standing advisory committee (SAC) created in 1962. The standing advisory committee was originally designed as a small brain trust which would consist of senior business leaders and act as the chief advisor to the president on issues of policy. It was a way of encouraging leaders of major business houses to participate in FICCI affairs without their having to contest elections and canvass for votes in order to play a meaningful role. At first it seemed as though the SAC would achieve its objective. Outsiders such as N. Dandekar, Sir Ramaswami Mudaliar, H. V. R. Iengar, and even Dharamsey M. Khatau were persuaded to participate. However, following a major rift within the federation over government charges of impropriety leveled at the Dalmia-Jain group in 1963 and the withdrawal of the Tatas and the Mafatlal from the federation, outsiders showed less interest in the federation. The SAC, composed of former presidents, senior committee members, and representatives of the larger industrial groups, became one more reflection of the old inner circle of the federation. It met quite frequently, with an average attendance of about twelve, discussed issues in great detail, and made recommendations to the committee for ratification.

When it appeared as though the SAC was becoming a means of preserving the control of the old guard, it began to generate controversy. Executive committee members questioned its vague and indefinite status. They charged that the SAC gave the top people too much say, with the result that the interests of two or three large houses got more attention than other pressing problems. They also charged that the existence of the SAC created two classes of committee members—the young and the old, that it did not give all committee members a chance to participate in basic decisions, that it acted as a supercabinet, and that its decisions usually were not even referred to the rest of the committee for ratification. In short, it was charged that the SAC was usurping the legitimate authority of the committee as the final decision-maker in the FICCI. Committee members cited specific examples of major issues which appeared on the agenda of the committee and were never acted on by the committee. Instead, those issues were simply referred to the standing advisory committee for action, without any charge that the SAC report back to the parent body.

Those who objected to the role of the SAC were, however, divided over how to reform it. One group felt the answer was to demand that younger people be added to the SACs membership. However, another group demanded either that it be abolished or that its role be more specifically defined. The leadership responded to the criticisms of the status of the SAC by attempting to co-opt some of the younger members and by accepting the principle that all members of the committee were free to attend meetings of the SAC. Thus, although an inner group continued to exist within the FICCI, the position of that group no longer went unchallenged.

The committee of the FICCI meets eight or ten times a year at different centers throughout India to discuss issues placed on the agenda by the president and the secretariat.[66] In dealing with resolutions which are to be submitted to the annual meeting, the committee receives recommendations from its member bodies who forward resolutions for consideration by the committee. The president of the federation sets up a screening committee to process the resolutions received from the members. Out of the hundred or more resolutions received annually, the screening committee selects ten to twelve dealing with critical topics, and from these four or five topical resolutions emerge.

Committee discussions are based on background notes prepared by the secretariat. Most members are highly dependent on these notes, because the notes represent the major source of information about the issues discussed. Following a detailed discussion of the issue, the president attempts to summarize the consensus of the group. Then the

[66] Committee members serve without pay. The committee meets about ten times a year at various major cities, and so each committee member must be prepared to spend a substantial amount of money for travel and hotels. The less affluent committee members have found it difficult to sustain these costs and have resigned. The same problem confronts FICCI presidents.

secretariat prepares a resolution or policy statement which embodies the essence of the consensus. The committee then reviews the policy statement or resolution and ratifies it.

The quality of discussions within the committee varies a great deal, depending upon the nature of the issue and the potency of the problem. Because of the necessity to balance off conflicting views and interests, there is a tendency for the committee to avoid issues on which there is a sharp disagreement—to either postpone consideration or leave it up to the discretion of individual members to decide what to do. Most committee members tend to view issues from a very narrow perspective, blinded by their own personal interests, rather than from the perspective of the industry or business at large. Perhaps the sole correcting force to this tendency is the secretariat, which tries to overcome this self-interest approach by placing the case in a larger context of the problems of the industry or the larger economy. Even so, many critics argue that policy pronouncements and resolutions tend to represent the lowest common denominator and that they therefore are vague, imprecise, and often contradictory.

Committee members tend to become divided over issues lying in four basic areas: political strategy, organizational values, conflicting interests, and clashes of personalities or primordial loyalties.

Politically, the FICCI elite is divided between the Birla strategy and the Bombay strategy. The Birla philosophy has always been that one should never confront or challenge government directly or openly. One should play along with government, step on their toes but not too hard, and try to work out agreements with government officials in private. The Bombay approach, especially that espoused by Swatantra party supporters in the FICCI, is that one should openly challenge and criticize government and speak out strongly and publicly on behalf of the private sector. This group argues that the FICCI should support and encourage the development of political parties that are willing to openly protect and espouse the business cause. Political differences between the Birla and the Bombay view exploded in 1970 when Babubhai Chinai, one of the top members of the committee and a man who was deeply involved in Congress party politics, resigned from the committee because of the committee's weak response to Mrs. Gandhi's nationalization of banks. His resignation reflected this larger division over political philosophy.[67]

[67] *The Economic Times* (Bombay), July 30, 1969. Babubhai Chinai was later elected an honorary member of the federation.

Similarly, on organizational issues there are those who feel that the FICCI should play a larger role in fostering a new image of business, by openly condemning any group accused of wrongdoing and isolating them from the "respectable" business community. This group also feels that the FICCI should sponsor groups to encourage the development of ethical practices. In short, business should play a larger role in policing itself and in developing a more acute social consciousness among the Indian business community. In addition, this group would like to see the FICCI and the chambers of commerce become a means of developing business leadership and political talent. The members of the committee and the president of the FICCI, they argue, should be chosen on merit and talent and not according to the number of companies owned or the size of their capital assets, because these positions have excellent potential as training grounds for later political activity. The majority of the FICCI committee members, however, see the FICCI as reflecting the realities of Indian business. Those realities, they believe, dictate that those who are willing to pay the cost of running the federation should have a dominant say in the policy and leadership selection. They feel it is not the job of business to police itself, and that whenever business is under attack it should be defended without apology or scapegoating. The reorganization of the federation in 1971 has tended to strengthen the hand of those who advocate a more open and public political posture and a more active role for business in building a new business image.

The majority of the conflicts within the committee are based on conflicting interests between trade and industry, modern and traditional industry, efficient and inefficient plants, and so forth. The trade versus industry struggle takes place largely at the annual meeting, for traders are still poorly represented in the committee. Moreover, both the traders and some industrial interests have a legitimate grievance. Because older Marwari houses had large investments in coal, sugar, and jute, these industries tended to get special consideration, even when their needs conflict with the more modern industrial sectors represented in the committee. Conflicts have also arisen between importers who want to continue to import goods and manufacturers who want to keep them out, between those who favor foreign collaboration and those who want an emphasis on indigenous or Swadeshi goods, and so forth. One of the most divisive recent issues cutting across all these interests was the dispute that took place within the FICCI over controls.

In the mid-1960s, Prime Minister Shastri decided to review all controls and eliminate those which no longer served any useful purpose.

In pursuit of this decision, Home Minister G. L. Nanda informed the federation, on May 29, 1965, that the government was studying controls, and he asked for recommendations as to which should be abolished. The committee of the federation met on June 28, but was unable to come up with any recommendations. A similar meeting was held on August 16, and again no agreement was reached.[68] Finally, on August 26, Prime Minister Shastri announced in the Lok Sabha that he was going to lift controls on some specific commodities to encourage production. When the committee met again on December 1, to discuss the issue of controls based on a note prepared by the secretariat, it was able to agree only on the need for the restoration of a market mechanism. As far as individual commodities were concerned, the committee passed the buck, leaving it up to the individual associations to make their own decisions. Within the committee, some members advocated a total abolition of controls, some wanted controls modified, and others opposed decontrol because it aided the profitability of their industries. Textiles, coal, and sugar interests within the committee most strongly opposed decontrol. The newer industries, such as engineering, favored a policy of total freedom from control. Thus, while the FICCI in theory stood for decontrol and a free market, each group opposed having such a policy applied to its industry. And so, despite the long-standing FICCI demand that government eliminate controls, internal divisions prevented the committee from making any recommendations and thereby influencing the direction of government policy. The committee seldom encounters difficulty in agreeing on demands for lower taxes, the need for greater incentives for investment, or whether to request government support for the private sector. But substantial disagreement regularly occurs over issues which have a more differential effect on the conflicting interests of which the federation is composed.

Another recent divisive issue within the committee concerned the problem of planning. During the formulation of the fourth Indian Five Year Plan, the committee could not agree on the appropriate size of the plan or on the levels of deficit financing that it should provide. Three distinct views were represented in the committee. The Bombay group in general favored a smaller plan and little or no deficit financing. The Birlas and Calcutta Marwaris favored a larger plan. A third group took the stand that deficit financing was acceptable if used for productive purposes. The dispute over planning had larger political overtones. The Bombay group feared that a larger plan and deficit

[68] FICCI, *Report of the Proceedings of the Executive Committee for the Year 1965* (Delhi: FICCI, 1965), pp. 98–99.

financing would enlarge the public sector and result in higher taxation. The Birla group looked upon a larger plan as a means of expanding their own facilities. As a result, numerous contradictory statements were issued individually by FICCI leaders.

Sometimes clashes of interest became embroiled in regional and personality conflicts. During the mid-1960s, India's textile industry was under severe strains because of recession and price controls. The committee of the FICCI decided to send a delegation to discuss the problem of the textile industry with government. The president of the Indian Cotton Mills Federation, who at the time also happened to be a member of the FICCI committee, objected strongly. He insisted that the problems of the textile industry should be handled by the Indian Cotton Mills Federation and not by the FICCI. The president of the Indian Cotton Mills Federation argued that the FICCI was not equipped to handle the complex issues involved in the textile industry. A group within the committee of the FICCI, however, argued that the textile issue had wider implications over which the FICCI, as a representative of both producers and distributors, clearly had jurisdiction. The president of the Indian Cotton Mills Federation threatened to resign from the committee if the issue were pressed. He was persuaded to withdraw his threat, but when, later, the FICCI insisted on passing a resolution on the subject at its annual meeting in 1968, the president of the Indian Cotton Mills Federation again refused to support it. The conflict over textile policy involved a jurisdictional dispute, a clash of personalities between the president of the Indian Cotton Mills Federation and other members of the committee, and a deeper clash between the big Bombay millowners who were not members of the FICCI and FICCI leaders. Although the Indian Cotton Mills Federation was unable to prevent the FICCI from considering the issue, it was still in a position to handle the issue separately if it chose to do so.

Thus, most FICCI resolutions and policy staements must be based on compromises. When the cleavages are minor, they can be ironed out. But when the clash of interest is strong or more direct, the committee is usually forced to postpone the issue or leave its members free to act on their own. As one committee member put it, "The decisions of the committee are after all only recommendations and are not really mandatory in any way. It really boils down to whether you are going to make a representation this way or some other way. Thus when a conflict develops the committee leaves it to government, and individual parties then use whatever influence they have with government to press their point of view."

The FICCI is a voluntary association, and its policy pronouncements are not binding in any legal way. The federation has no formal sanctions which it can employ against those who refuse to accept a particular federation decision. Individual members, on the other hand, control large capital assets, have their own source of influence, and their own contacts in government. They need not accept policy positions which they oppose. If they object very strongly, they can resign. Businessmen participate in FICCI politics as a means of gaining prestige and contact with government, from the desire to participate in an all-India body, and under pressure from others who would like to have them as allies. Thus, there are positive forces which work to keep the leadership together and to give a certain force of collectivity to FICCI policy pronouncements. Decision-making in the committee is thus based on personal influence, persuasion, and the balancing of interests designed to produce a consensus. The result is that many FICCI resolutions and policy pronouncements may represent the lowest common denominator of agreement—they may be left deliberately vague. Such resolutions do not provide much effective guidance to government policy-makers, but they may have some cathartic effect for business.

Although the committee is the chief policy-maker for the federation, the president, as the chief executive officer, is responsible for carrying out the policies laid down by the committee. The president has the power to speak on behalf of the federation, but he can be held accountable to the committee. The relationship of the president to the committee depends on the personality of the president. If the president is weak and does not like to make decisions, he makes frequent reference to the committee. A strong president resorts to the committee less frequently.

The president does not usually consult with the entire committee but rather with a small inner group which consists of its senior members, most of whom are former presidents. In recent times, however, observers can cite only one or two instances when a president made commitments which were unacceptable to important sectors of the committee. In these cases the committee was reluctant to make a public rebuttal, fearing to embarrass the president. The matter was handled internally.

The president is held in check not only by the committee but by the secretariat as well. The president is very dependent upon the secretariat for information and material, and he is constantly reminded by them as professionals that he represents the entire federation, not simply himself or the industry in which he has a dominant interest. The secretariat is also equipped to inform the president as to what past FICCI policy has been on a particular issue. Because the secretariat plays a major role as advisor to the committee as well as to the president, it is familiar with committee views on basic FICCI policies. It is especially aware of the interests and views of the dominant committee members who pay the bulk of the bills of the federation. Thus, even if a president has extensive experience in a particular industry, he is politely reminded that he must consult the industry. In this way, the secretariat attempts to overcome the narrow perspectives of FICCI leaders and the centrifugal tendencies of its diverse membership.

The pattern of oligarchical control over the federation achieved by big business in the past was partly a product of the uneven development of industry in India, which became reflected in federation membership. Yet it is also, in large part, brought about by the difficulties of mobilizing the Indian business community and a refusal on the part of those mobilized to pay the costs of an effective organ of collective action. The resistance to increases in fees by the ordinary members in the 1940s led to the adoption of the associate membership as a means of providing an elastic form of income. This economic power, however, was converted into voting power, which enabled a small group to gain and retain control over the committee and the presidency.

Patterns of control in the FICCI are changing. However, in the past such changes resulted in the emergence of a pattern of elite politics which reflected traditional cleavages within the business community and which, in time, resulted in an ever increasing disparity between the leadership and the rapidly expanding and changing membership. Although the elite might, only with difficulty, manage to balance the demands of influential families and regional groups, there was unanimity in their dedication to the needs of large-scale industry in India, and considerably less attention was paid to the problems of traders, small and medium business interests, and the newly developing regions.

With the increase in number and size of medium and small scale industrial units, the emergence of new giants, and the dispersion of new industrial development throughout the country as a result of government encouragement, all gradually reflected in a changing FICCI membership, pressure from these and other long ignored interests within the federation began to build up. The FICCI leadership found itself faced with demands for broader representation in the committee and for a larger voice in federation affairs and policy-making. The leadership has slowly responded to these demands, with the result that the FICCI is becoming more and more broadly based and truly reflective of the Indian business community as a whole.

PART THREE

Channels of Access and Influence

IX

PUBLIC OPINION AND BUSINESS

The mere mobilization and articulation of group interests does not guarantee the success or accomplishment of its goals. Having articulated its demands, an interest group must actively seek to gain access to decision-makers, in order to influence policy outcomes by so changing the perceptions of policy-makers that they accept the group's point of view, in whole or in part. Assuredly the effectiveness of an interest group depends on its ability to organize, to articulate real demands in unambiguous terms, and to gain access to relevant decision-makers. But ultimately the test of efficacy is the degree to which the group demonstrably influences public policy. This distinction between access and influence is often ignored or obscured.

Once demands are formulated, the group's next step is to secure access to decision-makers. The pattern of access, or how and where groups attempt to exert influence, varies from political system to political system. Access patterns conform to broad systemic factors, such as levels of modernization, structures of decision-making, and public policy, as much as they reflect the nature of the particular group which is, at any one time, exerting pressure at various points on the system. In general, however, groups focus their attention on those levels of decision-making that constitute the relevant locus or loci of power within that political system. Thus, a study of patterns of access also reveals the distribution of power within a system.

There are several points in the political process at which a group can bring influence to bear: public opinion, political parties and electoral campaigns, the legislative process, the cabinet, and the bureaucracy. Interest groups may also resort to direct action and violence. The strategy and tactics employed by a group seeking access depends on the political resources of the group, on the degree of direct representation the group enjoys within the decision-making structures, and on the distribution of power within the political system. Groups do not give equal attention to all levels of decision-making. In terms of time, energy, and resources, they devote their major efforts to securing access to the level of decision-making that will produce the most effective results. Although groups are ultimately interested in influencing those who are in a position to make authoritative decisions, they often find it necessary to intervene at an earlier phase of the policy process, by generating public suport for their position, by influencing the kinds of decision-makers selected for critical positions, and by building strong and close relations with actual or potential decision-makers.

In India, the abolition of direct functional parliamentary representation for business and other interest groups under the new constitution, and the centralizing of decision-making and the promulgation of planning as the guiding policy of the new government, added to the distrust of business which continues to permeate the political culture, persuaded business to concentrate its initial post-1947 strategy directly on the executive and on the higher echelons of the bureaucracy. Only recently—with the growing self-confidence of business and, for a brief time, the fragmentation of the decision-making structures resulting from changes in the party system—has this strategy been modified to the extent that business has organized itself to achieve access for its views by intervening at an earlier stage in the political process.

One of the most severe handicaps facing business in pressing its claims on government is the strong sense of suspicion and distrust of the private sector in India. "It is not just business rapport with government," argued one senior bureaucrat, "but it's rapport with the public at large which is poor. It is this lack of rapport with the public which is the chief factor in affecting business's ability to make representations to government." Most Indians have a robber baron image of private sector business. The private sector is said to be motivated solely by greed, interested primarily in quick returns, unconcerned with the welfare of its employees, lacking even a rudimentary sense of social consciousness, and guilty of nepotism and casteism in its employment practices.[1] Many of these popular stereotypes are as influential at the political and bureaucratic levels of decision-making as they are widespread among the population.

The low prestige of the private sector in India is a product of tradition, ideology, alleged past and present misdeeds, and actual business practices of some sectors of Indian business. Traditionally, Indian society has assigned the highest value to intellectual pursuit. The mer-

[1] For an excellent example of intellectual attitudes toward private sector business, see Mr. Justice P. B. Mukharji, *Social Responsibilities of Business* (Calcutta: Conference on Social Responsibilities of Business, 1967). For an excellent critique of Indian stereotyped images of business, see George B. Baldwin, *Industrial Growth in South India: Case Studies in Economic Development* (New York: Free Press, 1959), pp. 336–339.

chant has never been very high in the social scale. His "unremitting attention to money-making," noted Carstairs, earned the village bania many enemies. "It would be no exaggeration to say that they were the most hated community in this area. . . ." [2] This long-standing hostility toward the usurious village merchants has been transmitted to the modern industrial sector, a transferral that was facilitated by the traditional merchant caste origins of the vast majority of India's large entrepreneurial families,[3] and by the fact that industrialists like Ramkrishna Dalmia had been convicted of illegal operations very much in the image of the old stereotype. Thus, the low esteem of business is partly a result of traditional caste prejudices and past business practices.

Traditional images of business are reinforced by socialist and Marxist thought, which permeates the elite Indian political culture. In this atmosphere, as Erdman observes, "Few things elicit more derisive comment in contemporary India than support for laissez-faire capitalism." [4] Thus, a study by De Costa in 1956 of popular attitudes toward the public and private sectors showed that almost half of those interviewed considered private businessmen to be exploiters interested only in reaping large profits. These profits were viewed as unearned booty for private business. Such feelings were especially strong among young, urban, educated, middle-class intellectuals and were only slightly less pronounced in the rural areas.[5]

In sharp contrast to the negative image of the private sector, the survey revealed strong support for the development of a large public sector. The government-run public sector was generally believed to be primarily interested in the welfare of the people. Thus, there was considerable sentiment in favor of having the private sector replaced com-

[2] G. Morris Carstairs, *The Twice-Born* (Bloomington, Ind.: Indiana University Press, 1961), p. 120. See also Helen Lamb, "The Indian Merchant," in *Traditional India: Structure and Change,* ed. Milton Singer (Philadelphia: American Folklore Society, 1959), pp. 25–34; Leighton W. Hazlehurst, *Entrepreneurship and the Merchant Castes in a Punjabi City* (Durham, N. C.: Duke University Press, 1966).

[3] B. B. Misra, *The Indian Middle Classes: Their Growth in Modern Times* (London: Oxford University Press, 1961), pp. 251–357.

[4] Howard L. Erdman, *The Swatantra Party and Indian Conservativism* (Cambridge: Cambridge University Press, 1967), pp. 193–194.

[5] Indian Institute of Public Opinion, "The Structure of Urban Opinion on the Socialist Pattern of Society," *Monthly Public Opinion Surveys* I (1956): 36–39. Some sectors of business are very aware of these popular attitudes and feel they play a critical role in private sector development. See All-Indian Management Association, *Seminar: Business and Society,* September 1965 (Delhi: AIMA, 1965); and Prakash L. Tandon, "Management in India Today," Walchand Memorial Lecture Series (Bombay: Maharashtra Chamber of Commerce, 1968).

pletely by the public sector.[6] A study of the bureaucratic-political elite of Orissa in the early 1960s corroborated the De Costa results. The vast majority of those interviewed held strongly negative views of the private sector and supported a policy of substantial enlargement of the public sector.[7] Given these negative attitudes toward the private sector and the strong positive sentiment for the public sector, it is not surprising that Mrs. Gandhi's nationalization of private sector banks in 1969 elicited such an outpouring of enthusiasm and public support.[8]

A final factor which has helped to reinforce the strongly negative attitudes toward the private sector is the fairly widespread feeling that Indian business is dominated by greedy, unprincipled crooks who conduct their affairs in secret and engage in a wide variety of antisocial practices. As a result of illegal practices—including tax avoidance and evasion, profiteering, food adulteration, trafficking in licenses, permits and quotas, and manipulating of shares, accounts, and invoices—business is thought to have accumulated huge amounts of tax free "black money" which is used for ostentatious living. Only slightly worse, black money is considered by some to be the main source of corruption in public life, for businessmen are supposed to be adept at bribing public officials and politicians to achieve their ends.[9]

Finally, the Indian public is bombarded almost daily with authenticated and unauthenticated newspaper accounts of a variety of business misdeeds. Thus, popular attitudes are not totally unfounded. The question is whether malpractices should be attributed to the actions of a few black sheep or whether it is characteristic of the entire flock. Investigations conducted into the affairs of the Dalmia-Jain and Mundhra companies revealed widespread stock manipulation and tax evasion designed to fleece the shareholders of dividends and the government of

[6] Indian Institute of Public Opinion, "The Structure of Urban Opinion on the Socialist Pattern of Society," pp. 44–47; Mukharji, *Social Responsibilities of Business*, p. 5; Baldwin, *Industrial Growth*, pp. 336–339.

[7] Richard P. Taub, *Bureaucrats Under Stress: Administrators and Administration in an Indian State* (Berkeley and Los Angeles: University of California Press, 1969), p. 167.

[8] See *The Economic Times* (Bombay), April 20, 1969; April 27, 1969; and August 6, 1969.

[9] Mukharji, *Social Responsibilities of Business*, p. 64; Taub, *Bureaucrats Under Stress*, pp. 167, 169; Chester Bowles, *The New York Times*, April 25, 1969; and Myron Weiner, *The Politics of Scarcity: Public Pressure and Political Response in India* (Chicago: University of Chicago Press, 1962), pp. 124–125; Government of India, Ministry of Home Affairs, *Report of the Committee on Prevention of Corruption* (New Delhi: Government of India Press, 1964) (Santhanam Report); Surendranath Dwivedy and G. S. Bhargava, *Political Corruption in India* (New Delhi: Popular Book Services, 1967); John B. Montiero, *Corruption: Control of Maladministration* (Bombay: Manaktalas, 1966).

taxes.[10] Tax evasion is widely considered to be a major fiscal problem. Chester Bowles, former United States ambassador to India, said that India was losing hundreds of millions of rupees each year because penalties against tax evasion either were not heavy enough or were not enforced.[11] Nicholas Kaldor, an eminent Cambridge economist, was invited by the government of India to review the Indian tax system. Kaldor estimated that the sum lost as a result of tax evasion was between two and three hundred crores in 1953–1954. Of this, seventy to one hundred crores was due from the modern sector.[12] An official estimate made by the Central Board of Revenue placed the level of tax evasion in the high income brackets at forty-five crores per year. A more recent estimate made by the Direct Taxes Inquiry Committee estimated that income on which taxes were evaded for 1968–1969 was Rs 1,400 crores.[13] These estimates are probably not excessive. In Pakistan, the martial law regime of Ayub Khan, shortly after it came to power, succeeded in uncovering 134 crores (281.4 million dollars) of hidden wealth and collected 24 crores (50.4 million dollars) in taxes on excess income.[14]

According to many informed observers, however, the charges raised against Indian businessmen are exaggerated. A former British editor of the Indian business journal *Capital* insists that organized business in India is composed of a large, responsible, and public spirited group "whose merits have tended to be obscured by the misdemeanors of a few. . . ." [15] An American observer with extended experience in India reached a similar conclusion. "In my opinion," argued George Rosen, "the activities of Indian business do not approach those of American businessmen in the American 'robber baron' age; either many of the charges have never been proved and are based on unfounded gossip, or the activities mentioned were not illegal when carried out." [16]

Suspicion and distrust of the private sector has generated substantial

[10] "Mundhra Inquiry: The Full Story," *Free Press Journal* (January–February, 1958); Government of India, *Report of the Commission of Inquiry on the Administration of Dalmia-Jain Companies* (Vivian Bose Report), Ministry of Commerce and Industry, Department of Company Law Administration, Delhi, 1963.

[11] *New York Times*, April 25, 1969.

[12] Michael Kidron, *Foreign Investments in India* (London: Oxford University Press, 1965), p. 226.

[13] Montiero, *Corruption*, p. 47; *The Economic Times* (Bombay), March 21, 1972.

[14] Herbert Feldman, *Revolution in Pakistan: A Study of the Martial Law Administration* (London: Oxford University Press, 1967), p. 62.

[15] Geoffrey Tyson, *Nehru: The Years of Power* (New York: Praeger, 1966), pp. 61–62.

[16] George Rosen, *Democracy and Economic Change in India* (Berkeley and Los Angeles: University of California Press, 1966), p. 43.

support for the government's policy of permitting the private sector to function only under a system of tight regulation and control. Because it is believed that businessmen cannot be trusted to practice self-restraint, they must be externally restrained.[17] But as influential as the fear that business will cheat if government relaxes controls is the fear that a decision in favor of business will result in the decision-makers being attacked by the left as procapitalist and unprogressive. In India there is a feeling that the public stance of government must be one of aloofness and detachment. But when it comes to business, the relationship is more a matter of mutual suspicion and hostility than mere wary distance. Above all, too much close consultation is equated with collusion.

Businessmen in India are fully conscious of the hostile public attitude toward private sector business. The public image of business has had a significant effect on business behavior and even on its self-image. Most Indian businessmen are resentful over the failure of the public to give business sufficient recognition for its contributions to Indian development. They feel misunderstood as much as they feel maligned. Older businessmen are most likely to react indignantly when they feel they are being used as scapegoats for the failures of others. They display open contempt for politicians, the bureaucracy, and the public at large, and vow to carry out their affairs as they always have, dealing with government through the old style of quiet behind-the-scenes lobbying and wire-pulling, whether or not such procedures tend to confirm the suspicious public's view of their operations.

The post-World War II industrialists and a large number of the sons of India's unregenerate captains of industry who make up the new generation of educated owner-managers, on the other hand, are much more introspective and deeply concerned about the public image of business. S. S. Kanoria, a young Marwari business leader and former president of the FICCI, said, as early as 1957:

> The . . . question which troubles me is as to why the private sector, which is composed of intelligent people with ability and doing very hard work, lacks the admiration or even the respect of the other sectors of the community. Certainly it suggests that there is something seriously wrong with us. We cannot shut our eyes to the fact that whereas in the U.S.A. and other countries private enterprise is considered a *sine qua non* of democ-

[17] Taub, *Bureaucrats Under Stress*, p. 169.

> racy, freedom, and economic advancement, it is looked upon with contempt, hatred, and suspicion in our country. It is therefore no surprise that no political party in India ventured to advocate and support our case in the general elections. As things are now moving, we cannot deny that our days appear to be numbered and our system is on its way out in India. And, if the end comes, I am afraid it may go unwept, unsung, and unhonored. Whatever may be our own contention, we have failed to win the confidence of the people and identify ourselves with the awakening of the masses to the consciousness of poverty and degradation and the insistent demand for a better life. The general impression that we have made on the masses is that we are intoxicated with power and wealth, indulge in its vulgar show, and that our sole aim in life is to amass fortunes for ourselves regardless of national interests.[18]

Education and management training has given the younger generation of Indian owner-managers a sense of identity and professional status. As professionals, therefore, and not merely from a sense of pique, they refuse to be classified with the robber barons of old. This new self-image has made the younger generation determined to change the public image of the business community. To do so, they feel business must break out of its isolation, mix more freely with other sectors of the community, and participate more openly in politics and public affairs, even if it hurts.[19] Businessmen must show that they are responsible citizens interested in the larger problems of society. They concede, ironically, what the older generation of businessmen will not—that they were entirely too engrossed in making money, too greedy, and too concerned with living at peace with government regardless of the cost. Agreeing with their elders that business has made a substantial and positive contribution to Indian economic development, the younger generation is determined not to let the vast majority of the people remain unaware of it.

Business in India, therefore, has moved on several fronts to try to improve the image of private sector business, if only to create a more sympathetic climate of opinion to which it may appeal in times of need. A variety of essentially pilot programs have been launched, but there is still no consensus among Indian businessmen as to which mechanism

[18] FICCI, *Proceedings of the Thirtieth Annual Meeting, 1957* (Delhi: FICCI, 1957), pp. 15–16.

[19] "Should Businessmen Enter Politics?", *Industrial Times*, vol. X, no. 1 (January 1, 1968).

or combination of mechanisms will best accomplish the objective. Worse still, many of the programs have generated discord within the business community itself.

Perhaps the earliest effort to influence public opinion was an attempt by a group of Bombay businessmen to attack the problem at the ideological level by creating an organization to combat the collectivist sentiment in India by speaking out for the virtues of private enterprise. In 1956, shortly after the Congress party had committed itself to create a socialist pattern of society, A. D. Shroff and M. R. Masani, both of whom were at one time connected with the Tatas, and Murarji Vaidya of the All-India Manufacturers Organizations, created the Forum of Free Enterprise. This was designed as "a nonpolitical and nonpartisan organization," intended to educate the public "on the fundamentals of free enterprise and on the contributions which it can make to national welfare." [20] Free enterprise, according to the forum's manifesto, is an "integral part of democracy whose virtues were going by default due to sustained and unjustified attacks being made against it." [21]

The creation of the Forum of Free Enterprise generated such a violent reaction from the Indian political leadership that the organization felt compelled to issue a second document entitled "What the Forum Stands For." In this document the forum repudiated traditional laissez-faire doctrines and nineteenth-century capitalism as having "no place in contemporary Indian life." Such concepts, said the forum, were "as dead as the dodo." However, the forum also repudiated "the Marxist approach to socialism through state ownership of the means of production." In its place the forum supported the principle of "free enterprise operating within a planned economy." In short, the forum accepted the principle of a welfare state based on a planned economy in which both private and public sectors would exist together. The forum, however, warned that the public sector should not be permitted to expand to the point where it completely dominated the national economy, for such a development would lead to a "regimentation of life" that would hurt the individual as much as it would hurt business.

The Forum of Free Enterprise has remained a small but vocal organization which has focused the bulk of its attention on the college age generation of India. Although centers have been created in Ahmedabad, Bangalore, Calcutta, Madras, and New Delhi, its real base of support continues to be Bombay. The forum had a relatively mod-

[20] Forum of Free Enterprise, *Basic Documents* (Bombay: Forum of Free Enterprise, 1966).

[21] *Ibid.*

est budget of 220,000 rupees in 1967. These funds were received largely from contributions and membership fees. There are reports that it has encountered considerable difficulties in raising funds since the death of A. D. Shroff, one of its founders and most enthusiastic supporter. The forum's budget is used to support a variety of activities carried out by the Bombay headquarters and its regional centers. The forum publishes books, pamphlets, and articles for circulation to its members, student associations, Members of Parliament, educational institutions, and influential people in the community. It also has a program of donating book sets to college libraries. These include, among others, Freidrich Hayek's *The Constitution of Liberty,* R. Kelf-Cohen's *Nationalization in Britain: The End of a Dogma,* and Northcote Parkinson's *Parkinson's Law on the Pursuit of Progress.* Most of the forum's written material warns about the totalitarian implications of excessive government controls, heavy taxation, and government ownership of the means of production.

In addition to its book distribution and publication programs, the forum arranges public meetings to discuss topics of current importance. In 1967, the forum sponsored 139 such meetings in Bombay and at its regional centers. Attendance at forum meetings in Bombay is considered good, with an average audience level of about one hundred. However, meetings at the other centers have never generated the same enthusiasm. In New Delhi and Calcutta, for example, audiences usually seldom exceed twenty. Other programs of the forum include essay and elocution competitions specifically oriented toward students.

The forum admits that "it is difficult to assess the exact impact of our educational activities on public thinking . . . ," [22] and it may be that the ideology of the forum will have to be substantially revised and updated if it is to have any substantial impact on students or the Indian public. At present it appears to be an organization of believers, too closely identified with the Swatantra party and anti-Congress party opposition forces to have a very wide appeal to young or old.

Even within the business community, the political overtones of the forum created difficulties for the organization from the very beginning. Many of the forum's Bombay supporters attempted to have the FICCI endorse and support the forum as part of a federation drive to influence public attitudes toward business.[23] These overtures were rejected out-

[22] Forum of Free Enterprise, *Report and Accounts* (Bombay: Forum of Free Enterprise, 1967).

[23] FICCI, *Proceedings of the Thirtieth Annual Meeting, 1957* (Delhi: FICCI, 1957), pp. 18–19.

right, one delegate suggesting that the forum had been founded to "put up a fight and challenge the government." [24] In fact, the FICCI leadership refused open support to the forum because of its identification with anti-Congress forces, its close association with the Tatas, and its insistence on mixing politics with business. Even today, the business community remains divided on the utility, sponsorship, and philosophy of the forum. One pro-forum businessman stated the differences in the following terms: "The federation and Birlas feel that if the life of the private sector in India is to be twenty years then by a process of pressure on government one could at least extend the life of the private sector to thirty years. People in the forum, on the other hand, felt that the private sector should be a permanent institution and a permanent part of the society." But other businessmen feel that the forum itself has no future, that it could not withstand Nehru's violent reaction to it, and that it is ineffective except in Bombay. On pragmatic grounds, therefore, it would be unwise for the FICCI to associate itself with the Forum of Free Enterprise.

A second approach to changing popular attitudes toward the private sector has been the attempt to strengthen the process of self-regulation within the business community. The issue of self-regulation was originally raised by the Forum of Free Enterprise, which included among its basic documents a code of conduct for business. The issue became politically sensitive in the late 1960s as a result of the Dalmia-Jain scandal. Nor did the inflation and food shortages which followed in the wake of two successive crop failures improve the image of business. Government made numerous appeals to traders and shopkeepers to cooperate in trying to keep down prices and preventing artificial shortages. In response to the general concern over inflation and shortages, a group of Indian and foreign business concerns, in cooperation with the Indian International Center in New Delhi and other organizations, sponsored a series of public seminars on the social responsibilities of business.[25] As a result of these and other discussions, a group of businessmen and industrialists in Bombay attempted to formulate a set of fair trade practices which would be implemented by business on a voluntary basis through an organization known as the Fair Trade Practices Association (FTPA). The objectives of the FTPA were "to codify the existing fair trade practices, set up an effective machinery for their implementation in an organized manner and thereby create greater public confidence in and goodwill toward the business community."

[24] *Ibid.*, p. 21.

[25] Indian International Center, *Social Responsibilities of Business* (Bombay: Manaktalas, 1966). See also Mukharji, *Social Responsibilities of Business.*

Every member of the association accepted the following fundamental obligations:

(1) To charge only fair and reasonable prices and take every possible step to ensure that the prices to be charged to the consumer are brought to his notice.
(2) To take every possible step to ensure that the agents or dealers appointed by him do not charge prices higher than fixed.
(3) In times of scarcity, not to withhold or suppress stocks of goods with a view to hoarding and/or profiteering.
(4) Not to produce or trade in spurious goods or goods of standards lower than specified.
(5) Not to adulterate goods supplied.
(6) Not to publish misleading advertisements.
(7) To invoice goods exported or imported at their correct prices.
(8) To maintain accuracy in weights and measures of goods offered for sale.
(9) Not to deal knowingly in smuggled goods.[26]

By August 1968, the FTPA had two hundred members. Like the Forum of Free Enterprise, however, it was predominantly a Bombay-based organization. Among the major participants were the Tatas and Mafatlals and the large foreign business groups in India. The initiative behind the FTPA came from those Bombay business groups who feel that business can improve its image only through its own efforts to ostracize and impose sanctions against those who are dishonest. The idea is reminiscent of the caste panchayat, which keeps internal discipline by threats to cast out offenders.

As was true of the Forum of Free Enterprise, attempts to obtain FICCI endorsement and sponshorship of the FTPA failed. There is a very strong view within the federation that, because the FICCI has no real powers or sanctions to employ against those who violate codes of ethics, it is unwise to take the responsibility for implementing such codes. Although the federation can set down basic principles for business to which its members can subscribe, it must leave regulation and enforcement to government. Moreover, the FICCI feels that to introduce sanctions where they do not now exist would require a system of compulsory membership and licensing of member firms which would run contrary to the entire voluntary nature of the association and thus contrary to the philosophy and history of the federation.

[26] *The FTPA Bulletin*, vol. I, no. 1 (September–October, 1968).

Some members feel that the FTPA goes too far in the direction of self-regulation, and others feel it does not go far enough. They point out that the FTPA code makes no mention of tax evasion and other such "crimes" and that the organization has no real sanctions which it can employ. The enforcement provisions of the FTPA constitution are indeed vague. According to the constitution, every member of the association receives a seal upon joining the organization. The seal is to be a guarantee that the holder observes high business standards. Any complaints about a breach of the code are referred for investigation to a panel appointed by the executive committee of the association. If the panel finds that the charge is accurate and that the member has violated the code, the panel may take appropriate action, including termination of membership and withdrawal of the seal.[27] Withdrawal of the seal seems to be the only overt sanction, and yet, because the organization provides no screening methods for membership to begin with, the mere possession of the seal is meaningless. In short, the FTPA as presently constituted hardly seems an effective route to creating any sense of public confidence. The critics insist that the only way to make an organization like the FTPA effective is to have a code of ethics that can be upheld in court, if necessary.

A third approach to improving the image of business and influencing public opinion has been to reorient business associations to play a more constructive, active, and creative role. Traditionally business associations in India have functioned primarily as grievance bodies. The defensive stand has become almost automatic. But several attempts have been made to convert business associations into more active, research-oriented institutions capable of proposing concrete, constructive, and detailed alternatives to government policies and of acting as critics of government. The FICCI and several of its regional affiliates have moved much faster and further in this direction than has Assocham. In fact, the activities of the FICCI have changed dramatically in recent years, as its staff has increased and levels of professionalization within the federation have improved. Traditionally the federation reached the public largely through press releases, by passing and publicizing its resolutions, and by news coverage of its annual meeting. In recent years, however, the federation has substantially expanded its public information activities. The federation has begun to hold seminars on major issues of public policy, and leading government, industry, and academic specialists have been invited. It has created a separate research organiza-

[27] *Memorandum and Articles of Association of Fair Trade Practices Association*, Fair Trade Practices Association (Bombay, 1968), p. 8.

tion called the Economic and Scientific Research Foundation, which conducts both FICCI studies and other studies on a contract basis.[23] And it has begun to finance independent research by outside agencies, such as the Indian Council of Applied Economic Research. The federation has also sponsored trade fairs and industrial exhibitions to publicize the products of Indian industry and has recently expanded its headquarters in New Delhi to include a large exhibition hall for a permanent industrial exhibit designed for export promotion.

Although this represents an impressive list of activities, critics still feel that the federation is doing only a fraction of what needs to be done. Many of the old stereotypes still seem to carry weight. Arguments are still heard that business is not really interested in encouraging independent and objective research, that it still prefers to conduct its affairs in secret, and that the business community still remains too aloof from the rest of society. Moreover, most of the new federation activities are still conducted on such a modest scale that they must be substantially expanded if they are to make a real impact. There are some who feel that India needs an organization, similar to the Committee for Economic Development in the United States, which would do detailed studies of major issues of public policy and would recommend alternatives. There are also those who call for an organization somewhat similar to the Better Business Bureau. Yet some members of the federation argue that many of these new activities and the very independence which gives them credibility may jeopardize the business cause. For example, some years ago the federation sponsored a study of the managing agency system by the Indian Council of Applied Economic Research. Some members of the committee objected to such use of federation money because the federation would have no control over the recommendations made by the Council.

A fourth approach to improving the image of business has been to encourage and support a variety of subsidiary organizations, such as the management associations and the government-sponsored Indian Standards Institution and Productivity Councils. Professionalization of management is still relatively recent in India. The All-India Management Association was not founded until 1957, as Indian capital slowly began the process of separating ownership from management. In India, the professionalization of management—which has been encouraged principally by the bigger, more modern sectors of Indian and foreign business—could play an important role in changing public attitudes,

[23] See *Annual Report* 1966–1967, Economic and Scientific Research Foundation (New Delhi: Federation House, 1968).

particularly elite attitudes, toward business as business begins to recruit more and more talent from the professional middle class. At present, however, it is still generally assumed by most middle-class intellectuals that employment opportunities in the private sector are dominated by nepotism and casteism and that merit counts for little. There is a strong feeling that a management career based on merit is still not possible in the private sector of Indian business and that "until the government runs industry there will be too much weightage given to caste." [29] Unless business does something to correct this image, it is highly unlikely that it will gain the support of the Indian urban middle class. Although there are some indications that employment preferences among the Indian urban middle class are changing and that the coveted ICS-IAS positions no longer enjoy the status and glamor they once had, a business career is still not given serious consideration. Taub, for example, found that the dominant preference of a small sample of ICS officers was to see their sons not as government servants or as businessmen but as doctors, lawyers, or engineers.[30] Thus, the managerial revolution has not yet come to India, but when it does it will add much more respectability to a business career—provided, of course, it is based on real professionalism, for the white-collar crook is hardly preferable to the unscrupulous entrepreneur.

In addition to the ideological and image building approaches to changing the Indian business image, there are a hodgepodge of other suggestions. Some people argue that business should place more emphasis on its philanthropic activities, play a larger role in financing education, and focus greater attention on charitable activities. Similarly, business must pay more attention to publicizing its role in such areas as export promotion, development, and fulfilling plan targets. Others feel that the image of Indian business can be improved by placing greater emphasis on the mass media. The Indian business community might, for instance, set up a parallel newsreel service to combat the antibusiness propaganda which, it is argued, is constantly fed to the public by the government-controlled newsreel services. Still others feel that the image of Indian business can be improved only if the business community itself begins to change some of its priorities. Thus, the private sector might spend more time and money on research and industrial activities, for despite the existence of tax legislation designed to encourage research, very little research is actually done by Indian industry.

[29] Taya Zinkin, *Challenges in India* (London: Chatto and Windus, 1966), p. 214.
[30] Taub, *Bureaucrats Under Stress*, pp. 83, 85.

Another and persistent school of thought argues that the only way to improve the image of business is for business to become more politically active. There is a growing feeling among the younger generation that if business has a right to exist then business has a right to participate in politics and to influence elected representatives. As a result, there has been a greater trend toward lobbying and an increase in the participation of businessmen in party politics.

Indian business is in accord on the fact that it has an image problem, but thus far it has been unable to reach a consensus about the best way to change that image. A number of approaches have been tried, but the critics of each have prevented any one all-out effort on the problem. The ideological approach represented by the Forum of Free Enterprise has generated conflict because of the fear of either alienating the government, which was controlled by the dominant Congress party, or of destroying the political stability which only the Congress party seemed to be able to maintain. Perhaps even more controversial has been the issue of business ethics and the degree to which business should attempt to police itself by ostracizing the black sheep.

Ideological approaches and efforts to improve business ethics have generated a great deal of debate within business as ways to improve the business image. But there is little doubt that any attempt by business to become more active in the development of mass media would be met by strong public and governmental objections. The major Indian business houses already own almost all the important metropolitan newspapers and economic journals in the country. The *Times of India* (Bombay) and *Economic Times* (Bombay) are owned by Dalmia-Jain; the *Hindustan Times* (New Delhi) and *Eastern Economist* (New Delhi) are owned by the Birlas; the *Indian Express* and *Financial Express* are owned by Goenka; and the *Statesman* (Calcutta) and *Commerce* (Bombay) are said to be controlled by the Tatas and Mafatlal. The journal *Capital* in Calcutta tends to speak on behalf of British managing agency interests. The independent and left wing press, although represented, are no match for the giants controlled by the major business houses. Of the major metropolitan dailies, only the *Hindu* (Madras) is independently controlled. And of the major journals, only the *Political and Economic Weekly* is independent. The left wing press is represented by the *Patriot* (New Delhi) and *Link,* a weekly news magazine.[31]

Because of the pattern of newspaper ownership, the major news-

[31] See Registrar of Newspapers for India, *Press in India* 1968, pt. I (Delhi: Government of India Press, 1968).

papers are constantly referred to by the political left as the voice of monopoly capital. There has been increasing pressure on the government to apply to newspapers the principle of social control which was tried briefly with the banks before their nationalization. The argument goes that only some form of social control would enable the press in India to gain its independence from big business and promote genuinely professional journalism. The business-owned press has met these criticisms with the charge that government is trying to use such characterizations as an excuse to stifle criticism and gain control of the free press in India. Since the March 1971 Indian election, the volume of political criticism of the big metropolitan newspapers has led to renewed pressures for government action. The government has finally responded to these pressures by introducing legislation which would force big business to divest itself of control of the large metropolitan newspapers. Following this divestiture, the management of these newspapers would be reorganized through a complex formula of representation.[32]

The left in India has claimed that business is able to influence public policy, not so much through direct contact with decision-makers as through the indirect means of its control of the press. Press influence over decision-makers is, they argue, subtle and indirect. Newspapers, and their special correspondents in particular, are said to be able to make or break a politician by playing down or highlighting his role in government. They control the amount of publicity a politician or minister can get. Thus, ministers are said to seek out special correspondents and to try to establish a rapport that will guarantee them a good press.

The public image of business remains roughly what it was in the past. Yet for the present, at least, business functions in a hostile environment of suspicion and mistrust. This affects its strategy in dealing with the public, with political parties, and with government. What has changed is the self-image of business. The self-willed, often illiterate, but dynamic entrepreneurs who had the forethought to build the industrial base of modern India are giving way to an entirely different, younger generation that is well-educated, articulate, and aggressively determined to tell the real story of business to the public. This new self-image is beginning to give business the self-confidence it needs to perform a more active role in pressing its interests and correcting its image. Younger businessmen demanding a greater voice in public policy have come onto the scene at a time when Indian politics is in a

[32] *The Overseas Hindustan Times* (New Delhi), August 28, 1971.

critical state of flux. Many of the depressed sections of society have also become more self-confident and determined to mobilize their constituencies to push for their interests within the given system. As a result, one would expect that the competition for government attention in India in the future will increase substantially, and that the government of India, which has been relatively free of organized pressure, is now entering into a phase in which the articulation of demands will become a major function of groups in the larger society. Decision-making and public policy will no longer be free from pressure from below. Such pressure will now receive greater attention in the policy process.

X

POLITICS, ELECTIONS, AND BUSINESS

Although interest groups are primarily concerned with influencing decision-makers and shaping public policy items that specifically affect their interests, they may find it necessary to intervene at the recruitment stage of the political process to insure favorable policy outcomes and guarantee future access to the political leadership to present their views. Thus, interest groups support political parties whose views coincide with their own or are at least not totally at odds with theirs; they attempt to secure direct representation for group spokesmen by obtaining party endorsement for group candidates; and they may seek to influence party programs in ways which are favorable to the groups' interests. The support which any group is capable of providing depends on the political capital of the group. Business tends to control substantial economic power rather than large blocs of votes, and so one of the most potent sources of support business is able to provide is the financing of political parties and candidates.

The strategy employed by interest groups in supporting political parties is, to a large extent, determined by the nature of the party system and the types of parties that exist in that particular political system. The most significant feature of the party system in India in the post-independence period has been the capacity of the nationalist movement to transform itself into a dominant ruling party and retain that position of dominance despite internal crisis, schism, and external challenge. And so the most consistent dilemma of business has been the strategy it should pursue toward the ruling Congress party. Business cannot support the Congress party's long-term program of socialization, but business must come to terms with the necessity of not exacerbating in any way the present antibusiness stance of the Congress party.

The Indian National Congress, at the time of independence, was an extremely broad based political movement composed of a variety of groups. All those groups agreed on the imperative of gaining control of the national destiny, but each had a different image of the pattern of society the Congress party should establish for free India. The left wing of the Congress party supported a policy of state planning and economic growth through state-owned public sector investment; the right was committed more to private ownership with a large but subsidiary role for the state; the Gandhians preferred government support and encouragement for decentralized village and cottage industries organized into cooperatives.[1] Under pressure to satisfy each of these disparate tendencies, Congress party economic policies fluctuated erratically in the early years after independence. These fluctuations created a crisis of confidence in the business community which in turn resulted in a serious fall in industrial production and capital investment. Confidence was not restored until the mid-1950s when Congress party leadership managed to achieve a consensus on its policy of a socialist pattern of society, which even business welcomed as a policy with which it could deal. At least the continuation of the private sector seemed assured, and the threat of extensive nationalization of private sector facilities seemed virtually eliminated.[2] After 1955, the struggle within the Congress party was concerned less often with questions of whether or not there should be a private sector than with determining the size of the public relative to the private sector and a sufficient degree of dispersion of private sector growth among existing and potential entrepreneurs.

The relationship between business and the Congress party has fluctuated according to shifts in emphasis of Congress policy, from qualified support to partial alienation. To a very large extent the range from pragmatic support to rejection in post-independence business attitudes toward the Congress party has tended to coincide with pre-independence business orientations toward the nationalist movement. The strongest business support for the Congress movement came from Marwari and Gujarati capital. The Marwaris, led by G. D. Birla, supported the Congress, because they favored its nationalism and also because they viewed the Gandhian-led Congress as the best chance of keeping the left in India in check.[3] Although even G. D. Birla eventually became disillusioned with the Congress party, he remained convinced that it was the only party capable of providing political stability

[1] Stanley A. Kochanek, *The Congress Party of India: The Dynamics of One-Party Democracy* (Princeton, N.J.: Princeton University Press, 1968), pp. 164–181.

[2] Michael Kidron, *Foreign Investments in India* (London: Oxford University Press, 1965), pp. 74–97.

[3] G. D. Birla, *In the Shadow of the Mahatma* (Bombay: Orient Longman's Ltd., 1955), p. 48.

and preventing a Communist takeover.[4] Calcutta was the headquarters of most Marwari capital, a substantial portion of which was invested in the Communist stronghold of West Bengal. And so the Marwaris perceived that the major threat to the future of the private sector was in a possible Communist takeover rather than in Congress party socialism. Thus, although a large segment of big Marwari capital, including a section of the Birla family itself, rejected G. D. Birla's assessment of the political realities at the time of the 1967 general elections, their experience under the postelection Bengal United Front convinced them that G. D. Birla's notion of the realities and indispensability of the Congress party had been correct.

The older Bombay industrial elite led by Tata took an entirely different view. Bombay business, partially perhaps because it was more socially, educationally, and organizationally advanced than most Marwari capital, tended to be much more dogmatically committed to classical economic liberalism, which had flourished as the reigning ideology during the period of their capital formation. Located in the Congress party stronghold of Maharashtra and Gujarat where the radical left had made few inroads, these businessmen came to see Congress socialism, Congress taxation, and Congress controls as the major threat to private capital. Thus, they attempted to fight back at the ideological level, first through the Forum of Free Enterprise and finally through the creation of the Swatantra party as the first major party in India to challenge the dominant economic policy consensus of the Congress party.[5]

But the major strategy, and for most of the time the only strategy, of organized business was to work for its goals indirectly through the existing government, sometimes attempting to apply pressure, more often relying on persuasion. There were several phases in the relationship between business and the Congress party government: a period of uncertainty and conflict from 1947 to 1953, a period of accommodation from 1954 to 1963, and a period of renewed conflict culminating with a drift into opposition. From 1947 until shortly after the first general elections in India, the entire business community felt insecure. Business had faith in Congress party leaders as individuals but lacked confidence in their flexibility of purpose and administrative ability. Un-

[4] G. L. Nanda, Satyanarain Sinha, and G. D. Birla, *Government and Business* (Speeches delivered at the Indian Chamber of Commerce, Calcutta, April 10, 1965), (Calcutta: Indian Chamber of Commerce, 1965), pp. 7–8.

[5] Stanley A. Kochanek, "Interest Groups and Interest Aggregation: Changing Patterns of Oligarchy in the FICCI," *Economic and Political Weekly* 5 (1970): 1304–1306.

certainty arose, especially from the difficulty of ascertaining the probable final intentions of the new Congress government as various factions within the party attempted to push Congress party policy to the left. A crisis of confidence developed in which business felt unable to plan for the future while unable to predict the outcome of a wide range of public policy questions including controls, labor legislation, and proposed government regulation. The greatest anxiety, however, attached to the issue of nationalization of private property. A number of businessmen expressed their concern over this situation. "A great many discordant voices are being heard today," warned Sir Homi Mody in late 1947, "about the economic pattern India should adopt and the resultant uncertainty has discouraged enterprise both in industrial and investing field (sic)." [6] G. D. Birla pleaded with the new Congress government to declare its policy toward the private sector, because the drift that was creating a sense of fear and uncertainty among businessmen was also having a detrimental effect on the economy.[7]

The Congress government responded by calling a Tripartite Industrial Conference in December 1947. At that time government, industry, and labor agreed on an Industrial Policy Resolution. Although the Industrial Policy Resolution soon became government policy, conflicting views on economic policy expressed by various Congress party leaders prevented businessmen from ending their skepticism toward the government's intentions. "Businessmen," wrote Pratap Bhogilal, a Bombay industrialist, "are scared by talk of nationalization, perplexed by widely divergent statements by cabinet ministers, and irritated by the maze of ill-drawn and poorly administered regulations." [8] Business insecurity resulted in continued declines in industrial production. A slight improvement in production during the Korean War was canceled out by 1953 when Nehru, fresh from his massive victory in the first general elections, warned business that he did not consider private enterprise to be an essential part of domocracy. Nehru warned that "we are not willing to give private enterprise the high place which some countries have given it." In fact, he went on to say, "we are ready to view it with suspicion . . . if you imagine that we should keep private enterprise before us as an axiom or presumption you are mistaken." [9]

[6] D. R. Mankekar, *Homi Mody: A Many Splendored Life* (Bombay: Popular Prakashan, 1968), p. 230.

[7] FICCI, *Proceedings of the Twentieth Annual Meeting, 1947* (Delhi: FICCI, 1947), pp. 45–46.

[8] Unpublished letter, Pratap Bhogilal to the president of the Bombay Millowners Association, April 28, 1949.

[9] FICCI, *Proceedings of the Twenty-Fifth Annual Meeting, 1952* (Delhi: FICCI, 1952), pp. 33–34.

Nehru's harsh admonition on the heels of the sweeping Congress party victory at the polls led business leaders to reassess their approach to the Congress party. The Marwari-dominated FICCI, led by Birla, decided to adopt a much less critical and more conciliatory policy by offering its full cooperation to the government. B. M. Birla signaled the end of resistance and the beginning of resignation when he reminded the FICCI delegates that "a businessman is not a businessman unless he can adjust himself to changing conditions." [10] The precise nature of the adjustment business was expected to make was spelled out by G. D. Birla when he told the delegates at the annual meeting in 1954 that the FICCI resolutions were aimed as much at business as they were at government. Business must realize that changing times had given business and government "common objectives." There was plenty of scope for the private sector. Because its main function was to create employment and production, it could not "be just replaced by any planning authority," although it could "kill itself" through "its own defects." G. D. Birla conceded that businessmen might not like certain policies of government. "Because of their inexperience perhaps," he suggested, "they put forward policies which may not be quite helpful. But do not forget that their objective and our objective . . . is to build up the country, and if we build up the country, then, of course, everybody prospers." [11] Commenting on the FICCI proceedings, the Birla-owned *Hindustan Times* characterized G. D. Birla's remarks as more than a "clarion call" to business, for "it dared to recognize the bitter and unpleasant truths. Are businessmen so sure that they will be able to provide more employment even if government were to give them every facility they asked for? That was one of the questions which Mr. Birla bluntly asked." [12] His answer was, "Let us try."

The extent of the accommodation between the FICCI leadership and the Congress government was evident a year later, when Nehru's explanation of the Congress resolution committing the party to the objective of a socialist pattern of society was greeted by applause. Nehru told the FICCI that the new policy was not aimed at socializing the economy but at developing large-scale industry in the public sector. Even granting that Nehru had also gone out of his way to be conciliatory, the business reaction to his comments that the public sector need not grow at the expense of the private sector, because there was

[10] FICCI, *Proceedings of the Twenty-Seventh Annual Meeting, 1954* (Delhi: FICCI, 1954), pp. 8–20, 34.

[11] *Ibid.*, p. 101.

[12] Editorial in *The Hindustan Times* (New Delhi), March 9, 1954.

in fact room for both, was indeed a sign of the vast power of positive thinking.

The new era of cooperation was officially inaugurated with the initiation of the second Five Year Plan, which provided substantial scope for the growth of the private sector. By 1956 Nehru was complimenting the FICCI for its attempt to adjust to changed conditions. "I must say," he told the FICCI in March 1956, "I have been pleased that you have tried hard to appreciate the philosophy [of the government] and to adapt yourself to it. I think it does you credit." [13]

Even foreign business looked on the beginning of the second Five Year Plan as a key turning point in the economic development of post-independence India. The history of Bird and Company puts it this way:

> It is not surprising if those first years of independence appear in retrospect as a time of uncertainty and difficulty during which there is comparatively little of substantial progress, though much of effort and adjustment, to record. Gradually the firm began to see its way clearer. Then, in 1956, several definite things happened. The second Five Year Plan came into force: this, besides being a great deal more ambitious than the first, concentrated more of its attention on industry. Also the new Companies Act, dealing fairly comprehensively with the position of managing agents, took effect. For better or for worse, Birds now knew more clearly where they stood. About the same time the firm took certain very vital decisions about its future policy and actions.[14]

Bird and Company was not the only business house that felt able to move ahead again, and during the period of rapid expansion under the second Plan, business–government conflict continued to diminish along with the debate over the relative merits of public and private sector development.[15] By the early 1960s, the accommodation between business and the Congress government had reached such a point that in 1960 Nehru declared the friction between public and private sectors was unnecessary and harmful.[16] By 1962, the Jawaharlal Nehru who, in

[13] FICCI, *Proceedings of the Twenty-Ninth Annual Meeting, 1956* (Delhi: FICCI, 1956), pp. 23–24.

[14] Godfrey Harrison, *Bird and Company of Calcutta* (Calcutta: Anna Art Press Private Ltd., 1964), p. 249.

[15] See editorials in *The Times of India* (Bombay), March 27 and 28, 1960 and March 10, 1959.

[16] FICCI, *Report of the Proceedings of the Executive Committee for 1960* (Delhi: FICCI, 1960), p. 30.

1952, had been ready to view business with "suspicion," went so far as to tell the FICCI that he considered the private sector "a good thing for India." [17] Thus, business–government relations during the decade from 1952 to 1962 moved from one of confrontation to accommodation. Ironically, by this time the new accommodation was nearing its conclusion. Developments from 1963 to 1967 were to produce a total reversal in business attitudes toward the Congress party and the Congress government.

In fact, even during this extended period of wary goodwill, accommodation with the Nehru government had never been unanimous within the business community. It had been confined largely to the Marwari industrialists and to a sector of traditionally pro-Congress party Gujarati businessmen who together controlled the decision-making structure of the FICCI. These industrialists made a point of distinguishing between Nehru's actions and his rhetoric. Furthermore, they had easy access to Nehru, and whenever they could convince him of their point of view, he had followed up with the necessary action. And so they were favorably inclined toward him. Thus, as one former Congress party minister put it, "Nehru criticized business to a very great extent, but in fact he accommodated them. Business had access to Nehru and that access was never misunderstood." In other words, Nehru's socialist credentials were sufficiently strong so that no one would dare accuse him of selling out to private sector interests. Moreover business felt, as one industrialist put it, that "If you look back on the Nehru era it is clear that while Nehru talked a great deal about socialism, he never did anything to really affect business interests. Nehru had basically a split personality. He would talk one way, but act in another."

This duality and seeming ambivalence in Nehru's personality, which the more traditional sectors of business found perfectly understandable and acceptable, progressively alienated the more modernist sectors which had been by past tradition nonpolitical. It was the old Bombay industrial elite that was most strongly provoked by the incessant socialist rhetoric of Nehru and the Congress party and felt that its tendency to reinforce public suspicion and distrust of business could not be ignored. Furthermore, they insisted that its implications could not be ignored, regardless of the content of government policies which they believed were not as accommodating as some believed. They chafed under the tight government controls over the economy, they resented the constant need to lobby for favors, and they deplored the undesirable con-

[17] *Financial Express* (Bombay), March 25, 1962.

sequences on business morality. Finally, they could no longer participate in the FICCI policy of accommodation. As Homi Mody put it:

> We unreservedly accept the social objectives which the country has adopted through its government and Parliament. We fully accept the obligations cast on us to implement these objectives and help to create a social order in which there shall be equality of opportunities for all and a more equitable distribution of the good things in life.
>
> But if implementation of these objectives placed intolerable burdens on those engaged in the production of goods and services, and if the pace was so fast and the action so drastic that freedoms which were fundamental to the functioning of a democratic society were threatened, then it was clearly the duty of the business community as responsible citizens to raise their voice and point out where the country was drifting to.[18]

The counterattack by Bombay business was begun at the ideological level with the creation of the Forum of Free Enterprise. The creation of the Forum marked the beginning of the first open break between business and the Congress party and later led to the formation of the Swatantra party. Nehru deeply resented the Swatantra party and called it a party of "fossils, frustrated individuals, champions of vested interests and reactionaries" whose thinking was of the nineteenth century. Stung by Nehru's attack, Swatantra spokesmen retorted that it was Nehru's socialism which was the outmoded and obsolete concept. Nehru's policies, they argued, had limited Indian development and individual freedom by the creation of a permit, license, quota raj.[19] The Swatantra party would fight to bring an end to excessive governmental intervention in the economy and provide greater scope for individual initiative.

Many federation members may privately have accepted the Swatantra critique of Congress, but they were not as willing to challenge the ruling party so openly and blatantly. Their philosophy still rationalized a combination of limited public criticism of the Congress party and maximum maintenance of personal liaison with the government bureaucracy and the Congress party leaders. Thus, despite repeated pressure from some of its members, the federation refused to endorse either the Forum of Free Enterprise or the Swatantra party. As long as the

[18] Mankekar, *Homi Mody*, p. 240.
[19] *Ibid.*, p. 243.

economy was expanding rapidly and private sector growth continued within the framework of Congress party policy, anti-Congress sentiment within the FICCI remained latent, subdued but ready for mobilization. However, as the Nehru era began to draw to a close, a series of internal and external changes resulted in progressive alienation that terminated in a renewed conflict between business and government.

There was stress, strain, and crisis in almost all sections of Indian life during the years from 1963 to 1971. Indian development began to falter under the impact of two major wars, increased defense costs, two disastrous droughts, rampant inflation, and a manifestation of basic weaknesses in Indian planning itself. The culmination was a severe recession which brought economic growth to a halt in the midst of a major domestic political crisis. That crisis began with a struggle for succession after the death of Nehru and ended with the development of an open split in the Congress party.

Deterioration in relations between business and the Congress party began shortly after the Chinese invasion, in the fall of 1962. Like other sectors of Indian society, the business community rallied to the support of the government. Business contributed generously to the National Defense Fund, and business leaders appealed to the business community to cooperate with government in holding the price line.[20] However, once the immediate threat had passed, business began to feel the pinch of new government economic and fiscal policies designed to meet the need for more resources for defense. Thus, while Nehru called for prosperity for both the public and private sectors, business increasingly perceived new government taxes as an attempt to bolster the prospects of the one at the expense of the other.[21] These perceptions were reinforced by an apparent shift in Congress party policy to the left. The Congress party began to talk about the nationalization of private sector banks, warned about the dangers of the concentration of economic power in the hands of a small number of business houses, and increased government controls over distribution through state trading in a variety of commodities. FICCI leaders, breaking with the long-standing Birla philosophy, complained of a weakening of the government's pragmatic approach. With business claiming that the Congress party was trying to liquidate the private sector, there was open talk of withdrawing support from the Congress party and helping only those candidates acceptable to business in the 1967 elections. The high point of the business community's noisy public confrontation with the ruling

[20] *The Statesman* (Calcutta), October 23, 1962.
[21] *The Economic Times* (Bombay), March 17, 1963.

Congress party came at the time of the 1965 annual session of the FICCI, when K. P. Goenka, the president of the federation, delivered a vehement attack on the government. A series of resolutions introduced at the session were so critical of the government that the prime minister himself had to intervene to urge the federation to temper them. G. D. Birla also felt compelled to intervene personally to pacify and conciliate both sides. Again he counseled the business community that without the Congress party the country could not prosper.[22] Prime Minister Shastri, in turn, sent G. L. Nanda, one of his senior ministers, on a mission to major business centers to assure the business community that government was not out to destroy them and to urge them to recognize that a time of great crisis was not the time for such extreme criticism. Shastri's move had the effect of calming tempers and reducing the level of public criticism of his government by business. But a major turning point had been reached. The business community was on the verge of a major shift in its basic political strategy.

Business intervention in the 1967 general elections was primarily designed to humble the Congress party by reducing its massive majorities and making the party more amenable to business pressures. Business intervention took various forms—decreasing financial support to the Congress party, channeling the remaining Congress party funds through regional party bosses rather than through the central party office, increasing aid to opposition parties and independents, and engaging in a concentrated effort to elect to parliament more industrialists who could act as articulate and direct spokesmen for the private sector.

For a variety of reasons, most of which had little to do with the shift in business strategy toward the ruling party, the Congress party suffered a major defeat. Its majority at the center was substantially reduced, and the party lost its majorities in half the states. What is more, a large number of leading Congress party candidates were defeated at the polls. To the extent that they felt that the shift in business strategy had contributed its share to the Congress party debacle, many Congress party members who had been supporters of business were not at all happy with the results of the defection. The weakening of the Congress party at the center resulted in political instability and government indecision, which gravely complicated economic recovery. Business came under sharp attack both from the left and from factions within the ruling Congress party. Business in West Bengal was confronted by a Communist-dominated United Front Government which

[22] Birla, *Government and Business*, p. 4.

made life quite unpleasant for the majority of the Marwari industrialists. A large number of Marwari industrialists now felt that G. D. Birla was right in his political judgment.

Immediately after the election, business came under severe attack by both the left wing opposition and a group of Young Turks within the Congress party. The left perceived the business role in the 1967 election as an attempt to convert private sector economic power into political power, in order to gain control of the government and change the direction of the Indian economy. Although not necessarily opposed to the existence of the private sector, the Young Turks in the Congress party resented the pattern of business financial aid to the Congress party. They felt that pattern had strengthened the hand of the old guard bosses in the party. Thus, they joined with the left in a vehement attack on the private sector. They demanded strong measures to curb the growing economic power of the top business houses through monopoly legislation, they demanded the nationalization of private sector banks to deprive the big houses of control over credit for expansion, and, singling out Birla as guilty of a variety of corrupt practices, they demanded a complete government investigation of the activities of Birla House. Again the business community was placed on the defensive. The sharp attacks from the left created severe difficulties for the private sector, because both the bureaucratic and the ministerial levels were afraid to make decisions that might be viewed as a concession to vested interests. The issuing of industrial licenses slowed down, and a variety of major projects were held up in the bureaucratic pipeline, thereby halting business expansion and aggravating the economic recession.

The leadership of the FICCI tried desperately to restore harmony between the federation and the ruling party, but the federation became embroiled in the internal struggle for power in the Congress party between Mrs. Gandhi and the syndicate. When the Birla group decided to support Mrs. Gandhi, on the grounds that she offered the best hope for political stability, a major split in the federation was the result. Later, when the federation refused to condemn Mrs. Gandhi's summary nationalization of banks and nationalization of the cotton trade, Babubhai Chinai, a leading FICCI personality and the chief lieutenant of syndicate leader S. K. Patil, resigned from the federation along with some sectors of Bombay business.[23] At the same time the Birlas found a major effort being organized to undercut their power in the federation and so deprive them of the dominant role in federation decision-mak-

[23] *The Economic Times* (Bombay), July 30, 1969.

ing. When finally the Congress party split in two, there was also a substantial fragmentation of polical loyalties within the federation. The effect of that fragmentation was reflected in the 1971 mid-term elections. The outcome of the 1971 elections was the most uncertain in the post-independence period. Nevertheless, G. D. Birla and a large sector of the large Marwari houses supported Mrs. Gandhi, despite her radical rhetoric, in the hope that she could restore political stability. Thus, Mrs. Gandhi had little difficulty in collecting funds. But the opposition was also quite well financed, and more industrialists than ever before ran for public office—including Naval H. Tata and K. K. Birla.

After Mrs. Gandhi's overwhelming victory in the mid-term elections of 1971, the federation leadership renewed efforts to restore harmony with government. Mrs. Gandhi contributed substantially to this atmosphere of reconciliation when she reminded the business community that the private sector contributed over 85 percent of the national product of the country and that they obviously had a role to play in the future development of India.

The tone of accommodation on both sides was reminiscent of the 1953 to 1963 phase. The massive victory of the new Congress party meant that the only significant influence was influence which could be exerted through the ruling Congress party. Despite its more radical tone, business still had many friends in Mrs. Gandhi's government. At the same time the opposition parties, including the old Congress party, had been decimated and the potential business leverage of a Congress party government ruling with a narrow majority or a multiparty coalition of the right was lost. The massive Congress party majority had returned, and business—as it did in 1953—had to recognize this reality and adjust to it. This adjustment has not been easy, however, because of the strong pressure within the ruling Congress to push its policies further to the left and the increasing demand for the nationalization of private sector industries.

Direct Participation

As business finally became aware, maintaining close contact with the ruling Congress party was only one way to influence public policy outputs. One of the most important changes that has occurred in the Indian business community since independence has been the emergence of efforts to secure greater direct representation for business in Parliament. Thus far this strategy has failed.

Before independence, India had a system of functional representation for business in central and state legislatures. No such provision was included in the post-independence constitution, despite business objection. Businessmen and especially industrialists were reluctant to participate in politics based on mass franchise, and as a result they were fifteen years late in getting into politics. Although about 10 percent of Parliament has been composed of businessmen, these business representatives were mostly small traders and shopkeepers. Only a handful of industrialists—mainly those who had had a special relationship to the nationalist movement, like the Bajaj family or the Poddar family—were elected to Parliament. Most of the older generation of Indian businessmen were not interested in politics; there were several reasons for this. First, they considered their primary concern to be with business and not politics. "I do my business," was their slogan. Others felt that business and politics did not mix or that business was a full time job. They tended to be more interested in the expansion of their own business organizations than in public service or political activity. Thus, they lacked political experience. Furthermore, the older generation of businessmen, especially among the Marwaris, had received little formal education and so were not very articulate. Nor did they enjoy campaigning for votes. Thus, they were neither inclined nor equipped to participate actively in politics.

A second reason for the lack of interest in public office was that most of the older generation of businessmen had already developed close contacts with the older nationalist leaders, who had advised them to stay out of politics and let the Congress party look after their interests. The Congress party, they argued, was already swamped by demands for nominations or tickets, and the fewer claimants they had the better. Congress party members, moreover, had become professional politicians who would resent anyone trying to jump the queue, and businessmen were not prepared to stand in line. Finally, the average Congress party member did not think much of business and would not be likely to share a ticket with a businessman even if businessmen had participated in the nationalist movement. Congress party members tended to attribute apparent idealism to selfish motives. In addition, they felt that business connections with the nationalist movement had been perfunctory to the extent that businessmen had never really sacrificed for the cause as the truly dedicated nationalists had. Therefore, they resented the idea of business crashing into the political arena they had made possible.

A third reason for a lack of direct involvement of businessmen in politics was the handicap of the negative image and low status of business in India combined with the lack of a ready constituency to which a business candidate might appeal. As a result, businessmen, unlike princes and zamindars, had difficulty getting elected. Even Sir Homi Mody, who had been a very active business politician in the pre-independence period, was defeated when he tried to run for public office in the politics of mass franchise.

There was a fourth deterrent to direct participation in politics. As the new Congress government developed its policy of a planned, regulated, and controlled economy, most businessmen were afraid they would suffer reprisals—in the form of denied licenses, permits or other benefits—from a Congress-dominated government if they offended government by blatant electoral opposition. They also feared that the Congress party might use the official machinery of government to harass them over income tax and other bureaucratic matters. Initially there seemed to be little justification for business to participate actively in politics.

By 1967 this situation had changed. Business had decided it must participate and gain a direct voice in public affairs or it would never be able to influence government policy. This feeling was particularly strong among newer industrialists and the younger generation of the businessmen in the established business houses. The sons, grandsons, and the sons-in-law of the captains of industry were more highly educated, less preoccupied with expansion at any price, and more socially conscious, and they were anxious to do battle in the Indian political arena. They wanted to play a more active role in public life as respectable citizens. They were concerned about changing the low status and negative image of the Indian businessmen. They wished to convert the image so that businessmen would be seen as philanthropists rather than dishonest exploiters. They wanted Indian business organizations to be seen as modernized corporate structures independent of the state rather than as preserves of private profit. This self-confident new generation felt they had rights as citizens to participate in public life. Furthermore, they felt that the intellectuals and the haves had left Indian politics in the hands of the illiterates, the incompetents, and the have-nots. The country was suffering as a result. As one leading industrialist put it:

> The only way to save the country which was governed by the have-nots was to send out people such as economists, lawyers, and businessmen into politics. The businessmen in India have made a large amount of money and now must come to serve the country, but in practice they are cowards. They look only to their own individual losses and gains and not to the larger society. A citizen has a right to oppose government and business has a right to send

out its own people into government. We provide all the finances for the political parties and therefore we should have some of our own people in government.

Such businessmen contend, in addition, that business can make a positive contribution in the legislature, that business can actually have an impact on policy. All legislatures, Babubhai Chinai once argued, are rushing to put new laws on the books as though there was a competition.[24] The more voices heard in Parliament, he said, and the more views presented in Parliament, the more government will listen to Parliament, because government does take into consideration the views expressed in that body. Finally, a business presence could bring Parliament to a more realistic and pragmatic view of the role of businessmen. As one young business MP put it:

> Business is beginning to realize that it is impossible to keep away from politics because the business case is going by default. If a hundred wrong decisions are taken by government in relation to business, eighty of them are wrong due to the ignorance of the problem and only twenty involve differences over policy. Business has no other alternative but to gain adequate representation in Parliament by which it will be able to eliminate the eighty wrong decisions that go by default and at the same time make a positive contribution. Business has to perform a constructive role in India.

Thus, the younger generation takes a totally different view of politics than did their fathers.

Without minimizing the importance of playing a policy-making role, the younger generation of Indian business argues that political participation will help improve the business image by enabling business to explain its contributions to Indian development in the past two decades. It may even enable Indian business to establish closer relations with the masses.[25] Business, they argue, cannot afford to disdain five hundred million people. The gap between business and the masses must be closed. Survival requires it.

Although a large sector of business has thus changed its view about the importance of politics, the business community remains divided on how to implement their strategy. The younger businessmen reject the traditional methods of supporting a group of candidates indirectly.

[24] *Industrial Times*, January 1, 1968, p. 6.

[25] See Chapter IX.

They insist that effective political influence can be secured only by running for and holding public office. Because the job is too important to trust to others, businessmen must spend the time, the money, and the effort to do the job themselves. It has been proposed, therefore, that each of the top fifty families designate one of their younger members to devote his full time to a political career. Such a procedure would have a major impact on Indian political and government policy and would also encourage others to become active. As one advocate put it:

> If the big people don't want to commit themselves, then what happens to people who are smaller and who were not as well placed? If the sacrifices do not come from the top, then how can you expect them to come from the bottom? Political participation costs time and once you are in politics, you also have the possibility of incurring the displeasure of government and government officials. You cannot send others, you have to do the job yourself, or it is not going to get done.

Most businessmen agree that you should do the job yourself, but they prefer to send others. Prior to the 1967 election, both the FICCI and a group of Bombay businessmen actively considered proposals to increase the level of business representation in Parliament. The FICCI proposal called for an attempt to get at least one hundred businessmen elected to Parliament in 1967. Instead of acting directly to accomplish this goal, the FICCI would have established a higher level body to informally initiate negotiations with political parties and take other steps to insure proper representation in Parliament. The proposal generated a great deal of discussion, but it was finally agreed that the decision on electoral participation should be left up to individual members. A Bombay group held a similar discussion which broke down on the issue of financing. The problem was not raising funds to get representatives elected, but rather the difficulty of attracting top people to a job which paid fairly little by business standards and would actually require a major personal sacrifice for well-placed and talented persons. Thus the problem was how such a person could be supported with supplementary and legal income. Because no solution could be found to this problem, the project had to be dropped. Again the electoral issue was left to individuals.

There are some who feel that business should, through the federation, establish a federation committee which would select parties and find the right people for office. Business would then channel its funds through this committee. This is the procedure in Germany and it was, until recently, also used in Japan.[26] But the proposal received little support because of the influence of those who felt that business could not confront government in this way. They feel business associations should be kept aloof from direct intervention in electoral politics and should confine themselves to articulating and representing the views of business to government. Contributions should be left to individuals. Traditionally the FICCI has taken the view that it is an industrial and commercial body and, as one spokesman put it, "if we start indulging in politics also, our whole importance will be lost, and our organization will become a political body." [27]

Despite the lack of collective action, it is clear that the attitude of business toward political participation has changed. Business played an important role in seeking to elect more businessmen to Parliament in 1967, and in the 1971 mid-term election more major industrialists than ever before ran for public office. Among the candidates were some of the most illustrious names of Indian business, including Naval H. Tata, K. K. Birla, and Ramnath Goenka. However, because most of them contested either as independents or as non-new Congress party candidates, they went down to defeat in the new Congress landslide. Thus, direct participation has so far not proven to be very successful. But business is still in a strong position to play a role through its most important resource—the financing of political parties.

Party Finance

Without a party of its own and lacking even a solid body of representatives or spokesmen in Parliament, Indian business until 1959 was basically dependent on the Congress party to protect its interests. Its major source of influence within Congress was the support it provided the party and its leadership in the form of financial contributions. Elections in India have become progressively more costly over the years, partly because parties must now pay for what was once volunteered. As the memories and loyalties of the nationalist movement fade, the parties must reach the vast electorate through party mechanisms rather than through local notables or vote banks. Money is needed to pay for printing, gasoline, vehicles, and workers. All of these, because of the general inflationary spiral, have become more and more expensive. This inexorable trend toward increased electoral costs has made ex-

[26] Chitoshi Yanaga, *Big Business in Japanese Politics* (New Haven: Yale University Press, 1968), pp. 78–87.

[27] FICCI, *Proceedings of the Thirtieth Annual Meeting, 1957* (Delhi: FICCI, 1957), p. 30.

ternal financial support more necessary and potentially more influential.

In theory, India has placed a ceiling on the election expenses of candidates. Members of Parliament are limited to twenty-five thousand rupees; members of legislative assemblies may spend from six thousand to nine thousand rupees, depending upon local conditions. It is almost universally agreed that these ceilings are so unrealistic that they are surpassed by all but a few candidates. The evasion of electoral ceilings was simplified by changes in the election laws in 1956. These changes reduced the period of accountability for candidates and, more important, excluded expenses incurred by third parties. Thus, candidates evade the law by purchasing supplies in advance of the accountability period, by paying for them after the accountability period has ended, or by receiving direct services from third parties. In short, the ceilings are not only unrealistic, they are unenforceable.[28]

Election costs in India have soared since the first general elections. Although no precise figures are available, informal estimates indicate the trend. The really big increase followed the second general elections. By that time the Congress party image had begun to fade, party factionalism had increased internal competition, and opposition parties had succeeded in slowly eroding Congress party majorities. And so elections could not simply be won; they had to be fought. The 1957 elections were estimated to have cost parties and individual candidates about 25 million rupees. It is believed that expenditures increased tenfold from 1957 to 1962, so that 230 million rupees were spent in the 1962 elections. Estimates for the 1967 elections vary from 300 million to 660 million rupees, but it is widely believed that expenses increased at least 35 to 40 percent over 1962.[29] The estimates for the 1971 Lok Sabha election alone were put at 250 to 500 million rupees.[30]

Election costs for individual candidates may vary considerably, depending on the area, type of constituency, strength of the party organization, the candidate's familiarity to his constituency, and the nature of the opposition. A leading opposition MP admitted spending 130,000 rupees in 1967, to defeat a Congress party minister who is said to have spent 500,000 rupees trying to get reelected. In general, it is estimated that the average cost of electing a Member of Parliament is 100,000 to 150,000 rupees. It was even higher in the purely national election of

[28] R. P. Bhalla, "Economic Aspects of Elections in India," *The Indian Political Science Review* (Delhi), II (October 1967–March 1968): 57–58. A. H. and G. Somjee, "India," *Journal of Politics* 25 (1963): 686–702.

[29] *Ibid.*, p. 63.

[30] Editorial in *The Overseas Hindustan Times*, January 30, 1971.

1971, when MPs had to make up for the publicity local MLA (Member Legislative Assembly) candidates would have provided. This outlay for the election of a single officeholder represents an incredible lump sum of money in a poor country like India. Parties cannot possibly supply their candidates with the full sum. The result is that individual candidates must acquire additional funds from particular known fund raisers, party bosses, or their own efforts.

Election funds come from two sources. One source consists of party membership fees, contributions of candidates and their friends, and a levy on parliamentary income. This source produces no more than a fraction of the funds needed. The second source of funds is the business community. It is estimated that business provides about 90 percent of the election funds. Recently there have been numerous charges that foreign money has been contributed to election funds. The right wing charges the Communists with receiving funds from Moscow and Peking through fake subsidies to left wing publications and through their rupee trade accounts. The left wing charges the United States Central Intelligence Agency with using U. S. Public Law 480 funds for election purposes. So far no documentation has been produced to substantiate either of these charges.[31]

For the most part, then, the major source of funds has been business. Until the 1967 elections, the major recipient of election funds from business was the ruling Congress party. In the 1967 elections, although the Congress party still received the bulk of the funds, it had to watch a substantial distribution to other parties, especially the Swatantra party. Moreover, funds in 1967 tended to be directed to individuals within the party rather than to the party headquarters, thus undermining the power of the central party by depriving it of control over distribution. It is estimated that the Congress party spent 80 million rupees in 1962 and 150 million in 1967. And it is said that in 1971 Mrs. Gandhi had 100 million rupees at her disposal. The Swatantra party is said to have increased its expenditures from 5 million rupees in 1962 to 48 million rupees in 1967. The Jana Sangh moved from a relatively small expenditure in 1962 to approximately 35 million rupees in 1967.[32] Although even estimates are lacking, the opposition alliance in 1971 was obviously well financed. For parties like the Jana Sangh, the various

[31] The charge that foreign money has been used in Indian elections has been raised on numerous occasions. For example, the charge was raised repeatedly during the debate on banning company donations to political parties. See *The Patriot* (New Delhi), July 31, 1968 and August 15, 1968; *National Herald* (Lucknow and New Delhi), August 2, 1968 and August 7, 1968.

[32] Bhalla, "Economic Aspects of Elections," pp. 61–62.

Communist parties, and the SSP—each of which derives its strength from a corps of dedicated party workers of intense ideological loyalties —funds are not as important as they are for aggregative parties like the Congress, which seeks to run candidates in every constituency, or for elitist parties like the Swatantra, which has a relatively weak party organization.

Unlike business in Japan and Germany, business in India has no systematized method for giving contributions to political parties. Contributions are provided in several ways—through company contributions, through individual contributions, and through industry groups. Until recently a company in India was permitted, under Section 293A of the Companies Act, to contribute money to political parties provided its memorandum of association authorized such contributions. Such contributions, limited to 25,000 rupees or 5 percent of the average net profit of the company for the preceding three years, whichever was greater, were required to be disclosed in the company's annual profit and loss account. A study made by the government of India of company contributions showed that from 1962 to 1968 companies officially contributed 25,970,797 rupees to forty-seven political parties. The only two significant recipients were the Congress party, which received 20,552,798 rupees, and the Swatantra party, which received less than a quarter of the Congress party share or 4,602,553 rupees. The remaining forty-five parties combined received only 815,446 rupees. The largest sums were distributed around election time.[83]

Another study, conducted by the *Economic Times*,[84] showed that the leading 126 companies contributed 10,100,000 rupees to political parties in 1967. The Congress party received 7,370,000 rupees and the Swatantra party 2,520,000 rupees. The two biggest houses—Tata and Birla—together accounted for 34 percent of the total contributed by these 126 major companies. Both Tata and Birla gave money to the Congress party. Tata was much less generous to Congress than Birla, but Tata was conspicuous for its large contributions to the Swatantra party. Other major Swatantra supporters were Martin Burn, Bajaj, Khatau, Scindia, Walchand, and Thackersey. Of these, all except Bajaj play only a minor role in the FICCI.

The figures indicate that the Congress party has been the biggest beneficiary of company contributions, but they also demonstrate that its share was declining prior to 1971. In 1962–1963, the Congress party received 7,094,287 rupees, in 1967–1968 only 6,925,570 rupees. The

[83] *The National Herald* (Lucknow and New Delhi), August 14, 1968.
[84] *The Economic Times* (Bombay), December 5, 1967.

Swatantra party, on the other hand, increased its collections from 1,813,458 rupees in 1962–1963 to 2,452,999 rupees in 1967–1968. These figures are clear evidence of the trend toward more and more open contributions by business to the Swatantra party as disillusionment with the Congress party has increased.

Although company contributions represent only a fraction of the total business donations to political parties, they have been the most controversial. The Indian courts have questioned the practice on several occasions. Commenting in a case involving a request by Indian Iron and Steel Company to change its memorandum of association to enable it to contribute to political parties, Justice P. B. Mukharji commented that the request appeared to a cynic "to be a plea of the company to have legal sanction to bribe the government of the day, to induce policies that will help the company in its business." [35] Similarly, the Bombay High Court observed in a case involving Tata Iron and Steel:

> It is with considerable uneasiness and a sinking feeling in the heart that we approach this appeal. . . . But whatever our view may be as to the rightness or wrongness of what the Tata Iron and Steel Company proposes to do, however strongly we may feel [that] the danger of the corrupting influence of money must not be allowed to increase in this country and it must be strongly curbed, we could only be guided sitting in a court of law by legal principles, and not by our own views as to politics or morality.[36]

The issue of company contributions became politically explosive after the 1967 elections, when it developed into a source of factional conflict within the Congress party. The younger Congress MPs bitterly criticized the practice. They felt it strengthened bossism within the party, gave leaders from industrial regions an upper hand in the party, and tarnished the party's image.[37] They argued that money was going disproportionately to individuals and not being fairly distributed to all by the party. They pointed to the fact that the All-India Congress Committee (AICC) office had received only 700,000 rupees for the 1967 elections, although total company contributions to Congress party candidates were known to be many times that figure. Moreover, they argued that other parties now shared in the distribution of these company donations although the Congress party continued to suffer the

[35] Indian Iron and Steel Company Ltd., *All-India Reporter 1957* (Nagpur: All-India Reporter Ltd., 1957), Calcutta 234.

[36] Ketecha versus Tata Iron and Steel Company Ltd., *All-India Reporter 1958* (Nagpur: All-India Reporter Ltd., 1958), Bombay 155.

[37] *The National Herald* (Lucknow and New Delhi), July 26, 1968.

political price of approbation, because everyone assumed that the practice had been legalized in the first place solely to benefit the Congress party. This faction within the Congress party was determined to weaken some of the senior party leaders by reducing the amount of money they could distribute to their followers at election time. This pressure, reinforced by the public appeal of the proposal, succeeded. A bill prohibiting company contributions was passed in 1969.[38]

Company contributions, however, had never accounted for the bulk of political contributions from business. Estimates place company contributions at no more than 20 percent of the whole. The major source of political contributions were private contributions made directly to individuals. These private contributions took three forms. First, all major Congress party leaders, from the prime minister on down, collect funds for the party. In the early years, the outstanding fund collectors were Vallabhbhai Patel and Rajendra Prasad. Later the task became more decentralized. Central ministers like S. K. Patil, Manubhai Shah, and Morarji Desai performed the task in western India, and regional leaders like Atulya Ghosh, C. B. Gupta, Mohanlal Sukhadia, and K. Kamaraj took care of collections in their respective areas. The position of AICC treasurer had usually been held by someone from Bombay or Calcutta. Through the central ministers and the AICC office, money from individual Bombay and Calcutta businessmen found its way into the Congress party war chest. In the early years after independence, party leaders collected funds largely for party use, but there is evidence to substantiate the charges that in later years many had begun to use the funds collected to bolster their positions within the party. There is little doubt that men like Atulya Ghosh, C. B. Gupta, and S. K. Patil were able to consolidate their position within the party because of their ability to attract the funds needed to finance their supporters.

Individual contributions were also made directly to selected MPs. These MPs were influential Members of Parliament who provided easy access to the bureaucracy and particularly to ministers. They were also expected to argue specific cases for particular individuals, to provide advice on how to approach government, and to raise questions in Parliament that would bring pressure to bear on ministers or on the bureaucracy. Because of tight party discipline, the financing of individual MPs was regarded as a means of accomplishing specific objectives rather than as a way of influencing the formation of larger party policies. The Birla group, for example, in 1967 had a special relationship with

[38] *Capital* (Calcutta), May 29, 1969, pp. 1018–1019.

40 MPs that they had helped at the time of the fourth general elections.

Private business contributions were also used to support selected political figures who appeared to have bright futures but needed financing to build their careers. Aid was channeled in the form of campaign contributions and funds for publicity and supplementary expenses. The hope was, of course, that the bright young men who gained positions of authority would be sufficiently grateful to be a major asset to the individuals who had sponsored them.

By and large, then, political contributions stemming from business in India have been individual, not collective, and they have been given for individual and not collective benefits—that is, to ensure access for the purpose of obtaining an industrial license, permit, or other such benefits. But three things happened in the 1967 elections which indicated that business in India is beginning to think more in terms of collectively influencing political parties through contributions. First, pressure has begun to build up within the FICCI for more coordinated action by the business community. Although these efforts were not converted into action at that time, pressures for similar measures continue to be exerted within the federation and the business community at large.

The most successful collective business effort in 1967 was carried out by the cement industry through an organization called the Cement Allocation and Coordinating Organization (CACO). CACO had been set up to insure the orderly distribution of cement after the government decided to decontrol cement prices in January of 1966. CACO was responsible for arranging the sale of cement throughout India and received a limited amount of revenue which was part of a separate fund controlled by CACO. CACO used part of these funds in the 1967 elections to finance candidates who would oppose any attempt by government to again control cement. CACO paid out 3,415,355 rupees, of which the Swatantra party received 1,464,155, the Congress party received 1,006,000, Jana Sangh received 512,200, and the Jana Congress received 225,000.[39] CACO was in a unique position because it had an available fund which, although collected for other purposes, could be diverted to bolstering the political fortunes of the cement industry. If CACO is a portent of the future, India may be moving in the direction of Japan and Germany, where business has developed means of collective action in the realm of political contributions. One hears loose talk of funds being supplied by the jute, tea, and textile industries, but these are in reality references to collections of individual actions, not to collective contributions.

[39] *The Patriot* (New Delhi), April 3, 1968.

For the present, however, the pattern of individual contributions for individual benefit seems well established, although businessmen have differed in their assessments of the utility of such contributions. In the days when the Congress party enjoyed a monopoly of power, many businessmen felt that contributions to the Congress party were the equivalent of a compulsory levy. As one businessman said, "Politicians take it as their right to get contributions and feel no real sense of obligation in having taken them." Although they agree that politicians have short memories, most businessmen nevertheless believe that political contributions have three positive functions. First, they feel that, by strengthening those parties which are not opposed to the survival of the private sector in some form, they act as a bulwark against the Communists. Thus, except in the broadest ideological sense of supporting non-Communist parties, business feels that contributions have an individual, rather than a collective, impact on policy. Second, political contributions buy the insurance of a positive psychological orientation by preventing the development of resentment among top party leaders who are also the major party fund raisers. Finally, they make possible limited or specific individual benefits, such as access for purposes of obtaining licenses, permits, and import quotas.

Aside from the fact that the Congress party is the ruling party, most contributions go to Congress because businessmen feel that the other parties are worse or have no real standing. Because the Communists get money from abroad, businessmen argue, business must support the democratic parties. Defections from the Congress party are explained by reactions to Congress policies that were viewed as "designed to destroy the private sector."

Contributions are also believed to have a psychological function. This kind of contribution is made by check to political parties, and its impact is generalized rather than specific. Such contributions are said to give "insurance" or "general cover" or to see that "things do not go against you." In some cases such contributions are seen as unavoidable levies to prevent resentments or, as one individual put it, "to please a few ministers."

The third function of contributions is to obtain access for the purpose of gaining individual benefits. Generosity is a major consideration in securing important benefits. "Unless you give large contributions, they do not really count," said one businessman. A business MP defined "large" as somewhere in the realm of twenty to fifty lakhs. "Contributions up to one lakh," he argued, "mean nothing." Big contributions, however, "give considerable leverage on big issues," which he defined as starting a new plant, getting a permanent location, or getting a source of power. "If an individual helped a few ministers then he has easy access to those ministers and gets a sympathetic hearing from those ministers." The most helpful ministers are those whose careers you have helped build.

The impact of contributions on parties varies with the organization and discipline of the party. Until the period from 1963 to 1971, the Congress party was a well-organized and highly disciplined party. Thus business concentrated on trying to influence the party leadership, and most contributions went to party leaders. Helping individual MPs had limited but occasionally useful impact. As one industrialist put it, "An individual MP recognizes your contributions and yet his role is limited. The individual MP does not really have much power. He has to operate within the party, and the party places certain restrictions on his activities such as party discipline. All he can do is take your problem to the minister and in this sense he can help."

If the Congress party majority was reduced or a coalition government was in power, the status of the individual MP would be quite different. Ministers, less concerned with discipline and more concerned with maintaining support in the party, would be much more receptive to requests by MPs for action. Also, with decreased majorities, the threat of defection would become more important, for each vote would become critical in maintaining government majorities. Therefore individual influence with individual MPs would become more important as the role of the member himself becomes more critical to the leadership. The restoration of Congress party dominance has reduced this possibility for the present.

Patterns of funding, so critical to the maintenance of established parties, can also have a significant impact on attempts to build new political parties. As Erdman has observed:

> If resources are no problem, then the party leaders (or those who control the funds) can seek to set up those candidates who are most congenial to them, who are ideologically sympathetic, reasonably hard workers, and so on, or at least people who combine some of these qualities with local appeal. In the absence of ample funds, however, a high premium is put on self-financing candidates or on notable local figures who can win with a modest expenditure of funds. In this case, the central party organization becomes extremely dependent on such candidates and is not likely to establish substantial control over them.[40]

[40] Howard L. Erdman, *The Swatantra Party and Indian Conservatism* (Cambridge: Cambridge University Press, 1967), p. 171.

Thus, for the 1963 elections, the central office of the Swatantra party had originally promised to supply each MP about forty to fifty thousand rupees but was finally able to deliver only about thirty thousand,[41] forcing the Swatantra party candidates to supply a larger portion of their own funds. Under these circumstances the Swatantra MPs became much less amenable to party discipline than they might have been if they had been fully financed by the national organization.

Changes in the party system, in turn, have an impact on the role of contributions in the nominating process. The more decentralized and less disciplined the party, the greater the voice the political contributors will have in the distribution of party tickets. They may even insist that a party ticket be given to a family member in return for guaranteeing his funding and the funding of candidates for subsidiary offices in his constituency. They may, however, be content with specifying the selection of the right kind of candidate. Many businessmen made it clear to the Swatantra party leaders that they would be willing to support the party only if particular types of candidates were selected.[42] The private sector, they insisted, deserved articulate spokesmen such as Dandekar and Masani, and they got them.

Patterns of funding can also have an impact on factional politics in the constituency. For example, Ram Ratan Gupta, a Uttar Pradesh textile magnate, was able to secure the cooperation of Congress MLAs in his constituency, despite their initial attachment to the opposing Congress party faction, by promising to finance their campaigns.[43]

In its relationships with political parties, business uses its most potent resource—money. Business finances elections. It also finances the various party meetings which by tradition are held in rural settings. Substantial sums are required to build and provide facilities to house and feed the delegates to such meetings. The major functions of political contributions are to support ideologically acceptable parties, to ensure easy access to potential decision-makers, and to try to influence the nomination process. Political contributions in India are designed primarily for individual rather than collective benefit. The vast distributive capability of the Indian government makes access to decision-makers important and provides reason enough for continued contributions. Thus, while political contributions may ensure access and may aid in securing individual benefits, they do not guarantee that the business voice will dominate and determine public policy.

[41] *Ibid.*, p. 174.

[42] *Ibid.*, pp. 180, 183–184.

[43] Paul Brass, *Factional Politics in an Indian State* (Berkeley and Los Angeles: University of California Press, 1965), pp. 79–85.

XI

PARLIAMENT AND BUSINESS

The voice of business in the Indian Parliament was extremely weak during the first decade after independence. Functional representation had been abolished, mass franchise had been introduced, and there was no business party. "It is an unfortunate fact," said the president of Assocham as late as June 1965, "that, in the Indian Parliament as at presently constituted, the business viewpoint is inadequately represented. . . . The mere existence of this situation, the importance of Parliament activity, and the comparative ineffectiveness of business opinion therein, make it essential that the business community should find alternative means of publicizing its opinion and making its views heard." [1] Business had tended to be resigned to this situation during the 1950s. But system changes, combined with growing self-confidence, increased economic power, and changing attitudes toward politics and political participation within the business community, have brought about corresponding changes in business relations with Parliament.

For a variety of reasons, business activity in Parliament during the Nehru era was very limited. First, having accepted the principle of universal adult franchise, the constituent assembly also decided, despite sustained protest from business, to abolish the provisions for functional representation which had been instituted under the British.[2] This system of functional representation had served business well. Not only had it guaranteed business and commercial interests a voice, but it had also attracted to legislative service some extremely articulate business representatives, such as Sir Homi Mody and Sir Purshotamdas Thakurdas. In the absence of functional representation, the FICCI feared that "while in constituencies based on adult suffrage, labor would be adequately represented in the House of the People, . . .

[1] "The Associated Chambers of Commerce and Industry of India," a speech by H. K. S. Lindsay, president of Assocham (1964–1965), at the Rotary Club of Calcutta, June 8, 1965. Reprinted by Assocham, p. 2.

[2] Granville Austin, *The Indian Constitution* (Oxford: Clarendon Press, 1966), p. 152; FICCI, *Proceedings of the Twenty-First Annual Meeting, 1948* (Delhi: FICCI, 1948), p. 182; FICCI, *Report of the Proceedings of the Executive Committee for 1949* (Delhi: FICCI, 1949), pp. 58–59; FICCI, *Report of the Executive Committee for 1950* (Delhi: FICCI, 1959), pp. 79–80.

Indian commercial interests would not have any chance of being represented in the House under the constitution proposed."[3] Furthermore, with the abolition of functional representation and the introduction of mass franchise, few leading industrialists were willing to contest. And, unfortunately for the business commmunity, those who were elected tended to be less articulate as spokesmen for the private sector than their predecessors had been.

A second factor inhibiting business participation in Parliament was the fact that, until 1959 business had had no effective parliamentary mouthpiece in the form of an organized business party to speak clearly and authoritatively on its behalf. For years there seemed to be little hope of creating one, given the ideological climate, Congress party dominance, and the parliamentary bias created by the existence therein of "a strong section in the opposition and also in the Congress who had very strong prejudices against trade and industry and cast all sorts of aspersions against industry."[4]

But, and this is the third point, these attempts to gain access for business views by liaison and lobbying were hampered by the low level of legitimacy attached by the political culture to such activity and the consequent hostility of ministers and high civil servants to attempts to mobilize support in Parliament. The objection was not entirely to business lobbying as such. The norms of society and the political system viewed lobbying of any kind with suspicion and distrust, as an intrinsically equivocal if not illegal form of action.

When Nehru discovered that the FICCI had arranged a tour of Indian industry for the MPs elected in the first general election, to educate them about the activities of the private sector, he was so furious that the practice was stopped. Similarly, the civil service reaction to the news of lobbying activity was to work twice as hard to justify the government's decisions. Eventually the hostility of ministers and the higher civil servants to lobbying led many businessmen to feel that it was best not to function through Parliament lest such activity endanger the close liaison established at the executive level.

Yet the situation continued to trouble businessmen. L. M. Singhvi, a former MP, noted that:

> A strange ambivalence and lack of realism afflicts our attitudes on the role of the competing interest groups in the legislative

[3] FICCI, *Report of the Proceedings of the Executive Committee for 1949* (Delhi: FICCI, 1949), p. 59.

[4] G. D. Somani, *Confidential Report on the First Session of Parliament May 13, 1952 to August 12, 1952* (submitted to the Bombay Millowners Association, August 1952).

> process. On the one hand, we tend to look upon these pressure groups with dismay, disapproval, and suspicion; on the other hand, we know for a fact that interest groups do exist and operate in our society; and indeed we recognize that they have a right to exist and to operate because they represent a segment of public opinion. Our attitudes to pressure groups exemplify an unwholesome admixture of frosted and affected prudery and a passive and escapist permissiveness.[5]

Another MP put it this way:

> Until ten years ago there was no lobbying in India. We have the British attitude toward lobbying. The British are subtle and hypocritical about lobbying and so are we. If you visit an MP at his home and have tea with him, he is very friendly and cooperative. But if you see him in the central hall of Parliament and try to lobby him, he becomes very embarrassed. He feels lobbying is shameful.

Thus, despite constant alarms from business spokesmen in Parliament declaring that something had to be done to rectify this attitude, the obstacles seemed so formidable that little action was taken. In a memorandum to the committee of the Bombay Millowners Association summarizing the activities of the first session of India's post-election Parliament in August 1952, G. D. Somani, a business MP, warned:

> The important question I want to draw attention of the committee to is the fact that conditions have changed materially and although controls may be lifted sooner or later, the fact remains that our trade and industry will continue to be functioning under strict regulation and regimentation as indicated in the Planning Commission Report itself. It is essential that we should take measures to protect our interests in altered circumstances. Our case has gone by default on so many occasions, and even in matters where we had a very strong and genuine case we have not been able to educate either the MP or the general public outside, to show how on many occasions we have received unfair treatment from government and how all sorts of charges that are

[5] L. M. Singhvi, "The Legislative Process in India," *Journal of Constitutional and Parliamentary Studies* 4 (1970): 14.

> being leveled are mostly based on misunderstanding and prejudice. . . .
>
> Unless we are able to put forth our considered views in proper time it is quite likely that we may be deprived even of whatever reasonable modification or alternations we may otherwise secure.

Finally, business paid relatively little attention to Parliament, because the social and developmental legislation passed in the early 1950s had placed the bulk of the subsequent decisions affecting business in the hands of the bureaucracy. In a controlled and regulated economy, administrative action and not legislation is the day-to-day concern of the regulated party. Thus, it was more important for business to focus lobbying attention on the regulatory policies of the administration. This tactic seemed especially judicious, because individual Members of Parliament played only a minor role in the policy-making process. In the context of massive Congress party majorities and strict party discipline, the influencing of a few MPs would be meaningless. And yet, as Tyson has observed, the failure to inform the average MP of business aims and achievements may have been unwise.

> There have been one or two outstandingly able spokesmen for the private sector in the Lok Sabha from time to time, but in general the Congress back benchers have been ill informed about, and curiously indifferent to, the aims and achievements of privately owned Indian industry and business as a whole. As a result, some of the commercial legislation initiated and passed during the Nehru years has been more severe than wise.[6]

It was precisely this conviction that the legislation was unnecessarily severe and even unwise that finally turned business attention to Parliament in the later 1950s and early 1960s. By then business had begun to feel that it must begin to intervene earlier in the policy process, by concentrating on the content of legislation, if it was to avoid being saddled with a massive array of unacceptable legislation. Furthermore, Parliament was being used by the left as a forum to attack the private sector. The absence of an effective business counter-voice on the floor of Parliament enabled the left to hurl charges to which no reply could effectively be made. Business responded in two ways to this unsatisfactory situation. In 1958 the FICCI under the leadership

[6] Geoffrey Tyson, *Nehru: The Years of Power* (New York: Praeger, 1966), p. 64.

of Babubhai Chinai, a Congress party MP and lieutenant of the powerful Congress minister, S. K. Patil, decided to institutionalize a liaison and lobbying office within its secretariat. The office was to be staffed by a former employee of the Lok Sabha secretariat. A year later a sector of Bombay business not closely associated with the federation decided to encourage and openly support the formation of the Swatantra party as a spokesman for the private sector.

The decision by business to pay greater attention to Parliament, either directly by attempting to gain greater representation or indirectly by a process of lobbying, came at a very critical time. By the early 1960s Parliament had begun to play a much more important role as critic of government and as part of the policy process. Moreover, public policy itself began to change slightly. Under Prime Minister Shastri, a few steps toward dismantling the system of controls developed in the 1950s began.

The Legislative Process: The Select Committee

In India, all major legislation is initiated by the executive. There is almost no prior consultation between interest groups and the government on the form and content of legislation.[7] Executive initiative is especially marked in the case of legislation dealing with taxation and fiscal issues and slightly less so where the legislation derives from the report of a special commission of investigation. A legislative proposal usually embodies a variety of ministerial and bureaucratic compromises. But by the time a legislative proposal has been submitted to Parliament, the government has become publicly committed to it, in principle if not in detail. Thus, business has had a very difficult time even attempting to modify legislation once it has been submitted to Parliament, much less blocking it. Whatever influence business can bring to bear tends to be exerted at either or both of two points in the legislative process: during the select committee phase, and through Congress party members in Parliament. In most cases business resorts to neither body, unless efforts to persuade the executive have failed.

The Indian Parliament does not have a system of specialized committees—like those in the United States Congress—to which legislation is referred for detailed consideration. There is a system of parliamentary consultative committees which parallel the ministries of the government of India. But these committees are designed primarily to make possible a dialogue between MPs and government, thus

[7] Robert W. Stern, *The Process of Opposition in India: Two Case Studies of How Policy Shapes Politics* (Chicago: University of Chicago Press, 1970), pp. 151–160.

enabling government to explain the details of its policies to small groups of MPs. The Congress Party in Parliament has established a system of specialized committees, but they are used largely as study groups and do not play an active role in the legislative process. In the absence of an effective system of standing committees on legislation,[8] a select committee of the Lok Sabha or a joint committee of both the Lok Sabha and Rajya Sabha may be appointed to consider important legislative proposals submitted by government. A select committee regularly requests outside groups to provide both oral and written testimony. And so it is standard business strategy to ensure that legislation affecting commerce and industry is referred to a select committee. Business is thereby guaranteed direct access and formal consultation.

The members of a select committee are appointed or elected by the house or nominated by the speaker. Its membership is broad based and provides informally for the proportional representation of different political parties in the Lok Sabha. Although the size of a select committee is not fixed, it is usually small enough for a fairly intimate discussion. Members are not ordinarily subjected to party whips and directives, but the government is in a position to pressure its party members to expedite action if the bill is assigned a high priority by the government. The composition of the select committee is very important to those interested in attempting to influence the committee. If this committee is kept small and is staffed by the more articulate, influential, and knowledgeable MPs who have some expertise in the subject under consideration, business has been able to make an impact. Once a bill has been sent to a select committee, business may try one of two strategies. Blocking legislation is beyond the capacity of business because of its weak position in Parliament and among the Indian public, and so business tries either to delay the bill as long as possible or to press for modification in the most unacceptable clauses. The members of the select committee can be influenced, either through direct contact or indirectly through the chief minister, on whom the MP is dependent for a party ticket.

The effectiveness of business pressure on a select committee depends very heavily on the political power and personal commitment of the minister in charge of the bill. A strong minister can block attempts to change his bill if he or the civil service are not convinced of the validity of the need for the change. The ability to delay action is

[8] There are a few standing committees such as the Committee on Subordinate Legislation, the Estimate Committee, and so on, but they do not deal with legislation. See W. H. Morris-Jones, *Parliament in India* (Philadelphia: University of Pennsylvania Press, 1957), pp. 279–315.

similarly dependent on the minister, and also on the priority assigned to the legislation by the government and the degree of unity within the government as to the desirability of the action. For example, although a series of less prestigious and determined ministers had failed for over ten years to push through the revisions of the patent laws, Morarji Desai had sufficient political power and personal commitment to force the enactment of his bill on social control of banks and gold control despite strong efforts by business to delay passage of Morarji's proposals.[9]

Government is usually willing to make minor changes in legislation to meet strong criticism, provided such changes do not alter the major objectives of the legislation. In most cases these changes are made during the select committee phase in direct response to criticisms leveled at the proposals. For example, Minister of Finance T. T. Krishnamachari introduced in his budget speech, of May 15, 1957, a controversial and complex series of new tax measures which included a tax on wealth and an expenditure tax.[10] The wealth tax was applicable to both individuals and companies.[11] The finance minister defended these proposals in a public broadcast to the nation the same day,[12] but his budget came as a shock to the business community and the FICCI issued a strong press statement attacking the tax proposals on which it was based.[13]

Later meetings were held between FICCI representatives and the finance minister in Calcutta and Bombay. At the Calcutta meeting, G. D. Birla was among those included in the delegation. He urged that both the wealth tax and the expenditure tax as proposed by government be modified, because the wealth tax, on companies in particular, would inhibit productive wealth. The finance minister told the group that the government was committed to the broad structure of his tax proposals, but that adjustments of detail might be possible. These adjustments, he told the group, would be taken care of during the select committee stage of the finance bill.[14] The FICCI secretariat, therefore, prepared a detailed memorandum for submission both to the finance minister and to the select committee of Parliament. A small

[9] *The National Herald* (Lucknow and New Delhi), August 17, 1968.

[10] The budget is usually presented in February, but because of the 1957 elections it was delayed.

[11] Government of India, Publications Division, Ministry of Information and Broadcasting, *Speeches of T. T. Krishnamachari* (New Delhi: Government of India Press, 1957), pp. 22–23.

[12] *Ibid.*, p. 30.

[13] FICCI, *Correspondence for 1957* (Delhi: FICCI, 1957), pp. 389–395.

[14] *Ibid.*, p. 397.

delegation from the FICCI also testified before the select committee.

In response to the pleadings of the FICCI and other groups, the select committee made several changes in the bill. Among the important changes made by the select committee were: the exemption of shares held by one company in another company; the provision for a tax holiday of five years from the date of incorporation for new companies and new units of existing companies; and the exemption of the shipping industry from the wealth tax. Speaking before the Rajya Sabha on September 4, 1957, the finance minister reported that he had examined the original provisions of the wealth tax bill in the light of criticisms and representations received from various quarters. By and large these discussions had strengthened his sense of the need for such a bill, but he had accepted some of the recommended changes.[15] Although most of the changes accepted by T. T. Krishnamachari were minor, the exemption of shipping from the wealth tax was a major concession and the direct result of an intensive lobbying campaign carried out by the shipping industry. Shortly after his budget speech in May, representatives of the shipping industry had met with T. T. Krishnamachari and pleaded that the shipping industry be exempted from the wealth tax on the grounds that it would have a devastating impact on the future growth of the industry. At the time T. T. Krishnamachari flatly refused to grant the concession. Undaunted, the shipping industry began to mobilize its own resources. Shrimati Sumati S. Morarjee, president of the Indian National Steamship Owners Association (INSOA), went to Delhi to discuss the issue with various ministries. She returned and recommended to the committee of the INSOA that a special delegation be appointed to present the case of the industry to the select committee. A written memorandum was also prepared for submission to the government. Several days before the scheduled select committee meeting, Mrs. Morarjee and a small group from the INSOA arrived in Delhi to meet privately with ministers and influential members of the select committee.[16] "Friends in Delhi" advised her that the delegation should be strengthened by the inclusion of M. A. Master, a former director of Scindia and a recognized authority on the shipping industry. During these discussions, Mrs. Morarjee and her chief assistant, Navin Khandwalla, succeeded in gaining the support of Minister of Transport Lal Bahadur Shastri, Director-General of Shipping Nagendra Singh, and several key members of the select

[15] *Speeches of T. T. Krishnamachari*, p. 108.

[16] Scindia Steam Navigation Company, Ltd., *The Wealth Tax and the Shipping Industry* (Bombay: Commercial Department, Scindia Steam Navigation Company, Ltd., 1957), p. 35.

committee, especially Feroze Gandhi, husband of Prime Minister Nehru's daughter Indira. However, when Mrs. Morarjee and her INSOA delegation entered the committee room, the chairman, Mr. Asoke Sen, the law minister, told the delegation that the committee had already received the INSOA written memorandum and furthermore had heard testimony of Mr. B. P. Singh Roy of the FICCI and others, including a delegation from the Indian Merchants Chamber, who presented the views of the shipping industry. The chairman informed Mrs. Morarjee that, because "it is impossible at present to make a distinction between shipping companies and other companies," he saw little purpose in hearing the delegation.[17] At this point, Feroze Gandhi and Mr. M. R. Masani, another member of the select committee, requested the chairman to hear the delegation's case. After some hesitation the chairman agreed.

Master spoke for the delegation. He told the committee that shipping in India received no subsidy from the government and lacked the resources to finance even the modest development proposals for the industry under the second Five Year Plan. He argued that Indian shipping was at a disadvantage compared to British shipping because of its lower development rebate and investment allowance as well as its higher capital gains taxes. And now the government proposed to add the wealth tax. He argued that the shipping industry was a major foreign exchange earner for India, and that shipping could earn substantially more if permitted to grow more rapidly. He pointed out that this growth would be slowed if the industry could not generate the resources for expansion. Although the wealth tax on shipping might produce a small amount in terms of revenues for government, the industry would lose a substantial amount of money for purposes of investment, and the government would lose much more in the long run.[18]

Master's testimony made a deep impression on the select committee and on its chairman, for all his original hostility. Although other witnesses had been allotted no more than twenty minutes,[19] Master was listened to for fifty minutes "in rapt attention." [20] And when he finished, Mrs. Morarjee later wrote, "some members . . . rose to congratulate him there and then. Some like Shri Feroze Gandhi and others said that they were convinced they should not only be exempted from the operations of the wealth tax, but must be given further relief such as exemption from the capital gains tax, and so on." [21]

Support for the shipping industry came from quarters other than the

[17] *Ibid.*, p. 23.
[18] *Ibid.*, pp. 11–18.
[19] *Ibid.*, p. 22.
[20] *Ibid.*, p. 23.
[21] *Ibid.*, p. 23.

members of the select committee. Minister of Transport Lal Bahadur Shastri, shortly after the select committee meeting, discussed the matter favorably with the members of the Lok Sabha:

> The shipping companies have been strongly pleading for exemption being given to them from the new taxes proposed by the finance minister. I am told that the finance minister is greatly impressed with the evidence given by Mr. Master in the select committee. I do not know what his decision would be but, anyhow, I feel that perhaps he would be favorably inclined to agree to this proposal, because it is surely in the interest of the development of shipping which is so vital for our country.[22]

Shastri did not rest content with supporting the case of the shipping industry publicly. He also pressed the case privately with T. T. Krishnamachari.[23] As Master himself admitted, "Had it not been for the strong pressure that was brought from Shri Lal Bahadur Shastri . . . we may not have achieved the results that we have achieved today." [24]

Behind the exemption of the shipping industry from the wealth tax on corporations, then, there was a well-conducted process of lobbying which extended to the minister of transport as well as to the key members of the select committee and did not neglect the importance of making an effective presentation of the case. Despite his initial refusal to grant an exemption to the shipping industry, the finance minister was forced to bend before pressure from the Transport Ministry, the select committee of Parliament, and the industry. As Mrs. Morarjee later admitted,

> the factors that contributed to the change in the attitude of the finance minister were that I had met most of the members of the select committee and explained to them our case. Shri M. A. Master already had created a favorable opinion for exemption by his pamphlets and so forth, and his superb advocacy greatly strengthened our case. The support of the Transport Ministry also played a very important part, and ultimately what looked to be impossible did happen. For the first time, Indian shipping has been accorded a special recognition.[25]

The select committee phase of the legislative process is important, because it provides a recognized method—and a method recognized as

[22] *Ibid.*, p. 20.
[23] *Ibid.*, p. 42.
[24] *Ibid.*
[25] *Ibid.*, p. 28.

legitimate—for interest groups to gain direct access to Parliament. But most groups are not quite as successful as the shipping industry. The keys to success during the select committee phase are the attitude of the minister, the composition of the committee, and the nature of the issue. Fundamental changes in legislation require the ability to persuade either the minister or the higher echelons of the bureaucracy to accept the interest group's point of view. As the example of the shipping industry illustrates, business has resorted to lobbying in Parliament only after efforts at the executive level have failed.

But a great deal depends on the composition of the select committee and the nature of the issue. Select committees have been known to make bills even more stringent than originally proposed by government. Moreover, once an issue becomes controversial, then it becomes very difficult for business to achieve any changes. One of the most important checks on business lobbying in Parliament is the strong left-of-center lobby in Parliament. On numerous occasions that lobby has acted as a check on business, both within Parliament and in the Congress Party in Parliament. As long as India retains a dominant one-party system in which government controls massive majorities, lobbying in Parliament will have limited results. If government is agreed on a particular action, party discipline is all that is required to ensure its passage. If the government's majorities were substantially reduced, or if government were dependent on a coalition of parties—as was the case briefly prior to the 1971 elections—then the votes of individual MPs or small blocs of the MPs would count for much more and lobbying in Parliament would be much more effective.

The Congress Party in Parliament

The Congress Party in Parliament is second only to the select committee as an access point for business lobbying. The Congress Party in Parliament consists of all the Congress party members of the Lok Sabha and Rajya Sabha. The two most important organs of the Congress Party in Parliament are the general body and the executive committee. The general body is composed of all the Congress party members of Parliament. It meets frequently when Parliament is in session to discuss the broad policy dimensions of legislation. The executive committee plays a key role in deciding which amendments introduced by party members should be accepted before a bill reaches the floor of Parliament for final passage. Although Congress party MPs normally prefer to use private conversations to persuade ministers to accept changes in proposed legislation, party pressure may be exerted on ministers who are unreceptive to discreet requests for changes in a bill.

Attempting to influence legislation through the Congress Party in Parliament automatically brings business into conflict with the multiplicity of interests and ideological tendencies of which the Congress party is composed. Thus, on numerous occasions the pro-business right wing of the Congress has found itself held in check by the ever vigilant left wing of the party. The two most prominent examples of this pattern of group pressure can be found in the case of the Company Law Amendment and cement decontrol.

In 1956, India enacted the Companies Act, which was one of the most comprehensive and complex regulatory statutes in the country. The act has been repeatedly amended. Some of the most important changes in the act were proposed in 1963 and 1965, as an outgrowth of the Vivian Bose Commission Report on the activities of the Dalmia-Jain group of companies. The Bose Report had cited Dalmia for numerous malpractices in his operation. As a result, the government of India appointed Attorney General C. K. Dapthary and A. V. Viavanatha Sastri, a retired judge, to examine the Bose Report and recommend corrective and preventive action in the form of changes in the Companies Act. On the basis of Dapthary–Sastri Report, the government formed a comprehensive set of amendments to the Companies Act. Several of those amendments were highly controversial. One of the provisions most objectionable to business was a clause which gave government the right to convert its loan capital to private sector firms into share capital, thereby giving government a voice in the internal affairs of the company.[26] The FICCI charged that the government was proposing back door nationalization.[27]

The Company Law Amendments Bill was sent to a select committee of Parliament in December 1963. A group of Congress party members in the select committee succeeded in amending the conversion clause on loans by removing its retroactivity and making it applicable only to future loans. These Congress party members argued that past contracts should not be altered in such a drastic manner, because government might not use its power wisely. The very existence of such powers, they argued, gave the executive the power to browbeat those of its debtors whom it disliked. The select committee amendment came as a surprise to the finance minister and even to some of the Congress party members

[26] *The Economic Times* (Bombay), November 27, 1963.
[27] FICCI, *Correspondence for 1963* (Delhi: FICCI, 1963), p. 236.

on the select committee. The issue thereupon became embroiled in internal Congress party politics.

A group of socialist-oriented Congress party members, who were members of the select committee, challenged the validity of the amendment. Even though the majority of the select committee had approved the amendment, they called for a special meeting of the party executive to review the issue. They claimed that, because the party had never cleared the amendment, the party executive should review the select committee's action. At that special meeting with the excutive, however, the executive upheld the select committee's recommendations.[28] The defeated Congress members then circulated a petition demanding the convening of a full meeting of the general body of the Congress Party in Parliament. At that meeting they charged that some members of Congress, under the influence of big business lobbies, were trying to water down the bill.

The incident had occurred at a time when the Congress was in the midst of a major ideological debate. That debate involved a demand for a more radical form of socialism, to be demonstrated through the nationalization of banks and the adoption of a less equivocal resolution on democracy and socialism. The charges of undue influence, therefore, had a major impact, and the select committee changes aroused suspicion and ideological fervor among the Congress party rank and file. At the party meeting, even Nehru admitted that the finance minister had been embarrassed by the manner in which the select committee had made the change. He was reported to be annoyed about the whole controversy. To resolve the problem, some members of the party moved a resolution that the prime minister undertake the task of resolving the dispute. After consulting his cabinet, Nehru decided to reverse the decision of the Congress parliamentary party executive to support the select committee.[29] Later T. T. Krishnamachari disclosed that the loan provisions would actually affect only five companies. The government already held shares in two of the five. The other three were Tata Iron and Steel Company, Indian Iron and Steel Company, and Atul Products, each of which had an outstanding loan of ten million rupees.[30]

In the debate on the select committee report in Parliament, T. T. Krishnamachari announced that the government would not accept the select committee's recommendations on loans. However, the govern-

[28] *The Statesman* (Calcutta), December 12, 1963 and December 14, 1963.

[29] *Ibid.*

[30] *The Financial Express* (Bombay), December 14, 1963.

ment's actions by now had stirred up apprehensions among British interests as well as among Indian businessmen. In order to allay these fears, T. T. Krishnamachari assured the Lok Sabha that loans for financial institutions and the National Shipping Board were not included under the act. He went so far as to hint that action would not even be taken in the case of the two steel loans. In addition, he accepted an amendment whereby a copy of every order issued in regard to conversion had to be placed before the Lok Sabha within thirty days. In short, Parliament would have to approve any such conversion.[31] Thus, while business succeeded in modifying legislation through its friends on the select committee, their influence was cancelled out by strong pressure from the Congress left, pressure to which Prime Minister Nehru was quick to respond.

A similar incident occurred in the case of cement decontrol. But circumstances had changed, and the results were totally different. Midway through the third Five Year Plan, the Indian economy had begun to stagnate. The World Bank repeatedly advised that controls which served little purpose beyond inhibiting production should be lifted. And in 1963 the government decided to decontrol sixteen items. Believing that controls created artificial scarcity, Prime Minister Lal Bahadur Shastri committed himself, in the summer of 1964, to reviewing all controls and eliminating those which no longer served any useful purpose. In 1965 the government, on recommendation of a special committee, decided to decontrol steel. As Shastri began looking around for candidates for decontrol, cement seemed to be a prime candidate because of its importance as a basic industry. Despite acute shortages of cement in the mid-1960s, cement production was stagnant. The industry insisted that prices were simply not high enough to permit investment for expansion. Feeling that the private sector would be unable to meet the need for additional production, the government decided to enter the cement field and created the Cement Corporation of India, a public sector facility.[32]

At the same time discussions were taking place within the government, among the Planning Commission, the Committee of Economic Secretaries, and the Industry Subcommittee of the Cabinet Economic Affairs Committee, as to future government policy toward the cement industry. Some members of the Planning Commission and the Committee of Economic Secretaries were convinced that expansion of the

[31] *The Times of India* (Bombay), December 17, 1963; *The Financial Express* (Bombay), December 14, 1963.

[32] *The Statesman* (Calcutta), May 13, 1964.

public sector was the only solution to the problem. Others argued that expansion of the public sector was not feasible, because of foregin exchange shortages for the fourth Five Year Plan, because of the lack of expertise in the public sector cement corporation, and because it was cheaper to expand existing units than to start new units. When the issue of the feasibility of public sector expansion was raised in the cabinet, the Planning Commission responded by pointing out that the best way to produce cement in the public sector was to nationalize the industry. The Indian cabinet was unwilling to raise the issue of nationalization of cement at that time.[33] Thereafter, discussions focused on the industry's demand for a price increase. It was proposed that the industry be permitted to raise prices, provided the increase was used for expansion and not for higher profits and dividends. At this point, government economic advisors suggested that the industry should be completely decontrolled with the provision that certain informal safeguards be arranged. In short, government policy was receptive to the idea of decontrol, and once all other alternatives for expanding cement production in the public sector had been rejected, the cement industry seemed to be a good candidate.

Meanwhile, the leadership of the cement industry underwent an important change. In April 1965, D. M. Khatau stepped down as president of the Cement Manufacturers Association and was replaced by G. D. Somani, a former Congress party MP.[34] Aware that government was studying the problem of controls and trying to decide which industries to decontrol, Somani began working on Prime Minister Shastri, on T. N. Singh, the Union minister for industry, and on state Congress party leaders, to see that cement was decontrolled. He assured government that the industry was willing to guarantee safeguards which would protect the interests of both producers and consumers. In May 1965, a delegation of the cement industry met with T. N. Singh in Bombay, to discuss the industry's difficulties and in particular the industry's demand for a price rise. Although T. N. Singh was personally an unenthusiastic supporter of decontrol,[35] the delegation made a strong plea for lifting all controls on cement.[36] However, the industry began to press their case. In early August, the Cement Manufacturers Association broke with past policy to call openly for partial decontrol of cement as a means of generating extra

[33] *The Statesman* (Calcutta), December 10, 1965.
[34] *The Financial Express* (Bombay), April 25, 1965.
[35] *The Statesman* (Calcutta), December 10, 1965.
[36] Cement Manufacturers Association, *Fifth Annual Report 1965* (Bombay: Cement Manufacturers Association, 1965), p. 7.

funds for expansion. At the same time they accepted the responsibility for instituting some form of self-regulation within the industry.[37]

On August 26, Prime Minister Shastri abruptly announced in Parliament his decision to decontrol cement in principle, with the details to be worked out later. In defending the decision, T. N. Singh explained that the cement industry blamed controls for the tardy growth of the industry but that government had been receiving reports that existing controls were, in fact, ineffective. The government, he argued, was not wedded to controls for their own sake.[38] Later he told a consultative committee of Parliament that, as "an act of faith," the private sector was to be given a major role in expanding cement production. He also pointed out that the disruption of aid resulting from the Indian-Pakistan War of 1965 had made the role envisioned for the public sector cement corporation impossible to achieve.[39] Nevertheless, some members of the Parliament called the shift in policy a sellout to the private sector.[40]

Shastri faced strong opposition within his own party. Fearing that the policy change might mark the beginning of pressure from other sectors of industry, the executive committee of the Congress Party in Parliament expressed grave misgivings over the decontrol of cement. In reply, Shastri emphasized the need for more cement, and T. N. Singh assured members that the decision was taken only after consultation with chief ministers of the states had revealed that all of them supported the move. Some members urged reconsideration and if necessary a reversal of the decision. Instead, the minister of industries decided to hold informal discussions with MPs to try to allay any remaining fears.[41]

Thus, unlike Nehru, Shastri was not willing to give into pressure from the Congress party left wing. He decided to carry through with his decision. The key figure in calling Shastri's attention to cement and in making a convincing case for that industry was G. D. Somani, who lobbied for the industry through the Cement Manufacturers Association.

[37] *The Financial Express* (Bombay), August 7, 1965; *The Times of India* (Bombay), August 6, 1965.

[38] *The Times of India* (Bombay), September 3, 1965.

[39] *The Times of India* (Bombay), November 17, 1965.

[40] *The Statesman* (Calcutta), November 19, 1965.

[41] *The Economic Times* (Bombay), December 2, 1965; *The Times of India* (Bombay), December 4, 1965.

Lobbying

Although lobbying continues to be viewed with suspicion and equated with corruption, lobbying has been practiced increasingly in recent years. The quality of legislative lobbying, however, remains primitive by American standards. It is poorly organized, selectively applied, sporadically exercised, and tends to rely excessively on personal contacts. Lobbying by business in India works through four basic channels: elite representation, organized associations, private contractors, and business houses. Each has a different objective requiring a correspondingly different technique.

Elite representatives are business MPs. As Members of Parliament, they are in a position to promote their own interests apart from, or in conjunction with, the interests of the business community as a whole. As a Member of Parliament, the businessman enjoys complete and open access to ministers and other MPs on a daily, informal basis. He is in a position to persuade, mobilize support, and supply information. Although some MPs have been members of the committee of the FICCI and others have been associated with one of the major industry associations—such as jute, tea, sugar, cement, and textiles—or have come from prominent industrial families, their numbers have been too few from the present point of view of the FICCI. G. L. Bansal, the secretary-general of the FICCI, was a Congress party MP, but political divisions in the committee of the FICCI in the early 1960s prevented him from seeking reelection. Anti-Congress committee members insisted that he would have to resign from the FICCI if he accepted a party ticket. Today, however, a major objective of business has been to try to increase the level of direct representation in the hope that business would then be close to the source of policy and in a position to make a greater impact.

A second type of lobbyist comprehends the staff member of the major business associations. These lobbyists may stay in Delhi during sessions of Parliament, or they may make periodic trips to the capital to explain their organization's case and place its problems before selected MPs. This form of lobbying is relatively recent. Of all the business associations in India, only the FICCI has a full time parliamentary liaison man. The position was created in 1958. All the rest simply dispatch one of their regular staff members to Delhi for brief periods of time. Among the few industry associations which have accepted legislative lobbying, even in a limited way, are textiles, sugar, cement, and engineering. Of these, only the sugar industry maintains a permanent office in Delhi. Although several other associations have considered the possibility of creating a Delhi office, the cost has been a deterrent.

A third type of lobbyist works as an entrepreneur or private contractor who claims to have extensive contacts. He represents a variety of interests and receives a fee for his work. It is known that several MPs serve in this capacity. Some enterprising individuals have even gone so far as to create a need for their services by establishing an organization to represent a particular industry and then going out to solicit funds for this vital service.

The final type of lobbyists are those who represent India's largest business houses, sometimes masquerading as journalists or public relations men to lend greater legitimacy to their activities. Because most of the lobbying effort of the major houses is really aimed at the ministers and bureaucracy, the parliamentary lobbyist serves largely as a way to prod the executive into action on pending major projects. The Tatas, for example, lobbied continuously during the period preceding the government's approval of its huge Mithapur project.[42] Although all contact with Parliament in India is called lobbying, most of the work done by India's lobbyists would more properly be described as liaison work. That is, most representatives of business who have contact with Parliament serve primarily as listening posts, receiving information and passing it on to headquarters, rather than as partisans attempting to influence MPs to change the form and content of legislation.

Unlike Milbrath's Washington lobbyist, who spends most of his time in his office receiving and sending communications, the activity of a lobbyist in India is direct and personal.[43] The average Indian MP receives a large volume of written communications in the form of telegrams, letters, speeches, and resolutions from a variety of groups, associations and foreign embassies. But most MPs simply ignore these communications, and Indian lobbyists know it. The postal lobby, as it is called, is ineffective because of the volume of communications. The lack of staff to sort and classify such mail supplies a rationalization of the insuperability of the task of responding. The majority of MPs do not want to bother, anyway. MPs spend most of their time

[42] For example, see *The Times of India* (Bombay), November 9, 1968. The chief minister of Gujarat discussed the project with the prime minister and finance minister; *The Patriot* (New Delhi), August 7, 1968; *The Statesman* (Calcutta), July 11, 1968 reports a meeting between J. R. D. Tata and the minister of petroleum and chemicals.

[43] Lester Milbrath, *The Washington Lobbyist* (Chicago: Rand McNally, 1963), p. 121.

handling the multitudinous individual problems of their constituents. Helping their constituents get things done in Delhi usually means clearing their problems with the bureaucracy.

The most effective method of lobbying in India, therefore, is direct personal contact. When individuals want things done, they try first to tap the primordial loyalties of family, caste, or region. Lobbyists may also resort to the *quid pro quo*. One of the most effective means of lobbying to influence MPs is "to see those you've helped in the election." However, individual businessmen are reluctant to use their personal contacts for collective benefits. Business associations must therefore use different techniques. The technique used most frequently is socializing at tea parties, dinners, luncheons, and cocktail parties to which select groups of MPs are invited. At these intimate gatherings group spokesmen, usually association presidents and committee members, attempt to explain the problems of the particular group and ask for support. Support may take many forms, including pressing the case in private conversations with ministers and other MPs, making specific requests in speeches in Parliament or before party meetings, moving specific amendments in select committees, or raising questions in Parliament, party committee meetings, and consultative committees. To facilitate their efforts, cooperative MPs are provided with memoranda and other data essential to intelligent and effective support of the position advocated.

Lobbying tends to be primarily concerned with short-term problems rather than long-term policy. Groups lobby for immediate benefits in the form of higher prices, removal or reduction of a particular excise tax, subsidies, reduced control, and so on. Such lobbying tends to be extremely sporadic and lacks the continuity that lobbying for fundamental policy changes would require. People tend to show up only when something is bothering them and fail to maintain the kind of day-to-day contact which is the essence of sustained activity. So far, the parliamentary wing of the FICCI is the only organized business effort designed to build and maintain, through daily contacts, a relationship of trust with friendly MPs and, on an equally sustained basis, provide for the neutralization of potentially hostile forces. The purpose of the parliamentary wing of the FICCI is to establish direct contact with MPs in order to highlight the federation's case in regard to particular items of pending legislation or executive action. In many ways it can be said, even of the parliamentary office of the FICCI, that its primary function is liaison rather than lobbying. The FICCI representative serves as a listening post for business and as a channel for passing information on to Members of Parliament. The FICCI office supplies background notes and briefs on legislation, policy issues, and the budget to a select group of slightly less than one hundred (out of a total of some eight hundred) members of both houses of Parliament from all parties. Not only does the FICCI supply informational materials based on federation research, it prepares questions and supplementaries (that is, additional questions raised to supplement the original question and force government to explain its position or provide information) for use during question time and drafts amendments to pending legislation. Members of Parliament who use these materials, in whole or in part, are in a position to raise issues which might otherwise be neglected.

Rudimentary as its legislative lobbying and liaison efforts may seem, business has had even less success in generating grass roots pressures in support of the private sector, for the obstacles to indirect lobbying are almost insuperable. Transportation and communication problems make the mobilization of constituent pressure futile even where such efforts are possible. Telegraph and letter campaigns are resorted to only by business houses and business associates. Even in the urban areas, where the population is largely literate, the hostility to business is too universal to provide the basis for a truly mass effort. The FICCI has attempted to influence public opinion by using limited public relations campaigns with the usual mix of press releases, advertisements, and public speeches, but so far it is difficult to assess the impact of these efforts.

Recently the FICCI has employed indirect techniques of influencing Members of Parliament through the reorganization of the Diwan Chand Institute of National Affairs. This organization is financed partly by a trust, partly by the FICCI directly, and partly through business advertisements placed in its journal, *The Indian Recorder and Digest*. The Diwan Chand Institute of National Affairs arranges public discussions on important issues, invites speakers from government, Parliament, and the news media to address its public gatherings, and makes its facilities available as a daily gathering place where Members of Parliament can come to pick up information or discuss issues with the FICCI staff. The basic objective of all these activities, although they are open to the general public, is to educate Members of Parliament by attracting their attention to important issues. In 1968, for instance, the Diwan Chand Institute arranged a round table discussion on the proposed ban on company contributions to political parties. The session, which was attended by fifteen senior Members of Parliament, the president of Assocham, and six members of the FICCI committee, among others, received a great deal of publicity. The text of the resulting discussion was later circulated to brief other Members of Parliament. That same year the institute also sponsored talks on Czechoslovakia and on the Naga problem. Such programs are designed to give the Diwan Chand Institute, despite its very specific business-oriented objectives, an aura of broad public service—a very desirable image considering the general climate of literate opinion in India.

In spite of its expanded efforts to influence Parliament during the past decade, the FICCI has enjoyed limited results. Legislative opinion has proved resistant, not so much from active hostility as from total indifference. The many difficulties and the paucity of results have generated considerable opposition to extending the activities of the parliamentary wing of the FICCI secretariat. Some argue simply that the expenditure cannot be justified. Others continue to insist that it is poor tactics to lobby indifferent Members of Parliament when the risk of thereby alienating the executive and the bureaucracy has only diminished, not disappeared. As one secretary remarked, "If we find someone trying to pressure us through Parliament, we work twice as hard to prove our case." Nevertheless, given the growing importance of Parliament, its inadequate staff and secretarial facilities, and the lack of expertise of the average Member of Parliament, there is little doubt that a group like the FICCI could play a much more active and hardly more hazardous role in the parliamentary arena—if it is willing to pay the bill for converting a one-man show into a three-ring circus.

Business, however, tends to feel that its major problem in developing a successful lobbying effort is the weakness of the receiving end—that is, the attitude of the average Indian MP. The average Indian MP is at best indifferent. At worst he shows the general public distrust and suspicion of business. He is afraid to be identified with "vested interests" and has very little basic understanding of the kinds of issues which affect business. As one lobbyist bitterly complained,

> Most MPs do not read what you send them. The problem is that when it comes to issues like company law, finance, or taxation, the average MP does not even care to understand the detail and complexity of this kind of legislation and is willing to let it pass without paying much attention to it. However, if the issue involves something like language, then this is the kind of issue which he can understand and you get an intense struggle. In all other matters they are simply willing to follow the leader. The real problem in India is that there aren't enough intelligent peo-

> ple in Parliament to be able to deal with some of the more complex kinds of issues.

Business simply does not have a large enough group of businessmen or business supporters in Parliament to make much of an impact. Thus, the best they can do is try to select a list of potentially helpful MPs, try to persuade them of the justice of their case, and hope the persuasion will have some impact.

Even friendly MPs, however, have their reservations about the lobbying practices of business. They place the blame for ineffectiveness on business and not on the MP. Their first argument is that most of the material supplied by business associations to MP's is unusable. It is insufficiently detailed; it is one-sided and easily refuted; and it is unimaginative. Most business associations, it is charged, use a buckshot approach in their memoranda, instead of zeroing in on the most objectionable features of a government policy or legislative act to which they object. No one has time to read bulky memoranda. One MP asserted that, "The problem is that most associations really don't know how to brief an MP. . . . If they send a long memorandum to government, this is one thing. But this is not what the average MP wants or needs. The average MP is already swamped with paper. What he really needs is not more memoranda, but rather concise statements of what in fact is the problem." As another MP put it, in criticizing the FICCI's lobbying effort, "The FICCI uses a bull-headed approach. They attack every clause in a piece of legislation and you have to finally ask them to be a little more specific and to specify what they really object to since their memoranda attack everything without using any discrimination in the process." Others argue that business association memoranda use material too easily demolished by government. Furthermore, they point out, government would quickly smell a rat if too many speeches based on precisely the same limited data were suddenly delivered in Parliament. Yet business associations supply identical memoranda to as many as one hundred MPs. Thus, MPs argue that business associations must exert greater effort and imagination if they wish to make the most of the legislative lobbying opportunities that exist.

A second frequent complaint of legislators is that business is entirely too negative in its opposition. Business associations tend to adopt contrary positions without suggesting concrete alternatives. For a memorandum to be useful, argued one MP,

> it is not only important that an MP know the case against a bill, but he must also know the case which can be used against him.

> A business association cannot be satisfied by simply presenting their case. The MP must also know what case is being built up against the association so that he can reply in an effective way. Most associations never even apply their minds to this problem. They never ask themselves why it is that government is doing what it is doing. They never deal with the question of why government has decided to act and what counter arguments can be offered.

If business is to have an impact, say many MPs, business associations must pay greater attention to increasing their levels of professionalization and strengthening their research facilities, so that they are able to analyze problems in greater depth and offer plausible alternatives.

A third complaint is that business really does not know how to lobby and doesn't even try. As one business MP put it,

> In India, for the most part, if an industry or association has a problem, their normal inclination is to first contact the secretary and try to convert him. If that does not work, then they simply try to pay off at the lower levels of the bureaucracy. At the same time they then try to work through the state bosses, and if that too fails then the matter simply ends. They refuse to bother to pander to all of these mediocrities. One result of this is that many people find ways of introducing pinpricks into the trade simply to get money out of them.

A major Marwari industrialist put it this way: "There is very little lobbying in India. We have not yet learned how to lobby. In the old days, one had maharajas and the pattern was to secure his ear or that of his minister. We still act in this old way. We still use old methods."

Fourth, legislators complain that business does not establish and maintain a regular system of contact. Not only do businessmen come around only when they are in trouble; they appear when it is already too late to do much about their problem. As one businessman himself admitted, "The problem is that once a decision is taken in the government, it is very difficult to reverse it. Therefore, you must try to stop it before the decision is made and not after."

Finally, MPs complain that business hurts its own case when major houses seek to discredit each other in the eyes of the public. Conflicts between Birla and Dalmia-Jain, between Tata and Birla, and among smaller business groups have resulted in attacks in Parliament, denunciation of one house or another based on material supplied by the rival house. Risking the attempt to build a new collective image, business tries to discredit competitors in order to gain specific individual benefits in the form of industrial licenses, import licenses, and so on, and to block their issuance to others.

The recent attack on Coca-Cola India offers an excellent example. Strong anti-American sentiment developed as a result of shipments by the United States of arms to Pakistan despite the Pakistan government's suppression of the Bangladesh movement. Using this anti-American sentiment, Parry and Company pressed the government, through Parliament, to reduce drastically Coca-Cola's allowance of foreign exchange. Parry's purpose was to damage Coca-Cola's competitive position in relation to Parry's Gold Spot soda. Ironically, V. K. Krishna Menon was a major force behind the scenes in defending the Coca-Cola interests.[44]

The level and quality of lobbying in India, therefore, remain marginal by American standards. But the effectiveness of lobbying has been on the increase since the early 1960s. The death of Nehru, the growth of self confidence within the business community, the increased importance of Parliament in decision-making, and the switch to a more aggressive and open stance by business have all contributed to this increase. There continue to exist, however, a large number of checks which inhibit its further development. Business lobbying continues to be tainted by a very low level of legitimacy. The public, the bureaucracy, the ministers, and even the MPs view it with distrust and tend to equate it with corruption. In particular, leftist parties in Parliament and the left wing of the Congress party see such activity as attempts of vested interests to undermine progressive reforms. These groups, more than any others, act as a check on business in Parliament. Public suspicion and leftist rhetoric combined with traditional cultural attitudes toward business and the low level of direct representation of business in Parliament make it difficult for business to gain a hearing for the business view in the Indian Parliament. As if this were not enough, party discipline—especially in the ruling party—places severe limits on what a cooperative MP can do. As one Marwari industrialist put it, "MPs are not free. Their decisions are taken by the party bosses, not by the MPs."

For all these reasons, lobbying in Parliament remains weak and sporadic. Although business has been able to influence some noncontroversial economic issues and has had some success in delaying and

[44] *The New York Times*, August 8, 1971; *The Overseas Hindustan Times* (New Delhi), August 7, 1971.

modifying legislation, it has had almost no effect on major symbolic redistributive issues like tax policy, bank nationalization, and the creation of a large public sector. Most industrialists feel that business must pay more attention to "educating" MPs. Nevertheless, they find it more advantageous to concentrate their efforts at the ministerial and secretarial levels of decision-making. In fact, there are still some businessmen who argue that, because ministers and the higher echelons of the bureaucracy resent it, lobbying in Parliament is actually counterproductive.

XII

THE EXECUTIVE AND BUSINESS: PATTERNS OF FORMAL ACCESS

Despite the shift in emphasis in business strategy to extend its access and influence to newly emerging power centers such as Parliament and political parties other than the Congress party, the vast bulk of business resources and energy, both collective and individual, continues to be concentrated on the centers of power in the Indian political system—the prime minister, the cabinet, and the higher echelons of the bureaucracy. It is the executive in India which plays a dominant role, not only in initiating new policies but also in administering the vast powers delegated to it by the legislature in the planned and highly regulated Indian economy. Because the private sector is still responsible for producing 90 percent of the manufacturing output and for providing a large share of the planned investment in India's mixed economy, the government, as much as it might wish to do so, cannot treat the business community as a pariah. There exists in practice a strong reciprocal dependence, which has necessitated the creation of a close working relationship between business and government. Collectively through business associations and individually through the industrial embassies of major business houses, business thus enjoys a variety of direct formal and informal channels of access to government decision-makers.

Business lacks direct elite representation and has been unable, so far, to influence the selection of the top political leadership. And so business is forced to rely on indirect influence through formal and informal channels to government decision-makers. Because business played a behind the scenes role (so far as it played any role at all) in the freedom movement, the post-independence political leadership was drawn predominantly from the urban intellectual elite which had all along dominated the leadership of the Congress party. As one senior civil servant put it, "By training and background, the political leadership in India has no background in modern business. Perhaps the only exception was T. T. Krishnamachari. No other minister has had that kind of background. This has resulted in a lack of rapport between the political leadership and business."

Despite the lack of rapport stemming from lack of common experience, the absence of major business leaders in government has forced the business community to rely on its friends and contacts in the Congress party to protect its interests. However, even those who come close to sharing some of the views of business do not feel free to argue them within the government. The ideologues of the right are thus neutralized by the ideologues of the left. Into the vacuum rush demands emanating from every segment of the multi-interest Congress party and the larger society. Many of those demands are antithetical to business interests.

During the Nehru era, business was unable to influence the selection of leadership within the Congress party. Nehru, as the unchallenged leader of the Congress party, had an almost free hand in the selection of his ministers. The only course open to business was to come to terms with Nehru. Ironically, despite Nehru's public castigations of business, his particular brand of socialism did not require annihilation of the private sector. Nehru, in fact, was a close friend of Shri Ram, Singhania, and Tata, although his relations with the more obscurantist Marwaris like R. K. Dalmia and J. K. Birla were more strained. In his role as prime minister, Nehru refrained from nationalizing private productive facilities, he provided protection to Indian industry, and through the credit and investment facilities provided under the second Five Year Plan he laid the foundation for the expansion of the private sector as a major economic force in India. Although businessmen were far from happy with the elaborate system of controls and regulations, they learned to live with that system and they learned how to work through the bureaucracy to use it to their advantage.[1]

Following Nehru's death, business increasingly saw new opportunities to influence the selection of new political leadership. For the most part the political leadership in India has emerged out of a complex process of selection involving a trade-off among regional and linguistic factions in the Congress party. There were, however, indications that business attempted to influence the selection of the prime minister in 1966 and again in 1967.[2] At the time of the 1967 election, Morarji Desai claimed that "a few big business houses are taking undue interest" in the election.[3] After Mrs. Gandhi's election, the busi-

[1] D. R. Mankekar, *Homi Mody: A Many Splendored Life* (Bombay: Popular Prakashan, 1968), p. 212.

[2] Michael Brecher, "Succession in India 1967: The Routinization of Political Change," *Asian Survey* 7 (1967): 442.

[3] *The Patriot* (New Delhi), March 11, 1967.

ness community split over its strategy toward the top leadership. Some businessmen attempted to oust her from power, but others continued to support her in her battle against the syndicate.

Business so far has been as unsuccessful in determining the selection of top political leaders as in gaining direct elite representation at the ministerial level, and so it has been forced to place emphasis on securing access to the executive. The political leadership has not been completely unresponsive to these overtures, although it has been more inclined to establish close relations with individual business leaders than with the business community as a whole. Government relations with business associations tend to be formal and highly ritualized.

The process of achieving access to top bureaucracy has been even more precarious. Indian business did not enjoy the rapport with the colonial bureaucracy that English business easily maintained. Thus, there were no long-term personal contacts, no long-established strategies of access to fall back on when bureaucracy became, after independence, a center of power in its own right, by virtue of its pivotal position in a planned and controlled economy. Yet, in India, even more than in some developed countries, the vast majority of business attention is focused on the bureaucracy. The necessity of dealing with the bureaucracy has been one of the major reasons for the rapid growth of business associations and their bureaucratization and professionalization.

The formal structure of government provides for regularized contact between bureaucracy and various organized interests in India. But many other circumstances have combined to force business to focus intently on close liaison with the bureaucracy. First, a system of centralized planning—based on a mixed economy in which the private sector is tightly controlled and regulated—elevates the bureaucracy almost to the position of an independent center of decision-making and power. In India, as elsewhere, there has been a tendency for lawmakers to pass extremely broad enabling legislation. It is as important, therefore, for business to influence the rules drawn up under the legislation by the bureaucracy as it is for business to influence the legislation itself. Every day business is dependent upon literally hundreds of decisions which affect prices, distribution, raw material cost, plant location, and most every aspect of business activity. One official estimated that 75 percent of the decisions affecting business are made by the bureaucracy. The colonial raj has thus given way to what has been called "the permit, license, quota raj," and its princes are the top bureaucrats.

But even if dealing with the bureaucracy were not the only way to influence decisions, business would find it a valuable point of access. Business can function quietly and effectively at the bureaucratic level, despite the unfavorable public image of business and regardless of the status of the ideological debate going on at the political level at any given time. Some civil servants favor the public sector and others oppose the private sector. But most of the bureaucracy is neutral, and all of the bureaucracy is expected to function on the basis of what policy actually is rather than what they would prefer it to be. The bureaucracy, therefore, must operate in the context of a mixed economy, which means dealing with the private sector and with existing policy guidelines. Business might be too weak politically to challenge the basic policies and ideology of the regime, but it could still be influential in drawing up a definition of the policy that would expand its sphere of action to the very limits implied by the enabling legislation, thus strengthening its position vis-à-vis the public sector.

Finally, business must pay close attention to the bureaucracy because the bureaucracy is the source of many policy initiatives. Close contact with the higher echelons of the bureaucracy enables business to stop or modify government action at the formative phase, before positions become hardened by public debate.

Scope of Intervention

Although the Indian bureaucracy is remarkably accessible to individuals above a certain status level,[4] numerous factors set limits on the scope of group intervention in the bureaucracy. First, those who form the higher echelon of the Indian bureaucracy have internalized the long tradition of paternalistic independence developed by the old Indian Civil Service. They view themselves as independent guardians of the general welfare. As one secretary put it, "The majority of the people in India are poor, and this majority is not yet able to represent itself. Until the masses of India become more conscious, the bureaucracy must step in to protect their interests." In addition, the bureaucracy feels it must make decisions based on rational criteria corresponding to the basic national goals, needs, and resources of the society, not in response to pressures from organized vested interests. Speaking of pressures from business, one bureaucrat said, "We examine their demands but if they do not have a strong case we

[4] Richard P. Taub, *Bureaucrats Under Stress: Administrators and Administration in an Indian State* (Berkeley and Los Angeles: University of California Press, 1969), p. 51.

simply do not do what they want." Yet, even if bureaucracy were inclined to listen to business, it would be difficult to have a single course of action. As it is, bureaucrats insist, the advice they do get from business is so contradictory that their freedom of action is preserved more easily than if that advice was spoken by a united voice.

The bureaucracy is not always easy to influence, because its members are in many ways alienated from traditional society and its primordial loyalties. The bureaucracy is highly westernized and urbanized in its style and outlook; it shares many of the values and intellectual predispositions of the older generation of political intellectuals and is disposed to regard business as distrustfully as they. As if this were not obstacle enough for the businessman seeking to influence bureaucracy, there is a major status gap between the urban ICS-IAS officer and the more traditional Indian entrepreneur. However, a more satisfactory rapport is struck between the bureaucracy and the managers, owner-managers, and business association staff than with most of the older generation of Indian entrepreneurs. A common educational experience and cosmopolitan outlook overcome the suspicions generated by the political culture.

The bureaucracy has in its hands such tremendous power to regulate and control business that business is afraid to offend government by intervening excessively or tactlessly. Business is too dependent upon administrative actions to risk antagonizing government to the point of retaliation. There is too much that the bureaucracy in a controlled economy can do, or fail to do, in the way of regulatory, licensing, and enforcing actions. The majority of businessmen, therefore, still come to government as supplicants. Only the largest have begun to approach government in the manner of the self-confident industrialist; and threats, even on the part of the most powerful business interests, lack credibility. Bureaucrats argue that evidence has shown that in a tightly controlled economy industry will try to expand production regardless of the level of control imposed by government. Thus, for example, government did not take seriously the threat by the drug industry to stop production of particular drugs if price controls were imposed.[5] Nor does government quake when business talks of a strike in the capital market. Because most businessmen receive large portions of their funds from government credit agencies, this threat, too, lacked credibility.

Finally, the bureaucracy often prevails because government controls the most important sources of data—information and com-

[5] *The Economic Times* (Bombay), September 5, 1967.

munications. In some political systems, interest groups control data and channels of communications, and so government is dependent on interest groups for the materials that go into rendering technical decisions.[6] In India, however, the decision to embark upon a system of centralized planning resulted in the creation by government of its own sources of information and data collection.[7] Such data are used by all groups in India, including business and the press. Unfortunately, the quantities of data collected by government are so vast that the system is choked by its own volume. As a result, although a massive amount of information eventually becomes available, it lacks timeliness and lags behind need. Business could play a valuable role in filling this gap, but its organizations are not yet up to the task. When the FICCI secretary requests information from its member bodies and industrial units, his requests usually go unanswered. When business does manage to collect material, it is too often suspect, either sloppy or slanted, and government, therefore, feels it must be cross-checked. If the Indian Jute Mills Association claims that its estimates of the jute crop show a fall in production and a need to make arrangements for alternate supplies, government refuses to act on the data until it makes its own estimates. And the results of those estimates may become available too late to correct the resulting shortages.[8]

Although government regards the data generated by business associations with suspicion, it finds them to be a convenient—but not entirely reliable—channel of communications. One official observed, "It is easy to communicate a clear-cut directive through the federation, but the federation has not been successful in dissemination of background thinking." Other officials argue that business associations are not half as useful, as a channel of communications with their own members, as the press which "serves as a big government gazetteer."

A final factor which limits intervention in the bureaucracy has been the inability of modern economic and social interests to colonize the bureaucracy. The bureaucracy is independent, enjoys a very high social status, and is, above all, committed to accomplishing its own institutional missions. The bureaucracy enjoys its special status because of the ICS tradition of recruitment on merit. Merit is defined as intellectual attainment, which is highly valued in the Indian so-

[6] Joseph LaPalombara, *Interest Groups in Italian Politics* (Princeton, N.J.: Princeton University Press, 1964), pp. 349–393.

[7] For a discussion of the quality of Indian economic statistics, see George Rosen, *Democracy and Economic Change in India* (Berkeley and Los Angeles: University of California Press, 1966), pp. 141–153, 303; and *World Bank Report*, I, 21–22.

[8] For an example, see Indian Jute Mills Association, *Proceedings of the Annual Meeting April 1968* (Calcutta: IJMA, 1968).

ciety. The higher echelon of the bureaucracy, furthermore, is attractive to candidates of superior caliber, because its members are among the highest paid groups in Indian society and enjoy numerous privileges.[9] Thus, the recruitment process prevents modern social and economic interests from penetrating the bureaucracy directly. If penetration is to be made, it must be accomplished on the basis of particularistic relationships, personal friendships, or financial reward. Yet the traditions of the service also militate against these approaches.[10] The Indian bureaucracy and the ministries it staffs are most concerned with accomplishing their own institutional missions. As one businessman, who had come up against the bureaucracy, put it, "They are more concerned with the image of the ministry. What they do is in their interests and not in the interests of business. The image of the ministry is the key guide to what happens in that ministry. Thus for example, if the Commerce Ministry is charged with boosting exports, it will do all kinds of things to gain that end."

The bureaucracy is known to brief newspapers and to plant editorials to support the views of the bureaucracy. Bureaucrats have gone so far as to urge their clients to press a particular position with another agency, not excluding the prime minister, the Reserve Bank, or the finance minister. They have also encouraged business associations to push harder for more funds for their area of administration. Even a minister like V. K. R. V. Rao, who was known to have strong views in opposition to the private sector, publicly urged the Road Transport Association to push harder for more funds for road development when he was minister of transport. Thus, interministerial conflict, combined with a strong sense of bureaucratic mission, opens up important opportunities for business influence, even though that conflict may also be a major source of delay.

The scope of intervention in the bureaucracy is limited by strong traditions of independence enjoyed by the bureaucracy, the value system of the ICS-IAS elite, the ability of the bureaucracy to retaliate, its control over information and communications, the inability of modern groups to colonize the bureaucracy, and the strong sense of institutional mission which is part of the bureaucratic heritage. Although these factors set some boundaries on interest group activity, they do not mean that business cannot have any effect. Business enjoys a remarkable degree of access to the bureaucracy and enjoys many opportunities to influence decisions.

[9] Rosen, *Democracy and Economic Change*, p. 39.

[10] Myron Weiner, *Politics of Scarcity* (Chicago: University of Chicago Press, 1962), p. 122.

In consulting with business, the bureaucracy draws a distinction between receiving advice on matters affecting business and obtaining a representative view of business opinion or reactions. Because business associations reflect the lowest common denominator of business opinion, government consults associations when a representative view is needed. Advice, on the other hand, is sought from people who are "respected," "honest," and "know the subject." No one businessman is knowledgeable about all fields, and so business advice is solicited from various members of the business community. Often the advice is contrary to what might have been expected from the views expressed by the very association of which the adviser is a member. Expertise, of course, is not the only reason for such divergence. Businessmen, like the bureaucracy, tend to say things in private that could not be said in public. Therefore, in drawing up major policy statements, the bureaucracy often calls upon knowledgeable and trustworthy businessmen. This type of consultation, however, is purely at the discretion of the official involved. It does not always take place. The cement industry, for example, has complained on numerous occasions of a lack of prior consultation. Said the president of the Cement Manufacturers Association,

> Sometime in January 1963, the government announced an incentive scheme for the cement industry. The industry would have been happier if before announcing the scheme, the government had consulted it in the matter. If the objective behind the scheme is to achieve better production than the highest production achieved during the previous three years, it would have been in the fitness of things if the views of the industry had been ascertained before announcing the scheme.[11]

Again in 1964, the president complained that—despite rumors that cement would be decontrolled and that large public sector cement units were to be set up—the government failed to consult the cement industry in any way.[12]

Among Indian business associations, the apex organizations—FICCI, Assocham and AIMO—are considered to be the most prestigious, but

[11] Dharamsey M. Khatau, Speech delivered at the *Second Annual General Meeting of the Cement Manufacturers Association, Bombay,* June 14, 1963 (Bombay: CMA, 1963).

[12] Dharamsey M. Khatau, Speech delivered at the *Third Annual General Meeting of the Cement Manufacturers Association, Bombay,* August 14, 1964 (Bombay: CMA, 1964).

the specialized trade associations are said to give better and more useful advice within their own areas. Among the apex organizations, the FICCI is ranked first in prestige with government because of its size, diversity, and long identification with Indian interests. The fact that the FICCI is considered more representative than other groups because of its diversity of membership creates an image which the FICCI leadership cannot ignore. Although the Indian bureaucracy is well aware of the internal politics of the FICCI and its oligopolistic pattern of control, officials nevertheless tend to take the federation at face value. There is a growing respect in the bureaucracy for the FICCI secretariat. Yet the organization is still chided for the vagueness of its demands, which the bureaucracy recognizes are designed to satisfy the diverse interests represented by the federation, even at its leadership levels. Of the three apex organizations, the Assocham commands greatest respect within the bureaucracy because of its identification with professional management and its professional orientation. Part of this image is a product of the specialized associations affiliated with Assocham, especially the Indian Jute Mills Association and the Indian Tea Association. There are some in the bureaucracy, however, who continue to associate Assocham with foreign interests, because Assocham has made slow progress toward Indianization. The AIMO is identified with smaller business. Because its membership is heavily concentrated in Bombay, it is considered a sectional organization.

Although the apex associations are assigned the highest prestige, the bureaucracy finds the specialized associations more useful. They have fewer conflicting interests than the apex associations, and so they define their interests more clearly and their demands are more specific. The corollary is that the specialized agencies are not helpful in discussing major policy issues. Their perspective is too narrow. Thus, although the ministries which deal with the control and regulation of jute, textiles, drugs, and so on, find the specialized agencies most helpful, the Finance Ministry prefers to deal with the apex associations, which are better equipped to discuss broader issues of taxation and tax policy.

There is a growing respect in government for business associations in general, because officials have noticed a marked improvement in their performance over the past twenty years. As business associations have developed specialized secretariats, the scope and depth of their activity have increased. Today they are able to back up a case with independent research, specific information, statistics, and other data, and they are learning the value of following up the facts with strong representation. Whereas officials once found the representations of business so poorly drawn that the bureaucracy had no difficulty in refuting their claims, "they now do their homework," as one secretary put it. In addition, business has discovered ways to dress up particularistic demands in terms of the larger national interest. Finally, as one official reported, "They have stopped asking for petty things under the table." In short, there is a feeling within the bureaucracy that the performance of business associations has improved as they have become more bureaucratized and professionalized. Or perhaps it is just that one bureaucrat can always talk to another!

The image that officialdom has of the staffs of the business associations has improved, but the attitude of the bureaucracy toward business leadership remains critical. Although officials concede that they must deal with the leadership as it is, they question the character and public image of some of those selected to fill business association executive posts. Officials prefer to work with the professionally oriented managers or owner-managers than with the older generation of owner-financiers.

Patterns of Access: The Advisory Role of Business

Patterns of access to the political leadership and the higher echelons of the bureaucracy in India take three forms. First, drawing heavily on the British example, the Indian government has developed an extensive, highly structured, regularized, and formalized set of procedures for consulting various interests in the society through a bewildering array of statutory and nonstatutory advisory and consultative committees and commissions. The consultative bodies, which meet periodically at the initiative of government, enable business to present its case on matters of policy implementation directly to ministers and secretaries. The advisory groups, however, are not policy-making bodies. They are only policy-reviewing agencies,[13] and they function primarily as mechanisms for ascertaining the collective views of the business community and for propagating government views to business. Business, however, does not wait for government to call a meeting before acting. Exercising its right to petition and to make representations, business plays a direct advocacy role using a variety of mechanisms which are designed to place business demands before government decision-makers. Through its organized associations, business supplements its formal advisory role by initiating direct contact through written memoranda, personal deputation, petitions, correspondence, resolutions, meetings,

[13] Geoffrey Tyson, *Nehru: The Years of Power* (New York: Praeger, 1966), pp. 63–64.

seminars, and press releases. Business associates also maintain day-to-day contact with both the working level and the top echelons of the bureaucracy. Finally, because business associations do not handle individual problems of their constituencies, business firms and houses have found it necessary to supplement their collective approach to government by a system of administrative liaison and lobbying which is conducted through industrial embassies. This system of personal, informal contact is the least visible and most controversial aspect of business activity. It employs a variety of personal relationships based on status, school tie, caste, language, region, and system of direct benefits.

The government of India has established an elaborate array of hundreds of commissions, committees, and advisory councils to serve as channels of communication between business and government. Many of these bodies—such as the Advisory Committee on the Department of Commercial Intelligence and Statistics or the Central Advisory Committee on Lighthouses—are relatively unimportant. Others are specialized organizations recognized and approved by the government of India to function as instruments of export promotion. These organizations, which perform an executive function, include such groups as the Federation of India Export Organizations, the nineteen export promotion councils, and various commodity boards. Among the advisory and consultative bodies used as channels of communication with business, six are of particular importance: the Advisory Council on Trade, the Board of Trade, the Customs and Central Excise Advisory Council, the Direct Taxes Advisory Council, the Advisory Committee on Capital Issues, and—perhaps the most important of all—the Central Advisory Council of Industries (CACI). Unlike the others, the CACI is a statutory body created under the Industries (Development and Regulation) Act of 1951, one of the most important and far-reaching pieces of legislation dealing with the private sector in India. Unlike the non-statutory bodies which meet only periodically and merely furnish a forum for holding discussions and raising problems, CACI has specific statutory functions to perform.

The CACI, a conglomerate of interest group representatives, is composed of members drawn from apex business associations, employee groups, and consumer organizations. The bulk of the membership, however, is contributed by business. Some of India's leading industrialists are members, including the presidents of FICCI, Assocham, and AIMO. CACI *must* be consulted with respect to the making of rules under the Industries Act. Consultation on other matters is discretionary. The CACI meets about once a year. "It is customary at these meetings to have on the agenda a review of the general economic situation and also a review of one or two specific industrial sectors." [14] It is also customary for members to raise any issues which are of concern to them in addition to the items on the formal agenda.

The CACI also functions through two subcommittees, a standing committee which meets periodically to offer advice on major problems of development such as export expansion or power shortages, and the still more important reviewing subcommittee constituted under Rule 18 of the Registration and Licensing of Industrial Undertakings Rules, 1952, "to review all industrial licenses issued, refused, varied, amended, or revoked from time to time, and to advise the government on general principles to be followed in the issue of licenses for establishing new undertakings or substantial expansion of existing undertakings." [15]

It is very important to distinguish between these two levels of council functioning. The meetings of the CACI are ceremonial sounding boards of opinion, and they have come to function in a very stereotyped manner. The two sides—business and government—meet one day a year. They tend to confront one another with formal set speeches which have been exchanged in advance. There is little time for any real discussion, dialogue, or exchange of views. When a problem is raised, the minister simply asks the party who raises it to send him the details, because there is no time for detailed discussion. This is not to say that meetings of the CACI are useless. They perform essentially four functions. First, they are used by government to determine the representative view of business on policy issues, including specific issues of particular concern at that time. Thus, at the CACI meeting in November of 1967, business raised issues dealing with the recession, the Patents Bill, the Monopolies Bill, and various details of special industry problems. Government had an opportunity to reply to the year's accumulation of criticisms. Second, the CACI forces both sides to think about issues and find a way to articulate their positions. This enables both business and government to clarify their views for themselves and for one another. By testing new ideas and policies at CACI meetings, government can generate policy alternatives. Third, ideas raised in government speeches are examined and criticized by business at the session and in subsequent forums, meetings, and correspondence with government. Criticism of new policies enables government to see

[14] Government of India, Ministry of Industrial Development and Company Affairs, *Speech of F. A. Ahmed Before the Nineteenth Meeting of the Central Advisory Council of Industries* (New Delhi: November 10, 1967), p. 2.

[15] Government of India, Ministry of Industrial Development and Company Affairs, *Report, 1967–1968* (New Delhi: Government of India Press, 1968), pp. 26–27.

possible snags in their proposals. Fourth, CACI sessions provide a feedback mechanism, enabling business to present their grievances directly to government. "If you are responsive," said one official, "you are bound to respond to these pinpricks. After all, they are the people who wear the shoes and they know where it pinches." This kind of negative feedback is essential. Government could not function without it. In short, although CACI is not a decision-making or policy-making body, it provides an opportunity for business to influence government and vice versa. It is a consultative body designed to enable business to criticize the substance of government policy and raise questions about its implementation. Government in turn can explain its policies, test new ideas, and learn about the unintended hardships which policies may produce.

Many businessmen are highly critical of the CACI and other such advisory bodies. They say that such groups are a waste of time and money and charge that government takes no notice of them. This criticism is particularly characteristic of those who depend heavily on personal contacts in government and do not need established patterns of access. Others, conceding that these organizations are advisory and not decision-making bodies, insist that they do have a long-term impact on government thinking. They provide one of many forums for criticisms of government policy, and they force both sides to think about the implications of policy. They also help create an atmosphere of criticism—criticism that cannot be ignored.

The advisory bodies like CACI also function at another level, through a standing committee. In addition the CACI functions through its reviewing subcommittee. It is at the standing committee level that government and business can deal with more specific problems of policy and policy implementation. The standing committees of advisory bodies have become the key to how those bodies function. The standing committees of the CACI and other advisory bodies enable business to have an indirect influence on government policy.

For example, in 1962, the standing committee of the CACI urged government to focus attention on the expansion and development of existing units, instead of establishing new industries for production of the same items in order to realize economies of scale to enable Indian business to compete abroad for exports. Such a recommendation, clearly favoring existing producers,[16] had major policy implications at a time when government was trying to open up opportunities for new

[16] Matthew J. Kust, *Foreign Enterprise in India: Laws and Policies* (Chapel Hill, N.C.: University of North Carolina Press, 1964), p. 117.

entrepreneurs. In addition, the work of these standing committees becomes part of the evidence used by the bureaucracy when it prepares changes in administrative rules. It may also become the basis for changes in the legislation.

The reviewing subcommittee of the CACI plays an especially important role. It reviews the criteria and procedures used by government in issuing industrial licenses, and it makes recommendations for changes. These recommendations are usually accepted by government, and as a result a kind of case law is developed which has an influence on government policy. This kind of activity, argued one official, is "operationally much more important than all the memoranda of the FICCI."

In addition to creating the CACI, Section 6 of the Industry's (Development and Regulation) Act of 1951 authorized the government to establish, for any scheduled industry or group of scheduled industries, a development council consisting of persons capable of representing the interest of owners, employees, and consumers, and also persons having special knowledge of matters relating to technical or other aspects of the scheduled industries. Whereas the apex organizations represent business on the CACI, the specialized industry associations are represented on most of the development councils. The development councils are required to make recommendations regarding targets for production, coordination of production programs, norms of efficiency, optimum utilization of installed capacity, better marketing and distribution, standardization, development of new materials, and industrial research. In some industries, panels instead of development councils have been established, but they perform the same functions.

The development councils were viewed as the primary instrument for coordinating the private sector role in five year plan investment. The Planning Commission is associated with the work of the development councils. Their purpose was set forth in the first Five Year Plan as follows:

> The major instrument envisioned under the Act for establishing the necessary liaison between the public and private sectors and for insuring that private industry conforms more and more to the planned pattern of development is the Institution of Development Councils. The question of the development and regulation of industries is not one merely of how the government exercises certain powers, but the kind of machinery which can work from within each industry to help bring about a steady improvement in standards of productivity, quality of service, and management.

> Such a machinery should provide those interested in the industry, that is, the employers, the employees, and the public at large, a continuous opportunity to make a detailed study of the problems of the industry, including its various constituent units, and to implement a program of development in conformity with the needs of the industry and the overall pattern laid down in the Plan.[17]

The maximum strength of the development council is thirty members. The development officer of the Department of Technical Development concerned with that industry acts as secretary and provides all secretarial services to the council. Thus, the work of the development council is integrated with the chief technical unit of the government of India. A term on the council is for two years. Most of the members of the council are businessmen. The number of outside technical personnel is limited.[18] A study of the functioning of the development councils showed that the average size was about twenty-eight to thirty members, with absenteeism about seven to thirteen. Thus, one can assume that the actual attendance would be somewhere in the low twenties.

The bureaucracy appears to be pleased with the functioning of the development councils. The Mathur committee, for example, found that they

> can play a crucially important role in industrial development and offer the best forum for a "get-together" between the government, industry, and scientists and technologists for the identification of problems and for discovering lines of solving them in the best interest of the country. Discussions in these bodies can help bridge the gaps between policy and implementation, between theory and practical considerations, and between targets and actual production. We were impressed by the fact that, where development councils/panels received the right guidance, they contributed materially to the development of their sectors of industry. Considering all these factors, we would recommend that, as the one forum where development and production problems of an industry can be discussed with the different interest groups, development councils/panels should be established in all major sectors of industry except where development has already reached

[17] *Ibid.*, pp. 117–118.

[18] S. Subbaramaiah, "The Development Councils for Industries in India," *The Indian Journal of Economics* 43 (1963): 256.

> the stage beyond which it can hardly derive any benefit from such a body.[19]

Development councils help to decide where the lines between the public and the private sector should be drawn. Thus, as Kidron has noted, the development councils have far-reaching effects on government policy. He cites an example from the machine tool industry in which Minister of Production K. C. Reddy revealed the kind of policy decisions made:

> You must recall that the division of spheres between the government factory on the one hand and private industry on the other was settled after long discussions with the representatives of your association. We had made it clear to them that the state factory will not undertake production of lathes less than 8½ inches center, and we have no intention of going back on this agreement. On the contrary, after reviewing the position, particularly in the light of your general fears about lack of demand, the government has decided to produce only 400 of these lathes instead of the 1,200 originally envisaged.[20]

The role of the advisory councils in fact varies considerably, depending on the caliber of the membership and their personalities. If the minister knows his subject, the advisory councils can be useful. If, on the other hand, the minister is not interested in the detailed work of the ministry and is largely a political figure, then meetings become routine and no meaningful discussion takes place. Meetings also become very formal, because the minister is not equipped to carry on a dialogue with the group. The same is true of the quality of business representation.

Thus, the government of India has a very elaborate system of regularized and channeled access to government through advisory and consultative bodies. However, the roles of these bodies are carefully circumscribed and depend very heavily upon government initiative. At present government uses these advisory and consultative bodies to assess the views of the business community, not to obtain advice on policy. If these bodies are to become more effective, their activities

[19] Ministry of Industry and Supply, Government of India, *Report of the Study Team on Directorate General of Technical Development (Part II)* (New Delhi: Government of India Press, 1965), p. 76.

[20] Quoted in Michael Kidron, *Foreign Investments in India* (London: Oxford University Press, 1965), p. 91.

must be intensified. Meetings must be held more frequently and discussion must be less formal. In the meantime, government relies for advice on individual expertise and not on group consultation. Government–business relations at the individual level are very friendly, but at the group and public level they are pervaded by an atmosphere of distrust and suspicion. As Indian business associations come into their own and develop greater expertise, however, and as expertise becomes more widespread among the managerial and owner-managerial elite of business, the advisory council system should come into its own. Then government will be able to depend on the advisory and consultative bodies more than it has in the past.

Patterns of Access: The Advocacy Role of Business

Business does not sit back waiting for government to call a meeting before it ventures an opinion. Business also plays an advocacy role by freely exercising its right to petition and make representations. Business takes the initiative by formulating its views on a wide variety of issues and conveys those views to government decision-makers in various ways. Business invites ministers to address its meetings, it sends delegates of businessmen to meet with ministers and secretaries, it floods government offices with memoranda and correspondence, it conducts public seminars on major policy problems, and it maintains daily contact with the working levels of government through its professional secretariat.

The annual meetings of business associations play an important part in organizational maintenance. In addition, the annual meetings have become highly ritualized occasions for the exchange of views between business and government. Traditionally, just as the viceroy of old was invited to address the annual meeting of Assocham, the prime minister of India is invited each year to address India's premier business association, the FICCI. (Assocham must now be content with hearing a senior minister of the Indian government and only on rare occasions the prime minister. Other business associations usually invite the minister most directly connected with their industry.) These ministerial addresses are really one side of a dialogue, the government's carefully rehearsed role in an exchange of speeches in which business raises major points concerning broad government policy and government responds. On both sides the script is carefully prepared. Several weeks before the annual meeting, the association forwards the president's address to the government for study. The minister's speech is then written to answer those specific concerns raised by business and to present those points the government wishes to raise. Because business is informed of the content of the minister's speech before it is delivered, business has a chance to provide the last word in the dialogue through its ritual vote of thanks.

There is another long-standing custom. The business associations pass a series of four or five resolutions each year at the annual meeting, to highlight their major grievances. Although these resolutions are routinely forwarded to government, they tend to embody the most common denominator of diverse and conflicting interests of which the association is composed. This is especially true of FICCI resolutions. As a result, the resolutions are usually so general that they are quickly repudiated by businessmen in their individual discussions with government. In fact, the most important function of the resolutions may very well be whatever they contribute to organizational maintenance. The text of the resolution serves as a litany, and the vote serves as a ritual of participation by which the membership reaffirms its faith in the collectivity. Most government officials dismiss these resolutions as meaningless, and one official, perhaps accurately, characterized them as "teleological."

The most frequent form of initiative taken by business is the written memorandum followed by personal discussion with ministers and secretaries. As a former president of Assocham put it, "The process of representing the business viewpoint to government is of course a continuous one. The advisory bodies . . . meet only at specific intervals, and their deliberations are supplemented by frequent correspondence and, in addition, the president of the Associated Chambers pays numerous visits to New Delhi and engages in consultations at ministerial and secretarial levels."[21] These negotiations take place *in camera* through a process which Assocham likes to call private diplomacy. Most government officials feel that the personal follow-up of memoranda is essential, because it enables each to satisfy the other. The personal equation also helps to dispel latent conflict.

Memoranda deal with three types of issues: policy issues and legislation; administrative decisions and matters of administrative detail; and the impact of administrative rules and regulations. Policy issues and legislation may refer to planning, the managing agency system, delicensing, company law, and issues of that nature. Administrative decisions embrace the whole field of delegated legislation dealing with

[21] "The Associated Chambers of Commerce and Industry of India," a speech by H. K. S. Lindsay, president of Assocham (1964–1965), at the Rotary Club of Calcutta, June 8, 1965. Reprinted by Assocham, p. 9.

import policy, price policy, the issuing of licenses, or problems dealing with idle capacity. Administrative rules and regulations deal with the interpretation of existing law, the development of rules and regulations under the law, demands for modification of rules and regulations, and complaints of abuse of authority under the law.

As a general rule, in order for a memorandum to succeed, it must present a strong case and focus attention on the specific change that is desired in government policy to correct the alleged failure of policy. It is generally agreed in government that memoranda from business associations vary considerably in quality but that they have improved as business associations have strengthened their professional staffs and research sections. Even businessmen admit that they have not yet learned how to make an effective case. As one leading businessman put it, "We need a professional approach and we need broader vision." In stating its case, business is often excessively vague, subjective, and emotional. Businessmen cannot all agree on what they really want. And so they sidestep the difficulties by drawing up deliberately vague statements which boil down to the old complaint that government action has hurt business and government must help business overcome its difficulties. The chief cause of overgeneralization is that in any industry there are different layers or strata involving different interests, different sizes of units, different levels of development, and different levels of skill. All of these make it very difficult to develop a common case which can be accepted by all. But business also has a tendency to ask for more than is justified by the circumstances, or at least more than is supported by the evidence presented in the memorandum. In either case, government has heard it all before. A shoddy memorandum or a totally one-sided memorandum is simply ignored. But a memorandum from a business association is usually treated at a fairly high level of government if it is clear that a *prima facie* case exists. Such a memorandum must present a reasonably balanced view and must contain facts that truly support the case. The fate of a memorandum also depends on the credibility of the group which presents it. If the group has a reputation for doing a reasonably good job, the memorandum is treated seriously.

When memoranda are critically examined at different levels of government, personal discussions with interest group representatives are usually part of the process. A memorandum is given the greatest attention if the minister has shown a personal interest in it. Memoranda dealing with major policy issues may eventually be referred to the cabinet for action. Memoranda involving administrative decisions are studied and referred to the minister for decision. Memoranda dealing with administrative rules and regulations may be handled at the secretary level.

The vast majority of memoranda from business associations relate to administrative rules and regulations. It is estimated by some government officials that 90 percent of the activity of business associations is focused on the interpretation, development, and adjustment of administrative rules and regulations drawn up pursuant to legislation passed by Parliament. Like legislatures in most countries, but to an even greater degree, the Parliament of India passes broad enabling legislation, leaving it up to the government to work out the details. Some of India's most important legislation regulating the private sector is extremely terse.[22] Thus, the rules adopted pursuant to the legislation can have a critical impact on the operation of business and industry. Moreover, the rule-making functions take place in the solitude of the central secretariat, outside the glare of publicity. As a former president of Assocham once said,

> Very often, the rule-makers will have no direct experience of the problems to be covered by the rules. They are in need, therefore, of help and advice which chambers are particularly well qualified to provide. They speak normally for business as a whole rather than for a particular sectional interest. We believe that this kind of consultation, always detailed and often technical, is best handled by experts in the calm of committee rooms without any premature publicity which may prejudice the issue.[23]

Even the bureaucracy admits that the most useful role of business associations is as feedback mechanisms. They privately confess that some of the rules which government has developed are unworkable and that businessmen can often point out specific rules that are "silly." The bureaucracy argues that it is willing to make changes in rules and regulations in order to make them more acceptable or at least less painful, provided the changes do not distort the ultimate objective which the rules seek to accomplish. A representative example of this kind of detailed rule-making based on the clarification of complex details of government policy and legislation emerges from the following excerpt from the annual report of Assocham:

[22] For details see Kust, *Foreign Enterprise*, chapter 4.

[23] Lindsay, "The Associated Chambers," p. 9.

In December 1965, the Associated Chambers wrote to the Central Board of Direct Taxes seeking clarification of the interpretation to be placed upon Section 4A of the Preference Shares (Regulation of Dividend) Act, 1960, which section was inserted in the act by the Finance Act, 1965.

In pointing out that the effect of Section 4A was to limit the deduction of income tax from a preference share dividend to 25 percent of the stipulated dividend, the chambers explained that doubts had now arisen as to the meaning to be placed upon the term "stipulated dividend." Some companies had calculated tax liability with reference to the preference dividend prescribed in their articles of association plus the additional 11 percent of such dividend statutorily payable under Section 3(3) of the act. Certain shareholders, however, had maintained that "stipulated dividend" as used in Section 4A must be subject to the definition originally included in the act and that the 25 percent tax deduction should therefore apply only to the dividend fixed by the articles of association and not to the additional 11 percent prescribed under Section 3(3). In the light of the best opinion available, it appeared that the latter interpretation was the correct one, but the chambers doubted whether this had been the intention of the legislature in making the amendment since the effect would be that the additional 11 percent payable under Section 3(3) would be tax-free. The chambers accordingly sought clarification from the Central Board of Direct Taxes and also requested the board to consider whether, in the light of such clarification, any further amendment to the law was necessary.

Section 4A was subsequently withdrawn in the Finance Act, 1966.[24]

The business approach to administrative policy decisions is much more complex than its attempts to influence rule-making and therefore requires much greater expenditures of time and effort. An example of the process can be seen in the successful efforts of Assocham and its affiliate, the Indian Tea Association, to achieve a reduction in the government's excise duty on tea in 1968. Following the devaluation of the Indian rupee in 1966, the government of India imposed a special export duty on tea in an effort to prevent the tea

[24] *The Associated Chambers of Commerce and Industry of India, Forty-Seventh Annual Report, October 1966* (Calcutta: Assocham, 1966), p. 24.

industry from reaping windfall profits. The duty had been slightly modified in November 1966 and May 1967. However, the tea industry began pressing for substantial revision in the duty as a means of counteracting the repercussions of the devaluation of currency in Ceylon, another major tea exporter, and in the United Kingdom, the major tea consumer. Because both British and Indian tea interests in India were equally concerned about the issue, they joined together to form a special consultative committee to present a united front to the government.[25]

The Delhi office of Assocham worked very closely with the tea industry in its attempt to bring about a change in government policy. It was necessary to convince several high level bureaucrats in the Finance and Commerce Ministries of the legitimacy of the tea industry's demands, a task that was complicated by the fact that the two ministries had totally different views of the matter. The Commerce Ministry, which had the chief responsibility for maximizing exports and regulating the tea industry, was receptive to the demand for a decrease in the tax so far as it would prevent a loss of exports; the ministry was not without some concern about what the industry would do with its increased earnings. The Finance Ministry, on the other hand, was primarily concerned about the loss of revenue which a reduction in the tax would entail, and so it argued that the decline in tea exports was not caused by the high price of Indian tea but by a fall in demand resulting from reduced consumption. According to the Finance Ministry, therefore, no change in policy was necessary.

Assocham had succeeded in gaining the support of the Commerce Ministry by informally agreeing that any increase in profits which resulted from the decrease in taxes would be used to rehabilitate the tea industry through extensive replanting and modernization. After that agreement had been reached, the Commerce Ministry fought the industry's case with the Finance Ministry, arguing that economic considerations and the larger national interest far outweighed any loss in revenue that might occur.[26]

The major problem, said one of the participants in the talks, "was to convince people that the exchequer would gain more by a change in policy than by maintaining the policy which existed." Thus, after

[25] Although Assocham was willing to press merely for a reduction in the levy, the Indian producers insisted on total abolition of the tax. Thus, the consultative committee became committed to a policy calling for a total abolition of the tax, which Assocham considered to be a poor negotiating strategy. See *Economic Times* (Bombay), April 8, 1968.

[26] Editorial in *The Statesman* (Calcutta), October 9, 1968; *The Economic Times* (Bombay), September 29, 1968; and *Hindustan Times* (New Delhi), October 1, 1968.

a process of sustained and quiet negotiations and persuasion, the government through its ministerial bureaucracies agreed to a change of policy which amounted to a loss of one hundred million rupees in government revenue.

As a supplement to direct access to the higher echelons of government at the time of the annual meeting of business associations and through written memoranda and correspondence, business also employs several other approaches in attempting to press its views on government decision-makers. Small groups of five to six business leaders meet several times a year with the prime minister. These meetings are particularly characteristic of the FICCI. Based primarily on prepared agenda, these encounters involve broad policy issues rather than rule-making or administrative policy-making. Usually the prime minister gives the group thirty minutes to one hour of his or her time. Each member of the delegation is briefed to handle a specific item on the agenda. On November 26, 1964, for example, a delegation met with the prime minister to discuss the food situation, capital market, and industrial policy. This meeting was followed by a note to the prime minister "recapitulating the main points raised in the meeting in light of the observations and suggestions made by the prime minister on some of them." One contribution of the prime minister which the FICCI followed up was the suggestion that a liaison committee be created in important commercial centers, to bring about better understanding between the administration and the business community.[27]

Discussions with business leaders reveal that a variety of problems which do not appear on the record are raised at these meetings with the prime minister. These nonpublic items involve removing hardships or inequalities resulting from government action. During discussions the prime minister takes note of specific problems and may give specific guarantees that they will be corrected. It is also interesting to note that businessmen are frequently called upon by ministries and other bureaucratic agencies to push a particular point of view with the prime minister. Business, in turn, has its position reinforced by the stand taken by other ministers or by the Reserve Bank.

Throughout the year, the FICCI secretariat maintains day-to-day contact with various government ministers and with the bureaucracy. As a result of the rather close rapport which has been achieved between the secretariat and the bureaucracy, members of the FICCI staff have

[27] FICCI, *Report of the Proceedings of the Executive Committee for 1964* (Delhi: FICCI, 1964), p. 115.

been called on to serve on a number of special government committees. Finally, the FICCI has initiated a system of organized seminars on special topics, such as the managing agency system, the current Five Year Plan, import substitution, taxation, and the like. These seminars, which are attended by ministers and by secretaries within the relevant ministries, have proven quite useful in highlighting important issues. Some have even resulted in valuable concrete proposals.

Thus, business came to play both an advisory and an advocacy role in its relationship with the bureaucracy and its ministerial overseer. There is little doubt that business in India has achieved extensive access to government policy-makers, but mere contact does not guarantee acceptance of advice. In fact, there is a good deal of bitterness among businessmen arising from the feeling that their efforts are solicited only to be ignored. Administrators, on the other hand, tend to view these contacts as useful in working out the details of new policy and as a feedback mechanism to let the administration know where the policy, once made, pinches. Whether or not a new rule or a new law is designed to correct the situation depends on considerations of the state or the larger society—and in that sense organized business is only a minority group.

XIII

THE EXECUTIVE AND BUSINESS: LIAISON AND LOBBYING

The formal access to government, which has been institutionalized in the system of advisory bodies through which business associations are given direct access to ministers and the higher echelons of the civil service, is open and subject to formal description and analysis. There also exists, however, a vast subterranean system of individual contacts with government maintained by all the large business houses. Because this network is, more or less by mutual agreement, much less visible, it is more difficult to document than are the formal access patterns. Informal contacts are routed through the industrial embassies of the large business houses. According to the grapevine, these contacts range from a discreet exchange on the Delhi cocktail party circuit to the use of direct bribery to achieve business goals. In reality, however, the system of informal liaison and lobbying, designed to achieve individual distributive benefits and aimed at both the ministerial level and the higher echelons of the bureaucracy, is much more routinized than its critics imagine.

There are several reasons why almost every big business firm or house in India has found it necessary to establish some mechanism for liaison and lobbying with government. First, the complexity and comprehensiveness of government control and regulation necessitates the maintenance of a regularized channel of communication with relatively easy access to high government officials. Second, the problems of individual firms are not handled by business associations. Because chambers of commerce and specialized associations could not possibly handle all the government-related problems of their clients, they must confine themselves to general policy matters. Third, because business firms in India do not trust each other, they are unwilling to disclose their affairs to business associations for fear that others would then learn of their activities. They must, therefore, maintain their own liaison with government. Business firms also find it useful to maintain a listening post in Delhi to keep track of possible concessions made to other houses. Finally, and most important of all, the style and functioning of the Indian bureaucracy requires the creation and maintenance of a mechanism for insuring that files move through the bureaucracy without becoming bogged down, sidetracked, or forgotten, either deliberately or by accident. The upper echelons of the bureaucracy are so overwhelmed with paper and files handled in such an archaic manner that anyone who has any business to conduct with government must have someone who can expedite the process of pushing paper through the various levels of bureaucracy. The alternative is interminable delay and inaction. Even the state governments in India have found it necessary to establish Delhi offices for this purpose. In interviews in 1961–1962, Kidron found a fair number of examples of cases which took two years to go through the Industrial License, Capital Goods, Foreign Agreements, and Capital Issues Committees.[1] Studies by the FICCI showed similar delays. Also, competing firms have been known to do their best to see that the files of competitors are buried "accidentally."

Industrial embassies were first created to maintain contact with government during World War II, as the result of wartime scarcity and controls. The practice expanded rapidly after independence and especially after the introduction of the second Five Year Plan, with its concomitant increase in the level and variety of government regulation and control. The historian of Parry and Company recalled that

> the war and independence between them made a further radical change in the conditions of business in India. . . . The new Union government was at first—indeed still is—very chary of delegating its responsibilities to the states; in all matters of first-class importance, and in many of second-class or third or lower, control was centralized at Delhi. . . . Madras was no longer the "Governor in Council," in whom the last word and final prestige were vested. Delhi would not come to Madras, Madras must go to Delhi, and it soon became evident that in Delhi Parry's must have an office.[2]

Shaw Wallace, another large managing agency house, established a branch office in Delhi in 1955, because "it was soon found that the branch was increasingly needed in connection with calls on government officials, and it became clear that the post-independence trend made it necessary for the company to have a permanent high-level representative in Delhi to maintain contact with government." Once the Delhi

[1] Michael Kidron, *Foreign Investments in India* (London: Oxford University Press, 1965), p. 50.

[2] Hilton Brown, *Parry's of Madras: A Story of British Enterprise in India* (Madras: Parry & Company, Ltd., 1954), p. 310.

office was established, the company came to depend on it more and more.[3]

The industrial embassies perform three functions. First, they act as liaison mechanisms to push files and take care of minor correspondence, they provide a channel of communication with government, and they act as listening posts, collecting information and passing it on to the home office. Second, they provide a base for administrative lobbying which involves advocacy—that is, pleading the company's case for establishing new enterprises, expanding production, or solving other problems such as obtaining raw materials and foreign exchange. Finally, they keep channels of communication with government open continuously, so that easy access can be gained as needed for purposes of liaison and lobbying.

Big business draws a distinction between the liaison activities and lobbying by the Delhi office, which varies in composition and size according to the size of the firm and the extent of its activities. The largest firms conduct liaison through a special liaison man or a staff of liaison men, while medium sized firms use their Delhi public relations department or sales department to perform the function. In both cases the liaison function involves supplementing a routine system of work with specific assignments in relation to the operating levels of the bureaucracy. Liaison men confine their contacts to the deputy secretary level and below. They also maintain regular contact with offices in the development wing. Lobbying, by contrast, is carried out at the policy level of government—that is lobbying at the secretarial and ministerial level by the chief executive of the company or by a Delhi resident director who plays a role in company decision-making. Liaison for large and medium firms is carried out by regular company employees who have shown an aptitude for that kind of work or by people especially recruited for the job. Such people are selected because of their knowledge of government procedure or their ability to gain access because of former association with government, personal contacts based on school ties, and particularistic loyalties of caste, region, community, and language. Among the specially recruited personnel are former ICS and IAS officers, former members of the military or other government civil services. Smaller firms are dependent on free lance liaison men and lobbyists who claim to have good contacts with various ministries and agencies of government.

The recruitment of former government employees by business is

[3] Harry Townsend, ed., *A History of Shaw Wallace & Co. and Shaw Wallace & Co., Ltd.* (Calcutta: Sree Saraswaty Press Ltd., 1965), p. 170.

not an entirely new phenomenon in India, but has attracted widepread notice because of its increased frequency. The recruitment of former government employees by business first attracted attention as early as 1920. The government then in power seriously considered placing a ban on the acceptance of commercial employment by former government servants. (Before independence, both the India Jute Mills Association and the Tea Association employed former ICS officers.) Instead, it was decided to leave the matter to the individual's own discretion. The practice continued until 1946, when the government of India decided to require prior government approval before its former employees could take private positions after retirement.[4] The habit, however, was not eliminated. It first attracted attention again when the Estimates Committee of the Lok Sabha mentioned the problem in its report of 1953–1954. The Lok Sabha debated the issue in 1961; a resolution to ban such employment was introduced but got no further.[5] Two years later Nehru expressed his displeasure at the still growing custom of retired ICS officers accepting highly paid jobs with big business.[6] Like government, the public tends to view this practice as tantamount to corruption. Said the Santhanam committee,

> It is generally believed, that such employment is secured in many cases as a *quid pro quo* for favors shown by government servants while in service. It is also feared that high-placed government servants who accept such employment after retirement may be in a position, by virtue of their past standing, to exercise undue influence on those in service who might have been their colleagues or subordinates. The fact that some of these retired government servants who have accepted employment with private firms live in Delhi and perhaps operate as "contact men" has further heightened these suspicions.[7]

Clearly, former ICS people are hired because of their intimacy and familiarity with the bureaucracy. As one former ICS officer admitted, "It is easy for me to get an appointment because I know all the secretaries." It is not that the bureaucracy is inaccessible. The Indian bureaucracy is very accessible to people above a specific status. Yet groups do not want mere access, they want differential access, for ease of ac-

[4] Shriram Maheshwari, "Employment of Retired Government Officials in India," *Indian Journal of Public Administration* 12 (1966): 233.

[5] *Ibid.*, p. 240.

[6] *The Times of India* (Bombay), March 10, 1963.

[7] John B. Montiero, *Corruption: Control of Maladministration* (Bombay: Manaktalas, 1966), p. 63.

cess can save hours of time. Smaller businesses may get appointments with higher bureaucrats but they may have to sit for hours in an anteroom waiting for an opening. In addition to being able to secure firm appointments for their new employers, former ICS people can arrange informal parties attended by key ministry officials. Evidently they count on the old loyalties alone to see that some of the smaller bureaucratic details are taken care of. Most former government employees do not work for private firms for very long after retirement. The usual maximum is about five or six years. Presumably, by the end of that time most of their old contacts have been transferred to other assignments.

The activity of former government employees on behalf of the private sector does not necessarily involve corruption, although many in India believe it does. It is clear from discussions with businessmen and former government employees that the major reason for business to employ former government employees is their ability to achieve access, but they are not always successful. A leading business house employing a former ICS officer found him to be completely ineffective. One of their own men was much more adept at the job. However, it is also clear that former ICS people know which things they can ask for and which never to ask for. They realize from their experience as former bureaucrats that they lose their credibility if they push for the wrong things. In this sense they operate within self-imposed limits that protect the integrity of the system as much as the popular view asserts that they threaten it.

Whether he is a veteran of the private sector or a former ICS officer, the primary responsibility of a liaison man is to act as an expediter. Business is dependent on government approval for everything —even for its daily operating needs. Government permission comes in the form of permits and licenses, which must be secured to obtain the foreign exchange to import capital goods, raw materials, spare parts, and so on. Even domestically produced items like steel must be obtained through government allocation. Licenses and permits are secured from government by submission of an application. Such applications must also be filed to build new plants, undertake the major expansion of old plants, or make most other kinds of changes. The Delhi representative's job is to follow these papers through the bureaucracy from assistant secretary to deputy secretary, from deputy secretary to joint secretary, and from joint secretary to secretary. The purpose of having a representative is to reduce administrative delay. Plant production can be held up for weeks pending receipt of a license to import a spare part. The Delhi representative ensures that the application does not get misplaced, that the administrator does not forget about it, and that additional information is relayed promptly when requested. When an application is submitted to government, the Delhi representative takes a copy of the application to the appropriate government official and checks on the spot to see if the information is adequate and in the proper form. In the Indian bureaucracy, no paper can move or be processed to the next level until the missing information or necessary clarification has been provided. If more information or clarification is necessary, the representative is in a position to wire his head office by direct Telex and get the reply within twenty-four hours. Normal correspondence might take at least a week, and several days more would be lost just getting the letter delivered within the ministry itself. By developing close contact with administrators, the liaison men can even secure help in the preparation of applications and requests. A well-disposed administrator can show a business representative what to emphasize and how to strengthen his case.

The Delhi representative is also responsible for acting as a listening post, to ensure that concessions granted to one firm will also be available to others. Some houses even assign their liaison men the job of trying to delay or kill competitors' applications for new industries, additional capacity, or imports of raw materials and spare parts. In 1955, for example, Shri Ram of Delhi Cloth Mills learned that government was trying to encourage the production of sewing machines by small-scale industry in Punjab. To do this, the government was thinking of permitting these manufacturers to import some parts from abroad and was also contemplating setting a ceiling on the production of sewing machines by Jay Engineering, a Shri Ram affiliate. And so Shri Ram immediately sprang into action. By placing a ceiling on the production of sewing machines in his factories, he argued, government would hurt his company's ability to compete in foreign markets. His intervention succeeded, and the proposal was dropped.[8] Shri Ram also used his familiarity with government channels and his contacts in government to overcome threats from foreign competitors. When he learned that his major competitor, the Singer Sewing Machine Company, had been continually increasing its imports of spare parts, he complained to government that the practice should be stopped, because it was contrary to government efforts to curb foreign exchange expenditures and encourage domestic production. His real motive, however, was to undercut competition from Singer by crippling its attractive after-sales service.[9] Thus, the receipt of timely infor-

[8] Khushwant Singh and Arun Joshi, *Shri Ram: A Biography* (Bombay: Asia Publishing House, 1968), pp. 133–134.

[9] *Ibid.*, pp. 122–129.

mation allowed Shri Ram to protect his sewing machines from competition with both small-scale and foreign business. He was able to intervene to block pending action as well as to initiate beneficial governmental intervention.[10]

A third responsibility of a Delhi embassy is to hand carry all correspondence to government. This ensures safe and expeditious delivery to precisely the right person. The representatives also collect copies of government notifications, rules, regulations, and laws to be sent to the head office, where they might not be as readily available. Business must keep up with legislation and the related and ever proliferating rules and regulations, in order to know what to do.

Finally, the Delhi representative is responsible for some routine company business. He makes appointments for the head of the firm with secretaries and ministers. He entertains company directors when they are in Delhi, and he represents the company at social functions of the government of India. He arranges for passports and visas for company directors traveling abroad. The representative does a limited amount of local purchasing for the factory, and he takes care of a multitude of other minor administrative chores.

Although big and medium companies can afford to establish their own liaison men in Delhi, smaller firms must depend on free lance liaison men and lobbyists. Free lance liaison men are self-styled public relations men, Members of Parliament, journalists, former government employees, or company liaison men who moonlight in order to supplement their incomes. A free lance liaison man may represent two or three companies and, by charging a fee of three to four hundred rupees to each, he may average one to two thousand rupees per month. Small business cannot afford to do without someone on the spot to deal with all the complex government rules and regulations, but they do not always get what they think they are paying for. Some free lance lobbyists have a reputation for enjoying close contacts with a particular ministry or agency of government, such as the controller of exports and imports, or they may claim to have easy access to a particular minister. Others are charlatans who make grandiose claims but deliver very little.

The industrial embassy also serves as a focal point for the lobbying function of the firm. Lobbying is focused primarily on the secretary and minister in charge of the ministry, and it must be carried on by someone of equal rank in the business house. On major problems, it is usually the chief executive of the company or the Delhi resident di-

[10] Also Parry versus Coca Cola, Chapter XI.

rector who takes the issue up with government. It is the job of the chief executive of the company to try to build the image of his organization with government, so that when the company does have difficulties it can count on support from the government. If the chief executive is capable of establishing extremely close contacts, his advice will be actively sought by government. Thus it is the top leadership or owner of the firm—rather than the Delhi representative—who is responsible for pursuing with high government officials the firm's need for new company production or expansion, exploring tax or regulatory problems, and counteracting government policies which might hurt the firm or give an advantage to a competitor. Most large industrial houses, in fact, prefer to handle even problems of a policy nature on their own. They usually resort to the instrumentality of business associations only after their individual efforts have failed.

Access to ministers is secured through a variety of methods, many of which go back to the days of the freedom movement. In order to ensure easy access and a sympathetic hearing, business houses provide political contributions and financial support to individual ministers, and they offer warm and luxurious hospitality and provide jobs and patronage to relatives of ministers.

The tradition of providing financial support and hospitality to political leaders developed during the days of the freedom movement, when such acts were not only accepted but were considered patriotic. Indian business supplied funds to the Congress party for its political work and also helped to support the families of Congress party leaders who were imprisoned for their political activities. Purshottamdas Tandon, a former president of the Congress party and leading Uttar Pradesh politician, once described his relationship with Sir Padampat Singhania, one of India's major industrialists: "Padampat is an old friend of my family. I have known him all my life. When I went to jail against the British, he supported my wife and the family; and when I did not earn anything because I was too busy with politics, he helped me financially." [11]

Although such generosity was considered patriotic before 1947, today it would be classified in most societies as a conflict of interest. Yet the practice continues. S. K. Patil, for example, a leading Congress party politician and former minister, admitted publicly that the costs of some of the many trips he took to the United States were paid for by a business friend.[12]

Many businessmen who have tried to capitalize on their pre-inde-

[11] Taya Zinkin, *Challenges in India* (London: Chatto and Windus, 1966), p. 56.
[12] *The Free Press* (Bombay), September 28, 1967.

pendence role may achieve access, but they do not necessarily secure favorable results. For example, in writing to Finance Minister Morarji Desai requesting him to take a "personal interest" in the tax problems of a Muslim businessman, a "leftist" Muslim MP justified his intervention on the grounds that "the man concerned is one of the few Muslim business men, who even in the dark days of the Muslim League helped (sic) late Maulana Azad and the Muslim nationalists." Morarji did personally review the case. But, finding that the firm was in fact guilty of concealing income and evading custom duties, he refused to intervene.[13]

Although they continue to make political contributions to political leaders, most businessmen argue that the import of this investment is grossly overrated. The only contributions generally considered to bring results are those that benefit a politician on the way up. Party funds alone are unlikely to be sufficient for an ambitious young politician building his career. Business contributions allow him to carry out a personal election strategy and to support his fellows. This kind of backing is said to be given recognition if the politician in fact does succeed.

Another pre-independence tradition which has survived to become a means of securing access is the provision of hospitality and services to political leaders. Business houses in India maintain guest bungalows in various parts of the country. Given the lack of modern amenities and hotels in the Indian countryside, these bungalows provide facilities that are appreciated by touring ministers. Before independence even the Nehru family used the Singhania guest house at Mussoorie to escape the heat blanketing the north Indian plain in the summer.[14] Gandhi lived at the Birla house in New Delhi at intervals throughout his life, and it was there that he died at the hands of an assassin.

Perhaps the most elaborate hospitality is provided during meetings of the AICC and annual sessions of the Congress party. By tradition these meetings are held at out-of-the-way places in temporarily erected tent cities. Indian business provides funds for setting up these *tamashas,* feeding the ordinary delegates, supplying fleets of vehicles for party use, and also provides accommodation for VIPs, including chief ministers and members of the cabinet and council of ministers. For example, Birla's guest house manager and a staff of thirty were sent to cater to the needs of ministers at the Amritsar session of the Congress party in 1958.[15] At the Hyderabad session of the Congress party in

[13] Surendranath Dwivedi and G. S. Bhargava, *Political Corruption in India* (New Delhi: Popular Book Service, 1967), pp. 150–151.

[14] Taya Zinkin, *Challenges in India,* p. 55.

[15] *Ibid.,* p. 58.

January 1969, the local dealer for the Birla-owned Hindustan Motors provided a large fleet of new cars for use by VIPs. Hotels provided free rooms on the promise that their supplies of fixed-price, rationed sugar and rice would be increased.

Expense account entertainment is of course a worldwide phenomena. The Delhi cocktail party circuit is used to maintain contacts and at times to bring key company officials in contact with high level bureaucrats. Delhi representatives and company executives arrange private dinner meetings in Delhi's fashionable hotels, or they schedule small parties in hotel suites where detailed policy issues can be discussed in private. Because the benefits sought by business houses are much more tangible and direct, the amount of money available for entertainment and parties is much greater than most business association representatives are allowed. If a one hundred million rupee project is at stake, the cost of a few dinners and parties is considered a minimal investment.

Perhaps even more important is the patronage which business is capable of providing to the sons and nephews of those in power. In large business houses which have extensive holdings, it is not difficult for business to create a two thousand rupee per month job for a nephew or a grandson. As D. R. Gadgil once observed:

> [T]he range and field of activity of Indian businesses are now so large that they constitute today overwhelmingly the most important group of employers of personnel commanding high salaries . . . the relative position of government and business in this regard . . . greatly changed within the short span of eight years between 1948 and 1956. The direction of effort of those who want to get into the top [salaried groups] has consequently changed. Their goal is no longer to get into the highest official ranks but into the highest ranks of managers and technicians employed by large Indian and foreign businesses in India. This applies, among others, to sons and relatives of the highest officials as well as of prominent politicians. The pattern of behavior of officials on retirement has changed simultaneously. Formerly, these usually sought no employment and almost never employment with Indian business. Today the most highly placed officials very readily find highly rewarding positions within business. . . . We have thus arrived at the curious position that most officials who exercise large discretionary powers in relation to regulation of business might yet look on businessmen as potential

employers or patrons of their sons and relatives and even of themselves.[16]

Some of the most prominent examples of such employment are found in the families of S. K. Patil and Morarji Desai. At the time when S. K. Patil was a minister, his son was employed by the *Times of India* in their circulation department and his son-in-law was employed by Birla.[17] Morarji Desai's son was employed for some time by a foreign firm which, for some unexplained reason, continued to pay him a salary despite the fact that he had ceased working for the firm and had become a private secretary to his father.

Businessmen, in private, frankly admit that they use contacts of this nature to achieve access to government. "When you have a problem," they say, "the first thing you do is see those you've helped elect and the fathers whose sons you employ in your business."

It is popularly assumed that almost all contact between government and business involves bribery and corruption. Nowhere in the world is corruption as widely discussed as it is in India. Yet many of the devices used by business for maintaining access to ministers verge more on conflict of interest than outright corruption. Similarly, although it is generally admitted that government officials are presented with saris, whiskey, or alfanso mangoes as gifts for special occasions, just as American businessmen send gifts at Christmas time, it is very doubtful that a secretary of the government of India very eagerly sells out for a bottle of scotch. Few of the charges of corruption among central ministers and secretaries have been proven. Most corruption takes place at the lower levels of bureaucracy and tends to involve permits, licenses, tax evasion, selling supplies to government, or securing services from government. From 1957 to 1962, for example, 1,156 cases were filed by the Special Police Establishment against gazetted officers and 5,836 against non-gazetted officers. Of these, only twenty were at the highest levels of bureaucracy. Four cases involved under secretaries and sixteen were below the under secretary level.[18] Yet, given the propensity in India to view actions in terms of motives and the tendency to evaluate leaders in strictly moral terms, any such behavior will elicit the charge of corruption and will contribute to the tarnished image of business.

One of the most frequent forms of bribery in India is called speed

[16] Quoted in Kidron, *Foreign Investments*, p. 232.
[17] *The Free Press* (Bombay), September 28, 1967.
[18] Monteiro, *Corruption*, p. 43.

money. It is designed to expedite the processing of applications for licenses and permits. A secretary testifying before the Santhanam Committee on the Prevention of Corruption told the committee that, even after a decision had been made to grant a license and an official order had been actually issued, the order was not passed on to the applicant until he had paid the appropriate fee to the lower level clerk.[19] This kind of petty corruption is rampant throughout India.

In dealing with ministers and secretaries, access is not the equivalent of success by any means. For demands to be met, the issue must be legitimate, the case must be strong, and it must be substantiated with facts and figures. It also helps to state a case in terms of the national interest. Equally important, business must vary its strategy and tactics according to the minister, the secretary, the ministry, and the issue. Where the minister is strong and competent, as were Manubhai Shah, T. T. Krishnamachari, or Morarji Desai, direct consultation might be most appropriate. However, few ministers know so much about the subject of their jurisdiction. Nor have they the time, the talent, or the inclination to really run their ministry. Thus, they are very heavily dependent on the secretary in charge of the ministry for advice. In situations such as this, it is best to deal with the secretary. The responsibility of ministers also varies according to their institutional missions. The finance minister, for example, is primarily concerned with raising revenues and allocating foreign exchange. As one official put it, "Whenever people come here, they want something." The Finance Ministry is always in the driver's seat. But the Commerce Ministry plays a major role in export promotion and must seek the active cooperation of business. It is by its very nature, therefore, more susceptible to business demands. Other ministries which have primarily regulatory roles or major public sector roles tend to have equally characteristic postures which must be considered when business is mapping out a strategy of demands.

Most businessmen argue that it is absolutely essential to convince the secretary of the validity of your case, regardless of who the minister might be. As one business leader put it, "If the civil service sees your point of view, they will go all out to help you. But," he continued, "if the secretary is against you, you are lost." It is the secretary who prepares the case and makes recommendations to the minister. Thus, as another industrialist explained, "If you don't satisfy the secretary, the minister will not decide." The secretary is in a strong position to influence the decisions of the minister, and so it is generally agreed

[19] *Ibid.*, p. 32.

that "you can go and see the minister only after he clears it. You talk to the minister to inform him about what is happening but go to the secretary for a decision." Businessmen also agree that once a secretary has made a decision, it is certain that he will follow it up to ensure that the proper action is taken. "What a secretary says he means."

Individual and group access to government are both highly developed by Indian business. Of the two, personal access seems to produce the best results for individual business houses, but it is this very effective pattern of access that has come under the greatest attack. There is a general feeling, therefore, both within business and government, that greater reliance should be placed on business associations. The suggestion arises not only because the association route is safer but also because associations have come a long way in the past twenty years in professionalizing their staffs. As a result, they are potentially more effective than they were in the past.

In the past, as we have observed, government used business associations mainly to secure a representative view but turned to individual businessmen for advice. This pattern is also changing. One of the weakest aspects of most business associations has been the tendency to select leadership on the basis of the size of economic holding rather than selecting an articulate spokesman for business. This has been especially true of the FICCI. With the emergence of a new generation of owner-managers, there has been greater pressure to select leadership on the basis of talent, more concern for what the executive will be able to do for the collective, and less concern about what he has done in the past for himself.

Finally, it is quite evident that systemic factors place major checks on business influence with the executive. The hostile political culture, the decision-making system, and the public policy of regulation and control have meant that businessmen are consulted by government but are not able to negotiate from a position of strength for a specific set of demands. Business associations lack the cohesion needed to enforce agreements with government. Business is in too vulnerable a position to openly challenge decision-makers, because of the potential sanction of government and because business is unable to appeal to the wider public for support.

The most durable obstacles to smooth relations between business and government are not structural problems but attitudinal problems. Government does make an attempt to consult business, although this consultation does not necessarily eventuate in major changes in policy. Consultation is designed mainly to remove day-to-day impediments in the implementation of policy, and this it often does.

The real problems in business–government relations are endemic to the political culture and cannot easily be overcome by hard work or good behavior. Intellectual distrust, status differences, the negative business image, and antibusiness ideology intrude at every level to exacerbate the fear among officials that, if they make concessions to business, even legitimate concessions, they will be attacked as panderers to vested interests. In this atmosphere of mistrust, the personal factor becomes all the more important. If an individual comes to be trusted and respected, if he appears to know his business and does not exaggerate its importance in the scheme of things, he can go a long way toward overcoming the usual business handicap or at least toward making its results affect his own firms somewhat less oppressively.

XIV

PATTERNS OF ACCESS AND INFLUENCE

Clearly the obstacles to the business community's capacity to influence public policy on a major issue are nearly insuperable. However, a strong case managed with proper orchestration of persuasion at all levels of access can, under favorable circumstances, result in an outcome that is advantageous to private sector interests. To illustrate this point and to show the interaction of forces on all levels—forces which have been discussed abstractly and in isolation, two cases have been selected. In one case business achieved its objective; in the other it did not. The first case is a study of the successful effort by cotton traders to persuade the Indian government to decontrol the price of cotton in 1967. The effort succeeded largely because of the ability of the representatives of the cotton trade to form a broad based coalition of traders, growers, labor, and industrialists who forced the government to change its policies. The second case is a study of the ultimately successful twenty-year effort of the government of India to revise its patent legislation, despite sustained private sector opposition. Cotton decontrol remained largely a matter between government and business. But the campaign against patent law revision failed because the inevitable strong pressure from the Indian left was suddenly reinforced by public uproar over industrial pricing practices.

Toward the middle of the 1960s, growing stagnation in the Indian economy combined with pressure from the World Bank, major foreign aid donors, and Indian business, led the government of India to decide upon a major change in its traditional policy of maintaining tight controls over the pricing and distribution of major products. Sixteen items were decontrolled in 1963, quality steel and pig iron in 1965, and cement in 1966. In April 1967, however, despite the pleas of the East India Cotton Association,[1] Commerce Minister Dinesh Singh refused to extend the policy of decontrol to cotton. Under the leadership of a newly elected MP connected with the cotton trade, the cotton traders decided to embark on a major lobbying effort to pressure the govern-

[1] *The Economic Times* (Bombay), April 4, 1967.

ment to reverse its decision in time for the marketing of the fall 1967 crop.

The strategy for achieving decontrol of cotton used every possible forum to press the case on the unwilling government. Designated points of access included advisory bodies, Parliament, the Congress Party in Parliament, and both ministerial and bureaucratic components of the executive. Public meetings were also scheduled. But the most significant aspect of the strategy was the decision to mobilize all interested groups into a coalition that would demonstrate unanimous dissatisfaction with government policy at every level from producer to retailer.

This concentrated effort to press government to decontrol cotton continued unabated for several months. Thus, the commerce minister's refusal to accept the demands of the East India Cotton Association merely led the traders to press their case through a variety of other channels. By June 2, 1967, the traders had secured a unanimous recommendation for decontrol from the Cotton Advisory Board, a multi-interest advisory body established to advise government on cotton problems.[2] The Cotton Advisory Board's recommendation was reinforced two days later, when the Agricultural Prices Commission—a commission of experts appointed by the government to advise on the price policy for agricultural commodities—delivered itself of a similar recommendation.[3] In order to maintain the momentum and to impress upon government that all groups—traders, industry, labor, and growers—were unanimously behind a revision in government policy, the Indian Cotton Conference called a meeting in Bombay. The four hundred delegates to the conference demanded decontrol of cotton.[4]

These activities of early June had been focused on creating an image of widespread public support for decontrol. By late June the activity was shifted to the Parliament in New Delhi. All MPs interested in cotton were briefed by cotton trade experts and persuaded to participate in the debate on the annual Commerce Ministry budget. The debate was to take place the last three days of June. Each MP was urged to be sure to refer to the need to decontrol cotton in his speech concerning the general operations of the Commerce Ministry. Almost every MP cooperated. The Minister of Commerce was bombarded by references to the need for cotton decontrol. Similar efforts were made in the consultative committee of Parliament which dealt with the Ministry of Commerce.

[2] *The Financial Express* (Bombay), June 2, 1967.
[3] *The Economic Times* (Bombay), June 4, 1967.
[4] *The Economic Times* (Bombay), June 6, 1967.

The next part of the strategy called for making the point for decontrol to the prime minister. After the debate on the Commerce Ministry budget, a private meeting was held with all MPs from the important cotton producing state of Gujarat. They were scheduled to meet shortly with the prime minister to discuss state problems. The MPs were carefully briefed, so that they could refer knowledgably to the need to decontrol cotton during their talk with the prime minister. The prime minister, responding to the Gujarat delegation, promised that she would look into the matter. In a subsequent private meeting with MPs representing the cotton trade, the prime minister indicated that, because the government had declared in the president's speech that gradual removal of controls was to be a guiding policy of the government, she would examine the feasibility of the decontrol of cotton.

Discussions with the prime minister were supplemented by a careful lobbying campaign designed to convince each member of the cabinet that he must support a policy of decontrol. In order to strengthen their case with the ministers, the traders drafted a resolution demanding decontrol of cotton, and they succeeded in getting the Maharashtra Pradesh Congress committee to pass it. Thus, strong state party support was added to the previous official resolutions of support for decontrol. By the time the cabinet met as a body again, all ministers except one were either not interested in the issue, and therefore neutralized, or had agreed to support a policy of decontrol. The one holdout, however, was critical. He was Morarji Desai, a major power center in the cabinet who was also the finance minister. Morarji had resisted all pressures, including those of the chief minister of his home state of Gujarat.

All attention at this point, therefore, focused on changing Morarji Desai's position. A small group of eight Maharashtra MPs who were closely connected with the cotton growers met privately with Morarji. They threatened to resign from the Congress party unless the policy was changed. Given the relatively slim Congress party majority in Parliament, Morarji weakened and could not continue his course of active opposition to decontrol. At the cabinet meeting when the final decision to decontrol cotton was taken, Morarji simply sat in silence. The cabinet unanimously endorsed a change in the policy of cotton control.

Notice of the emerging shift in the government's position began to appear in the press shortly after a June 30 meeting between the Cotton Advisory Board and the Commerce Ministry. The press reported that an informal meeting was held July 4, 1967, between the Commerce Ministry and a group of traders, growers, labor representatives, and industry. At that meeting the possibility of a partial decontrol of cotton was discussed.[5] It was reported that the problem was to be examined for feasibility by a group of experts in the Commerce Ministry. By July 27, 1967, a twelve-point plan for decontrol had been evolved, and on July 28 there were reports in the press that the government expected to announce a policy of cotton decontrol within a week.[6]

In the first week of August, the scene shifted to the executive committee of the Congress party in Parliament. On August 3 and 4, the executive debated the problem of cotton decontrol. A large number of Congress Party MPs, led by Mohan Dharia of Maharashtra, one of a group of strongly socialist Young Turks, pleaded the case for decontrol as a way of aiding cotton growers. Among the others who spoke were A. G. Kulkarni, S. S. Deshmukh, S. R. Damani, Tulsidas Jadhav, S. N. Mishra, Tarkeshwari Sinha, and Ram Kishen. All supported decontrol.[7] In his reply to the debate, Commerce Minister Dinesh Singh assured the party executive that the government's new cotton policy, to be announced in Parliament in a few days, would be advantageous to the cotton growers. Singh declared that he was unable to make any commitment on the unanimous demand of the executive for complete decontrol, but he left the clear impression that a large measure of relaxation of cotton control could not be ruled out. The commerce minister insisted that he would have to talk to the textile commissioner and the millowners before the decision was actually made. A number of major problems, he observed, had to be taken into account. Any change in policy would have to ensure that consumer interests would be protected and that the textile industry would not raise prices on specific varieties. Sick textile units would have to be protected against the possibility that the larger, richer units would corner stocks of cotton by paying higher prices. Finally, government had to keep in mind the effects that cotton decontrol would have on other commodities, lest higher cotton prices result in diversion of too much crop land into cotton.

The difficulties were evidently not so impossible after all, for on August 10, 1967, just a few days after the commerce minister's remarks, the government announced its decision to decontrol cotton.[8] The annual report of the Ministry of Commerce explained the decision in the following terms:

[5] *The Economic Times* (Bombay), June 4, 1967.
[6] *The Economic Times* (Bombay), July 27, 1967 and July 28, 1967.
[7] *The Times of India* (Bombay), August 3, 1967 and August 4, 1967.
[8] *The Economic Times* (Bombay), August 11, 1967.

Cotton crop for the year 1967–1968 was expected to be better than the previous year and it was hoped that a reasonable level of prices would be maintained without recourse to statutory controls. Pricing of raw cotton in the country was considered to be subject to a particular asymmetry in that it was the only agricultural commodity for which statutory maximum prices had been fixed. It was apprehended that this asymmetry, if it persisted, would lead to distortions in the cropping pattern and in marketing practices. *Further, the grower, the trader, and the industry were also unanimous on the removal of the price controls on cotton.* The cotton policy for the current year was formulated in the light of the experience of the previous year, the factors mentioned above, and the two principal objectives, *viz.*, first to assure the grower a fair remuneration for his produce, and second to assure the consumer supplies of controlled varieties of cloth at reasonable prices, which in turn implied supply of cotton to the industry at appropriate prices. In terms of this policy the statutory ceiling prices of cotton were removed from September 1, 1967. However, in order to protect the legitimate interests of labor, the consumer, and the industry, certain safeguards such as stock control and credit control were kept in operation. Stock levels of cotton that may be held by mills in their own premises or with merchants/muccadums were prescribed at the beginning of the cotton season at 2½ months consumption in the case of mills at Bombay and Ahmedabad and 3½ months consumption in the case of mills situated elsewhere. Relaxation of these limits are also given to mills located at distant places at Assam or those which execute commitments to deliver for export 20% or more of their production or are required to execute orders for defense. Mills and other cotton licence holders are required to declare cotton stocks held by them at the end of each month in a prescribed form. Purchase and sales of cotton have also to be registered with the Indian Cotton Mills Federation, who send a monthly statement to the Textile Commissioner. A standing advisory board for cotton has also been constituted.

On the other hand, to provide an assurance to the farmer, minimum support prices for cotton were fixed at 5 to 10% over the corresponding floor prices in the previous year. It was declared that government would be prepared to buy whatever quantities of cotton were offered for sale at those prices.[9]

[9] Government of India, *Report 1967–1968: Ministry of Commerce* (New Delhi: Government of India Press, 1968), pp. 69–70. Italics mine.

The traders felt they had a strong case. The facts and figures demonstrated the failure of the existing policy and the reasonableness of their demands. Yet only their ability to put together a cohesive coalition and press their case on all possible fronts enabled them to eventually succeed. A similar effort by the drug industry in India, however, proved to be somewhat less successful.

Perhaps the best example of the deployment of foreign business pressure to influence government policy is the campaign of the drug industry against the twenty year effort of the government of India to revise the Indian patents laws. Indian laws pertaining to patents date back to 1856, when the Exclusive Privileges Act was enacted by the British to protect inventions in India. The act was amended several times and finally replaced in 1911 by the Indian Patents and Design Act which, with its amendments, still served as the basic patent law at the time of independence.[10]

Among the first orders of business of the post-independence government of India was a review of the patent laws to ensure that they were consistent with the national interest. In October 1948, the government of India appointed a patent inquiry committee to review the patent laws. In 1949 this committee submitted an interim report recommending immediate amendment of the 1911 act to provide for compulsory licensing to prevent the abuse of patent monopolies. This proposal was enacted in 1950. When the final report of the committee appeared that same year, its recommendations were incorporated into a new patents bill which was finally introduced into the Lok Sabha on December 7, 1953. As a result of heavy criticism from abroad, the bill was permitted to lapse. Four years later, in April, the government agreed to appoint a new committee to study the issue. This committee submitted its report in 1959, but no draft bill was forthcoming until 1963.

The patents bill of 1963 came under fire from a variety of directions. Within India, the chief opposition was mounted by Assocham. Speaking on behalf of Bombay drug firms, Assocham called for amendment on the grounds that the policies proposed in such vital areas as the life of patents, licenses of right, and government exemptions would be "damaging to the country's industrial economy."[11] The pressure exerted within India by Assocham was reinforced by direct pressure from abroad. During Prime Minister Shastri's visit to the United Kingdom in 1964, for instance, British business, in private meetings

[10] Matthew J. Kust, *Foreign Enterprise in India: Laws and Policies* (Chapel Hill, N. C.: University of North Carolina Press, 1964), pp. 419–420.

[11] *The Associated Chambers of Commerce and Industry of India, Forty-Seventh Annual Report, October 1966* (Calcutta: Assocham, 1966), p. 10.

with Shastri, warned that India would face a serious setback in foreign investment if the bill was not altered.[12] These warnings were also conveyed to the government of India through several foreign embassies.

In response to these pressures, the Shastri government delayed submitting the bill in Parliament pending its revision. The bill subsequently introduced in Parliament in September 1965 was quite different from the one passed by the Indian cabinet in April 1963. Although the new bill was a sharp departure from the Patents and Design Act of 1911, it contained several concessions to foreign business and especially the drug industry. The most important concessions involved the extension of the validity of patents for drugs, from seven years in the original bill to ten years in the revised draft. This still represented a drastic reduction from the sixteen year validity period under the 1911 act. Another important concession concerned royalties. Instead of reducing the royalty to 2 percent, the bill provided for a ceiling of 4 percent. This was done largely because the existing 50 percent tax on royalties would yield a net return of only 2 percent anyway.[13]

Despite these modifications, foreign business opposition to the patents bill continued. By this time, Assocham's criticism was being reinforced by criticism from the FICCI and the Organization of Pharmaceutical Producers in India (OPPI), a newly formed industry association affiliated with the Bombay chamber. In opposing the bill as an attempt to weaken patent protection for the pharmaceutical industry, OPPI warned that the bill would adversely affect prospects of continuing the foreign collaboration which had contributed so much to the rapid development of the drug industry in India. In less than two decades, the drug industry had been transformed from a processor of bulk imported drugs to a manufacturer of most of the major drugs known to the world. The value of production had jumped from 110 million rupees in 1948 to over 1.5 billion rupees in the mid-1960s.[14] OPPI insisted that patent protection, as a method of protecting industrial property right, was essential to the continued growth of the industry. Therefore, OPPI hoped that the government of India would give the industry further opportunity to present its case by referring the bill to a joint select committee of Parliament.[15] The alarm set off among the large multinational firms by the changes in the Patents Act went be-

[12] *The Economic Times* (Bombay), July 20, 1965.

[13] *Ibid.*

[14] Organization of Pharmaceutical Producers of India, *Supplementary Memorandum on the Patents Bill 1967* (Bombay: OPPI, 1967), pp. 3–8.

[15] *The Economic Times* (Bombay), September 22, 1965.

yond concern for the impact of such legislation on operations in India. There was real fear that there would be repercussions in other developing countries as well.

The joint committee of Parliament, which took up the government's patents bill in late 1965, considered representations from OPPI, Assocham, and the FICCI, and also from a wide variety of groups both in India and abroad. Altogether the committee received seventy written memoranda and heard evidence from forty-three associations. It took eight hundred pages of testimony from, among others, patent attorneys, major international drug companies, a large number of Indian organizations representing small-scale as well as large-scale business, and from major industrial associations in Britain, Germany, the United States, and Japan. Most of the large companies and foreign industry associations opposed any tampering with the existing patent laws. Small indigenous producers favored major changes in the legislation to curb the power of the foreign giants.[16]

The majority report of the joint committee, which was submitted to Parliament on November 1, 1966, basically accepted the government's bill. But there were strong dissents expressed by groups within the committee representing important segments of Indian opinion. The left rejected the government's bill in favor of complete abrogation of foreign patent privileges.[17] The right saw a number of provisions of the bill as striking "at some of the foundations of widely accepted principles in this field." [18] This division within the select committee of Parliament reflected the similar though not quite so extreme misgivings within the Indian government. Some experts in the Industry Ministry frantically urged revision of the bill because they feared that it would hurt industrial development and particularly foreign investment. Others felt that government had to proceed with the bill or face the charge that it had succumbed to foreign pressure.[19] Because of the deep divisions within the Parliament and the Indian government, the patents bill of 1965 was permitted to lapse.

The patents bill was reintroduced on August 12, 1967, and again sent to a joint select committee of Parliament. On this round, building on what had already been accomplished and using similar tactics, foreign business felt it had laid to rest the threat of total abolition of patents and was now in a position to rewrite the bill in a way which

[16] Lok Sabha Secretariat, *Joint Committee on the Patents Bill, 1965* (New Delhi: Lok Sabha Secretariat, 1966), two volumes.

[17] *Ibid.*, 16.

[18] *Ibid.*, 26.

[19] *The Statesman* (Calcutta), November 30, 1966.

would gain greater government recognition of patent rights as property. They therefore pressed for the following major changes: (1) No clause of the bill should have retrospective effect, as this would infringe on existing rights and attract constitutional issues having wide national and international repercussions. (2) The principle of compensation must be conceded for whatever purpose a patent is used. (3) The term of ten years for patents relating to food, medicines, and drugs, as compared to fourteen years for other classes of inventions, was discriminatory and inadequate. (4) The concept of "Licenses of Right" in the bill, applicable to patents for food, medicines, or drugs, was an entirely new concept. It effectively removed patent protection from this class of inventions and therefore should be dropped.

In addition, the industry opposed all statutory rates of compensation as arbitrary, discriminatory, unrealistic, and unfair and demanded that royalty rates should be fixed on the merits of each case. Moreover, the industry demanded that government use of patents for any class of inventions should only be under exceptional circumstances which should be explicitly set out in the bill. Finally, a right of judicial appeal must be granted in cases where the industry questioned particular executive decisions.[20]

Government uncertainty concerning the patents bill of 1967, in the face of continued foreign pressure against it, was demonstrated by the fact that the bill was not referred to a joint select committee of Parliament until late August 1968, over a year after its introduction. This delay was criticized by many MPs as a bending to pressure from foreign vested interests.[21] Once remanded to the joint select committee, the bill languished there nearly a year and a half.

The select committee report was finally presented to Parliament on February 27, 1970. It contained a number of additional concessions which were expected to go even further in meeting the criticisms of foreign business. In addition to raising the ceiling on royalty rates from 4 to 5 percent, the select committee suggested that all existing patents be totally exempt from the purview of the bill. Contrary to expectations, however, the committee cut the validity period of patents on food, drugs, and medicine from ten years to seven years. Again, all existing patents would remain in force for the full sixteen years provided under the old patent law. Finally, while supporting the government's right to patented formulas for public purposes, the select committee agreed with the drug industry that the government should

[20] OPPI, *Memorandum on the Patents Bill*, 1967.

[21] *The Patriot* (New Delhi), August 27, 1968.

pay royalties for such use.[22] From the select committee report it appeared that the efforts of the drug industry to modify the legislation had paid rich dividends. Yet the select committee report was the closest the drug industry would get to triumph for some time to come, if ever.

The select committee report on the patent bill reached Parliament at a most inopportune time. The patient lobbying efforts of business were suddenly threatened by a major public outcry against high drug prices. And a split had so factionalized the Congress party that the government became dependent on support from Socialist and Communist party votes in Parliament in order to stay in office. In early 1970, the government of India had decided to attempt to force down the price of drugs in the Indian market. Lack of adequate advance planning to implement the government's decision led to an almost chaotic situation. Prices of some drugs spiraled out of control, and other drugs disappeared from druggists' shelves. Angry MPs demanded immediate and firm action by government to force down the sudden rise in drug prices, only to be told by the helpless minister that the government's power to check drug prices was limited by the patent protection enjoyed by the industry.[23]

The sudden public upsurge of protest against the drug industry, which was reflected in Parliament coincided with the split in the Congress party and the emergence of a minority government led by Mrs. Gandhi—who was dependent on support of non-Congress party opposition parties in Parliament. A group of Socialist and Communist party members insisted that the government enact the long debated patent bill as the price for continued support.

Although there are some observers who discount the conjecture concerning the role of the Socialists and Communists in the passage of the bill and place greater emphasis on the drug pricing scandal, the sequence of events indicates that the government had responded precipitously to some stimulus, for the patents bill suddenly appeared on the agenda of a special holiday sitting of the Lok Sabha. At that special sitting of the Lok Sabha, a large group of hostile opposition party MPs succeeded in revising several of the concessions that had been granted to the drug industry by the select committee. The 4 percent limit on royalties was restored, and all attempts to change the seven year limit on drug patents were defeated. These changes and other provisions of the bill were deeply resented by foreign businessmen, and there were

[22] *The Economic Times* (Bombay), February 28, 1970.
[23] *Ibid.*

pervasive grumblings that the precipitous actions of the government would affect the climate for foreign investment in India.[24] At the moment, however, the government was more concerned with domestic politics than with foreign business prospects.

In fighting the patents bill, foreign business used a variety of organizations and tactics to delay, to modify, and to try to kill the bill. These efforts succeeded in delaying the legislation for twenty years. Twice the bill was introduced and twice it was permitted to lapse. Foreign business lost the final battle, however, for it could not prevail over the imperatives created by major changes in the Indian political system and the damage to its image caused by strong public reaction to high drug prices.

Foreign business had succeeded in delaying the patents bill largely because the government itself was divided and uncertain about the impact a change in the patent laws would have on economic development and foreign investment in India. In addition, because the patents bill was never accorded a very high priority by government, it was easily sidetracked by those who opposed it. Throughout its campaign against the bill, the pharmaceutical industry did its best to raise fears that the bill would have all kinds of devastating implications. Until 1965 the pharmaceutical industry relied largely on Assocham to represent its interests. In June of that year, however, the pharmaceutical industry created the OPPI. By employing modern lobbying techniques, the OPPI became one of the most dynamic industry associations in India.

The pharmaceutical industry felt that the special problems of the industry required an approach different from the old style representational methods and the quiet diplomacy of Assocham. The technical nature of the industry,[25] its strong foreign component, and the delicate problem of dealing with the emotionally charged accusation that the industry exploited the sick required a more aggressive strategy not limited to persuasive but polite conversation with the top echelons of the bureaucracy or ministries. The OPPI leadership, unlike that of Assocham, was anything but amateurish. It consisted of former ICS officers and industry leaders who could draw on long experience dealing with the Indian government. For example, J. N. Chaudhury, the

[24] *The Economic and Political Weekly* (September 26, 1970), p. 1586; and *The Economic Times* (Bombay), August 30, 1970.

[25] When the government of India sought the views of the Bengal chamber on the draft proposals of the 1953 patents bill, the chamber replied that due to the highly technical nature of the issue it was leaving it up to individual chambers to submit replies to government. See *The Associated Chambers of Commerce and Industry of India, Thirty-Fourth Annual Report, November 1952–October 1953* (Calcutta: Assocham, 1953), p. 7.

secretary of the OPPI was a former foreign service officer who had served as parliamentary assistant to Prime Minister Nehru at one time. He had also been an information officer at the Indian Embassy in Washington. In 1969, the president was Keith Roy, a former ICS officer turned drug executive.

The leadership of OPPI decided on a strategy that called for a massive public relations and education campaign to explain the nature of the drug industry to political leaders and to the public. In the process, of course, the campaign could also show how changes in the patent laws would adversely affect the industry. The objective was to blunt criticism or, as one official put it, to "at least eliminate the stupid and uninformed kind of criticism which arises in many sectors." The approach called for a public process of lobbying aimed at several influential groups, including among others top decision-makers. The first group was the Indian press. OPPI arranged for Indian journalists to tour its major plants. Tour guides were equipped with all kinds of information about the industry, and throughout each tour they attempted to answer all possible questions. From these tours emerged a series of articles in major Indian newspapers explaining the great progress that had been made in the drug industry since independence. These articles pointed out the modernity of drug producing facilities, the variety of drugs available in India, and the role the industry was playing in exports. They also discussed many of the "problems" faced by the industry. As a direct result of these tours, the drug industry for a time received a very favorable press in India.[26]

The second group which the industry was interested in educating were the Members of Parliament and especially the members of the select committee. As one official put it, "At a very early stage we accepted the idea that after the Nehru era MPs would become more important in provoking lines of policy and that every effort had to be made to keep them informed." The select committee on the patents bill in 1965 had already organized themselves into study groups to tour the major drug facilities. The objective of the OPPI was to maximize this opportunity by showing the MPs the nature and extent of the industry in India and explaining the industry's accomplishments. The idea was to try to remove the susceptibility to suspicion of those who

[26] Organization of Pharmaceutical Producers of India, *Annual Report, 1967* (Bombay: OPPI, 1967), p. 8. See, for example, *The Statesman* (Calcutta), November 10, 1967; *The Times of India* (Bombay), November 10, 1967; *The Hindustan Times* (New Delhi), November 11, 1967; and OPPI, *Press Comments on the Drug Industry* (Bombay: OPPI, 1967).

were not necessarily hostile to the industry but simply knew nothing about it. In this way, the industry felt it could avert mischievous, uninformed criticism of its activities. In addition, selected MPs were invited to go abroad to study the pharmaceutical industry. On tour, these MPs were very well taken care of by major multinational pharmaceutical firms.

Lobbying to influence MPs was a sharp shift from the tradition of Assocham, but it was justified by one OPPI leader in these words:

> In a democracy, if I do not blow my trumpet no one will do it for me. The tradition developed in India that any attempt to persuade an MP was immoral and antinational. . . . Business has failed to teach and educate MPs because they have been afraid. As a businessman in a democracy, I have a right to go to any MP and try to persuade him to my point of view. I have a right to do this openly and it should be done openly and I resent any charge that this process is corrupting. Yet the past traditions are strongly against it, the bureaucracy does not accept the legitimacy of this process of persuasion, and they view it as immoral. The average MP will be frightened to be seen with you in public or be seen with a representative of OPPI, because he fears he will be called antinational if he talks to representatives of the pharmaceutical industry which is so closely allied with foreign business. However, the sooner we all get up and say we have a right to tell Parliament about the industry the better it will be for all of us.

A third target was the bureaucracy. OPPI was very careful to see that discussions were held at all major levels of bureaucracy, from the deputy secretary on up. Care was taken to ensure that no one felt left out, that no one who "really counted" was ignored, and that no one "who could throw a monkey wrench into things" was missed. Informal meetings were held, not to present representations but to determine what common ground existed between government and the industry. Only then were formal memoranda prepared. Finally, the OPPI maintained close liaison with ministers and through contacts abroad ensured that the prime minister and other ministers of the Indian government were aware of the anxiety which proposed changes in the Indian patent laws had produced abroad.

In the end, however, none of these innovative tactics succeeded in obtaining what traditional Assocham methods could not achieve. The drug industry failed to obtain its maximum goals. When, suddenly, an issue that had been largely a concern of the elite in government became a public issue, the drug industry was unable to counteract public opinion.

The patent issue underscores the point that business in India has been most successful when it has been able to reduce issues to questions of detail and move them into the conference rooms to be handled by experts. Business to date has been unable to affect the course of broad national movements of opinion. It can influence to its profit only the detailed content of legislation and executive policy. In the final analysis, however, such rear guard victories are no longer considered to be enough. Therefore, foreign and Indian business in India is becoming much more vocal. In the past, the Indian government was able to count on indigenous capital to support its policies relating to foreign investment. This endorsement is no longer automatically forthcoming. As foreign capital gradually becomes more closely identified with indigenous capital, the old hostility between the two has been giving way to strong mutual support.

Partly as a result of this growing liaison with indigenous capital, foreign business in India is becoming more self-confident and aggressive, shifting from Assocham's techniques of quiet diplomacy, which focused attention on the higher echelons of the bureaucracy and ministries, to a greater concern with legislative lobbying, public relations, and even political parties. Some of the Indian managers of foreign concerns have even attempted to enter the political arena. This change in strategy can also be traced to the shift in the nature of foreign capital in India. Whereas the promoters of traditional forms of investment in tea and jute were, after independence, concerned simply with salvaging whatever remained of their ventures, the managers of the new manufacturing-oriented units are increasingly dedicated to an aggressive pursuit of their goals of rapid expansion and growth. The leadership of foreign capital, meanwhile, has also passed from the old British India hands to a new generation of Indian managers who are, psychologically, in a stronger position to push their demands.

Both of these case studies exemplify the considerable potential of interest groups which master the techniques of orchestrating the multiple points of access to decision-makers in India. At the same time, like all case studies, the examples can only be generalized up to a point. Both were settled during the years from 1967 to 1971, a period of substantial political uncertainty in India. The Congress party had been returned to power with a substantially reduced majority, so that the views of individual MPs or groups of MPs counted more than they had in earlier years. For this reason, the threat of resignations by a group of Maharashtra MPs was not only credible but an eventuality the Congress party could not afford. In the case of the patent legislation, the final decision came after the split in the Congress party placed Mrs. Gandhi in charge of a minority government dependent on support from the left in Parliament and especially from the Communists. Although the Communist party may have played an important role, the most critical factor seemed to be the appearance of the bill at a time of crisis, when the public uproar over the high prices of drugs quickly offset years of industry lobbying. The drug industry had lost the public sympathy it had tried to create. Yet the result need not be considered a total failure of twenty years of lobbying effort. The bill as finally passed was, from the business point of view, superior to earlier versions.

Interest group activity in the modern sector is beginning to grow within the Indian political system. However, most groups continue to be mobilized to fight a single issue. Each crisis group tends to disintegrate after it has won its point. Although one hears a great deal of talk about a farm lobby in Parliament, it is mainly an imaginary aggregate of individuals. The only interest that is organized on a permanent basis in India is business. This interest, however, faces numerous obstacles. Business has found that organization and organized effort alone may not be enough.

Neither foreign nor indigenous capital is capable of becoming a dominant force in India, now or for some time to come, if ever. The major check on business in India remains the strong left-of-center political culture which enthusiastically supports the government's socialist-oriented policies and its development and expansion of the public sector. Even when government seeks to make concessions to the private sector to meet the larger needs of economic growth, it is immediately faced by a barrage of criticism from an ever alert left wing opposition which sees any such concession as a sellout or as a corrupt, underhanded deal with vested interests. The split in the Congress party strengthened the position of the left wing parties who provided critical support to Mrs. Gandhi's minority government and even forced a divided and reluctant government to push through the patents bill despite the effects that bill might have on foreign investment in India. Business in India may retain its voice in shaping government policy, but its voice is still most effective when it can transfer major currents of national opinion for nationalization or radical redistribution to the regulatory arena—that is, a policy of regulation is preferable to nationalization. Then the issues can be discussed quietly and dispassionately by experts outside the glare of publicity and the ever-present criticism from the left wing of the Indian political spectrum, which at best tolerates the private sector and if possible would like to see it abolished.

Ironically, the only way that business can offset this public hostility is to abandon its excessive reliance on a suspicion-arousing closed-door method of explaining its demands. Above all, if business is to play a more important role in the Indian economy, it must improve its public image and convince the masses of the Indian society that it no longer stands for corruption, exploitation, or underhandedness, and that it has become socially conscious and concerned with the larger welfare of the society. Thus, in order to be successful or perhaps even to survive, business must adopt a two-fold strategy of continuing to deal with decision-makers on important issues facing the industry, while at the same time trying to improve its public image to the point where its legitimate claims will receive a sympathetic hearing.

Conclusion

XV

INTEREST GROUP PERFORMANCE AND PUBLIC POLICY

The extent of business influence in India is exaggerated by its enemies and understated by its friends. The source of these vastly disparate perceptions of a reality which lies somewhere in between—business is neither impotent not omnipotent—is traceable to a combination of factors. First, because the basic attitudes of the political culture are strongly antibusiness, business is viewed through a distorting glass of suspicion and distrust. Second, in the context of the government's commitment to a socialist pattern of society, almost any contact between business and government can be interpreted as abandonment of principle under pressure from vested interests. Yet in a mixed economy where the private sector contributes a substantial part of the gross national product, government cannot exclude businessmen as a ritually impure pariah caste, even though the least contact with business tends to be misunderstood. Finally, although much is surmised and asserted, very little is actually known about the organization of Indian business as an interest group, still less about its functioning as an organized interest, and least of all about what is presumed to be common knowledge—the extent of business influence on public policy.

In short, the evaluation of business influence in India has been based on an Alice-in-Wonderland sentence before trial process. And, because business is believed to enjoy unlimited access to all levels of government but especially to the political leadership and higher echelons of the bureaucracy, all of these are guilty, too, by association. Seldom are distinctions made between individual and collective action, legitimate consultation and corruption, allegation and proof of guilt. And it has been so taken for granted that virtually no effort has been made to measure and record actual changes in government position or policy as a result of business influence. Such a process of trial before sentence reveals that access is anything but synonymous with influence. To this finding the unplacable critics of business would have a reply. Because business operates quietly to achieve its ends, its "real" influence is almost impossible to determine. The true believer will not be convinced by this book, but others should find it helpful in understanding the trend from mixed economy to socialist pattern of society to socialization of banking in the Indian economy.

The perception of the extent and implications of business influence in shaping government policy varies according to the ideological perspective and expectations of the perceiver. The left conceives of India as a bourgeois dictatorship in which government decision-making is dominated by business. The very acceptance of the concept of a mixed economy is offered as proof, and further evidence is seen in the statements of many top political leaders that the private sector is needed to help develop India. Business maintains its influence, according to the left, by control over the press, by planting men in Parliament, by massive political contributions, by financial backing from foreign collaborators and western aid donors, and by connivance of members of the ICS–IAS who are looking forward to employment by private business after retirement. What business cannot get through these means it simply buys by drawing upon its vast hoard of "black money" to subvert public officials. Businessmen, then, are a breed of profiteers and exploiters who do not develop a nation but corrupt it.

The view of the right is completely antithetic to that of the left. The right argues that the tremendous resources of business have been dissipated by a combination of poor spirit and poor organization. Businessmen lack the strong convictions or personal courage to speak out in public in support of their views, the right explains. And in addition, according to the right, they do not even attempt to organize their potential supporters in the legislature. Thus, their aims go misunderstood in Parliament and in the country at large. Furthermore, they have failed to engage adequate professional staffs in their associations. They intervene in the decision-making process too late to be effective. They are too preoccupied with only a limited range of problems. And they are unlikely to improve their strategy or tactics, because each worries only about his own immediate personal interests and neglects the larger view of public policy as it affects business as a whole. In short, if business is weak, it is largely as a result of its own actions and especially because of its refusal to commit more resources to political parties of the right. In a sense, the right seems to be saying business could be as powerful as the left thinks it is already, if only it would try.

The actual situation lies somewhere between these dichotomized perceptions of business influence in India today. Perhaps as accurate a characterization as any was made by G. D. Birla, who asserted business has a "limited influence" which can have an impact if "it is correctly utilized."[1] Business in India has considerable political capital and resources to draw upon, and because it has been able to mobilize at least a portion of these resources, it has become the best organized interest group in the country. It is the only group in India capable of sustained action and continuous day-to-day contact with both the Parliament and ranking heads of government. Nevertheless, although business enjoys a high level of access to government decision-makers, its ability to convert this capital into influence is substantially held in check by a variety of internal organizational and external systemic restraints. Individual business houses have been successful in gaining specific, individual, distributive benefits, but business collectively has not been able to influence the broad outline and direction of public policy in India. For all that they have grown and become more effective institutions of collective action in the past twenty years, business associations in India are still too insufficiently organized, internally fragmented, oligarchically controlled, defensive, and reactive to exert maximum potential political influence. Both Assocham and the FICCI have built impressive headquarters buildings and filled them with small armies of clerks, typists, and chaprasis (office messengers) to assist a handful of professional analysts. But their level of professionalization is still woefully inadequate in comparison to similar organizations in Japan, Germany, France, and the United Kingdom. Although the staff of the FICCI is better trained than that of the Assocham, Assocham has the advantage of a more highly professionalized managerial leadership. The federation would do well to emulate Assocham by choosing its own leadership on the basis of personal and professional competence, rather than solely on the basis of the size of an individual's economic holdings. Barring two or three exceptions, the past leadership of the federation has been amateurish and inarticulate. This is a consequence of a selection process designed to perpetuate oligarchy and satisfy other internal needs instead of providing a strong leadership for the organization in its encounter with the government and the larger society. In its public performance this leadership, composed of the older traditionalist industrialists, became entirely too preoccupied with an extremely narrow range of problems, especially those centering on jute, tea, and textiles. Thus, because of its patterns of leadership selection, the federation has tended to represent the interests of the dominant elite rather than the business community as a whole.

There exists in the federation, as in Assocham, a strong minority

[1] G. D. Birla, *In the Shadow of the Mahatma* (Bombay: Orient Longman's Ltd., 1955), p. 60.

group which realizes the existence and the seriousness of these problems. Just as Assocham is slowly attempting a major reorganization to end the East India Company atmosphere—which pervades its Bengal headquarters—and to professionalize the association's bureaucracy, the federation has come under increasing pressure to change the existing pattern of leadership and control. The major reorganization of 1962 has been followed by changes in 1971 designed to dilute the power which large houses have been able to exercise through their financial contributions and the voting power of the associate membership.[2] Simply diluting the voting power of the big houses, however, will not solve the problem of organizational effectiveness. Past experience has shown that, although the whole gamut of traders, regional interests, and medium industry may be vocal when it comes to demands for representation at the leadership levels of the federation, the same groups are also the most outspoken opponents of increased fees. Yet better financing is essential if the trend toward greater professionalism and increased staff is to be continued.

Therefore, the major problem of the federation is to develop mechanisms for insuring that the wide diversity of interests which the organization represents are given a fair share in policy-making, without driving the major contributors to reduce their subscriptions. The federation has outgrown its existing organizational structure and needs a new, intermediate level policy-making body of about two hundred business representatives. This group could meet two or three times a year, to discuss major issues between annual meetings of the membership and to provide policy guidance to a small executive committee and the president. Such an arrangement, which has evidently worked rather well in other countries, would provide a level of meaningful participation for more of the interests composing the FICCI.

The greater professionalization of leadership, the restructuring of the internal decision-making process, and the development of larger secretariats must be accompanied by greater efforts to reconcile internal business conflicts, so that business demands can be more clearly articulated to government decision-makers. Many government decision-makers feel that the enunciations of business organizations are too quickly repudiated by individual business leaders and that business associations, because of their inability to secure the cooperation of their membership, are so unreliable in carrying through agreements that efforts to work things out between business and government are futile. At present, therefore, business associations can be used to obtain a repre-

[2] *The Economic Times* (Bombay), April 12, 1971.

sentative view, but they cannot be counted on to provide advice relating to any specific situation. The promise of cooperation from business associations, government decision-makers argue, must become reliable if business associations are to be treated as negotiating bodies.

Although conflicts based on primordial loyalties may be declining in India, they continue to be reflected indirectly in differences among businessmen over business ethics, business behavior, styles of dealing with government, and the degree of self-regulation appropriate to business. In addition, conflicts based on primordial loyalties also become reflected in patterns of elite politics, which still take on the form of competition among major business families. Superimposed on these traditional divisions are conflicting interests based on divergent economic functions. Thus, for example, although the cement industry succeeded in convincing the government to decontrol cement, the government was forced to reimpose controls because of a conflict between north Indian and south Indian cement factories over the system of freight equalization and the refusal of the maverick Dalmia group to cooperate with the other units in the industry.[3] Incidents such as this tend to confirm the belief among government officials that voluntary cooperation of a group of business units is unattainable and that coordination can only be insured by statutory regulation and control.

Problems of professionalism, leadership, and cohesion have been further complicated by the traditionally divisive, negative, and grievance-oriented style of business associations. Business tends to overstate its case and to neglect the larger context. In the words of one senior manager, "we do not study problems very carefully and as a result we appear subjective and emotional." The tendency is also to demand far more than the facts and data would justify. Carelessness might be explained by the lack of expertise, if business associations actually used to the utmost the limited professional staff they have acquired. But the problem is much more a matter of attitude than resources, for it really stems from the inability of business to take the analytical approach to economic realities that would lead them both to increase and really utilize professional staff.

What is needed by business, more than anything else, is a habit of mind and an organizational mechanism which is less reactive and more analytical. The government of India does not have a monopoly on talent, and certainly business has the resources to hire such talent. Most of the talent attracted by business today is bogged down in handling innumerable business-generated grievances, and so there is little

[3] See *The Financial Express* (Bombay), August 25, 1967; July 10, 1967.

time for long-range thinking and analysis. Yet the planning apparatus and the bureaucracy in India have been demonstrated to be capable of responding to imaginative ideas when such ideas are accompanied by thorough analysis and careful documentation. Only by increasingly devoting its best minds to such long-term considerations can business really expect to have a positive, as opposed to a negative, impact on government thinking. Such activity, of course, would require broader vision on the part of a more professionalized leadership, but it would also require much larger professional staffing of business associations, which in turn means the commitment of more resources. The issue of resources, however, inevitably brings one back to the problem of patterns of oligarchy and control.

The need to strengthen the organization of Indian business associations is becoming critical because of the difficulties being created by the enlargement of the entrepreneurial elite. The increase in numbers tends to clog individual channels of access. In addition, such vastly multiplied government business contacts generate even more suspicion among hostile observers. Working through business associations would reduce those occasions for misinterpretation considerably, especially if the government continues to dismantle some of its controls. Such a change in strategy may not be a matter of choice for business. Among both the ministers and the higher echelons of bureaucracy, the feeling is growing that it is "safer" to deal with business associations than with individual businessmen or business houses. It is safer, perhaps, from the point of view of public opinion. Yet it is risky to encourage business to work together. One of the least exploited yet potentially most promising means of increasing business influence on public policy would be the building of a coalition with other interests, to define common goals and confront government with a united front. This strategy, after all, was the key to success in securing the decontrol of cotton. Furthermore, business has managed to work in coalition with various institutional interests of the government of India. Such coalitions have sought private sector benefits as a by-product of enhancing the mission of the cooperating institution over that of other government bodies. This strategy might have some limited advantages in a system where institutional interests have played a disproportionate role. But the emergence of strong new functional interests, especially in the sector of Indian agriculture which has benefited from the green revolution, offers a potential for significant realignment of economic forces in India. For the foreseeable future, however, the impact of business on Indian public policy will continue to be held in check by a hostile political culture, a centralized and highly autonomous system of decision-making, and a pattern of public policy which gives government such a stranglehold over the private sector that business will be reluctant to challenge government authority too forcefully. Interest group behavior will be determined by systemic factors, and public policy will not be the result of some cash register calculus of subsystemic demands.

The specific Indian pattern of modernization grew out of an intersection of colonial rule and the traditional Indian social structure, which concentrated an emergent industrial elite drawn from just a few sections of Indian society in a limited number of geographic areas. Entrepreneurial pioneers whose ideological roots are in the nineteenth century have nevertheless benefited from the rapid growth of Indian economy under the post-independence government policy of planning, protection, and incentives. But their alleged monopoly position has made them the focus of attack by the vocal left wing of the Congress party and by the Socialist and Communist opposition, who tend to view them as the apotheosis of the traditionally despised Indian trader. "We have no real industrialists in this country," they sneer, "just a bunch of petty traders." Political attacks on business, which tend to take on caste overtones because of the origin of a large segment of the Indian industrial elite, have resulted in passage of monopoly legislation aimed at controlling the future growth of business and especially the growth of the big business houses. Government meanwhile has attempted, in various ways, to develop a more broadly based entrepreneurship, seemingly oblivious to the fact that the new industrialists must struggle alone in a hostile systemic environment which drives them to cooperate if they are to survive. Until now, the older and more powerful business houses have not given new business its due. But unless the interests of small-scale industry and new entrepreneurs can be expressed through existing business associations, which at present do not represent their interest, they will on their own initiative or on the encouragement of government create their own associations, thereby further fragmenting the business community. And if the business community is to have any substantial impact on public policy, it needs greater unity, not further internal competition. Yet business so far has been extremely vulnerable to the divide-and-rule strategy of government.

A political culture which is suspicious of the private sector and antagonistic to its values of maximization of profit and private gain will limit the ability of the business communities to appeal to the public for support. Such a political culture will also make it difficult if not impossible for business to develop its own political voice, either through direct representation or with development of a major business party.

The Swatantra party has so far been unable to make a substantial impact. Thus, for the foreseeable future, business will have to work through aggregative political parties and in particular the one now in power, the new Congress party led by Mrs. Indira Gandhi.

The recentralization of decision-making since the 1971 elections has substantially curtailed opportunities for business to work at many levels of the policy process which developed a certain autonomy during the period of uncertainty and decentralization from 1963 through 1971. The loss of many of its close supporters in the old Congress party who no longer enjoy positions of power, the reemergence of massive Congress party majorities, and the consolidation of decision-making in the office of a strong prime minister—all these factors signal the return to earlier patterns of securing access and influence. The passing of the old nationalist leadership and the emergence of a new generation of political leaders (some of whom, like Y. B. Chavan, have new sources of financial support) make it difficult for the old business houses to reestablish the previous close liaison with the top levels of government. They will, therefore, have to pay greater attention to formalized and regularized patterns of access established by the government for consulting the private sector. The old system of depending upon highly particularistic access based on blood relationships, personal friendships, and direct benefit will not disappear completely. But the newer patterns of growth and development and the increasingly technical complexity and sophistication of industrial development will require much more professionalized and regularized consultation. Given the preeminence of a planned, controlled, and regulated economy and the relatively uncorrupted pattern of strong political leadership which does not respond supinely to pressures from below, business groups will have to concentrate on trying to close the emotional and philosophical gap which separates the business elite from the governmental elite and the larger Indian public if it is to increase its influence on public policy.

In order to assess the success to date of the access business has achieved by its various approaches to government, one must distinguish among the kinds of public policy business seeks to influence. Business is not concerned with all public policy. Business, for example, takes very little interest in issues of foreign policy. Business involves itself only with those policies which have a redistributive, distributive, regulatory, or developmental impact on the private sector. Each type of policy requires of an interest group desiring to influence it different styles of action with a greater or lesser potential for success. In India, business is least likely to influence redistributive policy, has moderate success on distributive issues, and is most effective in influencing regulatory and developmental policy.

Business has never succeeded in blocking or even in modifying a major redistributive policy in India. When government itself has been united and determined to act and when it has detected strong popular support for any particular action, no amount of business pressure—whether on the prime minister, the cabinet, the Congress party, the Parliament, or the bureaucracy—can have any impact. Thus, business could not delay or modify the decision to nationalize life insurance[4] and most banks as part of a basic government program to bring all major credit facilities under government control in the mid-1950s. Business could not prevent the enactment of a variety of taxes on wealth, income, and expenditures—taxes designed to raise resources for development and to redistribute income in the name of socioeconomic change. It could not stop the creation of a massive public sector which came to dominate the entire capital goods industry of India. It could not stop the nationalization of private sector banks or general insurance. In short, business has a perfect record of failure in attempting to block or change any major redistributive policy of government in the last twenty years. What business *can* do, however, is to try to convert a redistributive issue into a regulatory issue in which its interest seems self-evident rather than self-serving.

Redistributive issues, once raised, tend to gain widespread public approval in a society committed to socialism and a redistribution of resources and wealth. And so business finds it advantageous in some cases to support greater government regulation and control as an alternative to total nationalization. Thus, when it became clear that public, party, and parliamentary pressures were strongly in favor of the nationalization of banks and general insurance, business was forced to view the government's already enunciated policy of social control as preferable. By transforming a redistributive policy calling for full nationalization into a regulative policy involving some more hazily defined social objective, business was able for a time to prevent total loss of its control over credit. At the same time it was able to shift considerations of credit allocation from the emotional arena to calm committees of experts where instrumental and pragmatic goals play a large role than ideological purity. The realistic approach, then, is to recognize the handwriting on the wall in time to shift attention from

[4] Bernard E. Brown, "Organized Business in Indian Politics," *The Indian Journal of Political Science* 23 (1962): 141.

the overall to the specific, from the visionary preamble to the technical clause, and so shift the locus of discussion from the forum to the tea table, where personal contact reinforced by personal and economic power count more than mass demonstrations.

Outside the area of those redistributive policy issues which have an all-compelling symbolic role in the Indian political system, business has been somewhat more successful in modifying or delaying, if not blocking, government action. Thus, business could not stop the enactment of one of the most comprehensive systems of company law in the world, or the enactment of the Industries (Development and Regulation) Act of 1951 which brought all private sector activities under strict government regulation and control. But business did succeed in making some useful if minor alterations. In fact, some of these alterations resulted in making parts of the legislation itself ineffective. For example, in 1963 the government—in the wake of the Dalmia-Jain scandal—introduced an amendment to the Companies Act. The amendment created a special tribunal with power to remove the management of a company for fraud. The purpose of the amendment was to overcome the difficulties presented by such removals under existing law.[5] At the select committee stage, the FICCI succeeded in modifying the amendment. The methods of appointment, the procedures, and the jurisdiction of the proposed tribunals were so altered[6] that within four years the government was forced to scrap the whole system. Although the original aim of these special tribunals had been to accomplish an expeditious investigation of the affairs of suspect companies, the FICCI changes deprived the findings of the tribunals of their finality. Therefore, instead of shortening the time required to dispose of a case, the process was extended by the need to refer cases to the courts. The tribunals were unable to achieve cooperation with their victims, and they also became imbroiled in all kinds of procedural wrangles. They were therefore abolished.[7]

Business pressure is most successful in influencing the timing and content of those policies on which government itself is divided. Where differences of opinion are considerable and the policy does not enjoy an especially high priority, business may be able to provide sympathetic government opponents of the policy with sufficient encouragement or

[5] *The Economic Times* (Bombay), November 27, 1963.

[6] FICCI, *Correspondence for 1963* (Delhi: FICCI, 1963), p. 273; *Report of the Proceedings of the Executive Committee for 1963* (Delhi: FICCI, 1963), p. 69.

[7] *The Financial Express* (Bombay), May 18, 1967. For an example of the problems found by the Tribunals, see the Bennett, Coleman case in Matthew J. Kust, *Supplement to Foreign Enterprise in India: Laws and Policies* (Chapel Hill, N.C.: University of North Carolina Press, 1966), pp. 68–69.

ammunition to achieve a remodeling or delaying action. Thus, business succeeded in delaying the abolition of the managing agency system for twenty years, and the revision of India's patent laws languished in a limbo of parliamentary and bureaucratic delay for over ten years before it was passed. Business, in the interim, was able to take advantage of the respite made possible by interministerial disagreement over the impact of patent legislation on foreign investment in India to secure some modifications of the legislation.

In short, the political culture in India is such that business is completely defenseless when the political leadership can state an issue in terms of the vested interests or can pit the haves against the have-nots. It has greater freedom of action on more complex issues, especially at the regulatory and developmental level and to a lesser extent on the distributive level. Within the corridors of the ministries and the bureucracy, moreover, decisions are based not on what groups within the Congress party or in the opposition feel government policy *should* be but on what it actually *is* at that moment in time. Here the character of the mixed economy and the delineation of the private sector's precise role within it are worked out on a pragmatic, not an ideological, basis. Here businessmen are regarded not as a pariah minority community but as a relatively powerful group responsible for a substantial amount of production. Their cooperation is needed, for the time being at least, in the national development effort, and their complaints, therefore, must be regarded as legitimate feedback enabling government to assess and adjust the impact of government policy. The excise tax on tea had to be reduced because business could show that it hurt exports. The shipping industry had to be exempt from the wealth tax on companies because that tax would have placed the industry at a competitive disadvantage internationally. Cement had to be decontrolled if production was to be increased.

Government is never able to prejudge the total impact of its complex regulatory and control powers, and so it has been willing to adjust its directives in the light of proven ambiguity or demonstrated hardship. In response to business petitions and according to the merits of the case government has, for example, extended deadlines for the exercise of import licenses to make up for delays caused by dock strikes. It has even acted to remove some ambiguities in the definition of a taxable income. In fact, hundreds of such cases fill the one thousand pages of correspondence between the FICCI and government each year.

In the case of development policy, government has granted concessions to business as part of its effort to accomplish broader public objectives. In such cases, there is almost a clientele relationship between business and government. Thus, the Commerce Ministry, which is charged with increasing exports, seeks to remove all barriers which impair the ability of the private sector to export its products. In the name of export promotion, the Commerce Ministry may even be found wrangling with the Finance Ministry over the granting of excise tax reductions to the tea or jute industry, for example, in order to accomplish its objectives. Government may also create attractive incentive schemes, tax rebates, and other concessions for business in an effort to enlist business cooperation in the accomplishment of other developmental objectives. Business and government, then, are not always in conflict, and business, naturally, is most likely to win the day when its interests are congruent with those of the government.

Despite the rhetoric aired in Parliament and in sections of the Indian press, the vested interests do not dominate the public policy-making process in India. They are held in check by a national consensus which is committed to a socialism based on rapid economic development and a more equitable distribution of resources, by a strong and independent bureaucracy, and by the restraints of a planned, regulated, and controlled economy. The political leadership derives its goals and its support from the larger society, the political system, and its own conception of what the national interest requires. The demands of any one particular group, especially business, come in a very poor fourth on the scale of influence. Yet, because government prefers to gain the widest possible acceptance and the full cooperation of all groups in the development effort, there is a genuine attempt to consult the various interests of which Indian society is composed—as long as it is understood that consultation does not commit the government to act in accordance with the advice it receives.

Business has been most successful in gaining frequent and sustained access to the executive and the bureaucracy, because public policy itself required such contact, because business could act outside the glare of hostile public opinion, and because it was at this level of personal contact that the political and economic power of business could be made to count. Business was quick to adjust to the structure of decision-making which emerged after independence, making the executive and the bureaucracy the effective centers of power. Access to these levels placed a premium on organization, bureaucratization, and non-agitational methods which suited business style and which business was in a position to finance. Thus, business emerged as the only organized group in Indian society capable of mounting a pattern of day-to-day contact with government. At the same time, business influence on Parliament and the political parties was constrained by larger systemic factors which made contact sporadic. The increased fragmentation of decision-making that resulted from the death of the nationalist leaders who had dominated Indian politics for almost twenty years and the splintering of party politics enabled business, for a brief period from 1963 to 1971, to play a larger role at party and parliamentary levels of government. But the return of massive Congress party majorities in 1971 placed new limits on such action. Meanwhile, it is still true that business—for all its access to the executive and the bureucracy, for all its occasional ability to modify or delay an objectionable policy—has not yet been able to convert its considerable economic power into truly effective political power.

The popular image of the underhanded, wirepulling capitalist is derived from the assumption that all contacts between government and business are attempts by vested interests to twist public policy in ways that will be contrary to the national interests and to those of the public at large. This view of the role of business interest groups tends to see business "pressure" as unidimensional. It obscures the actual dynamic interrelationships between government decision-makers and a particular sector of the society which is responsible for maintaining and generating increased employment and production. It is a view which is so preoccupied with the possibility of business attempts to subvert major redistributive policies that it ignores the entire range of distributive, regulatory, and promotional policy in which business has a legitimate interest. Most Indian decision-makers, when pressured to evaluate the performance of Indian business associations, confess first that business associations are weaker than is popularly supposed and second that business associations actually play a largely positive role in the policy process.

Business associations, then, are not dysfunctional even in a planned economy such as India has. They perform several positive functions for the political system. First, they provide a useful platform from which government may educate business and the public. They enable government decision-makers to explain and to justify existing government policies, to answer specific criticisms of such policies, and to test out new ideas on those who will be most affected by them. Second, business associations act as major corrective agents and feedback mechanisms. Decision-makers are not always able to project the detailed impact of particular government decisions, and business associations provide a mechanism for presenting another point of view. Furthermore, by telling government where the shoe pinches, business can provide concrete cases of undesirable consequences of existing government policies, thus enabling the government to take corrective action in order to accomplish the stated objectives without harmful or counter-productive side effects. Third, when responding to business criticism by speaking before business groups, decision-makers are forced to do their homework. They are constrained to review past policy decisions, assess the results, and justify their actions. Without the stimulus provided by organized groups, no such review would take place, and counterproductive policies might not be discerned so quickly. As one senior official put it, "The bureaucracy is very forgetful. They need constant reminding." Fourth, business associations are considered useful because they provide a mechanism for productive consultation. Whereas sustained consultation is possible with an organized group, it is extremely difficult to carry out systematic discussion with an anomic or agitational group. Fifth, the feeling by business that it is consulted does produce a sense of participation, even when the advice provided is not accepted. And that sense of participation helps to defuse dissatisfaction and total alienation. Sixth, business serves as a major link with private capital abroad and helps channel private foreign investment and technology to India. Finally, government cannot operate without the cooperation of the private sector in a variety of areas, including export promotion and the vast gray areas of business operations which are not covered by specific government controls or regulations. In short, the existence of organized business associations in India is largely functional to the long-term successful operations of a planned, democratic, socialistic political system.

One might even argue that it has been the very weakness of modern business associations which has proven to be dysfunctional. The pragmatic adjustments of Indian business to many aspects of public policy and administration, and their failure to professionalize as rapidly as they might have, resulted in major economic dislocations. Instead of doing its own analysis and its own planning, business became too dependent on government. As producers, businessmen allowed themselves to be paralyzed by the psychology of scarcity. The total dependence of business on government bound business irrevocably to government projections of what the economy would need during any five year period. These projections were based on elaborate econometric models, without any parallel effort to assess potential demand. Once government had announced the exact capacity that would be licensed to provide for those needs, each businessman fought to get as big a share of the total production as he could. Neither collectively nor individually did business attempt an independent analysis of the accuracy of the projection or the precise nature of the demand. Similarly, business became so totally dependent upon government protection and controls that it acquired a stake in the very controls it publicly opposed. The net result was the creation of high cost, inefficient industry. Domestic prices were high, and Indian products were unable to compete abroad and generate the foreign exchange which was necessary to the financing of the plan. If Indian business associations are becoming professionalized to the point where they can corroborate or challenge government planning figures, their new capacity will redress an imbalance.

The Indian case clearly demonstrates that the widely held assumption that modern interest groups are nonexistent in traditional and transitional societies is not entirely correct. More important, however, are the lessons to be learned from the process of group formation and institutionalization and how this relates to patterns of social differentiation and the emergence of new values. Primordial loyalties of family, caste, community, and region need not prevent the emergence of modern voluntary associations. In fact, these loyalties may serve as the building blocks of such organizations. They may inhibit the development of the association as a precise replication of foreign models, but the very creation of the association tends to assist in the breaking down and recomposition of these loyalties. The early Indian business associations were very closely connected with particular family and caste groups. Some of the members of those groups, despite their persistent primordial loyalties, saw good reason for trying to incorporate other sections of the business community. As business grew, as it moved from trade to complex industry, as it succumbed to a managerial and professional revolution, the effects on business associations were felt. The associations, in turn, became more modern and bureaucratized. Thus, although early forms of organization tended to institutionalize conflict built around primordial loyalties, these loyalties lost their preeminence over time. Modern functional differentiation emerged gradually from the social segmentation of traditional Indian society.

As in Germany, many business associations in India were family-dominated, because the pioneers of Indian industry built large business houses by mobilizing the resources of the joint family system. These same pioneering families were willing to put up the funds to develop mechanisms for collective action. FICCI deficits were made up by private contributions from members of the committee from 1927 until the creation of the associate membership in 1951. The creation of the associate membership, that enabled the federation to raise substantial resources to develop its professional secretariat, was essentially an institutionalization of the earlier practice. The bulk of the funds contributed continued to come from committee members, largely through the fees paid by their own companies which joined the federation as associate members. In return for this financial support, however, the FICCI elite demanded a dominant voice in the affairs of the organization. This pattern of family control of business associations continued as long as it survived as a force in the various business houses as well. But now the character of business itself has begun to change. Individual business houses have become too large and complex to be controlled in the traditional family style. The business community as a whole has grown in size and diversity. As business changed, so did its associations. The pioneer entrepreneurs are giving way to the managers and the bureaucrats. The relationships between business and government also changed in response to the changing internal character of business and the slow evolution and development of the major components of the Indian political system. The old patterns of individual and collective interaction between government and business developed as a result of the relationship between individual business families and the Indian National Congress, superimposed on the centralized system of decision-making for a public policy of planned development of the private sector, under strict control and regulation by the government. Under this system of public policy, the distributive capabilities of government were enormous. Government was in a position to provide a variety of direct benefits to individuals in the form of industrial licenses, permits, and other forms of administrative action which had to be obtained before the private sector could even begin to break ground for a new plant or keep an existing plant supplied with raw materials. These direct benefits were most likely to accrue to individuals who used a variety of family, caste, and personal relationships to obtain individual benefits. Petty favors from the lower echelons of the bureaucracy had to be obtained by payment of a *bakshish*.

Public policy, however, has always been another matter altogether. Most major decisions in India involve a complex interaction of institutional interests within the government. There is a balancing of interests among the Planning Commission, the Reserve Bank, the Finance Ministry, the Commerce Ministry, and the other ministries of the government, each reacting variably to demands from the Congress party, the opposition parties, and organized interest groups like business associations. The ministries and other organs of the government of India are staffed with professional bureaucrats, accountants, and economists who are committed to a concept of rational decision-making for accomplishing institutional missions. Facts and figures, a logical and effective case backed by supporting data—this is the way to impress the bureaucrats. When business became aware of the desire for a meaningful dialogue with government, the slow process of professionalizing its associations began. Meanwhile, government realized the necessity of establishing some form of regularized contact with the private sector in a mixed economy, especially because the very legislation which gave government the power to regulate and control the private sector included provisions for statutory consultations with the business community. The rapidly changing character of both business and government leadership elites, finally, has begun to strengthen these more formal, regularized patterns of consultation. The longstanding psychological gap, which tended to inhibit such consultation, is beginning to break down as business becomes more professional and managerial and government becomes more dependent on external advice in managing an increasingly complex and technologically sophisticated, mixed economy.

In short, the elaborate mechanism which has been developed over the past twenty years for consulting the private sector is slowly becoming energized as the size and diversity of the business elite begins to make the old system of individual wire-pulling more difficult to operate. Business may never fully make the transition from the "old lobbying" of personal contact to the "new lobbying" of organizations speaking and acting in the open. But it is moving in that direction[8] under the forces generated by internal and systemic change.

Other major functional interests in Indian society have not yet reached the same level of organization, professionalism, and autonomy which business has achieved. And so one of the greatest difficulties of business will be to avoid competition and to develop alliances with emerging functional interests in the society. So far, business has had to depend for external support solely on alignment with major institutional interests that need reinforcement in dealing with other institutional interests. In the immediate future, a more potent force would be to ally with the rapidly emerging agricultural lobbies. Such an alliance would increase private sector strength and would also ensure that the agricultural lobbies do not become hostile toward business interests. Such an alliance would also enable business to supplement its economic power with the voting power of the rural sector, which plays such a critical role in Indian electoral politics. So far business has been rather blind to these possibilities. It has, in fact, failed to mobilize support and encourage its closest potential allies, the vast

[8] Howard L. Erdman, *The Swatantra Party and Indian Conservatism* (Cambridge: Cambridge University Press, 1967), p. 207.

population of merchants, traders, and small-scale businessmen. Instead of encouraging the growth of small-scale industry by subcontracting to such units, the big houses have tried to control all the lines of production and credit. The major result has been to arouse fear of monopoly among the general population, thus further tarnishing the image of business. Although business is beginning to realize that preoccupation with its own expansion was a mistake, it has not yet taken the requisite corrective action.

In the long run, the very size of the private sector will ensure its survival for some time to come. Even today business and government are more interdependent than each is willing to admit. For all the verbiage about the incompatibility of private and public sector interests, the conflicts that have rent Indian politics for the last twenty years have been the caste, community, language, and regional interests in the traditional sector. Modern bureaucrats and business and political leaders in India may have more in common than either group may realize—the desire for increased production and economic development, without which the "politics of scarcity" might overwhelm the attempts to establish a secular democracy in India.

APPENDIX

A Brief Sketch of the Top Twenty Business Houses in India[1]

TATA (*Bombay*)

The Tatas are Parsis from Navsari in Gujarat. The founder, Jamsetji Tata, started his career in industry in the city of Bombay. There in 1869, he purchased an oil mill which he converted to a cotton mill. After World War I, the Tatas advanced from cotton, hotels, hydroelectric power, and steel into industrial banking, insurance, construction, soap, and cement. Next they went into aviation, chemicals, and engineering. Their major concentration is in the Bombay area.

The group comprises 53 companies. Their major business activities are: engineering, chemicals, trading companies, textiles, managing agents, iron and steel, electricity generation and supply, edible oils and foods, financing and investments, insurance, mining, nonferrous metals, and electrical goods. Tata was ranked number one, in 1965, with assets of 41,772 lakhs and gross sales of 32,498 lakhs.

Birla (*Calcutta*)

The Birlas are Maheshwaris from Pilani in Rajasthan. Shivnarain Birla started a small trading and money lending business in Bombay. The first Birla industrial venture was a cotton spinning mill established in 1916. By the 1930s Birla had gone into jute, cotton, sugar, publishing, and insurance. The base of their business is Calcutta.

The Birla group comprises 151 companies. The interests of the group are extremely varied: coffee and tea plantations, coal mining, bauxite mining, edible oils and foods, sugar, cotton and woolen textiles, jute, automobiles, bicycles, engineering, electrical goods, chemi-

[1] The information contained in these sketches is taken from company histories, R. K. Hazari, *The Structure of the Corporate Private Sector* (Bombay: Asia Publishing House, 1966), and Government of India, *Report of the Monopolies Inquiry Commission, 1965: Volumes* I and II (New Delhi: Government of India Press, 1965.). The expressions lakh and crore signify 100,000 and 10,000,000 respectively.

cals, cement, paper, shipping, investment, trading, publications, iron and steel, and other manufacturing.

The Birlas assets, in 1965, were 29,272 lakhs and their gross sales were 29,024 lakhs; they ranked number two.

Martin Burn (*Calcutta*)

Martin Burn is one of the oldest agency houses in India. It is descended from two old agency firms, Burn and Martin.

Burn was established in 1781 as a firm of architects and builders in Calcutta and engineers at Howrah. Martin was set up in 1892 to carry on business as engineers, builders, and contractors. In 1926 Martin acquired the firm of Burn, and in 1937 the group took up the manufacture of steel. Martin and Burn amalgamated in 1946, to form Martin Burn, a public limited company. Their base of concentration is Calcutta.

Both original firms were European, but a Bengali Brahmin, Sir Rajendra Mookerjee, came in as a partner before World War I. The present three controlling families in the group are the Martins, Mookerjees, and Banerjees, in that order.

The group consists of 21 companies. The industrial spheres in which it is active are: iron and steel, engineering (manufacturing railway wagons and cranes), electricity generation and supply, refractory products, and railway transport.

In 1965 the group ranked third and had assets of 14,961 lakhs and gross sales of 10,872 lakhs.

Bangur (*Calcutta*)

The Bangurs are Maheshwaris from Didwana in Rajasthan. Information is scanty, but it appears that the founder of the group, Mugneeram Bangur, established himself as a banker, property dealer, jute trader, and share broker in Calcutta in the 1920s. Through the 1940s the primary interest of the family remained finance and trade. They financed the ventures of the Somani family, which was industry-oriented and is now a part of the group.

During the earlier years, the only industrial ventures were two cotton mills in Bombay and Rajasthan and a cement company. After World War II, the industrial interests of the group expanded to include paper and jute. Financial activity remained the most important through the 1950s. Present areas of industrial activity are: jute, cotton textiles, sugar, cement, tea, chemicals, electrical goods, and paper.

The group is comprised of 81 companies. In 1965 they ranked fourth, with assets of 7,791 lakhs and gross sales of 6,529 lakhs.

The Associated Cement Companies, Ltd. (Bombay)

The Associated Cement Companies, Ltd. (ACC) is under the joint control of several business houses. The company was founded in 1936 by the amalgamation of 11 independent cement companies under the leadership of F. E. Dinshaw. The company grew out of earlier efforts of the cement industry to regulate prices and sales. The creation of a single company thus replaced a variety of industrywide associations. Today the principal interest of the company is the manufacturing of cement and cement-making machinery. It is also engaged in the manufacture of refractories (firebricks), refractory products, and coal mining. In 1965, ACC was ranked number five, with assets of 7,736 lakhs and gross sales of 4,413 lakhs.

Thapar (Calcutta)

The Thapars are Hindu Khatris from Ludhiana in Punjab. Most of their business is concentrated in the eastern region and in Bombay.

They were traders and coal agents in Calcutta in the early years of this century. In the 1930s the Thapars acquired some collieries and a paper mill, along with a bank and a life insurance company. In the 1940s they added a cotton mill.

Karam Chand Thapar & Bros. Pvt., Ltd. functions as managing agents, secretaries, and treasurers and engages in trading. Greaves Cotton & Co., Ltd. is engaged in the manufacture of paper cones and tubes, diamond drill bits and dressing tools, and also trade. Six other companies manufacture sugar (with its related activities such as import-export and dealing in sugarcane, molasses, and other by-products) and engineering goods (such as colliery equipment and tools, diesel engines and pumps, and textile machinery). They also are engaged in coal mining. Two companies manufacture paper; three manufacture electrical goods; and there is one company engaged in each of the following areas: producing starch and allied products, cotton textile, interstranded ropes and bandings, and chemicals. There is also an insurance company in the group. The rest of the companies are engaged in trading, investment, and owning properties.

Thapar comprises 43 companies: two are managing agency companies managing 23 companies, 19 more companies are under the control of the group master. Of the managed companies, 4 are also subsidiaries of the managing agency company, Greaves Cotton & Co. Ltd. In 1965, they were ranked number six, with assets of 7,190 lakhs and gross sales of 7,061 lakhs.

Dalmia Sahu Jain (Dalmia J., Dalmia, R. K., Sahu Jain, Shriyans Prasad Jain). (Calcutta, Bombay and Bihar)

Ramakrishna Dalmia, the founder of this group, is a Jain Bania from Rohtak in Punjab. He began, with his father, as a trader in the eastern region. In the early 1930s he set up a sugar mill (now the Rohtas Industries in Bihar) and acquired the minority interest in the management of South Bihar Sugar. Soon thereafter he entered the cement industry, and in 1938 he set up a small bank, the Universal Bank of India.

The 1940s was a period of rapid growth for the group. During this time Bharat Bank, Bharat Fire and General Insurance, Bharat Collieries, and Patiala Biscuit were set up. The group acquired control of Punjab National Bank, Bharat Insurance, Lahore Electric, Bennet Coleman, the Govan group of companies, two large cotton mills, a dairy, and three large Andrew Yule jute mills.

The group took up trading and financial activities which were viewed as malpractices and investigated. Some investigations are still continuing. It is contended that the group was partitioned between Ramakrishna Dalmia, his brother Jai Dayal Dalmia, and his son-in-law Shanti Prasad Jain, supposedly in 1948). There is no original legal document to this effect. Although there has been considerable separation of shareholding and clusters of companies, the separation is neither clear-cut nor complete.

The report of the Monopolies Enquiry Commission separates the group into four parts. Dalmia, R. is comprised of 11 companies whose main industrial interests are cement and edible oils and foods. It ranked seventy-fourth in 1965, with assets of 542 lakhs and sales of 542 lakhs. Dalmia, Jai Dayal is comprised of 15 companies. Their main industrial interests are cement, sugar, refractories, iron and steel, chemicals, and mining. In 1965 they ranked twenty-fifth with assets of 2,657 lakhs and sales of 1,907 lakhs. Sahu Jain is comprised of 26 companies. Its areas of main industrial activity are: cement, jute, paper, sugar, edible oil, chemicals, engineering, and mining. It ranked seventh, with assets of 6,779 lakhs and sales of 6,106. Shriyans Prasad Jain is composed of 12 companies. The main activity is the manufacture of chemicals; other activities are engineering and the manufacture of footwear products. It ranked sixty-second, with assets of 1,032 lakhs and sales of 764 lakhs.

Bird Heilger (Calcutta)

Bird Heilger is one of the oldest Calcutta agency houses. The original firms were set up as agency houses in the middle of the 1800s. Bird and Heilger were converted into private limited companies in 1928. Until recently the group was wholly controlled by the Benthall family, and some other British families held blocks of shares in a few companies.

After beginning in trade, Bird entered the jute industry in 1877 and had several more mills by 1910. They established an interest in coal in 1901, and they took up the supply of limestone and fireclay to the Tata steel plant when it went into operation. They then went into the supply of power for coal fields, timber, and engineering.

F. W. Heilger also began in trading. Their first industrial venture was Titaghar Paper in 1882, followed by coal mining. Their industrial interests are primarily in jute, coal, paper, engineering, fireclay, and power. There are 64 companies in the group. In 1965 their assets were 6,010 lakhs and their gross sales were 5,829 lakhs. They ranked eighth.

Juggilal Kamlapat (J. K. Singhania) (Kanpur)

The founders of this group were Juggilal Singhania and his son Kamlapat. The family, which belongs to the Aggarwal caste, migrated from Bikaner to Kanpur in the nineteenth century and set up business as merchants and bankers. They established a number of cotton gins and oil and flour mills, and in 1905 they opened a sugar factory and a distillery. These were followed by a cotton mill in 1919. In the 1930s they entered jute and engineering and acquired an insurance company.

The group is composed of 47 companies. They are engaged in the following industries: cotton, woolen and other textiles, jute, paper, chemicals, nonferrous metals, engineering, sugar, iron and steel, edible oils and foods, and mining. In 1965 they ranked ninth, with assets of 5,920 lakhs and gross sales of 5,443 lakhs.

Soorajmull Nagarmull (Calcutta)

This group was founded in 1900 by Seth Soorajmull Jalan, Seth Bansidhar Jalan, and Seth Nagarmull Bajoria. The Bajoria and Jalan families are Aggarwals from Ratangarh, Rajasthan. They began in jute and hemp baling and established several press houses. By World War I they were the leading exporter of hemp and jute. In 1927 they put up a jute mill, and they established two sugar mills in 1932–1933, in Bengal. Both mills are now located in Pakistan. In 1935–1936, Naskarpara Jute Mills and W. H. Harton, a rope manufacturing concern, were added to their industrial interests.

Presently the group is comprised of 77 concerns, 1 firm and 76 companies. Their industrial interests include: jute mills, engineering, cotton mills, chemicals (gas, oxygen, and acetylene), sugar mills, light railways, tea gardens, iron and steel, insurance, and banking. In 1965 the group ranked tenth, with assets of 5,737 lakhs and gross sales of 4,483 lakhs.

Walchand (Bombay)

The Walchands are Jains from Gujarat, but they have adopted Marathi as their language after having been settled in Sholapur for a number of generations. The family was originally in trade. In 1919 the founder, Walchand Hirachand, a very enterprising industrialist, set up Scindia Steam and Navigation Company, the first and largest Indian private shipping line. This was done in collaboration with Narottam Morarjee and Kilachand Devchand. Although the Walchands have always held the largest single block of equity, they have not established themselves as the dominant partner.

In the 1920s the group went into construction and allied activity. In the 1930s they took over Premier Construction, established two sugar mills, acquired majority interest in two engineering companies, and participated in the establishment of a small airline company.

At present the group's areas of industrial interest are: automobiles (including spare parts), engineering goods, sugar, edible oils and foods, refractories and ceramic goods, iron and steel, rubber goods, chemicals, and construction works. They are also insurance agents. In 1965 the group, comprised of 25 companies, had assets of 5,517 lakhs and gross sales of 5,402 lakhs. They ranked eleventh. Their industrial base is Bombay.

Shri Ram (New Delhi)

The Shri Rams are Aggarwals from Rohtak in Punjab. In the 1870s the family settled in Delhi and acquired a great deal of real estate in the area. Their first industry was the Delhi Cloth Mills. Now known as the Delhi Cloth and General Mills, it is the nucleus of the group and the largest diversified company in India. In the 1930s, Shri Ram took over Jay Engineering in Calcutta. This company manufactured sewing machines and fans. Presently it is one of the largest light engineering factories in Asia and the biggest manufacturer of electric fans in the world. Their industrial base remains Delhi.

Areas of industrial activity are textiles, chemicals, electrical goods, engineering (sewing machines, ball bearings, tungsten carbide products, capacitors), sugar, and ceramic goods. In 1965 the group assets were 5,468 lakhs and gross sales were 5,985 lakhs. The group comprises 18 concerns, of which 2 are firms and 16 are companies. The group is ranked twelfth.

Scindia (Bombay)

The Scindia Steam Navigation Co., Ltd., was established in 1919 by Narottam Morarjee, Walchand Hirachand, Lallubhai Samaldas, and Kilachand Devchand, to compete with foreign shipping. During the early 1920s it had to establish its right to its own coastal trade. Rate wars were waged by British shipping interests, but the company was able to survive. In 1933 a subsidiary company, Scindia Steamships (Burma), Ltd. was formed. A shipbuilding yard was established at Vishakhapatnam and moved in 1941 to Bombay, but its efforts were temporarily frustrated by World War II. In 1943 the group took over the management and obtained the controlling interest in Air Services of India, Ltd.

Following the war, a shipyard was reestablished at Vishakhapatnam. In 1945 the company's fleet consisted of thirteen cargo ships and two passenger vessels. Independence gave Indian shipping an important role in the economic life of the country. In 1952 the Scindia shipyard was nationalized.

Presently the group consists of 8 companies. Four companies are shipping companies. One company does marine insurance work; one is engaged in agency work; one is engaged in ship repairs and general engineering; and one is engaged in bunkering, clearing, forwarding, and painting.

This group ranked thirteenth in 1964, with assets of 4,696 lakhs and sales of 2,062 lakhs.

Goenka (Calcutta)

The Goenkas are Aggarwals from Dundlod Rajasthan. Members of the Goenka family made fortunes as employees of Ralli Brothers and Kettelwell Bullen. The most famous member of the family was Sir Badridas Goenka, who was a member of the Imperial Bank and the Reserve Bank and director of a large number of companies. Goenkas became actively associated with Duncan Brothers, a large British owned tea company, when it began to Indianize in 1948. Today Goenkas have 52 companies, with major holdings in jute, cotton, and wollen textiles, tea, electricity supply, chemicals, and coal mining. In 1965 the group ranked fourteenth, with assets of 4,695 lakhs and gross sales of 4,356 lakhs.

Mafatlal (Bombay)

The Mafatlals are Patels from Ahmedabad in Gujarat. The founder, Mafatlal Gagalbhai, was the son of a master weaver. Originally a small cloth trader, his industrial career began around the turn of the century when he was invited by a European manager to join in taking over a small, derelict mill. By 1920 the first company bearing his name existed. During the 1920s and 1930s he acquired 8 large cotton mills near Ahmedabad and in Bombay, a jute mill in Calcutta, and much real estate in Bombay. In the initial stages these take-overs were facilitated by moral and financial help from friends, who were rewarded by shares. The group became one of the most prosperous and well managed textile groups in the country. Since then, the group appears to have followed a policy of joint participation with other groups in new enterprises. Their industrial base is Ahmedabad.

The group is comprised of 22 concerns, 1 firm and 21 companies. Of these, 6 are engaged in the manufacture and processing of cotton textiles. Three companies manufacture chemical products such as dyestuffs, organic and inorganic chemicals, and petro-chemicals. Four are managing agents, while the remaining 8 companies are engaged in sugar, jute, and plywood and as insurance agents and textile engravers. In 1965 the group's rank was fifteenth, with assets of 4,591 lakhs and gross sales of 4,311 lakhs.

Sarabhai (Ahmedabad)

The Sarabhais are Gujarati (Jain Bania Shrimali) from Ahmedabad. The founder was the grandfather of Ambalal Sarabhai, the leading figure in the family. The Sarabhai family were indigenous bankers who helped establish Ahmedabad Manufacturing and Calico Printing Company. In 1880, when it failed, they were the major creditors and decided to run the enterprise themselves. The family was closely associated with Gandhi, and Ambalal's sister Anasuyabhen was a devoted follower of Gandhi.

Today the major holdings are in cotton textiles, drugs and pharmaceuticals, chemicals, and engineering. In 1965 the group ranked sixteenth, with assets of 4,316 lakhs and gross sales of 5,429 lakhs.

Andrew Yule (*Calcutta*)

This group is wholly foreign owned and is one of the oldest British managing agency houses in Calcutta. Established as an unincorporated trading firm in 1863 by Andrew and George Yule, it became a joint stock company when T. S. Catto joined in 1919. The Yule and Catto families, along with their American branches, control the group.

The first industrial venture was coal in the 1840s, when Bengal Coal was established. In the 1870s they set up another coal company and went into jute and two tea companies.

The main industrial interests of the group are coal mining, jute, and tea plantations. They also have interests in electricity, paper, engineering, and insurance. The group comprises 29 companies. In 1965 their assets were 4,189 lakhs and their gross sales were 3,430 lakhs. They ranked seventeenth.

Killick (*Bombay*)

In 1965 this group consists of 14 companies and has its principal interest in generation and supply of electric energy and the manufacture of textiles. They have other interests in mining, engineering, chemicals, and a variety of smaller ventures. The total assets of the group in 1965 were 4,150 lakhs and sales of 2,445 lakhs. It ranked eighteenth.

I.C.I. (*Bombay*)

This group consists of 5 companies, 4 of which are subsidiaries of the Imperial Chemical Industries of London. In 1965 its assets were 3,689 lakhs and gross sales were 3,816 lakhs. It ranked nineteenth.

Kilachand (*Bombay*)

This is a group of 12 companies involved in chemicals, cotton textile, and sugar. The caste of the Kilachand family is uncertain, but the principal location of their business activity is Bombay. In 1965 the assets of the Kilachand group totaled 3,513 lakhs and gross sales were 2,430 lakhs. It ranked twentieth.

BIBLIOGRAPHY

BOOKS

Almond, Gabriel A., and Powell, Bingham G., Jr. *Comparative Politics: A Developmental Approach.* Boston: Little, Brown, 1966.

Apter, David E., ed. *Ideology and Discontent.* New York: Free Press, 1963.

Aronson, R. L., and Windmiller, J. P., ed. *Labor Management and Economic Growth: Proceedings of a Conference on Human Resources and Labor Relations in Underdeveloped Countries.* Ithaca, N. Y.: Cornell University Press, 1954.

Austin, Granville. *The Indian Constitution.* Oxford: Clarendon Press, 1966.

Baldwin, George B. *Industrial Growth in South India: Case Studies in Economic Development.* New York: Free Press, 1959.

Basu, S. K. *The Managing Agency System: In Prospect and Retrospect.* Calcutta: World Press Private, Ltd., 1958.

Bauer, Raymond A., Pool, Ithiel de Sola, and Dexter, Lewis Anthony. *American Business and Public Policy: The Politics of Foreign Trade.* New York: Atherton Press, 1967.

Beer, Samuel H. *British Politics in the Collectivist Age.* New York: Knopf, 1965.

Berna, James. *Industrial Entrepreneurship in Madras State.* Bombay: Asia Publishing House, 1960.

Bhagwati, Jagdish N., and Desai, Padma. *India Planning for Industrialization: Industrialization and Trade Policies Since 1951.* London: Oxford University Press, 1970.

Birla, G. D. *In the Shadow of the Mahatma.* Bombay: Orient Longman's, Ltd., 1955.

Blake, George. *B. I. Centenary 1856–1956.* London: Collins Press, 1956.

Braibanti, Ralph, *et al. Asian Bureaucratic Systems Emergent from the British Imperial Tradition.* Durham, N. C.: Duke University Press, 1966.

Brass, Paul. *Factional Politics in an Indian State.* Berkeley and Los Angeles: University of California Press, 1965.

Braunthal, Gerhard. *The Federation of German Industry in Politics.* Ithaca, N. Y.: Cornell University Press, 1965.

Brecher, Michael. *India and World Politics: Krishna Menon's View of the World.* New York: Praeger, 1968.

———. *Nehru's Mantle: The Politics of Succession in India.* New York: Praeger, 1966.

Broomfield, J. H. *Elite Conflict in a Plural Society: Twentieth-Century Bengal.* Berkeley and Los Angeles: University of California Press, 1968.

Brown, Hilton. *Parry's of Madras: A Story of British Enterprise in India.* Madras: Parry and Company, Ltd., 1954.

Buchanan, Daniel Houston. *The Development of Capitalistic Enterprise in India.* New York: Macmillan, 1934.

Carstairs, G. Morris. *The Twice-Born.* Bloomington, Ind.: Indiana University Press, 1961.

Crick, Bernard. *The American Science of Politics: Its Origins and Conditions.* London: Routledge and Kegan, Paul, 1959.

Crouch, Harold. *Trade Unions and Politics in India.* Bombay: Manaktalas, 1966.

Das Gupta, Jyotirindra. *Language Conflict and National Development.* Berkeley and Los Angeles: University of California Press, 1970.

Das Gupta, L. R. *Indian Chambers of Commerce and Commercial Associations.* Calcutta: Eastern Chamber of Commerce, 1946.

Dwivedy, Surendranath, and Bhargava, G. S. *Political Corruption in India.* New Delhi: Popular Book Services, 1967.

Eckstein, Harry, and Apter, David, ed. *Comparative Politics: A Reader.* London and New York: Free Press, 1963.

Eckstein, Harry. *Pressure Group Politics: The Case of the British Medical Association.* Stanford: Stanford University Press, 1960.

Ehrmann, Henry W. *Organized Business in France.* Princeton: Princeton University Press, 1957.

———, ed. *Interest Groups on Four Continents.* Pittsburgh: University of Pittsburgh Press, 1958.

Erdman, Howard L. *The Swatantra Party and Indian Conservatism.* Cambridge: Cambridge University Press, 1967.

———. *Political Attitudes of Indian Industry: A Case Study of the Baroda Business Elite.* New York: Oxford University Press, 1971.

Feldman, Herbert. *Revolution in Pakistan: A Study of the Martial Law Administration.* London: Oxford University Press, 1967.

Gadgil, D. R. *Origins of the Modern Indian Business Class: An Interim Report.* New York: Institute of Pacific Relations, 1959.

Ghosh, P. C. *The Development of the Indian National Congress, 1892–1909.* Calcutta: Firma K. L. Mukhopadhyay, 1960.

Gillion, Kenneth L. *Ahmedabad: A Study in Indian Urban History.* Berkeley and Los Angeles: University of Caliornia Press, 1968.

Griffiths, Sir Percival. *The History of the Indian Tea Industry.* London: Weidenfeld and Nicholson, 1967.

———. *Modern India.* New York: Praeger, 1962.

Hanson, A. H. *The Process of Planning: A Study of India's Five Year Plans, 1950–1964.* London: Oxford University Press, 1966.

Hardgrave, Robert L., Jr. *The Nadars of Tamilnad.* Berkeley and Los Angeles: University of California Press, 1969.

Harris, F. R. *Jamsetji Nusserwanji Tata: A Chronicle of His Life.* Bombay: Blackie and Son (India) Ltd., 1958.

Harrison, Godfrey. *Bird and Company of Calcutta.* Calcutta: Anna Art Press Private, Ltd., 1964.

Harrison, Selig S. *India: The Most Dangerous Decades.* Madras: Oxford University Press, 1965.

Hazari, R. K. *The Structure of the Corporate Private Sector.* Bombay: Asia Publishing House, 1966.

Hazlehurst, Leighton W. *Entrepreneurship and the Merchant Caste in a Punjabi City.* Durham, N. C.: Duke University Press, 1966.

Heard, Alexander. *The Costs of Democracy.* Garden City, N. Y.: Doubleday, 1962.

Heidenheimer, Arnold J., ed. *Comparative Political Finance: The Financing of Party Organizations and Election Campaigns.* Lexington, Mass.: D. C. Heath, 1970.

Holt, Robert T., and Turner, John E. *The Political Basis of Economic Development: An Exploration in Comparative Political Analysis.* Princeton, N. J.: Van Nostrand, 1966.

Hutton, J. H. *Caste in India: Its Nature, Function, and Origins.* London: Oxford University Press, 1963.

Indian International Center. *Social Responsibilities of Business.* Bombay: Manaktalas, 1966.

International Bank for Reconstruction and Development. *India: A Review of Trends in Manufacturing Industry.* Washington: IBRD, 1970, 3 vols.

Irschick, Eugene F. *Politics and Social Conflict in South India: The Non-Brahman Movement and Tamil Separatism, 1916–1929.* Berkeley and Los Angeles: University of California Press, 1969.

Johri, C. K. *Unionism in a Developing Economy.* Bombay: Asia Publishing House, 1967.

Karnik, V. B. *Indian Trade Unions: A Survey.* Bombay: Manaktalas, 1966.

Kaushik, Rishi Jaimini. *Anandilal Poddar* (Hindi). Calcutta: Jaimini Prakashan, 1964.

———. *Shri Ramdev Chokhany* (Hindi). Calcutta: Jaimini Prakashan, N.D.

Kennedy, Van Dusen. *Unions, Employers, and Government: Essays on Indian Labor Questions.* Bombay: Manaktalas, 1966.

Kidron, Michael. *Foreign Investments in India.* London: Oxford University Press, 1965.

Kochanek, Stanley A. *The Congress Party of India: The Dynamics of One-Party Democracy.* Princeton: Princeton University Press, 1968.

Kornhauser, William. *The Politics of Mass Society.* New York: Free Press, 1959.

Kothari, Rajni. *Politics in India.* Boston: Little, Brown, 1970.

Kust, Matthew J. *Foreign Enterprise in India: Laws and Policies.* Chapel Hill, N. C.: University of North Carolina Press, 1964.

———. *Supplement to Foreign Enterprise in India: Laws and Policies.* Chapel Hill, N. C.: University of North Carolina Press, 1966.

LaPalombara, Joseph. *Interest Groups in Italian Politics*. Princeton: Princeton University Pres, 1964.

Mankekar, D. R. *Homi Mody: A Many Splendored Life*. Bombay: Popular Prakashan, 1968.

Mazumdar, D. L. *Toward a Philosophy of the Modern Corporation*. Bombay: Asia Publishing House, 1967.

Mehta, M. M. *Structure of Indian Industries*. Bombay: Popular Book Depot, 1961.

Milbrath, Lester. *The Washington Lobbyist*. Chicago: Rand McNally, 1963.

Misra, B. B. *The Indian Middle Classes: Their Growth in Modern Times*. London: Oxford University Press, 1961.

Modi, Balchand, *Desh-kee Itihas-mee Marwari Jatii-kaa Sthaan* (Hindi), Calcutta: Ragunath Prasad Singhania, 1940.

Montiero, John B. *Corruption: Control of Maladministration*. Bombay: Manaktalas, 1966.

Moraes, Frank. *Sir Purshotamdas Thakurdas*. Bombay: Asia Publishing House, 1967.

Morris-Jones, W. H. *The Government and Politics of India*. London: Hutchinson University Library, 1964.

———. *Parliament in India*. Philadelphia: University of Pennsylvania Press, 1957.

Mukharji, P. B. *Social Responsibilities of Business*. Calcutta: Conference on Social Responsibilities of Business, 1967.

Namjoshi, M. V., and Sabade, B. R. *Chambers of Commerce in India*. Bombay: Asia Publishing House, 1967.

National Council of Applied Economic Research. *The Managing Agency System: A Review of Its Working and Prospects of Its Future*. Bombay: Asia Publishing House, 1959.

Nayar, Baldev Raj. *Minority Politics in the Punjab*. Princeton: Princeton University Press, 1966.

Olson, Mancur, Jr. *The Logic of Collective Action*. Cambridge: Harvard University Press, 1965.

Pavlov, V. I. *The Indian Capitalist Class: A Historical Study*. Bombay: People's Publishing House Private, Ltd., 1964.

Punekar, S. D., and Madhuri, S. *Trade Union Leadership in India: A Survey*. Bombay: Lalvani Publishing House, 1967.

Pylee, M. V. *India's Constitution*. New York: Asia Publishing House, 1962.

Raman, N. Pattabhi. *Political Involvement of India's Trade Unions*. Bombay: Asia Publishing House, 1967.

Rice, A. K. *Productivity and Social Organization: The Ahmedabad Experiment*. Bombay: Tavistock Publications, Ltd., 1958.

Rosen, George. *Democracy and Economic Change in India*. Berkeley and Los Angeles: University of California Press, 1966.

Rudolph, Lloyd, and Rudolph, Susanne Hoeber. *The Modernity of Tradition: Political Development in India*. Chicago: University of Chicago Press, 1967.

Rungta, Radhe Shyam. *The Rise of Business Corporations in India: 1851–1900*. Cambridge: Cambridge University Press, 1970.

Rutnagar, S. M., ed. *Bombay Industries: The Cotton Mills*. Bombay: Indian Textile Journal, Ltd., 1927.

Seal, Anil. *The Emergence of Indian Nationalism: Competition and Collaboration in the Later Nineteenth Century*. Cambridge: Cambridge University Press, 1968.

Singer, Milton, ed. *Traditional India: Structure and Change*. Philadelphia: American Folklore Society, 1959.

Singh, Khushwant, and Joshi, Arun. *Shri Ram: A Biography*. Bombay: Asia Publishing House, 1968.

Stern, Robert W. *The Process of Opposition in India: Two Case Studies of How Policy Shapes Politics*. Chicago: University of Chicago Press, 1970.

Taub, Richard P. *Bureaucrats Under Stress: Administrators and Administration in an Indian State*. Berkeley and Los Angeles: University of California Press, 1969.

Thompson, J. Walter, Ltd. *Kothari and Sons*. Madras: Associated Printers, N. D.

Thompson, Edward, and Garratt, G. T. *Rise and Fulfillment of British Rule in India*. Allahabad: Central Book Depot, 1966.

Timberg, Thomas A. *Industrial Entrepreneurship among the Trading Communities of India: How the Pattern Differs*. Cambridge: Center for International Affairs, Harvard University, 1969.

Townsend, Sir Harry, ed. *A History of Shaw Wallace and Co. and Shaw Wallace and Co., Ltd*. Calcutta: Sree Saraswaty Press Ltd., 1965.

Truman, David. *The Governmental Process*. New York: Knopf, 1968.

Tyson, Geoffrey. *Managing Agency: A System of Business Organization*. Calcutta: Hooghly Printing Company, Ltd., 1961.

———. *Nehru: The Years of Power*. New York: Praeger, 1966.

Ward, Robert, ed. *Political Development in Modern Japan*. Princeton: Princeton University Press, 1968.

Weiner, Myron. *Party Building in a New Nation*. Chicago: University of Chicago Press, 1967.

———. *The Politics of Scarcity: Public Pressure and Political Response in India*. Chicago: University of Chicago Press, 1962.

———. *Party Politics in India*. Princeton: Princeton University Press, 1957.

———. *Political Change in South Asia*. Calcutta: Firma K. L. Mukhopadhyay, 1963.

Wootton, Graham. *Interest Groups*. Englewood Cliffs, N. J.: Prentice-Hall, 1970.

Yanaga, Chitoshi. *Big Business in Japanese Politics*. New Haven: Yale University Press, 1968.

Young, Roland, ed. *Approaches to the Study of Politics*. Evanston, Ill.: Northwestern University Press, 1958.

Zeigler, Harmon. *Interest Groups in American Society*. Englewood Cliffs, N. J.: Prentice-Hall, 1964.

Zinkin, Taya. *Challenges in India*. London: Chatto and Windus, 1966.

ARTICLES

Almond, Gabriel A. "A Comparative Study of Interest Groups in the Political Process." *American Political Science Review* 52 (1958): 270–282.

Beer, Samuel H. "Group Representation in Britain and the United States." *The Annals of the American Academy of Political and Social Science* 319 (1958): 130–141.

Bhalla, R. P. "Economic Aspects of Elections in India." *The Indian Political Science Review* (Delhi) 2 (October 1967–March 1968): 57–72.

Blue, Richard N. "Political Participation and Group Behavior of Indian Small Scale Entrepreneurs." *Asian Survey* 11 (1971): 900–915.

Brecher, Michael. "Succession in India 1967: The Routinization of Political Change." *Asian Survey* 7 (1967): 423–443.

Brown, Bernard E. "Pressure Politics in the Fifth Republic." *The Journal of Politics* 25 (1963): 509–525.

———. "Organized Business in Indian Politics." *The Indian Journal of Political Science* 12 (1962): 126–143.

Chopra, S. L., and Chauhan, O. N. S. "Emerging Pattern of Political Leadership in India." *Journal of Constitutional and Parliamentary Studies* 4 (1970): 119–127.

Cohn, Bernard S. "Recruitment and Training of British and Servants in India." In *Asian Bureaucratic Systems Emergent from the British Imperial Tradition,* edited by R. Braibanti, *et al.* Durham, N. C.: Duke University Press, 1966, pp. 87–140.

Dutt, R. C. "Hearing and Consultation Procedure in Public Administration." *Indian Journal of Public Administration* 4 (1958): 281–301.

Eckstein, Harry. "Group Theory and the Comparative Study of Pressure Groups." In *Comparative Politics: A Reader,* edited by H. Eckstein and D. Apter, pp. 389–397. London: Free Press, 1963.

Eldersveld, Samuel J. "Elections and Party System: Patterns of Party Regularity and Defection in 1967." *Asian Survey* 10 (1970): 1015–1030.

———. "The Political Behavior of the Indian Public." *Monthly Public Opinion Survey* 9 (1964): 4–9.

———. "American Interest Groups: A Survey of Research and Some Implications for Theory and Method." In *Interest Groups on Four Continents,* edited by H. W. Ehrmann, pp. 173–196. Pittsburgh: University of Pittsburgh Press, 1958.

Eulau, Heinz. "Lobbyists: The Wasted Profession." *Public Opinion Quarterly* 28 (1964): 27–38.

Finer, S. E. "The Federation of British Industries." *Political Studies* 4 (1956): 61–82.

———. "The Political Power of Private Capital." *Sociological Review*, 3 and 4 (Part I, December 1955, Part II, July 1956): 279–294 (I), 5–30 (II).

Frye, Charles E. "Parties and Pressure Groups in Weimar and Bonn." *World Politics* 17 (1965): 635–655.

Goel, M. Lal. "The Relevance of Education for Political Participation in a Developing Society." *Comparative Political Studies* 3 (1970): 336–346.

———. "Distribution of Civic Competence Feeling in India." *Social Science Quarterly* 51 (1970): 755–768.

Golembiewski, Robert T. "The Group Basis of Politics: Notes on Analysis and Development." *American Political Science Review* 54 (1960): 38–61.

Gusfield, Joseph R. "Political Community and Group Interests in Modern India." *Pacific Affairs* 36 (1965): 123–141.

Hagan, Charles B. "The Group in a Political Science." In *Approaches to the Study of Politics*, edited by R. Young, pp. 38–51. Evanston, Ill.: Northwestern University Press, 1958.

Hunt, Robert W. "Some Personal Roots of Modernity Among Small Industrialists in India." *Asian Survey* 11 (1971): 886–899.

Indian Institute of Public Opinion. "A Decade of Public Opinion Research: The Sociological Field." *Monthly Public Opinion Survey* 4 (1964): 24–36.

———. "After the Assembly Elections: 1972." *Monthly Public Opinion Survey* 17 (1972): i–x.

———. "The Fifth Lok Sabha Elections." *Monthly Public Opinion Survey* 16 (December 1970, January–February 1971): 82–90.

———. "Structure of Urban Opinion on the Socialist Pattern of Society." *Monthly Public Opinion Survey* 1 (May, June, and July 1956).

Ishida, Takeshi. "The Development of Interest Groups and the Pattern of Political Modernization in Japan." In *Political Development in Modern Japan*, edited by R. Ward, pp. 293–336. Princeton: Princeton University Press, 1968.

Ito, Shoji. "A Note on the 'Business Combine' in India." *Developing Economies* 4 (1966): 367–368.

Journal of Parliamentary Information, XVIII (1972), 372.

Kochanek, Stanley A. "Interest Groups and Interest Aggregation: Changing Patterns of Oligarchy in the FICCI." *Economic and Political Weekly* 5 (Special Number July 1970): 1291–1308.

Kothari, Rajni. "Continuity and Change in India's Party System." *Asian Survey* 10 (1970): 937–948.

Lamb, Helen B. "The Indian Business Communities and the Evolution of an Industrialist Class." *Pacific Affairs* 28 (1955): 101–116.

———. "The Development of Modern Business Communities in India." In *Labor Management and Economic Growth: Proceedings of a Conference on Human Resources and Labor Relations in Underdeveloped Countries*, edited by R. L. Aronson and J. P. Windmiller. Ithaca, N. Y.: Cornell University Press, 1954.

———. "The Indian Merchant." In *Traditional India: Structure and Change*, edited by Milton Singer, pp. 25–34. Philadelphia: American Folklore Society, 1959.

———. "Business Organization and Leadership in India Today." In *Leadership and Political Institutions in India,* edited by R. L. Park and I. Tinker, pp. 251–267. Princeton: Princeton University Press, 1959.

LaPalombara, Joseph. "The Utility and Limitations of Interest Group Theory in Non-American Field Situations." *Journal of Politics* 22 (1960): 29–49.

Latham, Earl. "The Group Basis of Politics: Notes for a Theory." *American Political Review* 46 (1952): 376–397.

Lowi, Theodore. "American Business, Public Policy, Case Studies, and Political Theory." *World Politics* 16 (1964): 677–715.

MacKenzie, W. J. M. "Pressure Groups: The Conceptual Framework." *Political Studies* 3 (1955): 247–255.

Macridis, Roy E. "Interest Groups in Comparative Analysis." *Journal of Politics* 23 (1961): 24–45.

Madsen, Douglas. "Solid Congress Support in 1967: A Statistical Inquiry." *Asian Survey* 10 (1970): 1004–1014.

Maheshwari, S. R. "The Minister-Secretary Relationship." *Journal of Constitutional and Parliamentary Studies* 4 (1970): 69–82.

Maheshwari, Shriram. "Employment of Retired Government Officials in India." *Indian Journal of Public Administration* 12 (1966): 232–254.

Malenbaum, Wilfred. "Politics and Indian Business: The Economic Setting." *Asian Survey* 11 (1971): 841–849.

March, James G. "An Introduction to the Theory and Measurement of Influence." *The American Political Science Review* 49 (1955): 431–451.

Medhora, Phiroze B. "Entrepreneurship in India." *Political Science Quarterly* 80 (1965): 558–580.

Milbrath, Lester. "Lobbying as a Communicative Process." *Public Opinion Quarterly* 24 (1960): 33–53.

Mazumdar, D. L. "Social and Economic Implications of the Companies Act, 1956." *Indian Journal of Public Administration* 3 (1957): 215–225.

Morris, Morris David, and Stein, Burton. "The Economic History of India: A Bibliographic Essay." *The Journal of Economic History* 21 (1961): 179–207.

Nayar, Baldev Raj. "Business Attitudes toward Economic Planning in India." *Asian Survey* 11 (1971): 850–865.

Paranjpe, H. G. "Government Regulation of Private Industry in India." *Indian Journal of Public Administration* 8 (1962): 297–316.

"The Role of Chambers of Commerce and Industry." *Industrial Times* 10 (1968).

Roth, Irvin. "Industrial Location and Indian Government Policy." *Asian Survey* 10 (1970): 383–396.

Rothman, Stanley. "Systematic Political Theory: Observations on the Group Approach." *American Political Science Review* 54 (1960): 14–33.

Rudolph, Lloyd I. "Continuities and Change in Electoral Behavior: The 1971 Parliamentary Election in India." *Asian Survey* 11 (1971): 1119–1132.

———. "Consensus and Conflict in Indian Politics." *World Politics* 13 (1961): 385–399.

Salisbury, Robert H. "An Exchange Theory of Interest Groups." *Midwest Journal of Political Science* 13 (1969): 1–32.

"Should Businessmen Enter Politics?" *Industrial Times* 10 (1968).

Singhvi, L. M. "The Legislative Process in India." *Journal of Constitutional and Parliamentary Studies* 4 (1970): 1–32.

Smith, David G. "Pragmatism and the Group Theory of Politics." *American Political Science Review* 58 (1964): 600–610.

Somjee, A. H. and G. "India." *Journal of Politics* 25 (1963): 686–702.

Subbaramaiah, S. "The Development Councils for Industries in India." *The Indian Journal of Economics* 43 (1963): 251–266.

Tandon, Prakash L. "Management in India Today." *Walchand Memorial Lecture Series*. Bombay: Maharashtra Chamber of Commerce, 1968.

Tata, J. R. D. "The Future of the Private Sector." *Journal of the Indian Merchants Chamber* 65 (1971): 43–47.

Verba, Sidney. "Organizational Membership and Democratic Consensus." *Journal of Politics* 27 (1965): 467–497.

Weiner, Myron. "Struggle Against Power." *World Politics* 8 (1956): 392–403.

———. "The 1971 Election and the Indian Party System." *Asian Survey* 11 (1971): 1153–1166.

PUBLIC DOCUMENTS: GOVERNMENT OF INDIA

All-India Reporter (1957): Calcutta 234 Nagpur: All-India Reporter Ltd., 1957. (Indian Iron and Steel Company Case.)

All-India Reporter (1958): Bombay 155 Nagpur: All-India Reporter Ltd., 1958. (Ketecha versus Tata Iron and Steel Company.)

Hazari, R. K. *Industrial Planning and Licensing Policy: Final Report*. New Delhi: Government of India Press, 1967.

———. *Industrial Planning and Licensing Policy: Interim Report to Planning Commission*. New Delhi: Government of India Press, 1967.

Home Department, Political. *Fortnightly Reports on the Internal Political Situation, 1932–1939*. New Delhi: Home Department, Government of India, 1932–1939. National Archives of India.

Lok Sabha Secretariat. *Joint Committee on the Patents Bill, 1965: Evidence (Volume I)*. New Delhi: Government of India Press, 1966.

———. *Joint Committee on the Patents Bill, 1965: Evidence (Volume II)*. New Delhi: Government of India Press, 1966.

———. *The Patents Bill, 1965 (Report of the Joint Committee)*. New Delhi: Government of India Press, 1966.

Ministry of Commerce. *Annual Report, 1967–1968*. New Delhi: Government of India Press, 1968.

Ministry of Commerce and Industry, Department of Company Law Administration. *Report of the Commission of Inquiry on the Administration of Dalmia-Jain Companies*. New Delhi: Government of India Press, 1963.

Ministry of Home Affairs. *Report of the Commission on Prevention of Corruption*. New Delhi: Government of India Press, 1968.

Ministry of Industrial Development and Company Affairs, *Annual Report 1967–68,* New Delhi: Government of India Press, 1968.

———. *Proceedings of the Nineteenth Meeting of the Central Advisory Council of Industries*. New Delhi: Government of India Press, 1967.

———. *Annual Reports of Development Councils*. New Delhi: Government of India Press, 1965–1966.

Ministry of Industry and Supply. *Report of the Study Team on Directorate General of Technical Development (Part I)*. New Delhi: Government of India Press, 1965.

Ministry of Information and Broadcasting. *Speeches of T. T. Krishnamachari*. New Delhi: Government of India Press, 1957.

Ministry of Law, Department of Company Affairs. *Report of the Managing Agency Enquiry Committee*. New Delhi: Government of India Press, 1966.

Ministry of Law. *The Companies Act, 1956*. New Delhi: Government of India Press, 1967.

———. *The Industries (Development and Regulation) Act, 1951*. New Delhi: Government of India Press, 1967.

Planning Commission. *Fourth Five Year Plan: 1969–1974*. Faridabad: Government of India Press, 1970.

Planning Commission. *The New India*. New York: Macmillan, 1958.

Registrar of Newspapers for India. *Press in India, 1968: Part I*. New Delhi: Government of India Press, 1968.

Report of the Industrial Licensing Policy Inquiry Committee. New Delhi: Government of India Press, 1969.

Report of the Monopolies Inquiry Commission, 1965: Volumes I and II. New Delhi: Government of India Press, 1965.

PUBLICATIONS OF BUSINESS ASSOCIATIONS IN INDIA

A. *Histories of Major Business Associations*

Andhra Chamber of Commerce. *Andhra Chamber of Commerce Souvenir, 1963*. Madras: Andhra Chamber of Commerce, 1963.

Bengal National Chamber of Commerce and Industry. *Souvenir Volume: 1887–1962*. Calcutta: Bengal National Chamber of Commerce and Industry, 1962.

Bharat Chamber of Commerce. *Golden Jubilee Souvenir: 1900–1950*. Calcutta: Alliance Press, 1950.

Federation of Indian Chambers of Commerce and Industry. *Silver Jubilee Souvenir:* 1927–1951. Bombay: India Printing Works, 1951.

The Indian Bank Limited. *The Indian Bank Limited Golden Jubilee: 1907–1957*. Madras: Associated Printers Private, Ltd., 1957.

Indian Merchants Chamber. *Fifty Years, 1907–1957*. Bombay: Indian Merchants Chamber, 1958.

Madras Chamber of Commerce Centenary Handbook, 1836–1936. Madras: The Madras Chamber of Commerce, 1936.

Saklatvala, S. D. *History of the Millowners Association: Bombay 1875–1930*. Bombay: For private circulation, 1930.

Southern India Chamber of Commerce. *Southern India Chamber of Commerce Golden Jubilee: 1910–1960*. Madras: Commercial Printing and Publishing House, 1960.

Sulivan, Raymond J. *One Hundred Years of Bombay: History of the Bombay Chamber of Commerce, 1836–1936*. Bombay: Times of India Press, 1937.

Tyson, Geoffrey. *The Bengal Chamber of Commerce and Industry 1853–1953 Centenary Survey*. Calcutta: The Bengal Chamber of Commerce, 1953.

B. Annual Reports and Proceedings

All-India Manufacturers Association. *Annual Report*. Bombay: AIMO, 1947–1970.

———. *Proceedings of the Annual Meeting*. Bombay: AIMO, 1947–1970.

Associated Chambers of Commerce and Industry. *Annual Report*. Calcutta: Assocham, 1946–1970.

———. *Proceedings of the Annual Meeting*. Calcutta: Assocham, 1920–1970.

Bengal Chamber of Commerce and Industry. *Proceedings of the Annual General Meeting*. Calcutta: Bengal Chamber of Commerce and Industry, 1947–1970.

———. *Report of the Executive*. Calcutta: Bengal Chamber of Commerce and Industry, 1947–1970, vols. I and II.

Bombay Chamber of Commerce and Industry. *Annual Report*. Bombay: Bombay Chamber of Commerce and Industry, 1947–1970.

Cement Manufacturers Association. *Annual Report*. Bombay: Cement Manufacturers Association, 1961–1970.

———. *Presidential Addresses Delivered at the Annual General Meeting*. Bombay: Cement Manufacturers Association, 1961–1970.

Economic and Scientific Research Foundation. *Annual Report*. New Delhi: Federation House, 1967–1970.

Fair Trade Practices Association. *The FTPA Bulletin* 1 (1968).

Federation of Indian Chambers of Commerce and Industry. *Proceedings of the Annual Session*. New Delhi: FICCI, 1932–1972.

———. *Report of the Proceedings of the Committee of the Federation for the Years 1932–1972*. New Delhi: FICCI, 1932–1972.

———. *Important Correspondence and Documents*. New Delhi: FICCI, 1936–1972.

Forum of Free Enterprise. *Report and Accounts*. Bombay: Forum of Free Enterprise, 1967–1970.

Indian Jute Mills Association. *Proceedings of the Annual Meeting*. Calcutta: IJMA, 1968–1970.

Indian Merchants Chamber. *Annual Report*. Bombay: Indian Merchants Chamber, 1931–1970.

Organization of Pharmaceutical Producers of India. *Annual Report*. Bombay: OPPI, 1966–1970.

C. *Documents, Memoranda, and Special Pamphlets*

All-India Management Association. *Seminar on Business and Society*. New Delhi: AIMA, 1965.

Associated Chambers of Commerce and Industry. *The Associated Chambers of Commerce and Industry: Talk by H. K. S. Lindsay, President, 1964–1965, at the Rotary Club of Calcutta June 8, 1965*. Calcutta: Assocham, 1965.

———. "Articles of Association of the Associated Chambers of Commerce and Industry of India." *The Associated Chambers of Commerce and Industry, Forty-Eighth Annual Report*. Calcutta: Assocham, 1967.

Bombay Millowners Association. Unpublished Papers Relating to the Creation of the Indian Cotton Mills Federation. 1946–1958.

Democratic Group. *Constitution of the Democratic Group*. Bombay: The Democratic Group, n. d.

Federation of Indian Chambers of Commerce and Industry. *Memorandum and Articles of Association*. New Delhi: FICCI, 1962; rev. ed., 1970.

———. *Federation of Indian Chambers of Commerce and Industry: Organization and Functions*. New Delhi: FICCI, 1965.

Fair Trade Practices Association. *Memorandum Articles of Association*. Bombay: FTPA, 1968.

Forum of Free Enterprise. *Basic Documents*. Bombay: Forum of Free Enterprise, 1966.

Indian Chamber of Commerce, Calcutta. *Government and Business*, text of speeches delivered by G. L. Nanda, Satyanarain Sinha, and G. D. Birla at the Indian Chamber of Commerce, Calcutta, April 10, 1965. Calcutta: Indian Chamber of Commerce, 1965.

Organization of Pharmaceutical Producers of India. *Memorandum on the Patents Bill*. Bombay: Tata Press Ltd., 1967.

Organization of Pharmaceutical Producers of India. *Supplementary Memorandum on the Patents Bill 1967*. Bombay: OPPI, 1968.

Scindia Steam Navigation Co. Ltd. *The Wealth Tax and the Shipping Industry*. Bombay: Commercial Department, Scindia Steam Navigation Co. Ltd., 1957.

Somani. G. D. *Confidential Report on the First Session of Parliament, May 13, 1952*. Submitted to the Bombay Millowners Association, August, 1952.

NEWSPAPERS AND JOURNALS

A. *Newspapers*

Economic Times (Bombay)
Financial Express (Bombay)
Free Press Journal (Bombay)
Hindustan Times (New Delhi)
New York Times (New York)
Overseas Hindustan Times (New Delhi)
Patriot (New Delhi)

National Herald (Lucknow and New Delhi)
The Statesman (Calcutta)
Times of India (Bombay)

B. *Journals*

Capital (Calcutta)
Commerce (Bombay)
Eastern Economist (New Delhi)
Economic and Political Weekly (Bombay)
Link (New Delhi)

INDEX

Lightning Source UK Ltd.
Milton Keynes UK
UKHW010804091021
391926UK00001B/83